EXPLORING MDX

USING

MICROSOFT SQL SERVER 2012

ASHIM MAZUMDER

eGurus

Irving, Texas 75063 USA

EXPLORING MDX USING MICROSFT SQL SERVER 2012
Author: Ashim Mazumder

ISBN: 978-1-62367-000-9
Library of Congress Control Number: 2012945131

Published by:
eGurus, Irving, Texas 75063, USA
Email: publication@eGurus.com, Website: http://www.eGurus.com,Twitter: eGurusDotCom
First Edition: September, 2012.

This book is dedicated to four most important persons in my life
my wife Anjana, son Arnav, parents Nikunja and Ranjita
for their encouragement, advice and patience.
-Ashim Mazumder

CREDITS

Author

Ashim Mazumder has been working as designer, architect and trainer of various software and databases for last two decades. He studied undergraduate in computer engineering at NIT, Kurukshetra, India and pursued graduate studies in computer science and automation at IISc, Bangalore, India. He continues to have special interest in database, business intelligence, data analysis and sharepoint.

Technical Reviewers

Roberto Pozo, MVP on SQL Server, is a Chilean engineer, who lives in Mérida - Venezuela. He's a professional IT Technology with several years of experience. Recognized as Windows Azure Champion and Developer. You can follow Roberto on Twitter @angaroasoft or visit his blog SQL Server http://angaroasoft.wordpress.com.

Thiago Zavaschi (MVP) is master in computer science and currently is a Microsoft Premier Field Engineer focused in SQL Server and Business Intelligence Technologies based in Brazil. Former Microsoft MVP and works actively in technical communities, as speaker (TechEd), writer (SQL Server MVP Deep Dives 2) and blogger (Zavaschi.com).

Miguel Egea Gomez (MVP), is an Engineer in IT with more than 19 years. He work as Associate Mentor for SolidQ Spain. He was MVP from 2001-2009 and from 2011-2012. He work as external DBA and developing BI projects for large companies in Spain. The last five years has been working with the Microsoft BI Suite, SSIS and SSAS mainly.

Jeff Cates, (PMP, MCITP) is a Business Intelligence expert - consulting in SSAS, SQL, and MDX since 2001. He can be reached at catesgroup.com.

Ron Olson, has over 20 years of IT experience as a Developer, Development Manager, QA manager and Project Manager. His background includes database design and testing work.

Tobiasz Koprowski (MVP, SQL Server), Community leader focused on SQL Server, SharePoint, security, collaboration, and Change Management, Disaster Recovery, Business Continuity Management and Service Level Agreement. Microsoft Certified Trainer, Freelancer, consultant. Conducts audit projects, consulting and implementation in Poland and across Europe. Technical Team Leader in Global IT Community Association, where he also serves as Vice-Chair in EMEA. Member of such Microsoft Terminology Community, Friends of RedGate, PASS Programm Committee and co-founder of Azure SQL PASS Virtual Chapter. Member of the ISSA, ACM and several communities in the world. Since July 2010 awarded as Most Valuable Professional for SQL Server. Currently president of the Polish SQL Server User Group. For several years, the conference organizer of SQLDAY. Speaker at group meetings and conferences. Runs several blogs: IT Pro, aimed at the SQL and SharePoint, a blog about licensing, and several private blogs. In his spare time journalist and music critic, photographer and concert promoter.

Contents

Acknowledgements

So many people are involved in writing this book, without whom this would never be possible to complete this book.

First of all, I'd like to thank Carrie Pedraza for her encouragement and support . I'd like to thank reviewers, Ron Olson, Roberto Pozo, Thiago Zavaschi, Miguel Egea Gomez, Tobiasz Koprowski, Raman Gupta, Lydia Lewis, Jeff Cates for detail reviews and various feedbacks.

I would like to thank Panchanan Das, Usha Das, Indranil Ganguly, Mithu Goswami, Arindam Paul , Suguna Paul, Milind Kulkarni, Rashmi Kulkarni, Shrikant Gupta, Abhijit Das, Shilpa Das, Ritwik Ganguly, Aditya Paul and all of my students and microsoft forum members for their contribution, advice and encouragements.

My special thanks to Vaibhav Gupta and Devendra Gupta for contribution in the cover photograph.

Last but not the least, I'd like to thank my family members; this could not be possible without their unconditional support.

Hopefully, I have not forgotten anybody, but if I have, it was an oversight.

-Ashim Mazumder

Preface

This book is for anybody who wants to learn MDX language. We have assumed that you have got some relational database design and SQL language experience, and know basic concepts of Data warehouse and SQL Server Analysis Services (SSAS). Throughout the book, we used practice database "Adventure works", which is very popular among users of Microsoft SQL Server environment. Inside this book, you will find:

- More than 350 MDX queries.
- MDX functions are explained with simple examples.
- Some topics like "All Level" explained in detail with various examples.
- Detail analysis of each component of queries.
- MDX query architecture explained in detail with examples.
- Contains simplified definition of functions with examples and their possible values.
- Performance tuning and best practices.

This book is an important and valuable reference for those interested in learning and improving their MDX skill.

Organization of the Book

This book is divided into ten chapters and an appendix.

- Chapters from one to eight chapter explains MDX query functions with examples.
- Ninth chapter explores data definition and data manipulation statements for MDX.
- Tenth chapter has fifteen tips for performance tuning and best practices in MDX.
- Appendix I consist of solutions of exercise queries of each chapter.
- Queries in chapters are executed in the same order throughout the book. If the result of a query does not match with the result by a reader, please check the order of the query and any update in the cube.

This is a practical book that contains many screen shots, diagrams and around 350 MDX queries. Many screen shots, and steps used to explain MDX development in a simplified way. All source codes are real codes tested by the author and have been included in this book directly from source files.

Explanation techniques used in this Book

- Steps: Instead of solving complex query in one step, multiple steps help readers understand one step at a time and reach the solution easily.
- Screen shot: Screen shots for tasks give readers easy to understand the task.
- Strategies: Strategies before each query gives readers idea of how to solve the query.
- Analysis: Detail analysis after each query gives a detail explanation of each component of a query.
- Definition: Definitions of MDX functions are short and simple with example of each parameter.
- Exercises: To learn a language, it is very important to practice. Exercises at the end of each chapter provide readers with opportunities to apply the skills they learned.

Chapter 1: Introduction to MDX

Agenda

MDX stands for **M**ulti **D**imensional e**X**pressions, a language that query and manipulate multi-dimensional OLAP (Online Analytical Processing) cubes. MDX is not only used by Microsoft Corporation but also adopted by the wide range of OLAP vendors like MicroStrategy, NCR, Oracle Corporation, SAS, SAP, Teradata, Whitelight etc. Other languages in SQL Server Analysis Services (SSAS) include XMLA (XML for Analysis), used for client application to access SQL Server Analysis Services, DMX (Data Mining eXpressions), used to access data in Data Mining Models and DAX (Data Analysis eXpressions) used in SSAS tabular models.

The first section of this chapter describes environment set up to practice MDX, which includes the download of "Adventure Works" sample database, creating and processing of SSAS database from the downloaded project. The next section explores some basic concepts of MDX, like dimension, fact, tuple, set and hierarchies, which are necessary to understand components of MDX. Other topics include basic structure of MDX, writing first MDX query, default measure, attribute hierarchy, user defined hierarchy and different cases of "All Level". Apart from exploring more queries related to sorting, counting, this chapter also compares SQL with MDX. For readers of this book with SQL experiences, comparing MDX queries with corresponding SQL will provide some level of comfort. Not all SQL code can be translated to corresponding MDX, but some basic translations are explained in this chapter.

Environment Set Up

Step 1: Install Microsoft SQL Server 2012.

You should install at least following components of SQL server 2012 in your machine:

- SQL Server Database Engine
- SQL Server Analysis Services
- SQL Server Reporting services in native mode

If not installed yet, you can download evaluation version of SQL Server 2012 from following location,
http: //www.microsoft.com/sqlserver/en/us/get-sql-server/try-it.aspx
The trial version of SQL Server 2012 is good for 180 days.

Step 2: Download "Adventure Works DW" database and analysis services project for SQL Server 2012 from following location:
http: //msftdbprodsamples.codeplex.com/releases/view/55330,
For future versions of SQL server, search for "Adventure Works DW" in the website
http: //msftdbprodsamples.codeplex.com/

Figure 1-1: Download location for AdventureWorks database.

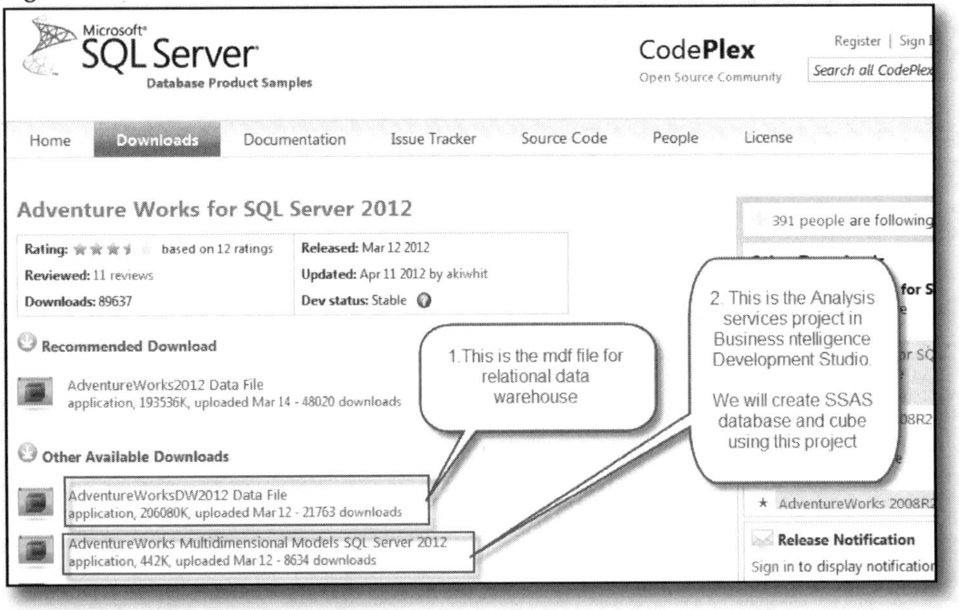

There are two files:

- AdventureWorksDW2012_Data.mdf: This is the "mdf" file for relational data warehouse database.
- AdventureWorks Multidimensional Models SQL Server 2012.zip: This zip file consists of analysis services project for SSAS database.

Step 3: Attach relational data warehouse database.

1 Create a directory on your machine, C: \SSAS_2012_DB.
2 Copy the file "AdventureWorksDWDW2012_Data.mdf" in this directory.
3 Open SQL Server Management Studio, login to "Database Engine".
4 Right click on "Databases", Select "Attach".
5 Click "Add" button and select the file AdventureWorksDWDW2012_Data.mdf.
6 Click on the log file and then click on the "remove" button at the bottom of the screen.

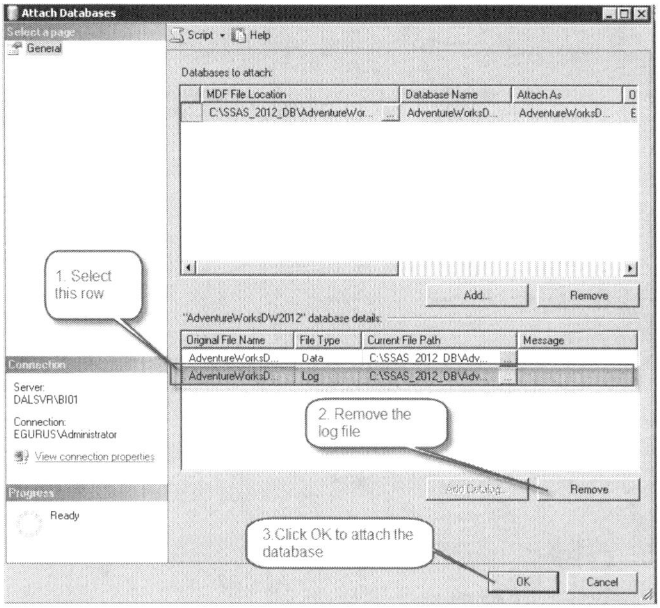

Figure 1-2: Attach relational data warehouse database.

7 Click "OK" button, this will attach the database "AdventureWorksDW2012".

Step 4: Open SQL Server Analysis Services project and configure deployment server.

1 Create a directory "C:\Projects", unzip the zip file "AdventureWorks Multidimensional Models SQL Server 2012.zip" in "C:\Projects\AdventureWorks Multidimensional Models SQL Server 2012" directory.
2 Open the directory C:\Projects\AdventureWorks Multidimensional Models SQL Server 2012.
3 Open the directory "AdventureWorks Multidimensional Models SQL Server 2012".
4 Open the directory "Enterprise".
5 Open the Visual Studio solution file "AdventureWorksDW2012Multidimensional-EE".
6 Select on the project "AdventureWorksDW2012Multidimensional-EE" just below the solution "AdventureWorksDW2012Multidimensional-EE" in solution explorer.
7 From top menu click "Project" and then select properties.
8 Click on "Deployment" tab.
9 Populate your appropriate server in "Server" field, in my case it is "DALSVR\BI01", where DALSVR is the server name and BI01 is the name of the SQL Server named instance.

Figure 1-3: Deployment configuration and Data Source.

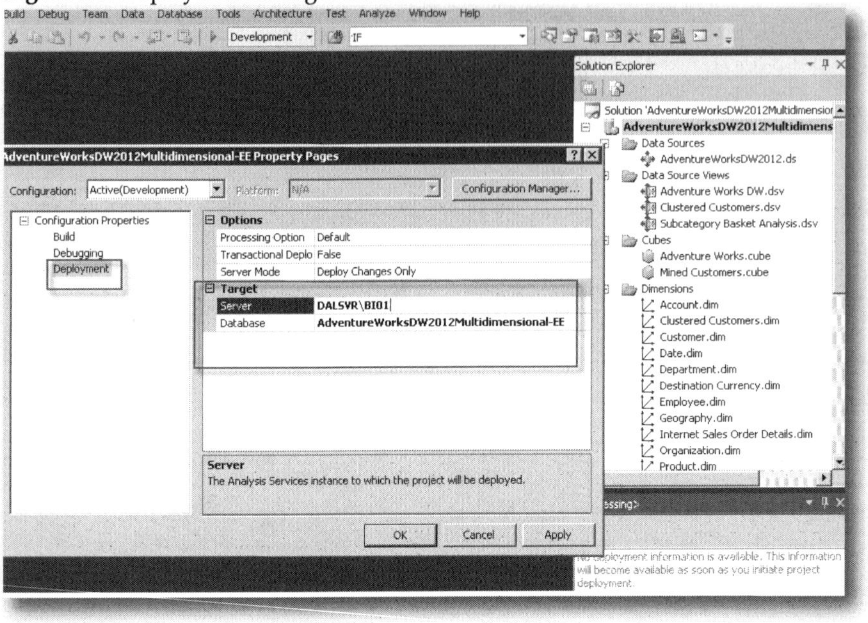

Step 5: Configure data source.

1 In solution explorer, just below the project name "AdventureWorksDW2012Multidimensional-EE", expand the folder "Data Sources", and double-click on "AdventureWorksDW2012.ds".

2 Click on "Edit" button and select appropriate server, in my case "DALSVR\BI01".

3 Make sure the database name in "Connect to a database" is "AdventureWorksDW2012".

4 To make sure database connection is good, click on "Test Connection", and then click OK.

Step 6: Process SSAS database.

1 In solution explorer, right click on "AdventureWorksDW2012Multidimensional-EE" project and select "Rebuild".

2 After "Rebuild" completes, right click on "AdventureWorksDW2012Multidimensional-EE" and select "Process".

3 Click "Yes". This will start deployment to the server.

4 When "Process" window shows up, click on "Run". This will take several minutes, and you will see a screen that shows "Process succeeded". Close the "Process" window and Visual Studio solution.

Step 7: Verify SSAS database is created.

1 Open SQL Server Management Studio and connect to Analysis services to the server (in my case "DALSVR\BI01").

2 Expand the "Databases" node and verify the SSAS database "AdventureWorksDW2012Multidimensional-EE" exists.

This completes the environment set up.

Basic Terms & Concepts

This section explains some basic concepts of MDX and SQL Server Analysis Services.

Tuple

- Tuples are members of an ordered set.
  Let us consider a set "Countries":
  Countries = {[United States], [United Kingdom], [Canada], [France], [Germany], [China], [India]}
  Some tuples of set "Countries" are:
  t1 = ([United States])
  t2 = ([United Kingdom])
  t3 = ([Canada])
  t4 = ([France])
- Tuples are enclosed by parenthesis ().
- Tuples can have more than one member.
  Let us consider three sets as follows:
  Countries = {[United States], [United Kingdom], [Canada], [France], [Germany], [China], [India]}
  Sports = {[Tennis], [Baseball], [Football], [Cricket]}
  Languages = {[English], [French], [German], [Mandarin], [Hindi]}

  Some tuples with two members are:
  A1= ([United States], [Football])
  A2= ([United States], [Baseball])
  A3= ([United Kingdom], [Tennis]) ,
  A4= ([United Kingdom], [Cricket])

  Some tuples with three members are:
  B1= ([United States], [Football], [English])
  B2= ([Germany], [Tennis], [German])
  B3= ([France], [Tennis], [French])
  B4= ([India], [Cricket], [English])
  B5= ([India], [Cricket], [Hindi]).
  Similarly, you can create tuples with four members, tuples with five members, etc.
- A tuple can have only one member from a particular set.
  This means, in the previous example, you cannot have tuples like
  - ([United Kingdom], [Tennis], [United States])
    Because, two members are from set "Countries".
  - ([United States], [Baseball], [Football])
    Because, two members are from set "Sports".

  In other words, a tuple cannot have more than one member from a set.
- Tuple follow the sequence of members in a tuple.
  This means, in tuple ([United States], [Football], [English]), the sequence is (Country, Sport, Language), and this tuple is not same as ([Football], [United States], [English]), which has different sequence.

Set

- A set is a collection of similar tuples.
  From previous examples
  - Tuples A1, A2, A3 and A4 can belong to same set.
    S1 = {A1, A2, A3, A4}, because all tuples have same template (Country, Sport)
  - Tuples A1, B2 cannot belong to same set, because the template of tuple A1 and tuple B2 is different. Template of A1 is (Country, Sport) and template of B2 is (Country, Sport, Language).
  - Tuples (United States, Football, English) and (Football, United States, English) cannot belong to same set, because the sequence of the members are not same.
- Sets are enclosed by curly brackets {}.

Dimension

- Dimension defines business objects. For example, Product, Date, and Person etc.
- Each dimension object is uniquely identified by a key value.

Hierarchy

- A hierarchy defines relationships between two or more levels within a given dimension.
  For example, in "Calendar" hierarchy of [Date] dimension.
  - [Date] level rolls up to [Month] level.
  - [Month] level rolls up to [Calendar Quarter] level.
  - [Calendar Quarter] level rolls up to [Calendar Semester] level.
  - [Calendar Semester] level rolls up to [Calendar Year] level.

Level

In the previous example, some levels in the hierarchy "Calendar" are Date, Month, "Calendar Quarter" , "Calendar Semester" and "Calendar Year" etc.

Member

Each level of a hierarchy consists of members. A Member is an instance of a level. For example, a member of level "Month" in the hierarchy "Calendar" is [Date].[Calendar].[Month].&[2008]&[2].

Fact Table /Measure Groups

- Fact tables record a process or an event.
- Create one fact table per process or event type. For example, "sale" is a process, "booking a ticket" is a process.
- A fact table connected with dimension tables via foreign keys.
- Level of detail in a fact table is known as grain of the fact table.
- Design your fact table for the lowest level of data, then you will be able to aggregate data for higher level.
- Fact table exist in relational data warehouse.
- A fact table may have one or more facts.
- Measure groups are representation of "Fact Tables" in the corresponding cube.
- A measure represents a fact in a fact table.

Structure of MDX query

Basic structure of an MDX query is shown in the figure.

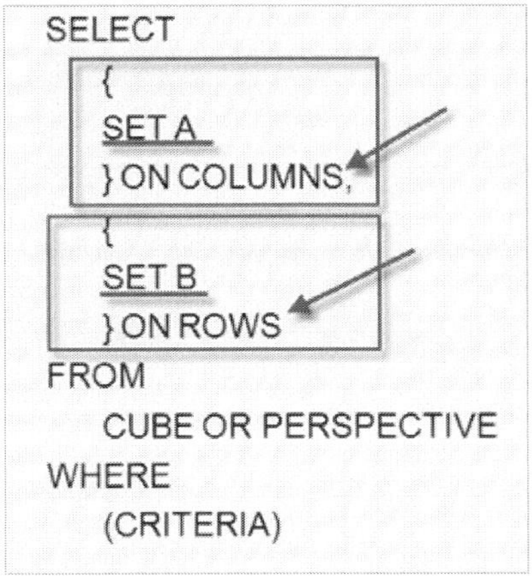

Figure 1-4: Structure of MDX query.

- "SET A" display data in **columns**.
- "SET B" display data in **rows**.
- Sets are enclosed by {} and separated by coma.
- Columns come first then rows.
- You cannot define an axis without defining its predecessors.
- Means, you cannot display rows without displaying columns.
- **"From"** clause has the cube name or perspectives.
- **"Where"** clause limits the query with certain criteria.

Axes

You can name axes in three different ways, named axes, numbered axes and AXIS with a parenthesis as below:

Named Axes	Numbered Axes	Numbered with AXIS
Columns	0	AXIS(0)
Rows	1	AXIS(1)
Pages	2	AXIS(2)
Sections	3	AXIS(3)
Chapters	4	AXIS(4)

Query#1.01: First MDX Query

Goal: Find Total "Internet Sales Amount" for the company "Adventure Works".

MDX	Result
SELECT { [Measures].[Internet Sales Amount] } ON COLUMNS FROM [Adventure Works]	Internet Sales Amount $29,358,677.22

Analysis:

- In above query, "Internet Sales Amount" is total internet sales ever done by fictitious company "Adventure Works".
- You can replace "COLUMNS" with 0 or axis(0).

Query#1.02:

Goal: Find [Internet Sales Amount] for each fiscal year.

Strategy:

- Display [Internet Sales Amount] on columns.
- Display [Fiscal Year] on rows.

<table>
<tr><th></th><th>Option 1</th><th>Option 2</th></tr>
<tr><td>MDX</td><td>SELECT
{
[Measures].[Internet Sales Amount]
} ON COLUMNS,
{
[Date].[Fiscal].[Fiscal Year]
} ON ROWS
FROM
[Adventure Works]</td><td>SELECT
{
[Measures].[Internet Sales Amount]
} ON COLUMNS,
{
[Date].[Fiscal Year].[Fiscal Year]
} ON ROWS
FROM
[Adventure Works]</td></tr>
<tr><td>Result</td><td><table><tr><th></th><th>Internet Sales Amount</th></tr><tr><td>FY 2005</td><td>(null)</td></tr><tr><td>FY 2006</td><td>$7,072,084.24</td></tr><tr><td>FY 2007</td><td>$5,762,134.30</td></tr><tr><td>FY 2008</td><td>$16,473,618.05</td></tr><tr><td>FY 2009</td><td>$50,840.63</td></tr><tr><td>FY 2010</td><td>(null)</td></tr><tr><td>FY 2011</td><td>(null)</td></tr></table></td><td><table><tr><th></th><th>Internet Sales Amount</th></tr><tr><td>FY 2005</td><td>(null)</td></tr><tr><td>FY 2006</td><td>$7,072,084.24</td></tr><tr><td>FY 2007</td><td>$5,762,134.30</td></tr><tr><td>FY 2008</td><td>$16,473,618.05</td></tr><tr><td>FY 2009</td><td>$50,840.63</td></tr><tr><td>FY 2010</td><td>(null)</td></tr><tr><td>FY 2011</td><td>(null)</td></tr></table></td></tr>
</table>

Analysis:

- [Measures].[Internet Sales Amount] displayed on columns.
- To display fiscal years on rows, it can be done in two ways:
  1. **Option 1:** Using user defined hierarchy [Date].[Fiscal].
     This hierarchy has five levels, [Fiscal Year], [Fiscal Semester], [Fiscal Quarter], [Month] and [Date].
     The year level can be expressed as [Date].[Fiscal].[Fiscal Year].
  2. **Option 2:** Using attribute hierarchy [Date].[Fiscal Year].
     This hierarchy has two levels "All Level" and "Individual Level".
     The year level can be expressed as "Individual Level", which is [Date].[Fiscal Year].[Fiscal Year].
- The result shows null values for fiscal years FY 2005, FY 2010 and FY 2011, because there is no "Internet Sales Amount" for these years.

Query#1.03:

Goal: Find [Internet Order Quantity] for each product category for each fiscal year.

Strategy:

- Display all [Product Categories] on columns.
- Display all [Fiscal Years] on rows.
- Add [Internet Order Quantity] in "Where" clause.

MDX

```
SELECT
  {
  [Product].[Product Categories].[Category]
  } ON COLUMNS,
  {
  [Date].[Fiscal].[Fiscal Year]
  } ON ROWS
FROM
  [Adventure Works]
WHERE
  ( [Measures].[Internet Order Quantity] )
```

Result

	Accessories	Bikes	Clothing	Components
FY 2005	(null)	(null)	(null)	(null)
FY 2006	(null)	2,206	(null)	(null)
FY 2007	(null)	3,222	(null)	(null)
FY 2008	34,319	9,777	8,665	(null)
FY 2009	1,773	(null)	436	(null)
FY 2010	(null)	(null)	(null)	(null)
FY 2011	(null)	(null)	(null)	(null)

Analysis:

- [Product Categories] is a user defined hierarchy in dimension "Product", consists of three levels, [Category], [Subcategory] and [Product].
- [Product] rolls up to [Subcategory].
- [Subcategory] rolls up to [Category].
- [Product].[Product Categories].[Category] represents all product categories.
- "Where" clause sets the current Measure context to [Internet Order Quantity].
- Only one measure displayed in this query, which is [Measures].[Internet Order Quantity].
- You can display other measures like [Measures].[Internet Tax Amount], [Measures].[Internet Sales Amount] instead of Internet Order Quantity.

Query#1.04:

If you remove the "Where" clause from the previous query and run the query, the result will be as shown below:

MDX

```
SELECT
  {
  [Product].[Product Categories].[Category]
  } ON COLUMNS,
  {
  [Date].[Fiscal].[Fiscal Year]
  } ON ROWS
FROM
  [Adventure Works]
```

Result

	Accessories	Bikes	Clothing	Components
FY 2005	(null)	(null)	(null)	(null)
FY 2006	$36,814.85	$15,018,534.07	$66,327.53	$1,166,765.32
FY 2007	$124,433.35	$22,417,419.69	$750,716.33	$4,629,101.14
FY 2008	$410,049.73	$28,866,427.79	$960,796.98	$6,003,210.20
FY 2009	(null)	(null)	(null)	(null)
FY 2010	(null)	(null)	(null)	(null)
FY 2011	(null)	(null)	(null)	(null)

Question: In the above result, what is the value displaying in the result?
Answer: The value displayed in the result is called "Default Measure", every cube has a default measure and in this case, the default measure is "Reseller Sales Amount".

Goal: Find name of the default measure of the cube [Adventure Works].

MDX

```
WITH
MEMBER [Measures].[DefaultMeasure] AS
[Measures].DefaultMember.Name
SELECT
  {
  [Measures].[DefaultMeasure]
  }ON COLUMNS
FROM
  [Adventure Works]
```

Result

DefaultMeasure
Reseller Sales Amount

How to change a Default Measure?

Goal: Change the default measure of [Adventure Works] cube to "Internet Sales Amount".

Steps:

1 Open "SQL Server Data Tools".

2 Open Analysis Services Database, "AdventureWorksDW2012Multidimensional-EE". As shown in the Figure 1-5.

3 Open the cube "Adventure Works". (Steps are shown in the Figure 1-6)

4 Right click on "Adventure Works" in Measures tab, select Properties.

5 Set "DefaultMeasure" property as "Internet Sales Amount"

6 Save the project by clicking "Save" button, this will take few minutes and will save the configuration to the server.

7 Using MDX, verify the default measure is changed.

Figure 1-5 : Connect to SSAS database.

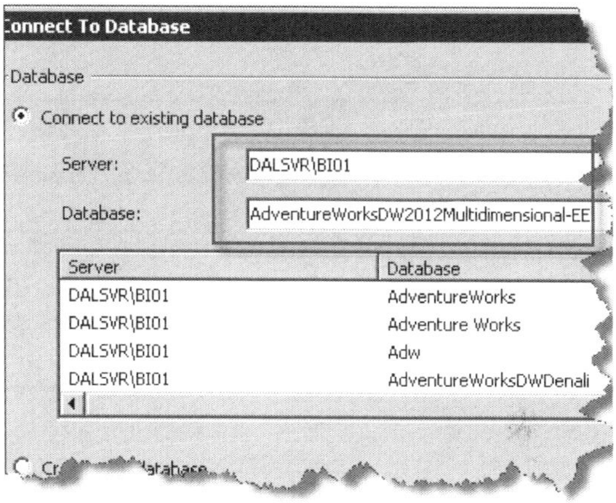

Figure 1-6 : Change default measure.

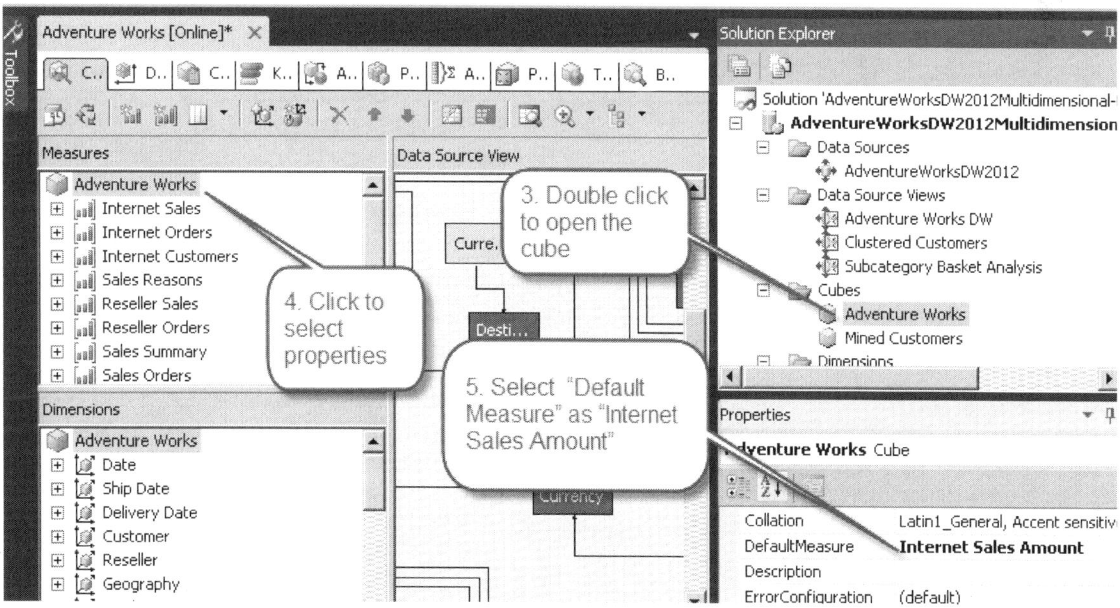

Query#1.05:

Goal:

- Find [Internet Sales Amount] for each product category for each fiscal year.
- Do not show null values.

Step 1:

- Find [Internet Sales Amount] for each product category for each fiscal year.

MDX

```
SELECT
  {
  [Product].[Product Categories].[Category]
  } ON COLUMNS,
  {
  [Date].[Fiscal].[Fiscal Year]
  } ON ROWS
FROM
  [Adventure Works]
WHERE
  [Measures].[Internet Sales Amount]
```

Result

	Accessories	Bikes	Clothing	Components
FY 2005	(null)	(null)	(null)	(null)
FY 2006	(null)	$7,072,084.24	(null)	(null)
FY 2007	(null)	$5,762,134.30	(null)	(null)
FY 2008	$667,015.32	$15,483,926.11	$322,676.62	(null)
FY 2009	$33,744.64	(null)	$17,095.99	(null)
FY 2010	(null)	(null)	(null)	(null)
FY 2011	(null)	(null)	(null)	(null)

Analysis:

- "Internet Sales Amount" is null for FY 2005, FY 2010, FY 2011 for all product categories.
- "Internet Sales Amount" is null for product category "Components" for all fiscal years.

Step 2:

- Do not show null values.

Strategy:
You can achieve the result in two ways:

- **Solution 1:** Using the key word "NON EMPTY". "NON EMPTY" returns non empty values for a row or a column. The statement, "Do not show null values" has two meanings:
  - Do not show years in rows, if value is null.
  - Do not show the product category in columns, if value is null.
- **Solution 2:** Using the function "NonEmpty". "NonEmpty" function return non empty values of a given measure for a set. The statement, "Do not show null values" has two meanings:
  - Do not show a year in rows, if all product categories have null "Internet Sales Amount" for that year, for example, FY 2005, FY 2010, FY 2011.
  - Do not show a product category in columns, if all years have null "Internet Sales Amount" for that product category, for example "Components".

Solution 1: Using key word "NON EMPTY".

MDX

```
SELECT
  NON EMPTY
  {
  [Product].[Product Categories].[Category]
  } ON COLUMNS,
  NON EMPTY
  {
  [Date].[Fiscal].[Fiscal Year]
  } ON ROWS
FROM
  [Adventure Works]
WHERE
  [Measures].[Internet Sales Amount]
```

Result

	Accessories	Bikes	Clothing
FY 2006	(null)	$7,072,084.24	(null)
FY 2007	(null)	$5,762,134.30	(null)
FY 2008	$667,015.32	$15,483,926.11	$322,676.62
FY 2009	$33,744.64	(null)	$17,095.99

Solution 2: Using function "NonEmpty".

MDX

```
SELECT
  {
  NonEmpty
    (
    [Product].[Product Categories].[Category],
    [Measures].[Internet Sales Amount]
    )
  } ON COLUMNS,
  {
  NonEmpty
    (
    [Date].[Fiscal].[Fiscal Year],
    [Measures].[Internet Sales Amount]
    )
  } ON ROWS
FROM
  [Adventure Works]
WHERE
  [Measures].[Internet Sales Amount]
```

Result

	Accessories	Bikes	Clothing
FY 2006	(null)	$7,072,084.24	(null)
FY 2007	(null)	$5,762,134.30	(null)
FY 2008	$667,015.32	$15,483,926.11	$322,676.62
FY 2009	$33,744.64	(null)	$17,095.99

Attribute Hierarchy and "All Level"

Let us consider three attributes of dimension "Product", viz. "Product", "Subcategory" and "Category". By default, each attribute has an attribute hierarchy, with the same name as attribute name and consists of two levels:

- "All Level" and
- "Individual Level"

For example, attribute hierarchy "Product" of dimension "Product" has two levels:

- "All Level": Name of the "All Level" of product dimension is "All Products".
- "Individual level": Name of individual level of attribute hierarchy "Product" is "Product".

The expression, [Product].[Product].[Product] means:

- First [Product] is the name of the **dimension**.
- Second [Product] is the name of the attribute or also known as attribute **hierarchy**.
- Third [Product] is the **level** within the attribute hierarchy [Product].
- [Product].[Product].[Product] will return list of all products.

- "All Level" is the default level of a hierarchy. This means, if you do not mention the level in a hierarchy, by default it will return "All Level".
- [Product].[Product] will return "All Products", because by default, level of attribute hierarchy "Product" is "All Products".

Query#1.06:

Goal: Find [Internet Sales Amount] for [Product].[Product] and [Product].[Product].[Product].

<table>
<tr><th>[Product].[Product]</th><th>[Product].[Product].[Product]</th></tr>
<tr><td>As level not mentioned it returns "All Level"</td><td>This is the individual level, returns all individual products</td></tr>
<tr><td>SELECT
{
[Measures].[Internet Sales Amount]
} ON COLUMNS,
{
[Product].[Product]
} ON ROWS
FROM
[Adventure Works]</td><td>SELECT
{
[Measures].[Internet Sales Amount]
} ON COLUMNS,
{
[Product].[Product].[Product]
} ON ROWS
FROM
[Adventure Works]</td></tr>
<tr><td>

	Internet Sales Amount
All Products	$29,358,677.22

</td><td>

	Internet Sales Amou
All-Purpose Bike Stand	$39,591.00
AWC Logo Cap	(null)
AWC Logo Cap	(null)
AWC Logo Cap	$19,688.10
Bike Wash - Dissolver	$7,218.60
Cable Lock	(null)

</td></tr>
</table>

User Defined Hierarchy and "All Level"

In Product dimension, there is a hierarchy called "Product Categories", this hierarchy is a user defined hierarchy and can be described as:

- The hierarchy [Product Categories] has three levels [Product], [Subcategory] and [Category].
- [Product] level rolls up to [Subcategory] level.
- [Subcategory] level rolls up to [Category] level.
- [Category] level rolls up to "All Level".

Following queries shows an example of "All Level" and a level in user defined hierarchy.

Query#1.07:

Goal: Find [Internet Sales Amount] for hierarchy [Product Categories] and for [Subcategory] level.

[Product].[Product Categories]	[Product].[Product Categories].[Subcategory]
As level not mentioned it returns "All Level"	Subcategory level returns all subcategories
SELECT { [Measures].[Internet Sales Amount] } ON COLUMNS, { [Product].[Product Categories] } ON ROWS FROM [Adventure Works]	SELECT { [Measures].[Internet Sales Amount] } ON COLUMNS, { [Product].[Product Categories].[Subcategory] } ON ROWS FROM [Adventure Works]
	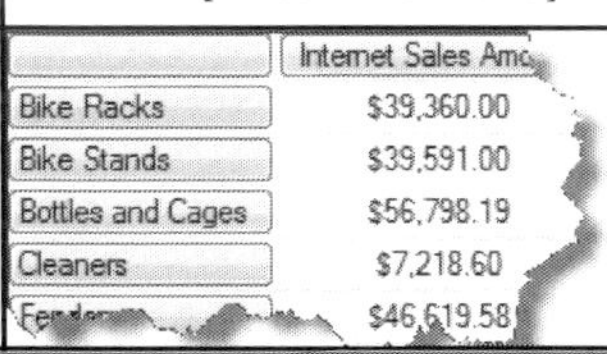

Change name of "All Level"

The name of "All Level" is configurable, there are two locations, where you can configure the name of the "All Level":

- Field "AttributesAllMemberName" of properties of a dimension, this "All Level" name applies to all attribute hierarchies of the dimension.
- Field "AllMemberName" of properties of a user defined hierarchy, this "All Level" name applies to only that user defined hierarchy.

Some more points regarding "All Level":

- "All Level" name of attribute hierarchies is different from "All Level" name of user defined hierarchy.
- "All Level" name is same for all attribute hierarchies in a dimension, because attribute hierarchy uses "All Level" name of dimension.

Goal: Change the name of "All Level" of dimension "Product" from "All Products" to "All Test Products".

Steps:

1. Open "SQL Server Data Tools".
2. Open analysis services database, "AdventureWorksDW2012Multidimensional-EE".
3. Open dimension "Product" and right click on "Product" in "Attributes" tab, select properties.
4. Find "AttributesAllMemberName", change name from "All Products" to "All Test Products".
5. Save the project, close "SQL Server Data Tools".
6. Open a new SQL Server Management Studio, select SSAS database "AdventureWorksDW2012Multidimensional-EE", open new query, expand the dimension "Product", expand "Product" attribute, expand "Members".
7. Verify that the "All Level" name of product dimension changed from "All Products" to "All Test Products".
8. After verification, change "All Level" name back to "All Products".

Goal: For user defined hierarchy "Product Categories" of dimension "Product", change the name of "All Level" from "All Products" to "All My Products".

Steps:

1. Open "SQL Server Data Tools".
2. Open analysis services database, "AdventureWorksDW2012Multidimensional-EE".
3. Open dimension "Product" and right click on "Product Categories" hierarchy, select properties.
4. Find the property "AllMemberName", change name from "All Products" to "All My Products".
5. Save the project, close "SQL Server Data Tools".
6. Open SQL Server Management Studio, open new query, expand the dimension "Product", expand "Product Categories" hierarchy , expand "Members".
7. Verify that the "All Level" name of user defined hierarchy changed from "All Products" to "All My Products".
8. After verification, change "All Level" name back to "All Products".

Members of a Hierarchy

"Members of a hierarchy" means **all members from all levels** of hierarchy and is applicable to both user defined hierarchies and attribute hierarchies.

For example, [Product].[Product Categories].Members will show all members from following levels:

- "All Level"
- Category
- Subcategory
- Product

Similarly, [Product].[Category].Members will show all members from following levels:

- "All Level"
- Category

Query#1.08:

Goal: Find [Internet Sales Amount] for [Product].[Product Categories].Members and [Product].[Category].Members.

[Product].[Product Categories].Members

```
SELECT
  {
  [Measures].[Internet Sales Amount]
  } ON COLUMNS,
  {
  [Product].[Product Categories].Members
  } ON ROWS
FROM
  [Adventure Works]
```

	Internet Sales Amoun...
All Products	$29,358,677.22
Accessories	$700,759.96
Bike Racks	$39,360.00
Hitch Rack - 4-Bike	$39,360.00
Bike Stands	$39,591.00
All-Purpose Bike Stand	$39,591.00
Bottles [illegible] Cages	[illegible]

[Product].[Category].Members

```
SELECT
  {
  [Measures].[Internet Sales Amount]
  } ON COLUMNS,
  {
  [Product].[Category].Members
  } ON ROWS
FROM
  [Adventure Works]
```

	Internet Sales Amount
All Products	$29,358,677.22
Accessories	$700,759.96
Bikes	$28,318,144.65
Clothing	$339,772.61
Components	(null)

Analysis:

- [Product].[Product Categories].Members will return all members from "All Level" , [Category], [Subcategory] and [Product] level.
- [Product].[Category].Members will return all members from "All Level" and [Category] level.

Children of a Hierarchy

"Children of a hierarchy" is not a valid statement, because children can only be possible for a member. However, that is also not completely true, because:

Children of Hierarchy = Children of Default Member of Hierarchy

- You can set default member of a user defined hierarchy using "Alter Cube" statement in calculation.

  ALTER CUBE [Adventure Works]

  UPDATE DIMENSION [Product].[Product Categories],

  DEFAULT_MEMBER = [Product].[Product Categories].[Category].[Bikes];

  In this case [Product].[Product Categories].Children = Children of "Bikes"= Subcategories of "Bikes".
- By default, "Default Member" of a Hierarchy = "Default Member" of topmost level (i.e. Category).

  "Default Member" of Category level = "All Level"

  [Product].[Product Categories].Children = Children of "All Level" i.e. all product categories.

Note: "Level of a Hierarchy" and members of "Level of a Hierarchy" returns all members of that level. This means, [Product].[Product Categories].[Category] and [Product].[Product Categories].[Category].Members will return all product categories.

Query#1.09:

Goal: Find [Internet Sales Amount] for [Product].[Product Categories].Children and [Product].[Category].Children. Both will return all product categories.

[Product].[Product Categories].Children

```
SELECT
  {
  [Measures].[Internet Sales Amount]
  } ON COLUMNS,
  {
  [Product].[Product Categories].Children
  } ON ROWS
FROM
  [Adventure Works]
```

	Internet Sales Amount
Accessories	$700,759.96
Bikes	$28,318,144.65
Clothing	$339,772.61
Components	(null)

[Product].[Category].Children

```
SELECT
  {
  [Measures].[Internet Sales Amount]
  } ON COLUMNS,
  {
  [Product].[Category].Children
  } ON ROWS
FROM
  [Adventure Works]
```

	Internet Sales Amount
Accessories	$700,759.96
Bikes	$28,318,144.65
Clothing	$339,772.61
Components	(null)

Query#1.10:

Goal: Find [Internet Sales Amount] for [Product].[Product Categories].[Category] and [Product].[Product Categories].[Category].Members. Both will return all product categories.

[Product].[Product Categories].[Category]

```
SELECT
        {
        [Measures].[Internet Sales Amount]
        } ON COLUMNS,
        {
        [Product].[Product Categories].[Category]
        } ON ROWS
FROM
        [Adventure Works]
```

	Internet Sales Amount
Accessories	$700,759.96
Bikes	$28,318,144.65
Clothing	$339,772.61
Components	(null)

[Product].[Product Categories].[Category].Members

```
SELECT
 {
 [Measures].[Internet Sales Amount]
 } ON COLUMNS,
 {
 [Product].[Product Categories].[Category].Members
 } ON ROWS
FROM  [Adventure Works]
```

	Internet Sales Amount
Accessories	$700,759.96
Bikes	$28,318,144.65
Clothing	$339,772.61
Components	(null)

SQL versus MDX

Not all MDX can be translated to corresponding SQL and vice versa, but some of the very fundamental MDX can be translated to SQL and vice versa. Consider following SQL, which displays the name of employees from department "Marketing":

```
SELECT
      FirstName + ' '+ LastName AS EmployeeName
FROM
      dbo.DimEmployee
WHERE
      DepartmentName = 'Marketing'
```

To translate above SQL to MDX, consider following points:

- The "Employee" dimension in [Adventure Works] cube represents dbo.DimEmployee table.
- Select [Employee].[Employee Department].[Employee], to display all employee names.
- In "From" clause, use the cube [Adventure Works], instead of a table name.
- Use "Where" clause to filter DepartmentName = "Marketing" by following MDX,
  WHERE [Employee].[Department Name].&[Marketing]

Query#1.11:

Goal: Display first name and last name of employees from department "Marketing".

<table>
<tr><th>SQL</th><th>MDX</th></tr>
<tr><td><pre>SELECT
  FirstName + ' '+ LastName
  AS EmployeeName
FROM
  dbo.DimEmployee
WHERE
  DepartmentName = 'Marketing'</pre></td><td><pre>SELECT
  {
  } ON COLUMNS,
  {
  [Employee].[Employee Department].[Employee]
  } ON ROWS
FROM
  [Adventure Works]
WHERE
  [Employee].[Department Name].&[Marketing]</pre></td></tr>
<tr><td>
<table>
<tr><th></th><th>EmployeeName</th></tr>
<tr><td>1</td><td>Kevin Brown</td></tr>
<tr><td>2</td><td>David Bradley</td></tr>
<tr><td>3</td><td>David Bradley</td></tr>
<tr><td>4</td><td>Sariya Hampadoungsataya</td></tr>
<tr><td>5</td><td>Mary Gibson</td></tr>
<tr><td>6</td><td>Jill Williams</td></tr>
<tr><td>7</td><td>Terry Eminhizer</td></tr>
<tr><td>8</td><td>Wanida Benshoof</td></tr>
<tr><td>9</td><td>John Wood</td></tr>
<tr><td>10</td><td>Mary Dempsey</td></tr>
</table>
</td><td>Kevin F. Brown
Mary A. Dempsey
Wanida M. Benshoof
David M. Bradley
David M. Bradley
Jill A. Williams
John L. Wood
Mary E. Gibson
Sariya E. Hampadoungsataya
Terry J. Eminhizer</td></tr>
</table>

Query#1.12:

Goal: Modify the last query and sort by employee name.

SQL

```
SELECT
  FirstName + ' '+ LastName
  AS EmployeeName
FROM
  dbo.DimEmployee
WHERE
  DepartmentName = 'Market-
ing'
ORDER BY EmployeeName
```

MDX

```
WITH
MEMBER [Measures].[EmployeeName] AS
[Employee].[Employee Department].CurrentMember.Name
SELECT
  {
  } ON COLUMNS,
  {
  ORDER
    (
    [Employee].[Employee Department].[Employee],
    [Measures].[EmployeeName],
    BASC
    )
  } ON ROWS
FROM
  [Adventure Works]
WHERE
  [Employee].[Department Name].&[Marketing]
```

SQL result

	EmployeeName
1	David Bradley
2	David Bradley
3	Jill Williams
4	John Wood
5	Kevin Brown
6	Mary Dempsey
7	Mary Gibson
8	Sariya Hampadoungsataya
9	Terry Eminhizer
10	Wanida Benshoof

MDX result

David M. Bradley
David M. Bradley
Jill A. Williams
John L. Wood
Kevin F. Brown
Mary A. Dempsey
Mary E. Gibson
Sariya E. Hampadoungsataya
Terry J. Eminhizer
Wanida M. Benshoof

Analysis:

- The second parameter of "Order" function cannot be [Employee].[Employee Department].[Employee], because [Employee].[Employee Department].[Employee] is a level and "Order" function is looking for an expression.
- A new calculated member [Measures].[EmployeeName] is created, which is an expression and can be used for sorting the set.
- The third parameter is BASC instead of ASC. BASC means break hierarchy and then sort, if you use only ASC, "Order" will sort the members within the same level of hierarchy. More detail about break hierarchy is discussed in Chapter 2.

Query#1.13:

Goal: Find total employees count.

SQL	MDX
SELECT COUNT (DISTINCT EmployeeKey) AS Employees_Total_Count FROM dbo.DimEmployee	WITH MEMBER Measures.Employees_Total_Count AS COUNT ([Employee].[Employee Department].[Employee]) SELECT { Measures.Employees_Total_Count } ON COLUMNS FROM [Adventure Works]
Employees_Total_Count 1 296	Employees_Total_Count 296

Query#1.14:

Goal: Find total employees count in department "Marketing".

SQL	MDX
SELECT COUNT (DISTINCT EmployeeKey) AS Employees_Total_Count FROM dbo.DimEmployee WHERE DepartmentName='Marketing'	WITH MEMBER Measures.Employees_Total_Count AS COUNT (FILTER ([Employee].[Employee Department].[Employee], [Employee].[Department Name].CurrentMember.Name ="Marketing")) SELECT {Measures.Employees_Total_Count } ON COLUMNS FROM [Adventure Works]
Employees_Total_Count 1 10	Employees_Total_Count 10

Query#1.15:

Goal: Find "Reseller Sales Amount" for each state of United States.

SQL

```
SELECT
  G.StateProvinceName,
  SUM(F.SalesAmount) AS SalesAmount
FROM
  dbo.DimGeography G
  JOIN dbo.DimReseller S
  ON S.GeographyKey = G.GeographyKey
  JOIN dbo.FactResellerSales F
  ON F.ResellerKey = S.ResellerKey
WHERE G.EnglishCountryRegionName
='United States'
GROUP BY G.StateProvinceName
ORDER BY G.StateProvinceName
```

	StateProvinceName	SalesAmoun...
1	Alabama	45429.029
2	Arizona	1432585.5
3	California	9764270.70
4	Colorado	2395913.84
5	Connecticut	1125700.40
6	Florida	2299888.8
7	Georgia	1044577.79
8	Idaho	227301.751
9	Illinois	607939.96
10	Indiana	1073388.587
11	Kentucky	163713.839
12	Maine	479865.529
13	Massachusetts	107353.8

MDX

```
SELECT
  {
  [Measures].[Reseller Sales Amount]
  }ON COLUMNS,
  {
  [Geography].[Geography].[State-Province]
  }ON ROWS
FROM
   [Adventure Works]
WHERE
  [Geography].[Country].&[United States]
```

	Reseller Sales Amount
Alabama	$45,429.03
Arizona	$1,432,585.57
California	$9,764,270.71
Colorado	$2,395,913.84
Connecticut	$1,125,700.41
Florida	$2,299,888.87
Georgia	$1,044,577.80
Idaho	$227,301.75
Illinois	$607,939.97
Indiana	$1,073,388.59
Kentucky	$163,713.84
Maine	$479,865.53
[illegible]	(null)

Notes:

- SQL only returns those rows, which have "Reseller Sales Amount" value.
- MDX may return some rows with null values, because:
  - MDX first returns all possible states.
  - And then finds "Reseller Sales Amount" for each state.

EXERCISES

Exercise 1.1: Find [Reseller Sales Amount] for each product category for each country.

Exercise 1.2: Display sorted list of all states of "United States".

Exercise 1.3: Find the number of cities in the state of Florida.

Chapter 2: Set Functions

Set functions are essential part of MDX.This chapter is divided into four parts. The first part of this chapter explores some basic set functions like Head, Subset, TopCount, TopPercent, Order, UnOrder, Distinct and TopSum, explained with simple examples.

One of the most important functions of the second part is the Descendants function. This function has four different forms, and the descendant flag can have seven possible value. Each of the forms and their corresponding results are explained with examples. In addition to the Descendants function, the second part of the chapter explains some interesting functions like Union, Intersect, Except, Filter, etc.

The third part of the chapter explores frequently used functions like CrossJoin, Range, Extract, NonEmptyCrossJoin, Exists and Generate. NonEmptyCrossJoin function is deprecated, and it is retained only to maintain backwards compatibility. You should use Exists and NonEmpty functions instead of NonEmptyCrossJoin function. An example shows how to convert from NonEmptyCrossJoin to NonEmpty and Exists function. Other important functions are Generate and Exists. "Generate" function is used to loop through a set and "Exists" function check for existence of tuples of a set in another set. These functions are explained in detail with various examples, and I hope you will enjoy this chapter. Last, but not least, "Exercises", will help you to practice some MDX queries.

Agenda

Head, Subset, TopCount, TopPercent, Order, UnOrder, Distinct, TopSum

Descendants, AddCalculatedMembers, StripCalculatedMembers, MeasureGroupMeasures, Filter, Union, Intersect, Except

CrossJoin, Extract, NonEmptyCrossJoin, Range, Exists, Generate

Exercises

Query#2.01:

Goal: Display "Reseller Sales Amount" for first 5 products from the list of all products.

Strategy:

- [Product].[Product Categories].[Product] returns the list of all products.
- Alternatively, you can use [Product].[Product].[Product] to list all products.
- Return first 5 products means, return from beginning of the list without any sorting criteria.

MDX

```
SELECT
  {
  [Measures].[Reseller Sales Amount]
  }ON COLUMNS,
  {
  Head
    (
    [Product].[Product Categories].[Product],
    5
    )
  }ON ROWS
FROM
  [Adventure Works]
```

Result

	Reseller Sales Amount
Hitch Rack - 4-Bike	$197,736.16
All-Purpose Bike Stand	(null)
Mountain Bottle Cage	(null)
Road Bottle Cage	(null)
Water Bottle - 30 oz.	$7,476.60

Analysis:

- "Head" function returns items from beginning of a list.
- First parameter of "Head" function is a list.
- Second parameter of "Head" is the number of items you want to return.

Head **(<Set> [, <Count>])**

<Set>:

- An expression that returns a valid set, e.g. [Product].[Product Categories].[Product].

<Count>:

- Number of members you want to return from the set <Set>, e.g. 5.
- This is an optional parameter, if no value is passed, Head function will return first member of the set <Set>.

The Result:

- This returns items from beginning of a list.

Query#2.02:

Goal: Display [Reseller Sales Amount] for 5 products from third position from the list of products.

Strategy:

- You cannot use "Head" function, because "Head" function always return items from beginning of a list.
- Use "Subset" function to get the expected result.

MDX

```
SELECT
  {
  [Measures].[Reseller Sales Amount]
  }ON COLUMNS,
  {
  Subset
    (
    [Product].[Product Categories].[Product],
    2,
    5
    )
  }ON ROWS
FROM
  [Adventure Works]
```

Result

	Reseller Sales Amount
Mountain Bottle Cage	(null)
Road Bottle Cage	(null)
Water Bottle - 30 oz.	$7,476.60
Bike Wash - Dissolver	$11,188.37
Fender Set - Mountain	(null)

Analysis:

- Subset function return items from any part of a set.
- Second parameter of Subset function is starting location with 0 based indexes.
- Third parameter of Subset function is the number of items you want to return.

Subset **(<Set>, <Start> [, <Count>])**

<Set>:

- An expression that returns a valid set, e.g. [Product].[Product Categories].[Product].

<Start>:

- The start location within the set <Set>, e.g. 2.

<Count>:

- Number of members from the set <Set>, e.g. 5.
- This is an optional parameter, if no value is passed, Subset function will return the rest of the set from <Start> location.

The Result:

- This returns items from any part of a set.

Query#2.03:

Goal: Display "Top 5 products" from the list of all products sorted by "Reseller Sales Amount".

Strategy:

- Sort the list of products by "Reseller Sales Amount" in descending order.
- Then, select first 5 products from the sorted list.

MDX

```
SELECT
  {
  [Measures].[Reseller Sales Amount]
  }ON COLUMNS,
  {
  TopCount
    (
    [Product].[Product Categories].[Product],
    5,
    [Measures].[Reseller Sales Amount]
    )
  }ON ROWS
FROM
  [Adventure Works]
```

Result

	Reseller Sales Amount
Mountain-200 Black, 38	$1,634,647.94
Mountain-200 Black, 38	$1,471,078.72
Road-350-W Yellow, 48	$1,380,253.88
Touring-1000 Blue, 60	$1,370,784.22
Mountain-200 Black, 42	$1,360,828.02

Analysis:

- First parameter of "TopCount" function is the list of all products.
- Second parameter of "TopCount" function is the number of items you want to return.
- Third parameter of "TopCount" function is the expression for sorting the set.

TopCount **(<Set>, <Count> [, <Numeric_Expression>])**

<Set>:

- An expression that returns a valid set, e.g. [Product].[Product Categories].[Product].

<Count>:

- Number of members from the set <Set>, for example, 5.

<Numeric_Expression>:

- A numeric expression to sort the set <Set>.
- This is an optional parameter, if no value passed, TopCount will act like Head function and will return <Count> items from beginning of the set <Set>.

The Result:

- This returns items from beginning of a list sorted by <Numeric_Expression> in descending order.

Query#2.04:

Goal: Display "Top 15% products" from the list of all products sorted by "Internet Sales Amount".

Strategy: Using "TopPercent" function means:

- Sort products list by "Internet Sales Amount" in descending order.
- Select first 15% products from the above list, which means, total sum of "Internet Sales Amount" of selected products equal or more than 15%.

Step 1: Find total "Internet Sales Amount"

MDX	SELECT
	{
	[Measures].[Internet Sales Amount]
	}
	ON COLUMNS
	FROM
	[Adventure Works]

Result	Internet Sales Amount $29,358,677.22

Note: 1% of total "Internet Sales Amount" = $293,586.77

Step 2: Display "Top 1% products" from the list of all products sorted by "Internet Sales Amount".

MDX	SELECT { [Measures].[Internet Sales Amount] } ON COLUMNS, { TopPercent ([Product].[Product Categories].[Product], 1, [Measures].[Internet Sales Amount]) } ON ROWS FROM [Adventure Works]
Result	| Internet Sales Amount Road-150 Red, 48 | $1,205,876.99

Analysis:

- Only one row shows in the result, because "Internet Sales Amount" in the first row is more than 1% of total [Internet Sales Amount].

Step 3: Display "Top 15% products" from the list of all products sorted by [Internet Sales Amount].

MDX

```
SELECT
  {
  [Measures].[Internet Sales Amount]
  } ON COLUMNS,
  {
  TopPercent
    (
    [Product].[Product Categories].[Product],
    15,
    [Measures].[Internet Sales Amount]
    )
  } ON ROWS
FROM
 [Adventure Works]
```

Result

	Internet Sales Amount
Road-150 Red, 48	$1,205,876.99
Road-150 Red, 62	$1,202,298.72
Road-150 Red, 52	$1,080,637.54
Road-150 Red, 56	$1,055,589.65

Analysis:

- 1% of total "Internet Sales Amount" = $293,586.77.
- 15% of total "Internet Sales Amount" = $293,586.77*15 = $4,403,801.55.
- Sum of the all rows from above result = $4,544,402.90.
  Which is just crossed 15% of total [Internet Sales Amount].

TopPercent (<Set>, <Percentage>, <Numeric_Expression>)

<Set>:

- An expression that returns a valid set, e.g. [Product].[Product Categories].[Product].

<Percentage>:

- This is the percentage of total value, for example, 15%.

<Numeric_Expression>:

- A numeric expression to sort the set <Set>.

The Result:

- This returns items from beginning of a list sorted in descending order based on <Numeric_Expression>. Accumulated value of selected items are just greater than or equal to <Percentage> of total <Numeric_Expression> for the set <Set>.

Query#2.05:

Goal: Find "Internet Sales Amount" for each Product Category, and sort by "Internet Sales Amount" in descending order.

MDX	

```
SELECT
 {
 [Measures].[Internet Sales Amount]
 } ON COLUMNS,
 {
 ORDER
  (
  [Product].[Product Categories].[Category],
  [Measures].[Internet Sales Amount],
  DESC
  )
 } ON ROWS
FROM
 [Adventure Works]
```

Result

	Internet Sales Amount
Bikes	$28,318,144.65
Accessories	$700,759.96
Clothing	$339,772.61
Components	(null)

Analysis:

- The second parameter is the name of the field by which the result will be sorted.
- The third parameter describes how you want to sort the result. Possible values are ASC, DESC, BASC or BDESC. BASC & BDESC means break hierarchy before sorting.
- In this case, DESC and BDESC will return same result because all product categories are in the same level.

What is "Break" of Hierarchy?

Let us assume there are four levels in a hierarchy L1, L2, L3 and L4 and consists of following members:

- Members in level "L1": A-L1, B-L1, C-L1.
- Members in level "L2": A-L2, B-L2, C-L2.
- Members in level "L3": A-L3, B-L3, C-L3.
- Members in level "L4": A-L4, B-L4, C-L4.

If you order by the member name, here are four possible cases:

- **Case#1 (ASC)** - Sorting within each level:
  <u>A-L1, B-L1, C-L1,</u> <u>A-L2, B-L2, C-L2,</u> <u>A-L3, B-L3, C-L3,</u> <u>A-L4, B-L4, C-L4</u>.

- **Case#2 (BASC) -** Do not depend on level:
  A-L1, A-L2, A-L3, A-L4, B-L1,B-L2,B-L3,B-L4, C-L1,C-L2,C-L3,C-L4.

- **Case#3 (DESC) -** Sorting within each level:
  C-L1, B-L1, A-L1, C-L2, B-L2, A-L2, C-L3, B-L3, A-L3, C-L4, B-L4, A-L4.
- **Case#4 (BDESC) -** Do not depend on level:
  C-L4, C-L3, C-L2, C-L1, B-L4, B-L3, B-L2, B-L1, A-L4, A-L3, A-L2, A-L1.

Order **(<Set>, <Numeric_Expression>|<String_Expression> [,{ASC|BASC|DESC|BDESC}])**

<Set>:

- An expression that returns a valid set, e.g. [Product].[Product Categories].[Product].

<Numeric_expression>:

- A valid numeric expression, for example, [Measures].[Internet Sales Amount].

<String_expression>:

- A valid string expression, for example, [Measures].[EMail Address], which is the email address of an employee.

ASC|BASC|DESC|BDESC:

- This is the sorting type.
- This is an optional parameter, if no value is passed, the default value is ASC.

The Result:

- This returns a sorted set.

Following query displays list of all employees:

```
SELECT
  {
  } ON COLUMNS,
  {
  [Employee].[Employee Department].[Employee]
  }ON ROWS
FROM
  [Adventure Works]
```

To sort all employees list by employee name, you **cannot** use following code:

```
SELECT
  {
  } ON COLUMNS,
  {
  Order
    (
    [Employee].[Employee Department].[Employee],
    [Employee].[Employee Department].[Employee],
    ASC
    )
  }ON ROWS
FROM
  [Adventure Works]
```

The second parameter of "Order" function is a level expression, not a numeric or string expression. Instead, you should create a calculated member, which evaluates the name of the current employee.

Query#2.06:

Goal: Display name of all employees, and sorted by employee name in descending order.

Strategy:

- Use "Order" function to sort the employee list.
- As Employees belongs to different levels of hierarchy, use BDESC instead of DESC.

MDX	WITH MEMBER [Measures].[Employee Name] AS [Employee].[Employee Department].CurrentMember.Name SELECT { } ON COLUMNS, { **Order** ([Employee].[Employee Department].[Employee], [Measures].[Employee Name], BDESC) }ON ROWS FROM [Adventure Works]
Result	

Analysis:

- Sorting using BDESC breaks the hierarchy.
- [Measures].[Employee Name] is a string expression and used to sort the set of all employees.
- [Employee].[Employee Department].[Employee] is a level and cannot be used for sort the set of all employees.

UnOrder

"UnOrder" function does not have any effect in result of a query but "Unorder" function is used as a hint to MDX Query Engine that ordering is not required for this set expression, and these hint can improve the performance of the query. For example, following MDX query hints SQL Server that no sorting required for the set [Product].[Product Categories].[Category].

```
SELECT
  {
  [Measures].[Internet Sales Amount]
  }
  ON COLUMNS,
  {
  UnOrder
    (
    [Product].[Product Categories].[Category]
    )
  }
  ON ROWS
FROM  [Adventure Works]
```

Distinct

Distinct function returns unique set of values and does not show any duplicate values, following query shows use of "Distinct" function. Named set "My Product Categories" consists of duplicate product categories "Bikes" and "Clothing". "Distinct" function will remove the duplicates.

MDX	WITH
	SET [My Product Categories] AS
	  {
	  [Product].[Product Categories].[Category].[Accessories],
	  [Product].[Product Categories].[Category].[Bikes],
	  [Product].[Product Categories].[Category].[Bikes],
	  [Product].[Product Categories].[Category].[Clothing],
	  [Product].[Product Categories].[Category].[Clothing],
	  [Product].[Product Categories].[Category].[Components]
	  }
	SELECT
	  { [Measures].[Internet Sales Amount] } ON COLUMNS,
	  { Distinct ([My Product Categories]) } ON ROWS
	FROM
	  [Adventure Works]

Result	| Internet Sales Amount Accessories | $700,759.96 Bikes | $28,318,144.65 Clothing | $339,772.61 Components | (null)

Query#2.07:

Goal: Show top products which have at least "Internet Sales Amount" value $3,000,000 cumulatively.

MDX

```
SELECT
  {
  [Measures].[Internet Sales Amount]
  } ON COLUMNS,
  {
  TopSum
    (
    [Product].[Product Categories].[Product],
    3000000,
    [Measures].[Internet Sales Amount]
    )
  } ON ROWS
FROM
 [Adventure Works]
```

Result

	Internet Sales Amount
Road-150 Red, 48	$1,205,876.99
Road-150 Red, 62	$1,202,298.72
Road-150 Red, 52	$1,080,637.54

Analysis:

- The criteria is cumulative value of internet sales amount is equal or just crossed $3,000,000.
- As the value increases, it adds items in descending order.
- Here is the order of steps:
  - Add topmost product, Road-150 Red, 48($1,205,876.99) = Total $1,205,876.99 < $3,000,000
  - Add 2nd topmost product, Road-150 Red, 62($1,202,298.72) = Total $2,408,175.71 < $3,000,000
  - Add 3rd topmost product, Road-150 Red, 52($1,080,637.54) = Total $3,488,813.25 > $3,000,000
- TopSum and BottomSum break the hierarchy.

TopSum (<Set>, <Value>, <Numeric_Expression>)

<Set>:

- An expression that returns a valid set, e.g. [Product].[Product Categories].[Product].

<Value>:

- This is the value against which tuples are compared, for example, 3,000,000.

<Numeric_expression>:

- A valid numeric expression, typically a measure, e.g. [Measures].[Internet Sales Amount].

The Result:

- This returns items from beginning part of a list sorted in descending order based on <Numeric_Expression>. Accumulated value of selected items is just greater than or equal to <Value>.

Descendants

There are four forms of "Descendants" function, as follows:

FORM-1

Descendants (<Member>, <Distance>, <Descendant_Flag>)

<Member>:

- Member of a hierarchy, for example, [Geography].[Geography].[Country].&[United States] is a member of hierarchy [Geography].

<Distance>:

- Distance of level from the first parameter, for example, 2.

<Descendant_Flag>:

- This flag indicates, what should be included in the resultant set.
- Possible flags are SELF, AFTER, BEFORE, SELF_AND_AFTER, SELF_AND_BEFORE, SELF_BEFORE_AFTER and LEAVES.
- Detail explanations of flags are as follows:

  SELF

  The self is the level defined in second parameter or a level that located at distance <Distance> from member/set defined in first parameter.

  For example, if "United States" is the member (first parameter) and distance is 1, then SELF means all "State-Province" of "United States".

  AFTER

  This means all descendants of SELF.

  BEFORE

  BEFORE means anything before SELF and up to member or set defined in first parameter.

  BEFORE includes the member or set defined in first parameter.

  BEFORE does not include SELF.

  SELF_AND_AFTER

  This set consists of all members of SELF and AFTER.

  SELF_AND_BEFORE

  This set consists of all members of SELF and BEFORE.

  SELF_BEFORE_AFTER

  This set consists of all members of SELF, BEFORE and AFTER.

  LEAVES

  This means all nodes of the SELF.

The Result:

- This returns descendants of member <Member> for a given <Distance> for <Descendant_Flag>.

FORM-2

Descendants **(<Member>, <Level>, <Descendant_Flag>)**

<Member>:

- Member in a hierarchy, e.g. [Geography].[Geography].[Country].&[United States].

<Level>:

- Level in hierarchy, e.g. [Geography].[Geography].[State-Province].

<Descendant_Flag>:

- Same as described in FORM-1.

The Result:

- This returns descendants of <Member> for a given <Level> for <Descendant_Flag>.

FORM-3

Descendants **(<Set>, <Distance>, <Descendant_Flag>)**

<Set>:

- Set of members from same level of a hierarchy, for example,
  {[Geography].[Geography].[Country].&[United States],
  [Geography].[Geography].[Country].&[Canada]}

<Distance>:

- Distance from first parameter, e.g. 2.

<Descendant_Flag>:

- Same as described in FORM-1.

The Result:

- This returns descendants of set <Set> for a given <Distance> for <Descendant_Flag>.

FORM-4

Descendants **(<Set>, <Level>, <Descendant_Flag>)**

<Set>:

- Set of members from same level of a hierarchy, for example,
  {
  [Geography].[Geography].[Country].&[United States],
  [Geography].[Geography].[Country].&[Canada]
  }

<Level>:

- Level in hierarchy, for example,
  [Geography].[Geography].[State-Province]

<Descendant_Flag>:

- Same as described in FORM-1.

The Result:

- This returns descendants of set <Set> for a given <Level> for <Descendant_Flag>.

Query#2.08:

Goal: Find all cities of "United States". [Hint: use Descendants function, (FORM 1)].

MDX	SELECT
	  {
	  } ON COLUMNS,
	  {
	  DESCENDANTS
	    (
	    [Geography].[Geography].[Country].&[United States],
	    2,
	    SELF
	    )
	  }ON ROWS
	FROM
	  [Adventure Works]

Result	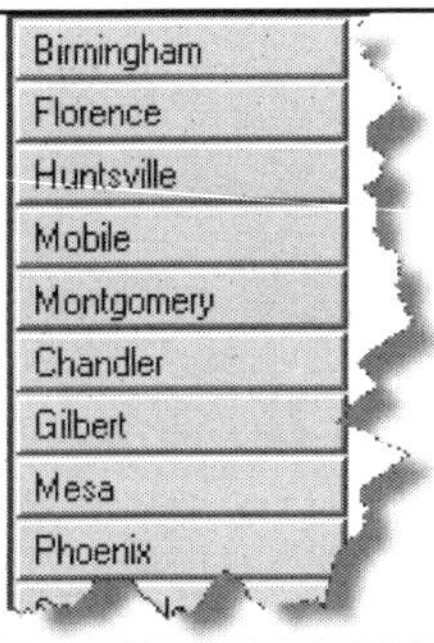

Analysis:

- The first parameter of "Descendants" function is a member expression. [Geography].[Geography].[Country].&[United States]
- The second parameter is the distance from the first parameter. Value passed is 2.
- The third parameter is an optional parameter. If not passed, the default parameter is SELF. Here are the results for all possible values of Descendant_Flag:
  - SELF: Distance = 2, means two levels below the first parameter, that means, "All cities of United States".
  - AFTER: All descendants after "SELF", that means all postal codes of United States.
  - BEFORE: "United States and all states of United States", because:
    - Before SELF and up to member defined in the first parameter.
    - BEFORE includes the member defined in the first parameter.
    - BEFORE does not include SELF.
  - SELF_AND_AFTER: "All cities of United States" and "All postal codes of United States".
  - SELF_AND_BEFORE: "All cities of United States", "United States" and "All states of United States".
  - SELF_BEFORE_AFTER: "All cities of United States", "United States", "All states of United States" and "All postal codes of United States".
  - LEAVES: "All cities of United States".

Query#2.09:

Goal: Find all states and cities of "United States". [Hint: use Descendants function (FORM 2)].

MDX

```
SELECT
  {
  } ON COLUMNS,
  {
  DESCENDANTS
    (
    [Geography].[Geography].[Country].&[United States],
    [Geography].[Geography].[City],
    SELF_AND_BEFORE
    )
  -
  [Geography].[Geography].[Country].&[United States]
  }ON ROWS
FROM
  [Adventure Works]
```

Result

Analysis:

- The first parameter is a member expression [Geography].[Geography].[Country].&[United States].
- The second parameter is a level which is [Geography].[Geography].[City].
- The third parameter is an optional parameter. If not passed, the default parameter is SELF. Here are the results for all possible values of Descendant_Flag:
  - SELF: Members of the level passed in the second parameter = "All cities of United States".
  - AFTER: All descendants after "SELF", that means "All postal codes of United States".
  - BEFORE: "United States" and "All states of United States", because:
    - Before SELF and up to member defined in the first parameter.
    - BEFORE includes the member defined in first parameter.
    - BEFORE does not include SELF.
  - SELF_AND_AFTER: "All cities of United States" and "All postal codes of United States".
  - SELF_AND_BEFORE: "All cities of United States", "United States" and "All states of United States".To get the expected result, remove "United States" from this set, which will give "All cities" and "States of United States".
  - SELF_BEFORE_AFTER: "All cities of United States", "United States", "All states of United States" and "All postal codes of United States".
  - LEAVES: All cities of United States.

Query#2.10:

Goal: Find all cities of "United States" and "Canada". [Hint: use Descendants function (FORM 3)].

MDX	Result
(see code below)	(see result below)

```
SELECT
  {
  } ON COLUMNS,
  {
  DESCENDANTS
    (
      {
      [Geography].[Geography].[Country].&[United States],
      [Geography].[Geography].[Country].&[Canada]
      },
    2,
    SELF
    )
  }ON ROWS
FROM
  [Adventure Works]
```

Analysis:

- The first parameter is the set of two countries, United States & Canada.
- The second parameter is the distance from the set in the first parameter. The value is 2.
- The third parameter is an optional parameter, default parameter is SELF. If not passed, the default parameter is SELF. Here are the results for all possible values of Descendant_Flag:
  - SELF: Two levels from the first parameter, which means, all cities of United States and Canada.
  - AFTER: All descendants after "SELF", that means all postal codes of United States and Canada.
  - BEFORE: Means, "United States and Canada" and "All States of United States and Canada":
    - Before SELF and up to the set defined in first parameter.
    - BEFORE includes the set defined in first parameter.
    - BEFORE does not include SELF.
  - SELF_AND_AFTER: All cities and postal codes of United States and Canada.
  - SELF_AND_BEFORE: United States and Canada, all cities and all states of United States and Canada.
  - SELF_BEFORE_AFTER: United States and Canada, all cities, postal codes and states of United States and Canada.
  - LEAVES: All cities of United States and Canada.

Query#2.11:

Goal: Find States and Cities of "United States" and "Canada". [Hint: use Descendants function (FORM 4)].

MDX

```
SELECT
  {
  } ON COLUMNS,
  {
  DESCENDANTS
    (
      {
      [Geography].[Geography].[Country].&[United States],
      [Geography].[Geography].[Country].&[Canada]
      },
    [Geography].[Geography].[City],
    SELF_AND_BEFORE
    ) -
    {
    [Geography].[Geography].[Country].&[United States],
    [Geography].[Geography].[Country].&[Canada]
    }
  }ON ROWS
FROM
  [Adventure Works]
```

Result

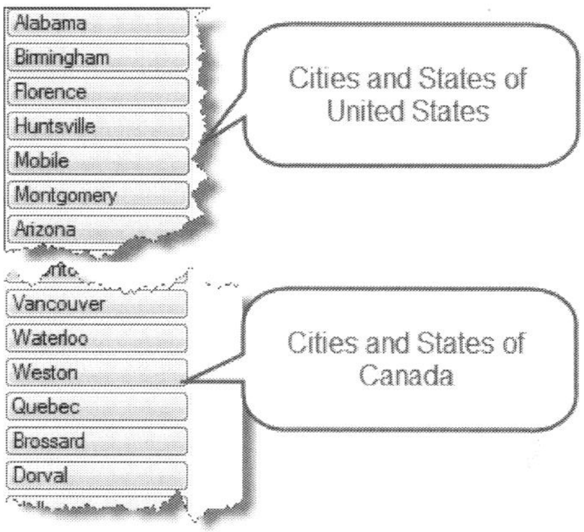

Analysis:

- The first parameter is a set, consists of United States and Canada.
- The second parameter is the level, [Geography].[Geography].[City].
- The third parameter is an optional parameter. If not passed, the default parameter is SELF. Here are the results for all possible values of Descendant_Flag:
  - SELF: The level passed in the second parameter,that is all cities of United States and Canada.
  - AFTER: All descendants after "SELF", that means all postal codes of United States and Canada.
  - BEFORE: "United States and Canada" and "All states of United States and Canada", because:
    - Before SELF and up to set defined in the first parameter.
    - BEFORE includes the set defined in the first parameter.
    - BEFORE does not include SELF.
  - SELF_AND_AFTER: All cities and postal codes of United States and Canada.
  - SELF_AND_BEFORE: United States and Canada, all cities and states of United States and Canada.
  - SELF_BEFORE_AFTER: United States and Canada, all cities, postal codes and states of United States and Canada.
  - LEAVES: In this case, "All cities of United States and Canada".

Query#2.12:

Goal: Find all calculated measures of [Adventure Works] cube.

MDX	SELECT { } ON COLUMNS, { AddCalculatedMembers ([Measures].Members) - [Measures].Members }ON ROWS FROM [Adventure Works]
Result	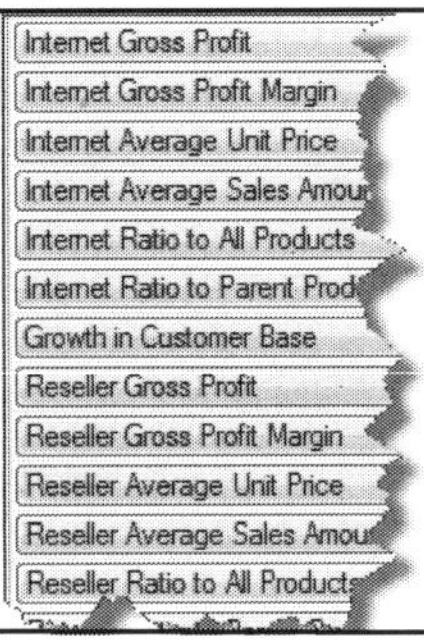

Analysis:

- [Measures].Members does not include calculated members.
- The function, "AddCalculatedMembers" adds all calculated members.
- Similarly, "StripCalculatedMembers" function removes calculated members from a set.

AddCalculatedMembers (<Set>)

<Set>:

- An expression that returns a valid set, for example, [Measures].members.

The Result:

- This function returns the union of <Set> and all calculated members of <Set>.

AddCalculatedMembers not only applies to "Measures" dimension but also to any other dimensions. Following steps creates a calculated member [Product].[Category].[Clothing and Accessories], and display using the function AddCalculatedMembers,

Steps:

1 Open SQL Server Data Tools.
2 Open analysis services database "AdventureWorksDW2012Multidimensional-EE".
3 Open the cube "Adventure Works".
4 Go to "Calculations" tab.

5 Click "Script View" button in the tool bar to toggle to script view of "Calculations".

6 Go to the end of the "Calculations" and add following code:

```
CREATE MEMBER CURRENTCUBE.[Product].[Category].[Clothing and Accessories] AS
    SUM
      (
        {
        [Product].[Category].[Accessories],
        [Product].[Category].[Clothing]
        }
      )
```

This code will create a calculated member "Clothing and Accessories" in "Product" dimension.

7 Save and close "SQL Server Data Tools".

8 Run following MDX queries.

Without AddCalculatedMembers

```
SELECT
  {
  [Measures].[Internet Sales Amount]
  } ON COLUMNS,
  {
  [Product].[Category].Members
  } ON ROWS
FROM
  [Adventure Works]
```

	Internet Sales Amount
All Products	$29,358,677.22
Accessories	$700,759.96
Bikes	$28,318,144.65
Clothing	$339,772.61
Components	(null)

With AddCalculatedMembers

```
SELECT
  {
  [Measures].[Internet Sales Amount]
  } ON COLUMNS,
  {
  AddCalculatedMembers
    (
    [Product].[Category].Members
    )
  } ON ROWS
FROM
  [Adventure Works]
```

	Internet Sales Amount
All Products	$29,358,677.22
Accessories	$700,759.96
Bikes	$28,318,144.65
Clothing	$339,772.61
Components	(null)
Clothing and Accessories	$1,040,532.57

Calculated Member

Query#2.13:

Goal: Display only non-calculated members from the following set of measures:

```
{
[Measures].[Internet Sales Amount],
[Measures].[Internet Order Quantity],
[Measures].[Internet Gross Profit]
}
```

Note: [Measures].[Internet Gross Profit] is a calculated member.

Without StripCalculatedMembers

```
SELECT
  {
  [Measures].[Internet Sales Amount],
  [Measures].[Internet Order Quantity],
  [Measures].[Internet Gross Profit]
  } ON COLUMNS,
  {
  [Product].[Product Categories].[Category]
  } ON ROWS
FROM
  [Adventure Works]
```

	Internet Sales Amount	Internet Order Quantity	Internet Gross Profit
Accessories	$700,759.96	36,092	$438,674.57
Bikes	$28,318,144.65	15,205	$11,505,796.50
Clothing	$339,772.61	9,101	$136,412.58
Components	(null)	(null)	(null)

With StripCalculatedMembers

```
SELECT
  {
  StripCalculatedMembers
    (
      {
      [Measures].[Internet Sales Amount],
      [Measures].[Internet Order Quantity],
      [Measures].[Internet Gross Profit]
      }
    )
  } ON COLUMNS,
  {
  [Product].[Product Categories].[Category]
  } ON ROWS
FROM
  [Adventure Works]
```

	Internet Sales Amount	Internet Order Quantity
Accessories	$700,759.96	36,092
Bikes	$28,318,144.65	15,205
Clothing	$339,772.61	9,101
Components	(null)	(null)

StripCalculatedMembers **(<Set>)**

<Set>:

- An expression that returns a valid set, for example,
  [Product].[Product].Members
  [Measures].Members

The Result:

- This function returns a set by removing any calculated members from a given set <Set>.

Query#2.14:

Goal: Display name of all measures of the measure group "Internet Sales".

MDX

```
SELECT
  {
  }  ON COLUMNS,
  {
  MeasureGroupMeasures("Internet Sales")
  }  ON ROWS
FROM
  [Adventure Works]
```

Result

Internet Sales Amount
Internet Order Quantity
Internet Extended Amount
Internet Tax Amount
Internet Freight Cost
Internet Total Product Cost
Internet Standard Product Cost

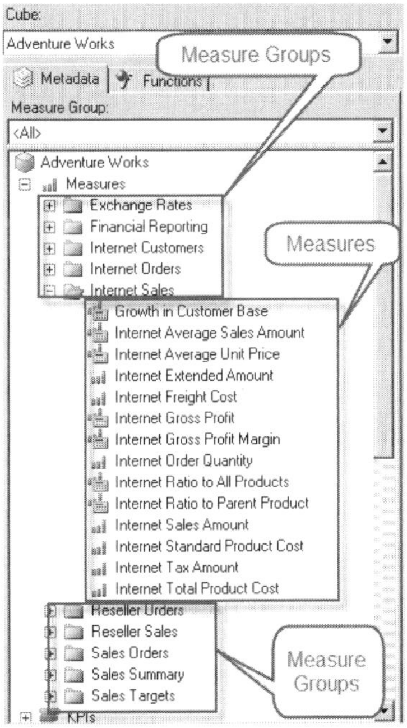

Figure 2-1: Difference between Measure and Measure Groups.

- Measure Groups typically represent a Fact table.
- You can have one or more measures in a measure group.
- Measures are fields in a fact table.

MeasureGroupMeasures **(<MeasureGroupName>)**

<MeasureGroupName>:

- A valid measure group name.

The Result:

- This function returns all measures of a given measure group.

Query#2.15:

Goal: Show only those product categories for which "Internet Sales Amount" exceed $500,000 for fiscal year 2008.

Showing all product categories

```
SELECT
  {
  [Measures].[Internet Sales Amount]
  } ON COLUMNS,
  {
  [Product].[Product Categories].[Category]
  } ON ROWS
FROM
  [Adventure Works]
WHERE
  [Date].[Fiscal].[Fiscal Year].&[2008]
```

	Internet Sales Amount
Accessories	$667,015.32
Bikes	$15,483,926.11
Clothing	$322,676.62
Components	(null)

Showing only filtered product categories

```
SELECT
  {
  [Measures].[Internet Sales Amount]
  } ON COLUMNS,
  {
  FILTER
    (
    [Product].[Product Categories].[Category],
    [Measures].[Internet Sales Amount] >500000
    )
  } ON ROWS
FROM
  [Adventure Works]
WHERE
  [Date].[Fiscal].[Fiscal Year].&[2008]
```

	Internet Sales Amount
Accessories	$667,015.32
Bikes	$15,483,926.11

Filter (<Set>, <Logical_Expression>)

<Set>:

- Expression returns a valid set.
  For example, [Product].[Product Categories].[Category].

<Logical_expression>:

- An expression evaluates true or false.

The Result:

- This returns a set consists of members from <Set> which returns true for <Logical_expression>.

Query#2.16:

Goal: Find cities, which are in top 10 reseller sales either in fiscal year 2007 or 2008.

Strategy:

- Set1 = Cities that are in top 10 sales for fiscal year 2007.
- Set2 = Cities that are in top 10 sales for fiscal year 2008.
- The expected result is the union of sets, Set1 and Set2.

MDX

```
WITH
SET [Top 10 Cities in FY 2007-2008] AS
UNION
   (
   TopCount
      (
      [Geography].[Geography].[City],
      10,
         (
         [Measures].[Reseller Sales Amount],
         [Date].[Fiscal].[Fiscal Year].&[2007]
         )
      ),
   TopCount
      (
      [Geography].[Geography].[City],
      10,
         (
         [Measures].[Reseller Sales Amount],
         [Date].[Fiscal].[Fiscal Year].&[2008]
         )
      )
   )
SELECT
   {
   [Measures].[Reseller Sales Amount]
   } ON COLUMNS,
   {
   [Top 10 Cities in FY 2007-2008]
   } ON ROWS
FROM
   [Adventure Works]
```

Top 10 cities for 2007

Reseller Sales Amount

Reseller Sales Amount for FY 2007

Top 10 cities for 2008

Result

	Reseller Sales Amount
Toronto	$4,460,477.69
London	$1,935,729.92
Nashua	$1,103,370.47
Paris	$1,452,049.41
Memphis	$1,104,968.39
Seattle	$1,494,860.53
Richmond	$1,258,920.00
Garland	$1,123,139.92
Burnaby	$1,304,163.69
Orleans	$989,510.13
Montreal	$1,129,784.47
Sand City	$534,956.28
Vancouver	$790,199.30

Analysis:

- [Measures].[Reseller Sales Amount] is the total Reseller Sales Amount .
- ([Measures].[Reseller Sales Amount], [Date].[Fiscal].[Fiscal Year].&[2007]) is the "Reseller Sales Amount" for fiscal year 2007.

Union (<Set1>, <Set2> [,...n][, ALL])

The Result:

- Returns union of two or more sets.
- If "ALL" parameter is passed, union will retain to duplicate members.

Alternate Syntax

- <Set1> + <Set2> [,...n]
- {<Set1>, <Set2> [,...n]}

Query#2.17:

Goal: Find cities, which are in top 10 reseller sales in fiscal year 2007 as well as in fiscal year 2008.

Strategy:

- Set1 = Cities that are in top 10 sales for fiscal year 2007.
- Set2 = Cities that are in top 10 sales for fiscal year 2008.
- The expected result is the intersection of sets, Set1 and Set2.

MDX

```
WITH
SET [Top 10 Cities in FY 2007-2008] AS
INTERSECT
   (
   TopCount
      (
      [Geography].[Geography].[City],
      10,
         (
         [Measures].[Reseller Sales Amount],
         [Date].[Fiscal].[Fiscal Year].&[2007]
         )
      ),
   TopCount
      (
      [Geography].[Geography].[City],
      10,
         (
         [Measures].[Reseller Sales Amount],
         [Date].[Fiscal].[Fiscal Year].&[2008]
         )
      )
   )
SELECT
   {
   [Measures].[Reseller Sales Amount]
   } ON COLUMNS,
   {
   [Top 10 Cities in FY 2007-2008]
   } ON ROWS
FROM
   [Adventure Works]
```

Top 10 cities for 2007

Reseller Sales Amount for FY 2007

Top 10 cities for 2008

Result

	Reseller Sales Amount
Toronto	$4,460,477.69
London	$1,935,729.92
Paris	$1,452,049.41
Seattle	$1,494,860.53
Richmond	$1,258,920.00
Burnaby	$1,304,163.69
Orleans	$989,510.13

Intersect (<Set1>, <Set2> [,...n][, ALL])

The Result:

- Returns intersection of two or more sets.
- If "ALL" parameter is passed, the intersection will retain to duplicate members.

Query#2.18:

Goal: Find cities which are in "Top 10 list" of reseller sales in fiscal year 2007 but could not make in to "Top 10 list" for fiscal year 2008.

Strategy:

- Set1 = Cities that are in top 10 sales for fiscal year 2007.
- Set2 = Cities that are in top 10 sales for fiscal year 2008.
- Except "Set2" from "Set1" will return required result.

MDX

```
WITH
SET [Top 10 Cities in FY 2007-2008] AS
EXCEPT
   (
   TopCount
      (
      [Geography].[Geography].[City],
      10,
         (
         [Measures].[Reseller Sales Amount],
         [Date].[Fiscal].[Fiscal Year].&[2007]
         )
      ),
   TopCount
      (
      [Geography].[Geography].[City],
      10,
         (
         [Measures].[Reseller Sales Amount],
         [Date].[Fiscal].[Fiscal Year].&[2008]
         )
      )
   )
SELECT
   {
   [Measures].[Reseller Sales Amount]
   } ON COLUMNS,
   {
   [Top 10 Cities in FY 2007-2008]
   } ON ROWS
FROM
   [Adventure Works]
```

Result

	Reseller Sales Amount
Nashua	$1,103,370.47
Memphis	$1,104,968.39
Garland	$1,123,139.92

Except (<Set1>, <Set2> [, ALL])

The Result:

- Remove tuples from the <Set1> that exist in the set <Set2>.
- If "ALL" parameter is passed, the result will retain to duplicate members.

Alternate Syntax

- <Set1> - <Set2>

Query#2.19:

Goal: For each reseller, find "Reseller Sales Amount" for each product category for each year.

Step 1: Find "Reseller Sales Amount" for each product category.

MDX

```
SELECT
  {
  [Measures].[Reseller Sales Amount]
  } ON COLUMNS,
  {
  [Product].[Product Categories].[Category]
  } ON ROWS
FROM
  [Adventure Works]
```

Result

	Reseller Sales Amount
Accessories	$571,297.93
Bikes	$66,302,381.56
Clothing	$1,777,840.84
Components	$11,799,076.66

Step 2: Find "Reseller Sales Amount" for each product category for each year.

To find product categories for each year, use the "CrossJoin" function. Cross join is Cartesian product of two sets. For example, let us consider two sets:

- SetA = {(A1), (A2), (A3)}
- SetB = {(B1), (B2)}

Then,
SetA CrossJoin SetB = {(A1, B1), (A1, B2), (A2, B1), (A2, B2), (A3, B1), (A3, B2)}
Similarly, to find product category for each fiscal year, you can use cross join of {Product categories} and {Fiscal Years}.

MDX

```
SELECT
   {
   [Measures].[Reseller Sales Amount]
   } ON COLUMNS,
   {
   CrossJoin
      (
      [Product].[Product Categories].[Category],
      [Date].[Fiscal].[Fiscal Year]
      )
   } ON ROWS
FROM
   [Adventure Works]
```

Result

		Reseller Sales Amount
Accessories	FY 2005	(null)
Accessories	FY 2006	$36,814.85
Accessories	FY 2007	$124,433.35
Accessories	FY 2008	$410,049.73
Accessories	FY 2009	(null)
Accessories	FY 2010	(null)
Accessories	FY 2011	(null)
Bikes	FY 2005	(null)
Bikes	FY 2006	$15,018,534.07
Bikes	FY 2007	$22,417,419.69
Bikes	FY 2008	$28,866,427.79
Bikes	FY 2009	(null)
Bikes	FY 2010	(null)
Bikes	FY 2011	(null)

Step 3: For each Reseller, find "Reseller Sales Amount" for each product categories for each year.

MDX

```
SELECT
  {
  [Measures].[Reseller Sales Amount]
  } ON COLUMNS,
  {
  [Reseller].[Reseller Type].[Reseller]
  *
  [Product].[Product Categories].[Category]
  *
  [Date].[Fiscal].[Fiscal Year]
  } ON ROWS
FROM
  [Adventure Works]
```

Result

			Reseller Sales Amount
A Great Bicycle Company	Accessories	FY 2005	(null)
A Great Bicycle Company	Accessories	FY 2006	(null)
A Great Bicycle Company	Accessories	FY 2007	(null)
A Great Bicycle Company	Accessories	FY 2008	(null)
A Great Bicycle Company	Accessories	FY 2009	(null)
A Great Bicycle Company	Accessories	FY 2010	(null)
A Great Bicycle Company	Accessories	FY 2011	(null)
A Great Bicycle Company	Bikes	FY 2005	(null)
A Great Bicycle Company	Bikes	FY 2006	$8,532.68
A Great Bicycle Company	Bikes	FY 2007	$469.79
A Great Bicycle Company	Bikes	FY 2008	(null)
A Great Bicycle Company	Bikes	FY 2009	(null)
A Great Bicycle Company	Bikes	FY 2010	(null)
A Great Bicycle Company	Bikes	FY 2011	(null)
A Great Bicycle Company	Clothing	FY 2005	(null)
A Great Bicycle Company	Clothing	FY 2006	$15.56

CrossJoin (<Set1>, <Set2> [,...n])

Set_expression (<Set1>, <Set2> ...n):

- Expression returns a valid set, for example, [Product].[Product].[Product Category Name].

The Result:

- This returns Cartesian product of two or more sets.

Alternate Syntax:

- <Set1> * <Set2> * <Set3> * ...n.

Query#2.20:

Goal: From the last cross join, list all distinct years.

MDX

```
SELECT
   {
   [Measures].[Reseller Sales Amount]
   } ON COLUMNS,
   {
   Extract
     (
       {
       [Reseller].[Reseller Type].[Reseller]
       *
       [Product].[Product Categories].[Category]
       *
       [Date].[Fiscal].[Fiscal Year]
       },
     [Date].[Fiscal]
     )
   } ON ROWS
FROM
   [Adventure Works]
```

Result

	Reseller Sales Amount
FY 2005	(null)
FY 2006	$16,288,441.77
FY 2007	$27,921,670.52
FY 2008	$36,240,484.70
FY 2009	(null)
FY 2010	(null)
FY 2011	(null)

Analysis:

- The first parameter of "Extract" function is a set created by a CrossJoin.
- The second parameter of "Extract" function is a hierarchy, which is [Fiscal Year].
- The "Extract" function extracts current member of the hierarchy from the set.

Similarly, following query shows extract product categories from the last cross join.

MDX

```
SELECT
   {
   [Measures].[Reseller Sales Amount]
   } ON COLUMNS,
   {
   Extract
     (
       {
       [Reseller].[Reseller Type].[Reseller]
       *
       [Product].[Product Categories].[Category]
       *
       [Date].[Fiscal].[Fiscal Year]
       },
     [Product].[Product Categories]
     )
   } ON ROWS
FROM
   [Adventure Works]
```

Result

	Reseller Sales Amount
Accessories	$571,297.93
Bikes	$66,302,381.56
Clothing	$1,777,840.84
Components	$11,799,076.66

Extract (<Set>, <Hierarchy1> [, <Hierarchy2>, ...n])

<Set>:

- Expression returns a valid set, typically a CrossJoin in this case.
  For example, {[Product].[Product Categories].[Category] * [Date].[Fiscal].[Fiscal Year]}.

<Hierarchy1>, <Hierarchy2> ...n:

- These are hierarchies and typically, sub part of <Set>.

You can also extract more than one hierarchy from the last cross join. Following query shows extract all product categories and fiscal years from the last cross join.

MDX

```
SELECT
   {
   [Measures].[Reseller Sales Amount]
   } ON COLUMNS,
   {
   Extract
      (
         {
         [Reseller].[Reseller Type].[Reseller]
         *
         [Product].[Product Categories].[Category]
         *
         [Date].[Fiscal].[Fiscal Year]
         },
      [Product].[Product Categories],
      [Date].[Fiscal]
      )
   } ON ROWS
FROM
   [Adventure Works]
```

Result

		Reseller Sales Amount
Accessories	FY 2005	(null)
Accessories	FY 2006	$36,814.85
Accessories	FY 2007	$124,433.35
Accessories	FY 2008	$410,049.73
Accessories	FY 2009	(null)
Accessories	FY 2010	(null)
Accessories	FY 2011	(null)
Bikes	FY 2005	(null)
Bikes	FY 2006	$15,018,534.07
Bikes	FY 2007	$22,417,419.69
Bikes	FY 2008	$28,866,427.79
Bikes	FY 2009	(null)
Bikes	FY 2010	(null)
Bikes	FY 2011	(null)
Clothing	FY 2005	(null)
Clothing	FY 2006	$66,327.53
Clothing	FY 2007	$750,716.33
Clothing	FY 2008	$960,796.98
Clothing	FY 2009	(null)
Clothing	FY 2010	(null)
Clothing	FY 2011	(null)
Components	FY 2005	(null)
Components	FY 2006	$1,166,765.32
Components	FY 2007	$4,629,101.14

Analysis:

- If the set expression is {[Product].[Product Categories].[Category] * [Date].[Fiscal].[Fiscal Year]}, you cannot use [Reseller].[Reseller Type] as hierarchy expression because this hierarchy does not exist in the set expression.
- Typically, the set expression is a cross join, but if you have a set which is not a cross join, for example, [Product].[Product Categories].[Category], the only one hierarchy expression you can use for extract is [Product].[Product Categories].

Query#2.21:

Goal: Find "Reseller Sales Amount" for each product category for each year, only show non empty values or show only those values that have association.

With CrossJoin

```
SELECT
  {
  [Measures].[Reseller Sales Amount]
  } ON COLUMNS,
  {
  CrossJoin
    (
    [Product].[Product Categories].[Category],
    [Date].[Fiscal].[Fiscal Year]
    )
  } ON ROWS
FROM
  [Adventure Works]
```

		Reseller Sales Amount
Accessories	FY 2005	(null)
Accessories	FY 2006	$36,814.85
Accessories	FY 2007	$124,433.35
Accessories	FY 2008	$410,049.73
Accessories	FY 2009	(null)
Accessories	FY 2010	(null)
Accessories	FY 2011	(null)
Bikes	FY 2005	(null)
Bikes	FY 2006	$15,018,534.07
Bikes	FY 2007	$22,417,419.69
Bikes	FY 2008	$28,866,427.79
Bikes	FY 2009	(null)

With NonEmptyCrossJoin

```
SELECT
  {
  [Measures].[Reseller Sales Amount]
  } ON COLUMNS,
  {
  NonEmptyCrossJoin
    (
    [Product].[Product Categories].[Category],
    [Date].[Fiscal].[Fiscal Year]
    )
  } ON ROWS
FROM
  [Adventure Works]
```

		Reseller Sales Amount
Accessories	FY 2006	$36,814.85
Accessories	FY 2007	$124,433.35
Accessories	FY 2008	$410,049.73
Bikes	FY 2006	$15,018,534.07
Bikes	FY 2007	$22,417,419.69
Bikes	FY 2008	$28,866,427.79
Clothing	FY 2006	$66,327.53
Clothing	FY 2007	$750,716.33
Clothing	FY 2008	$960,796.98
Components	FY 2006	$1,166,765.32
Components	FY 2007	$4,629,101.14
Components	FY 2008	$6,003,210.20

Note: NonEmptyCrossJoin function is deprecated, and you should not use this function. It is retained only to maintain backwards compatibility. You should use Exists and NonEmpty functions instead.

NonEmptyCrossJoin (<Set1> [, <Set2>, ...] [,<Count>])

<Set1>:

- Expression returns a valid set, e.g. [Product].[Product Categories].[Category].

<Count>:

- This is an optional parameter, if this value is passed; only <Count> number of sets will return.
- NonEmptyCrossJoin (SetA, SetB, SetC, SetD, 2) will return only SetA and SetB.

The Result:

- This returns only non-empty values of a CrossJoin.
- All calculated members will be excluded by this function.

Query#2.22:

Goal: Modify Query#2.21 and replace "NonEmptyCrossJoin" using NonEmpty function.

MDX

```
SELECT
  {
  [Measures].[Reseller Sales Amount]
  } ON COLUMNS,
  {
  NonEmpty
    (
      {
      [Product].[Product Categories].[Category]
      *
      [Date].[Fiscal].[Fiscal Year]
      },
    [Measures].[Reseller Sales Amount]
    )
  } ON ROWS
FROM  [Adventure Works]
```

Result

		Reseller Sales Amount
Accessories	FY 2006	$36,814.85
Accessories	FY 2007	$124,433.35
Accessories	FY 2008	$410,049.73
Bikes	FY 2006	$15,018,534.07
Bikes	FY 2007	$22,417,419.69
Bikes	FY 2008	$28,866,427.79
Clothing	FY 2006	$66,327.53
Clothing	FY 2007	$750,716.33
Clothing	FY 2008	$960,796.98
Components	FY 2006	$1,166,765.32
Components	FY 2007	$4,629,101.14
Components	FY 2008	$6,003,210.20

Query#2.23:

Goal: Modify Query#2.21 and replace "NonEmptyCrossJoin" using "Exists" function.

MDX

```
SELECT
  {  [Measures].[Reseller Sales Amount]  } ON COLUMNS,
  {
  Exists
    (
      {
      [Product].[Product Categories].[Category]
      *  [Date].[Fiscal].[Fiscal Year]
      },
      {
      [Product].[Product Categories].[Category]
      *  [Date].[Fiscal].[Fiscal Year]
      },
    "Reseller Sales"
    )
  } ON ROWS
FROM  [Adventure Works]
```

Result

		Reseller Sales Amount
Accessories	FY 2006	$36,814.85
Accessories	FY 2007	$124,433.35
Accessories	FY 2008	$410,049.73
Bikes	FY 2006	$15,018,534.07
Bikes	FY 2007	$22,417,419.69
Bikes	FY 2008	$28,866,427.79
Clothing	FY 2006	$66,327.53
Clothing	FY 2007	$750,716.33
Clothing	FY 2008	$960,796.98
Components	FY 2006	$1,166,765.32
Components	FY 2007	$4,629,101.14
Components	FY 2008	$6,003,210.20

Exists (<Set1>, <Set2> [, <MeasureGroupName>])

<Set1>:

- An expression that returns a valid set, e.g. [Product].[Product Categories].[Category].

<Set2>:

- Expression returns a valid set, typically, a subset of <Set1>. If <Set1> and <Set2> are same, the result will return all members of <Set1>.

<MeasureGroupName>:

- This is an optional parameter.
- This is a measure group name in quotes.

The Result:

- This returns tuples of <Set1> that exists in <Set2>.
- If <MeasureGroupName> value is passed, it will return tuples of <Set1> that exist in <Set2> and associated with the MeasureGroup specified in third parameter.

Inspect the following query:

Without Exists Function	With Exists Function

SELECT
{
[Measures].[Internet Sales Amount]
} ON COLUMNS,
{
[Product].[Product Categories].[Category]
} ON ROWS
FROM
[Adventure Works]
	SELECT
	{[Measures].[Internet Sales Amount]} ON COLUMNS,
	{
	Exists
	(
	[Product].[Product Categories].[Category],
	{
	[Product].[Product Categories].[Subcategory].[Road Bikes],
	[Product].[Product Categories].[Subcategory].[Touring Bikes],
	[Product].[Product Categories].[Subcategory].[Gloves],
	[Product].[Product Categories].[Subcategory].[Shorts]
	}
	)
	} ON ROWS
	FROM [Adventure Works]

Without Exists Function result:

	Internet Sales Amount
Accessories	$700,759.96
Bikes	$28,318,144.65
Clothing	$339,772.61
Components	(null)

With Exists Function result:

	Internet Sales Amount
Bikes	$28,318,144.65
Clothing	$339,772.61

Analysis:

- "Exists" function limits the list of product categories.
- Only shows those product categories, which have subcategories listed in second set.

Query#2.24:

Goal: Show "Internet Sales Amount" for each month from February, 2008 to September, 2008, for the state of "Texas".

Strategy:

- Given months are from the same dimension ([Date]), same hierarchy ([Calendar]) and same level ([Month]).
- The best way to create set of months is using range operator.

MDX

```
SELECT
   {
   [Measures].[Internet Sales Amount]
   } ON COLUMNS,
   {
   [Date].[Calendar].[Month].&[2008]&[2]
   :
   [Date].[Calendar].[Month].&[2008]&[9]
   } ON ROWS
FROM
   [Adventure Works]
WHERE
   [Geography].[Geography].[State-Province].&[TX]&[US]
```

Result

	Internet Sales Amount
February 2008	$1,462,479.83
March 2008	$1,480,905.18
April 2008	$1,608,750.53
May 2008	$1,878,317.51
June 2008	$1,949,361.11
July 2008	$50,840.63
August 2008	(null)
September 2008	(null)

Analysis:

- Colon between two values defines the range.
- Both the members should be from the same dimension, same hierarchy and same level.
- If the first parameter is null, it starts from beginning of the list.
- If the second parameter is null, it will return the list from first member to end of the list.

Composite Keys:

- [Date].[Calendar].[Month].&[2008]&[2] identifies February, 2008. The key of Month level is a collection of two attributes "Calendar Year" and "MonthNumberOfYear".
- [Geography].[Geography].[State-Province].&[TX]&[US] identifies state of "Texas" (TX) of United States (US). The key of [State-Province] level is a collection of two attributes "StateProvinceCode" and "CountryRegionCode" and that is the reason, the expression is:
  [Geography].[Geography].[State-Province].&[TX]&[US] instead of
  [Geography].[Geography].[State-Province].&[TX]

Following steps demonstrates the key of [State-Province] level is a collection of two attributes "StateProvinceCode" and "CountryRegionCode".

Steps:

1 Open "SQL Server Data Tools".

2 Open Analysis Services Database, "AdventureWorksDW2012Multidimensional-EE".

3 Open the cube "Adventure Works".

4 Double-click on "Geography" dimension in solution explorer.
5 Right click on the attribute "State-Province" in attribute's tab.
6 Select properties.
7 Find "Key Columns" and click on the ellipse of "Collection".
8 Verify the key is made up of "StateProvinceCode" and "CountryRegionCode"

Figure 2-2 : Key collection of a level

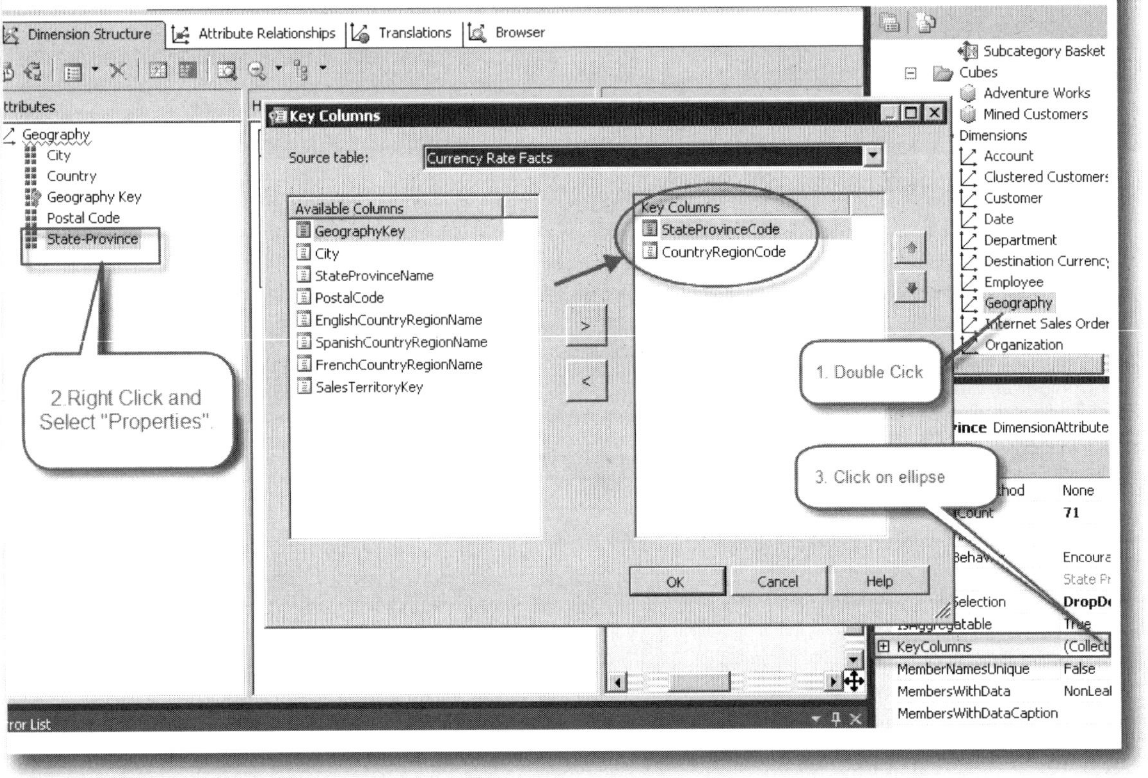

It is very important to understand why the key is not one attribute but collection of attributes:

- Only state code is not enough to identify a state, because there may be another state with the same name in another country. To make the key unique, the key of State-Province level is a combination of Country code and state code.
- Similarly, only "MonthNumberOfYear" is not enough to identify a month, because there is another month with the same name in another year. Hence, the key of month level is a combination of "Calendar Year" and "MonthNumberOfYear".

Generate

The "Generate" function returns a set by applying "one set" to "each member of another set". This function has two forms as described below:

FORM 1

Generate (<Set1>, <Set2> [, ALL])

<Set1>:

- Expression returns a valid set, e.g. [Product].[Product Categories].[Category].

<Set2>:

- Expression returns a valid set. Typically <Set2> depends on <Set1>.

ALL:

- This is an optional parameter.
- If this value is passed, the result will be returned without removing duplicates.

The Result:

- If <Set2> depends on <Set1>, <Set2> applies to each member of <Set1>.
- If <Set2> does not depend on <Set1>, this will return <Set2> times number of members in <Set1>.
- Union them all and return the set.
- If third parameter "ALL" is passed, duplicate values will be returned else distinct values will be returned.

FORM 2

Generate (<Set>, <String> [, <Delimiter>])

<Set>:

- Expression returns a valid set, e.g. [Product].[Product Categories].[Category].

<String>:

- Expression returns a string. Typically, <String> depends on <Set>.

<Delimiter>:

- This is an optional parameter.
- If no third parameter is passed, the string will be just concatenated with no delimiter.

The Result:

- If <String> depends on <Set>, <String> applies to each member of <Set>.
- Concatenate them all.

Query#2.25:

Inspect the following query:

MDX	Result

WITH
MEMBER [Product].[Product].[P1] AS "P1"
MEMBER [Product].[Product].[P2] AS "P2"
MEMBER [Product].[Product].[P3] AS "P3"
SET [SETP] AS
{
[Product].[Product].[P1],
[Product].[Product].[P2],
[Product].[Product].[P3]
}
MEMBER [Reseller].[Reseller].[R1] AS "R1"
MEMBER [Reseller].[Reseller].[R2] AS "R2"
MEMBER [Reseller].[Reseller].[R3] AS "R3"
 	
SET [SETR] AS
{
[Reseller].[Reseller].[R1],
[Reseller].[Reseller].[R2],
[Reseller].[Reseller].[R3]
}
SELECT
{
} ON COLUMNS,
{
GENERATE ([SETP],[SETR])
} ON ROWS
FROM
[Adventure Works]
	R1
	R2
	R3

Analysis:

- In Generate function
  - Set1 = SETP
  - Set2 = SETR, Set2 does not depend on Set1
  - It will loop through Set1 three times, as it has three items, and returns {(R1),(R2),(R3)} for each loop.
  - As the third parameter "ALL" is not passed, it will return {(R1), (R2), (R3)} one time instead of three times.

Query#2.26:

Inspect the following query:

MDX	Result

WITH
MEMBER [Product].[Product].[P1] AS "P1"
MEMBER [Product].[Product].[P2] AS "P2"
MEMBER [Product].[Product].[P3] AS "P3"
 	
SET [SETP] AS
{
[Product].[Product].[P1],
[Product].[Product].[P2],
[Product].[Product].[P3]
}
MEMBER [Reseller].[Reseller].[R1] AS "R1"
MEMBER [Reseller].[Reseller].[R2] AS "R2"
MEMBER [Reseller].[Reseller].[R3] AS "R3"
 	
SET [SETR] AS
{
[Reseller].[Reseller].[R1],
[Reseller].[Reseller].[R2],
[Reseller].[Reseller].[R3]
}
SELECT
{
} ON COLUMNS,
{
GENERATE ([SETP],{[SETP].Current}*[SETR])
} ON ROWS
FROM
[Adventure Works]
	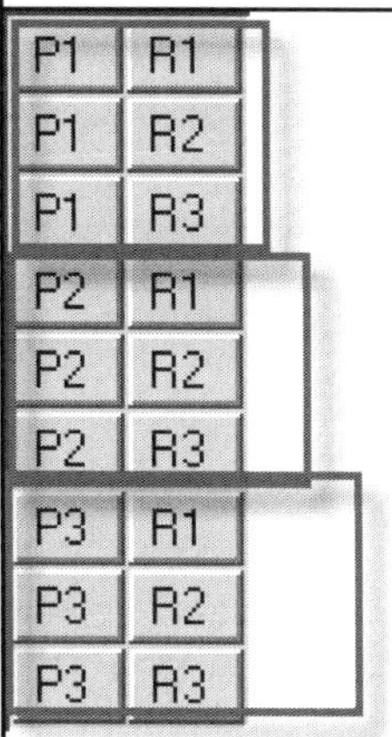

Analysis:

- Two sets SETP and SETR are created, and these sets do not depend on each other.
- In Generate function
  - Set1 = SETP
  - Set2 = {[SETP].CurrentMember}*[SETR]}, that means Set2 depends on Set1.
  - It will loop through each member of Set1 and generate the result as shown in the screen shot.

Query#2.27:

Inspect the following query:

MDX	Result

WITH
MEMBER [Product].[Product].[P1] AS "P1"
MEMBER [Product].[Product].[P2] AS "P2"
MEMBER [Product].[Product].[P3] AS "P3"
SET [SETP] AS
{
[Product].[Product].[P1],
[Product].[Product].[P2],
[Product].[Product].[P3]
}
MEMBER [Reseller].[Reseller].[R1] AS "R1"
MEMBER [Reseller].[Reseller].[R2] AS "R2"
MEMBER [Reseller].[Reseller].[R3] AS "R3"
 	
SET [SETR] AS
{
[Reseller].[Reseller].[R1],
[Reseller].[Reseller].[R2],
[Reseller].[Reseller].[R3]
}
SELECT
{
} ON COLUMNS,
{
GENERATE ([SETP],[SETR],ALL)
} ON ROWS
FROM
[Adventure Works]
	R1
	R2
	R3
	R1
	R2
	R3
	R1
	R2
	R3

Analysis:

- In Generate function
  - Set1 = SETP
  - Set2 = SETR, Set2 does not depend on Set1.
  - It will loop through Set1 three times, as it has three items, and returns {(R1), (R2), (R3)} for each loop.
  - As the third parameter, "ALL" is passed, it will return {(R1), (R2), (R3)} three times.

Query#2.28:

Goal: For each month of fiscal year 2008, find "product category" which has highest "Internet Sales Amount" for that month.

Step 1: Find "Internet Sales Amount" for each month of fiscal year 2008 for each product category.

MDX

```
SELECT
  {
  [Product].[Product Categories].[Category]
  } ON COLUMNS,
  {
  DESCENDANTS
    (
    [Date].[Fiscal].[Fiscal Year].&[2008],
    3,
    SELF
    )
  } ON ROWS
FROM
  [Adventure Works]
WHERE
  [Measures].[Internet Sales Amount]
```

Result

	Accessories	Bikes	Clothing	Components
July 2007	$14,468.20	$865,692.78	$6,507.86	(null)
August 2007	$52,056.61	$772,021.51	$23,335.39	(null)
September 2007	$52,149.72	$931,963.95	$26,144.46	(null)
October 2007	$54,595.17	$999,928.88	$25,925.53	(null)
November 2007	$54,832.02	$1,116,620.90	$25,528.19	(null)
December 2007	$65,607.99	$1,635,373.24	$30,806.54	(null)
January 2008	$56,456.93	$1,254,568.27	$29,219.75	(null)
February 2008	$56,995.90	$1,377,419.13	$28,064.80	(null)
March 2008	$60,097.80	$1,392,038.07	$28,769.31	(null)
April 2008	$62,673.58	$1,514,048.73	$32,028.22	(null)
May 2008	$71,880.47	$1,775,296.95	$31,140.09	(null)
June 2008	$65,200.93	$1,848,953.70	$35,206.48	(null)

Analysis:

- The result shows all product categories for all months of fiscal year 2008.

Step 2: For each month of fiscal year 2008, find "product category" which has highest "Internet Sales Amount" for that month.

Strategy:

- Show "Internet Sales Amount" in columns.

- Show months of fiscal year 2008 in rows.
- Show the name of top product category of that month in rows.

MDX

```
SELECT
   {
   [Measures].[Internet Sales Amount]
   } ON COLUMNS,
   {
   GENERATE
      (
      DESCENDANTS([Date].[Fiscal].[Fiscal Year].&[2008],3,SELF),
      [Date].[Fiscal].CurrentMember
      *
      TopCount
         (
         [Product].[Product Categories].[Category],
         1,
            (
            [Measures].[Internet Sales Amount],
            [Date].[Fiscal].CurrentMember
            )
         )
      )
   } ON ROWS
FROM
   [Adventure Works]
```

Set1

Set2

1. Internet Sales Amount for Current Month.

2. Returns product category which have maximum Internet Sales Amount for current month.

3. Current month. CrossJoin with current month makes the Set2 depends on Set1.

Result

		Internet Sales Amount
July 2007	Bikes	$865,692.78
August 2007	Bikes	$772,021.51
September 2007	Bikes	$931,963.95
October 2007	Bikes	$999,928.88
November 2007	Bikes	$1,116,620.90
December 2007	Bikes	$1,635,373.24
January 2008	Bikes	$1,254,568.27
February 2008	Bikes	$1,377,419.13
March 2008	Bikes	$1,392,038.07
April 2008	Bikes	$1,514,048.73
May 2008	Bikes	$1,775,296.95
June 2008	Bikes	$1,848,953.70

Analysis:

- Show "Internet Sales Amount" in columns.
- In "Generate" function:
  - Set1: All months of fiscal year 2008.
  - Set2:
    - Set2 depends on Set1.

- Set2 finds top product category of that month.

- ([Measures].[Internet Sales Amount], [Date].[Fiscal].CurrentMember) is "Internet Sales Amount" for the current month.

Query#2.29:

Goal: Display all product categories in a string separated by "-".

MDX

```
WITH
MEMBER [Measures].[Product Categories String] AS
GENERATE
   (
   [Product].[Product Categories].[Category],
   [Product].[Product Categories].CurrentMember.Name,
   " - "
   )
SELECT
   {
   [Measures].[Product Categories String]
   } ON COLUMNS
FROM
            [Adventure Works]
```

Result

Product Categories String
Accessories - Bikes - Clothing - Components

Analysis:

- The "Generate" function is in FORM 2.
- The second parameter is a string, and is name of the current product category.
- The third parameter is the delimiter of the string which is "-".
- It loops through all product categories and creates the string.

EXERCISES

Exercise 2.1: Find "Bottom 5% products" based on "Internet Sales Amount" from the list of all products for fiscal year 2008. Do not include empty "Internet Sales Amount" values.

Exercise 2.2: Find "Reseller Sales Amount", "Reseller Sales Quantity" for Texas , Florida and New York for fiscal years 2007, 2008 for product categories "Bikes" and "Clothing".

Exercise 2.3: Find the number of days between 01/20/2008 and 03/15/2008.

Exercise 2.4: Display "Reseller Sales Amount" for each product category for each country. Also sort the result by country and then by product category.

Exercise 2.5: Using "Exists" function display name of states which have following cities: Columbus, San Jose, Tampa.

Chapter 3: Navigation Functions

Navigation functions are used for browsing through attribute hierarchies and user defined hierarchies in a cube.

The first section of this chapter explores parent and child navigation functions, like, "find the parent of a member", "find first child of a member", "find if a given member is an ancestor of another member or not?", "find if a member is a leaf or not?" etc. One interesting function is "CurrentOrdinal", which returns the location of the member within a set. The "CurrentOrdinal" function is explained with a complex example, which I hope you will enjoy . Another interesting topic in this section is the discussion on the difference between "Current" and "CurrentMember" functions.

The second section of this chapter explores browsing members in the same level. For example, "find siblings of a member", "find if two members are siblings or not?", "find first and last sibling of a member", "find a cousin of a member" etc.

The third section of this chapter explores miscellanous functions, including "DataMember" and "LinkMember" along with other functions. The "LinkMember" function links a member from two different hierarchies of same dimension. The "DataMember" function returns a system generated member, which is very useful to distinguish individual member value and from an aggregated value for non-leaf nodes. Last, but not least, "Exercises" will help you to revise the chapter contents and practice MDX queries based on this chapter.

Agenda

Current, CurrentMember
Parent, Children, Ancestor
Ancestors, Ascendants,
FirstChild, LastChild,
IsAncestor, IsLeaf,
CurrentOrdinal

Siblings, IsSibling,
FirstSibling, LastSibling
Lead, Lag, NextMember,
PrevMember, Cousin

DefaultMember,
IsGeneration, LinkMember,
DataMember,LookupCube
UnknownMember,
Properties

Exercises

Query#3.01:

Goal: List all product categories in one string and separated by a dash (-).

Strategy:

- Loop through the set of all product categories.
- Read each product category and concatenate in a string, delimited by "-".

MDX

```
WITH
SET [The Product Categories] AS
[Product].[Product Categories].[Category]

MEMBER Measures.[Product Categories Str] AS
GENERATE
  (
  [The Product Categories],
  [The Product Categories].CURRENT.ITEM(0).NAME,
  " - "
  )

SELECT
  {
  Measures.[Product Categories Str]
  } ON COLUMNS
FROM
  [Adventure Works]
```

Result

Product Categories Str
Accessories - Bikes - Clothing - Components

Analysis:

- Created a named set "The Product Categories", which consists of all product categories.
- Created a member "Product Categories Str", to hold the result string.
- "Generate" function is used to iterate through the set "The Product Categories".
- To get the current member of the set, use the function "Current".
- In "Generate" function:
  - The first parameter is the set "The Product Categories", the function is looping through this set.
  - The second parameter is the string [The Product Categories].CURRENT.ITEM(0).NAME, which depends on the first parameter.
  - ITEM(0).NAME is the product category name.
- Difference between "Current" and "CurrentMember":
  - "Current" returns the current tuple from a **set** during iteration.
  - "CurrentMember" returns the current member from a **hierarchy** during iteration.

Query#3.02:

Goal: Find "Internet Sales Amount" for all product Subcategories of product categories "Bikes" and "Clothing".

Solution 1:

Step 1: Find "Internet Sales Amount" for all Product Subcategories.

MDX

```
SELECT
  {
  [Measures].[Internet Sales Amount]
  } ON COLUMNS,
  {
  [Product].[Product Categories].[Subcategory]
  } ON ROWS
FROM
  [Adventure Works]
```

Result

	Internet Sales Amount
Bike Racks	$39,360.00
Bike Stands	$39,591.00
Bottles and Cages	$56,798.19
Cleaners	$7,218.60
Fenders	$46,619.58
Helmets	$225,335.60
Hydration Packs	$40,307.67
Lights	(null)
Locks	(null)
Panniers	(null)
Pumps	(null)
Tires and Tubes	$245,529.32

Step 2: Find "Internet Sales Amount" for Product Subcategories that belong to product categories "Bikes" and "Clothing" by limiting subcategories list using "Where" clause.

MDX

Same hierarchy appeared twice
NOT ALLOWED

```
SELECT
   {
   [Measures].[Internet Sales Amount]
   } ON COLUMNS,
   {
   [Product].[Product Categories].[Subcategory]
   } ON ROWS
FROM
   [Adventure Works]
WHERE
   {
   [Product].[Product Categories].[Category].&[1],-- Bikes
   [Product].[Product Categories].[Category].&[3] -- Clothing
   }
```

Result

```
Executing the query ...
The Product Categories hierarchy already appears in the Axis1 axis.
Execution complete
```

Solution:

There are multiple solutions to this issue,

- Change the hierarchy in "Where" clause from user defined hierarchy [Product].[Product Categories] to attribute hierarchy [Product].[Category].

The new "Where" clause will be:

```
WHERE
  {
  [Product].[Category].[Bikes],
  [Product].[Category].[Clothing]
  }
```

MDX

```
SELECT
  {
  [Measures].[Internet Sales Amount]
  } ON COLUMNS,
  {
  [Product].[Product Categories].[Subcategory]
  } ON ROWS
FROM
  [Adventure Works]
WHERE
  {
  [Product].[Category].[Bikes],
  [Product].[Category].[Clothing]
  }
```

Result

	Internet Sales Amount
Mountain Bikes	$9,952,759.56
Road Bikes	$14,520,584.04
Touring Bikes	$3,844,801.05
Bib-Shorts	(null)
Caps	$19,688.10
Gloves	$35,020.70
Jerseys	$172,950.68
Shorts	$71,319.81
Socks	$5,106.32
Tights	(null)
Vests	$35,687.00

- A very similar alternate solution is to change hierarchy in rows from [Product].[Product Categories] to [Product].[Subcategory]. The code for rows will look like:

```
{
[Product].[Subcategory].[Subcategory]
} ON ROWS
```

- Both of these solutions will return same result, but are arranged in different order, as the two solutions use two different hierarchies.
- Some other common solutions are:
  - Using "Descendants" functions.
  - Using "Exists" function.

Solution 2:

Using "Descendants" function:

MDX

```
SELECT
   {
   [Measures].[Internet Sales Amount]
   } ON COLUMNS,
   {

   DESCENDANTS
      (
       {
       [Product].[Product Categories].[Category].&[1],-- Bikes
       [Product].[Product Categories].[Category].&[3] -- Clothing
       },
      1,
      SELF
      )

   } ON ROWS
FROM
   [Adventure Works]
```

Result

	Internet Sales Amount
Mountain Bikes	$9,952,759.56
Road Bikes	$14,520,584.04
Touring Bikes	$3,844,801.05
Bib-Shorts	(null)
Caps	$19,688.10
Gloves	$35,020.70
Jerseys	$172,950.68
Shorts	$71,319.81
Socks	$5,106.32
Tights	(null)
Vests	$35,687.00

Solution 3:

Using "Exists" function:

MDX

```
SELECT
   {
   [Measures].[Internet Sales Amount]
   } ON COLUMNS,
   {
   EXISTS
      (
      [Product].[Product Categories].[Subcategory],
         {
         [Product].[Product Categories].[Category].&[1],-- Bikes
         [Product].[Product Categories].[Category].&[3] -- Clothing
         }
      )

   } ON ROWS
FROM
   [Adventure Works]
```

Result

	Internet Sales Amount
Mountain Bikes	$9,952,759.56
Road Bikes	$14,520,584.04
Touring Bikes	$3,844,801.05
Bib-Shorts	(null)
Caps	$19,688.10
Gloves	$35,020.70
Jerseys	$172,950.68
Shorts	$71,319.81
Socks	$5,106.32
Tights	(null)
Vests	$35,687.00

Query#3.03:

Goal: Modify solution 1 of the last query to find "Internet Sales Amount" for product subcategories for product categories "Bikes" and "Clothing" **for fiscal year 2008.**

Strategy:

- Add new condition in "Where" clause for fiscal year 2008, i.e. [Date].[Fiscal].[Fiscal Year].&[2008]

MDX

```
SELECT
   {
   [Measures].[Internet Sales Amount]
   } ON COLUMNS,
   {
   [Product].[Product Categories].[Subcategory]
   } ON ROWS
FROM
   [Adventure Works]
WHERE
   {
   [Product].[Category].&[1],-- Bikes
   [Product].[Category].&[3], -- Clothing

   [Date].[Fiscal].[Fiscal Year].&[2008]

   }
```

Two types of objects in a set
NOT ALLOWED

Result

```
Executing the query ...
Members, tuples or sets must use the same hierarchies in the  function.

Execution complete
```

Analysis:

- You cannot have more than one type of objects in a set, because this violates the rule of a set.
- Two different types of objects in the "Where" clause are, "product category" and "fiscal year" and are not allowed.

Solution:

- You should be able to define a set of similar objects tuples.
- Define tuple with ("product category", "fiscal year"). The modified "Where" clause will look like this:

```
WHERE
  {
   (
   { [Product].[Category].[Bikes],[Product].[Category].[Clothing] },
   [Date].[Fiscal].[Fiscal Year].&[2008]
   )
  }
```

The corrected query and result are shown below:

MDX

```
SELECT
  {
  [Measures].[Internet Sales Amount]
  } ON COLUMNS,
  {
  [Product].[Product Categories].[Subcategory]
  } ON ROWS
FROM
  [Adventure Works]
WHERE
    (
     {
     [Product].[Category].[Bikes],
     [Product].[Category].[Clothing]
     },
    [Date].[Fiscal].[Fiscal Year].&[2008]
    )
```

Result

	Internet Sales Amount
Mountain Bikes	$6,397,228.51
Road Bikes	$5,241,896.55
Touring Bikes	$3,844,801.05
Bib-Shorts	(null)
Caps	$18,834.05
Gloves	$33,379.87
Jerseys	$165,066.21
Shorts	$67,050.42
Socks	$4,881.57
Tights	(null)
Vests	$33,464.50

Analysis:

- Create a set using similar objects:

```
{
[Product].[Category].[Bikes],
[Product].[Category].[Clothing]
}
```

- Then create a tuple with dissimilar objects:

```
(
  {
  [Product].[Category].[Bikes],
  [Product].[Category].[Clothing]
  },
[Date].[Fiscal].[Fiscal Year].&[2008]
)
```

Query#3.04:

Goal: Modify the last query to find "Internet Sales Amount" for product subcategories for product categories "Bikes" and "Clothing" for fiscal year 2008. Also show product category name for each product subcategory.

Strategy:

- [Product].[Product Categories].CurrentMember will return the current member of the hierarchy [Product].[Product Categories], which is a product subcategory.
- Parent of the current "product subcategory" will be a "product category".
- Create a calculated member, "The Product Category", to find product category name and display in columns.

MDX

```
WITH
MEMBER [Measures].[The Product Category] AS
[Product].[Product Categories].CurrentMember.Parent.Name

SELECT
  {
  [Measures].[Internet Sales Amount],
  [Measures].[The Product Category]
  } ON COLUMNS,
  {
  [Product].[Product Categories].[Subcategory]
  } ON ROWS
FROM
  [Adventure Works]
WHERE
  {
   (
    {
    [Product].[Category].[Bikes],
    [Product].[Category].[Clothing]
    },
    [Date].[Fiscal].[Fiscal Year].&[2008]
   )
  }
```

Result

	Internet Sales Amount	The Product Category
Mountain Bikes	$6,397,228.51	Bikes
Road Bikes	$5,241,896.55	Bikes
Touring Bikes	$3,844,801.05	Bikes
Bib-Shorts	(null)	Clothing
Caps	$18,834.05	Clothing
Gloves	$33,379.87	Clothing
Jerseys	$165,066.21	Clothing
Shorts	$67,050.42	Clothing
Socks	$4,881.57	Clothing
Tights	(null)	Clothing
Vests	$33,464.50	Clothing

CurrentMember

<Hierarchy>.CurrentMember

<Hierarchy>:

- Expression returns a valid hierarchy. For example, [Product].[Product Categories].

The Result:

- This returns the current member of a hierarchy during iteration.

Notes:

- "CurrentMember" will return from any level of a hierarchy.
  For example,
  - While iterating through [Product].[Product Categories].[Subcategory] , [Product].[Product Categories].CurrentMember will return the current "product subcategory" e.g. "Road Bikes".
  - While iterating through [Product].[Product Categories].[Category], [Product].[Product Categories].CurrentMember will return the current "product category" e.g. "Bikes".
  - While iterating through [Product].[Product Categories].[Product], [Product].[Product Categories].CurrentMember will return the current product e.g. "Road-150 Red,44".

Parent

<Member>.Parent

<Member>:

- Expression returns a valid member.
  For example, [Product].[Product Categories].[Subcategory].&[2].

The Result:

- This returns the parent of a member.

Notes:

- You cannot write [Product].[Product Categories].[Subcategory].Parent, because [Product].[Product Categories].[Subcategory] is a level not a member.
- [Product].[Product Categories].[Subcategory].&[2].Parent is a valid expression as [Product].[Product Categories].[Subcategory].&[2] is a member.
- Parent of a product category e.g.[Product].[Product Categories].[Category].&[1] is "All Level".
- Parent of "All Level" of a hierarchy is null.

Query#3.05:

Goal: Find "Reseller Sales Amount" for each state of Australia.

Strategy:

- The user defined hierarchy "Geography" has five levels "All Level", [Country], [State-Province], [City] and [Postal Code].
- One member of [Country] level is [Geography].[Geography].[Country].&[Australia].
- Use "Children" function to get all states of Australia.

MDX

```
SELECT
  {
  [Measures].[Reseller Sales Amount]
  } ON COLUMNS,
  {
  [Geography].[Geography].[Country].&[Australia].Children
  } ON ROWS
FROM
  [Adventure Works]
```

Result

	Reseller Sales Amount
New South Wales	$1,129,270.79
Queensland	$39,071.48
South Australia	$71,602.27
Tasmania	(null)
Victoria	$354,390.84

Children

<Member>.Children

<Member>:

- Expression returns a valid member.
  For example, [Product].[Product Categories].[Subcategory].&[2]

The Result:

- This returns a set of children of the member <Member>.

Analysis:

- You cannot write [Product].[Product Categories].[Subcategory].Children, because [Product].[Product Categories].[Subcategory] is a level not a member.
- You cannot get grand-children using children function, for example, you cannot write [Product].[Product Categories].[Category].[Bikes].Children.Children, because [Product].[Product Categories].[Category].[Bikes].Children is **not a member but a set**.

Query#3.06:

Goal: Display "Reseller Sales Amount" for all cities of the state of Texas and compare with the Country's "Reseller Sales Amount" for fiscal year 2008.

Step 1: Display "Reseller Sales Amount" for all cities of the state of Texas for fiscal year 2008.

Strategy:

- In user defined hierarchy "Geography", cities rolls up to states. This means that children of Texas will return all cities of Texas.
- Use "Where" clause to limit data "for fiscal year 2008".

MDX

```
SELECT
  {
  [Measures].[Reseller Sales Amount]
  } ON COLUMNS,
  {
  [Geography].[Geography].[State-Province].&[TX]&[US].Children
  } ON ROWS
FROM
  [Adventure Works]
WHERE
  [Date].[Fiscal].[Fiscal Year].&[2008]
```

Result

	Reseller Sales Amo
Arlington	(null)
Austin	$230,176.48
Baytown	$6,103.29
Carrollton	(null)
Cedar Park	$1,376.99
College Station	$237,808.91
Corpus Christi	$142,459.42
Dallas	$37,443.72
Fort Worth	$1,700.26
Garland	$366,908.33
Hillsboro	(null)
Houston	$324,477.26
Humble	$157,107.55
[illegible]	$303,6[illegible]

Step 2: Display "Reseller Sales Amount" for all cities of the state of Texas and compare with the Country's "Reseller Sales Amount" for fiscal year 2008.

Strategy:

- Find corresponding country:
  - Grandparent of a city is the country.
  - You can also use "Ancestor" function to find the country.
- [Measures].[Reseller Sales Amount] is the "Reseller Sales Amount" without any condition.
- [Reseller Sales Amount] for the country Australia is:

```
(
[Measures].[Reseller Sales Amount],
[Geography].[Geography].[Country].&[Australia]
)
```

- [Reseller Sales Amount] for the country where the city of Irving belongs:

```
(
[Measures].[Reseller Sales Amount],
[Geography].[Geography].[City].&[Irving]&[TX].Parent.Parent
)
```

MDX

```
WITH
MEMBER [Measures].[RSA For Country] AS
 (
 [Measures].[Reseller Sales Amount],
 ANCESTOR
 ([Geography].[Geography].CurrentMember,2)
 )
MEMBER [Measures].[PCT Of Country] AS
[Measures].[Reseller Sales Amount]/
[Measures].[RSA For Country],
FORMAT_STRING = "Percent"
SELECT
 {
 [Measures].[Reseller Sales Amount],
 [Measures].[PCT Of Country]
 }
 ON COLUMNS,
 {
 [Geography].[Geography].[State-
Province].&[TX]&[US].Children
 }
 ON ROWS
FROM
 [Adventure Works]
WHERE
 [Date].[Fiscal].[Fiscal Year].&[2008]
```

Result

	Reseller Sales Amount	PCT Of Country
Arlington	(null)	(null)
Austin	$230,176.48	1.10%
Baytown	$6,103.29	0.03%
Carrollton	(null)	(null)
Cedar Park	$1,376.99	0.01%
College Station	$237,808.91	1.14%
Corpus Christi	$142,459.42	0.68%
Dallas	$37,443.72	0.18%
Fort Worth	$1,700.26	0.01%
Garland	$366,908.33	1.75%
Hillsboro	(null)	(null)
Houston	$324,477.26	1.55%
Humble	$157,107.55	0.75%
Irving	$303,633.72	1.45%
Killeen	$12,071.31	0.06%
La Marque	$18,772.68	0.09%
Laredo	(null)	(null)
Mesquite	$281,844.75	1.35%
Plano	$2,930.55	0.01%
Round Rock	(null)	(null)
San Antonio	$292,375.13	1.40%
Stafford	(null)	(null)
Sugar Land	$4,471.81	0.02%

Ancestor (<Member>, <Level> | <Distance>)

<Member>:

- Expression returns a valid member.
  For example, [Product].[Product Categories].[Subcategory].&[2].

<Distance>:

- Distance from the <Member> level to the ancestor's level.

<Level>:

- This is the level of an ancestor.

The Result:

- This returns the ancestor of the member <Member> at level <Level>.
- Or this returns the ancestor of the <Member> at a level at a distance <Distance>.

Analysis:

- ANCESTOR ([Geography].[Geography].[City].&[Irving]&[TX] , 2) will return ("United States"), because, the distance between the country level and the city level is 2.
- Also,
  ANCESTOR ([Geography].[Geography].[City].&[Irving]&[TX], 2)
  = [Geography].[Geography].[City].&[Irving]&[TX].Parent.Parent
  = ANCESTOR
  (
  [Geography].[Geography].[City].&[Irving]&[TX],
  [Geography].[Geography].[Country]
)
  All of the above statements will return "United States".
- If the second parameter is a level lower than the first parameter, the function will not return any error but will not return anything.
  For example, this code will not return anything:
  ANCESTOR
  (
  [Geography].[Geography].[City].&[Irving]&[TX],
  [Geography].[Geography].[Postal Code]
)
- If the second parameter is a distance less than zero, which is not a valid distance, the function will give an error "The numeric expression evaluates to an unusable distance."
- There is another function called "Ancestors" which returns the same result as "Ancestor" does, but "Ancestor" returns one member and "Ancestors" returns a set, which has only one member.

Ancestors **(<Member>, <Level> | <Distance>)**

<Level>:

- Expression returns a valid level, e.g. [Geography].[Geography].[Country].

<Distance>:

- This is an integer, e.g. distance between the country level and the city level is 2.

The Result:

- "Ancestor" and "Ancestors" returns same result but "Ancestor" will return one member and "Ancestors" will return a set, which has only one member.
- For example,
  - If "Ancestor" function returns ("United States"), which is a member or a tuple.
  - Then "Ancestors" will return {("United States")}, which is a set that has only one member.
- Note: Microsoft SQL Server Analysis Services does not support multiple parents.

Query#3.07:

Goal: Find "Reseller Sales Amount" for the city of Plano and all of its Ancestors for fiscal year 2008.

Strategy:

- Use "Ascendants" function to find all ancestors of the city of Plano.
- Add "Where" clause to implement the condition "for fiscal year 2008".

MDX

```
SELECT
  {
  [Measures].[Reseller Sales Amount]
  } ON COLUMNS,
  {
  ASCENDANTS
    (
    [Geography].[Geography].[City].&[Plano]&[TX]
    )
  } ON ROWS
FROM
  [Adventure Works]
WHERE
  [Date].[Fiscal].[Fiscal Year].&[2008]
```

Result

	Reseller Sales Amount
Plano	$2,930.55
Texas	$2,421,662.16
United States	$20,927,177.22
All Geographies	$36,240,484.70

Analysis:

- Above query returns all ancestors of the city of Plano.
- The Geography hierarchy has five levels, viz.
    - [All Level]
    - [Country]
    - [State-Province]
    - [City]
    - [Postal Code]

Ascendants (<Member>)

<Member>:

- Expression returns a valid member.
  For example, [Product].[Product Categories].[Subcategory].&[2].

The Result:

- This returns all ancestors of the member <Member>.

Query#3.08:

Goal: Find "Reseller Sales Amount" for the state of Texas for the first and last month of fiscal quarter Q1 of 2008.

Strategy:

- Use "FirstChild" and "LastChild" function to find the first and the last month of Q1, 2008.
- Add "Where" clause to limit the data for the state of Texas only.

MDX

```
SELECT
    {
    [Measures].[Reseller Sales Amount]
    }
    ON COLUMNS,
    {
    [Date].[Fiscal].[Fiscal Quarter].&[2008]&[1].FirstChild,
    [Date].[Fiscal].[Fiscal Quarter].&[2008]&[1].LastChild
    }
    ON ROWS
FROM
    [Adventure Works]
WHERE
    [Geography].[Geography].[State-Province].&[TX]&[US]
```

Result

	Reseller Sales Amount
July 2007	$160,992.21
September 2007	$299,028.76

Analysis:

- "Fiscal year 2008" starts from "July, 2007" and ends in "June, 2008".
- Different levels of user defined hierarchy "Fiscal" are [Fiscal Year], [Fiscal Semester], [Fiscal Quarter], [Month] and [Date].
- Similarly, to find the first day of "September, 2008", you can use following expression: [Date].[Fiscal].[Month].&[2008]&[9].FirstChild
- Also, to find the last day of "February, 2008", you can use following expression: [Date].[Fiscal].[Month].&[2008]&[2].LastChild
- You cannot use [Date].[Fiscal].[Month].FirstChild or [Date].[Fiscal].[Month].LastChild, because [Date].[Fiscal].[Month] is a level, not a member .

FirstChild

<Member>.FirstChild

<Member>:

- Expression returns a valid member, e.g. [Date].[Fiscal].[Month].&[2008]&[2].

The Result:

- This returns the first child of a member.

LastChild

<Member>.LastChild

<Member>:

- Expression returns a valid member, e.g. [Date].[Fiscal].[Month].&[2008]&[2].

The Result:

- This returns the last child of the member <Member>.

Query#3.09:

Goal: From the set of all ancestors of postal code "75061", identify leaf members.

Strategy:

- Use "IsLeaf" function to find if the current member is a leaf or not.

MDX

```
WITH
MEMBER [Measures].[IsLeaf] AS
IsLeaf ([Geography].[Geography].CurrentMember)

SELECT
 {
 [Measures].[IsLeaf]
 } ON COLUMNS,
 {
 ASCENDANTS
   (
   [Geography].[Geography].[Postal Code].&[75061]&[Irving]&[TX]
   )
 } ON ROWS
FROM
 [Adventure Works]
```

Result

	IsLeaf
75061	True
Irving	False
Texas	False
United States	False
All Geographies	False

IsLeaf (<Member>)

<Member>:

- Expression returns a valid member, e.g. [Date].[Fiscal].[Month].&[2008]&[2].

The Result:

- This returns true if the member <Member> is a leaf and false if it is not a leaf.

Query#3.10:

Goal: From the set of all countries, identify the countries which have the city of Dallas.

Strategy:

- Use "IsAncestor" function to find if a country is ancestor of city "Dallas" or not.
  Note: The expression for "City of Dallas" is [Geography].[Geography].[City].&[Dallas]&[TX].

MDX

```
WITH
MEMBER [Measures].[IsAncestor] AS
IsAncestor
  (
  [Geography].[Geography].CurrentMember,
  [Geography].[Geography].[City].&[Dallas]&[TX]
  )
SELECT
  {
  [Measures].[IsAncestor]
  } ON COLUMNS,
  {
  [Geography].[Geography].[Country]
  } ON ROWS
FROM
  [Adventure Works]
```

Result

	IsAncestor
Australia	False
Canada	False
France	False
Germany	False
United Kingdom	False
United States	True

IsAncestor (<Ancestor>, <Member>)

<Ancestor>:

- Expression returns a valid member, e.g. [Date].[Fiscal].[Fiscal Year].&[2008].

<Member>:

- Expression returns a valid member, e.g. [Date].[Fiscal].[Month].&[2008]&[2].

The Result:

- If <Ancestor> is an ancestor of <Member> then returns true else false.
- Both <Ancestor> and <Member> should be from same hierarchy of a dimension.

CurrentOrdinal

<Set>.CurrentOrdinal

<Set>:

- This is not a set expression but a **named set**.
  For example,
  WITH
  SET [The Product Categories] AS
  {
  [Product].[Product Categories].[Category]
  }

The Result:

- While iterating through the named set <Set>, "<Set>. CurrentOrdinal" will return the current iteration number.

Query#3.11:

Goal: Using "Generate" function, iterate through [Product].[Product Categories].[Category] and list all product categories.

MDX	Result

SELECT
{ } ON COLUMNS,
{
GENERATE
(
[Product].[Product Categories].[Category], ← Set 1
{
[Product].[Product Categories].CurrentMember
} ← Set 2
)
}
ON ROWS
FROM
[Adventure Works]
	Accessories
	Bikes
	Clothing
	Components

Notes:

- The second parameter is a set and you cannot use [Product].[Product Categories].CurrentMember. Instead, you need to use curly brackets to qualify as a set

```
{
[Product].[Product Categories].CurrentMember
}
```

- [Product].[Product Categories] is a user defined hierarchy and [Product].[Product Categories].CurrentMember is the current member of the hierarchy.
- You cannot use "Current" for set [Product].[Product Categories].[Category], because "Current" can only be used with **a named set**.

Query#3.12:

Goal: Using "Generate" function, iterate through the **named set** of "The Product Categories" and list all product categories using "Current" function.

MDX

```
WITH
SET [The Product Categories] AS
{
[Product].[Product Categories].[Category]
}
SELECT
    { } ON COLUMNS,
    {
    GENERATE
        (
        [The Product Categories],
            {
            [The Product Categories].Current
            }
        )
    }
     ON ROWS
FROM
    [Adventure Works]
```

Result

Accessories
Bikes
Clothing
Components

Note:

- "Current" and "CurrentOrdinal" functions can only be applied to a named set.

Query#3.13:

Goal: For each state of "United States", find the number of months needed by resellers to sell $500K worth of products in fiscal year 2008.

Step 1: For each state of United States, display "Reseller Sales Amount" for each month of fiscal year 2008. Display zero for null "Reseller Sales Amount".

MDX

```
WITH
MEMBER [Measures].[NN Reseller Sales Amount] AS
Coalesceempty
   (
   [Measures].[Reseller Sales Amount],
   0
   )
SELECT
   {
   DESCENDANTS
      (
      [Date].[Fiscal].[Fiscal Year].&[2008],
      [Date].[Fiscal].[Month]
      )
   } ON COLUMNS,
   {
   NonEmpty
      (
      [Geography].[Geography].[Country].&[United States].Children,
      [Measures].[Reseller Sales Amount]
      )
   } ON ROWS
FROM
   [Adventure Works]
WHERE
   [Measures].[NN Reseller Sales Amount]
```

Treat zero for null values

All months of FY 2008

Exclude states which have all empty Reseller Sales Amout for FY 2008

Result

	July 2007	August 2007	September 2007	October 2007	November 2007
Alabama	0	4180.446	2183.64	0	2901.234
Arizona	216303.1752	10648.7524	61566.8564	167493.8497	6049.584
California	326144.3683	330169.8591	395376.2663	288046.3517	270032.386
Colorado	64785.1614	200242.3144	50524.4273	30922.3536	166991.7817
Connecticut	68192.3965	47559.8519	12423.5249	72704.1853	26898.792
Florida	128555.7901	67695.0832	64395.1066	100563.7773	57550.4771
Georgia	37025.4946	35523.087	12790.0517	48732.1454	26898.234
Idaho	41100.9589	0	0	57866.274	0
Illinois	10981.0997	9604.7969	1669.032	14693.91	5900.412
Indiana	52302.4308	1918.56	2.748	47749.0453	5451.354

Step 2: For each state of United States, show "Running Total Reseller Sales Amount" for each month of fiscal year 2008.

Strategy:

- Modify calculated member [NN Reseller Sales Amount] to [Running Total Reseller Sales Amount].

MDX

```
WITH
MEMBER [Measures].[Running Total Reseller Sales Amount] AS
SUM
   (
   PeriodsToDate
      (
      [Date].[Fiscal].[Fiscal Year],
      [Date].[Fiscal].CurrentMember
      ),
   Coalesceempty([Measures].[Reseller Sales Amount],0)
   )
SELECT
   {
   DESCENDANTS
      (
      [Date].[Fiscal].[Fiscal Year].&[2008],
      [Date].[Fiscal].[Month]
      )
   } ON COLUMNS,
   {
   NonEmpty
      (
      [Geography].[Geography].[Country].&[United States].Children,
      [Measures].[Reseller Sales Amount]
      )
   } ON ROWS
FROM
   [Adventure Works]
WHERE
   [Measures].[Running Total Reseller Sales Amount]
```

Running Total

Analysis:

- "PeriodsToDate" function used to calculate "Running Total Reseller Sales Amount".
- In this case,
  - Current members of [Date].[Fiscal] hierarchy are months of fiscal year 2008.
  - Following code will return all months from beginning of the fiscal year 2008 to current month.

    PeriodsToDate
      (
      [Date].[Fiscal].[Fiscal Year],
      [Date].[Fiscal].CurrentMember
)
- "Sum" function will add up "Reseller Sales Amount" for all months from beginning of the fiscal year to current month, which is equal to "Running Total Reseller Sales Amount".

Result

	July 2007	August 2007	September 2007	October 2007	November 200
Alabama	0	4180.446	6364.086	6364.086	9265.32
Arizona	216303.1752	226951.9276	288518.784	456012.6337	462062.217
California	326144.3683	656314.2274	1051690.4937	1339736.8454	1609769.231
Colorado	64785.1614	265027.4758	315551.9031	346474.2567	513466.038
Connecticut	68192.3965	115752.2484	128175.7733	200879.9586	227778.750
Florida	128555.7901	196250.8733	260645.9799	361209.7572	418760.234
Georgia	37025.4946	72548.5816	85338.6333	134070.7787	160969.0127
Idaho	41100.9589	41100.9589	41100.9589	98967.2329	98967.2329
Illinois	10981.0997	20585.8966	22254.9286	36948.8386	42849.2506
Indiana	52302.4308	54220.9908	54223.7388	101972.7841	107424.13

Step 3: Modify the last query to show only those states which sold at least $500K in the fiscal year 2008.

Strategy:

- Create a member "Yearly Reseller Sales Amount" to calculate the total "Reseller Sales Amount" for each state for fiscal year 2008.

```
WITH
MEMBER [Measures].[Yearly Reseller Sales Amount] AS
SUM
  (
  [Date].[Fiscal].[Fiscal Year].&[2008],
  CoalesceEmpty ([Measures].[Reseller Sales Amount], 0)
  )
```

- To show only those states which sold at least $500K as "Yearly Reseller Sales Amount", use following filter:

```
FILTER
  (
  NonEmpty
    (
    [Geography].[Geography].[Country].&[United States].Children,
    [Measures].[Reseller Sales Amount]
    ),
   [Measures].[Yearly Reseller Sales Amount] >500000
  )
```

Following is the modified query and result.

MDX

```
WITH
MEMBER [Measures].[Yearly Reseller Sales Amount] AS
SUM
   (
   [Date].[Fiscal].[Fiscal Year].&[2008],
   Coalesceempty([Measures].[Reseller Sales Amount],0)
   )
MEMBER [Measures].[Running Total Reseller Sales Amount] AS
SUM
   (
   PeriodsToDate([Date].[Fiscal].[Fiscal Year],[Date].[Fiscal].CurrentMember),
   Coalesceempty([Measures].[Reseller Sales Amount],0)
   )
SELECT
   {
   DESCENDANTS([Date].[Fiscal].[Fiscal Year].&[2008],[Date].[Fiscal].[Month])
   } ON COLUMNS,
   {
   FILTER
      (
      NonEmpty
         (
         [Geography].[Geography].[Country].&[United States].Children,
         [Measures].[Reseller Sales Amount]
         ),
      [Measures].[Yearly Reseller Sales Amount] >500000
      )
   } ON ROWS
FROM
   [Adventure Works]
WHERE
   [Measures].[Running Total Reseller Sales Amount]
```

Show only those states that sold ateast $500k in FY 2008

Result

	July 2007	August 2007	September 2007	October 2007	November 2007
Arizona	216303.1752	226951.9276	288518.784	456012.6337	462062.217
California	326144.3683	656314.2274	1051690.4937	1339736.8454	1609769.23
Colorado	64785.1614	265027.4758	315551.9031	346474.2567	513466.0384
Florida	128555.7901	196250.8733	260645.9799	361209.7572	418760.23
Michigan	64718.4206	122818.8882	189510.8322	235160.9232	277528.408
Missouri	76318.9816	180201.4324	274855.7679	346147.0028	450464.54
New Hampshire	70004.8376	77412.5336	182917.9327	251539.0709	254107.952
New York	0	84683.4029	204245.6036	204245.6036	262549.56
North Carolina	0	130258.099	156519.8061	156519.8061	246272.31
Or[illegible]	3290[illegible]6223	113057.7694	[illegible]85308[illegible]948	33[illegible]31.3868	368168.0

Step 4: Modify the last query to show a string that a concatenation of all "Running Total Reseller Sales Amount"values delimited by "-". Also show CurrentOrdinal of months in parentheses.

Strategy:

- Use "Generate" function to loop through each month of the year .
- "Where" clause no longer needed as [Measures].[Running Total RSA String] displays the content of a cell.

MDX

```
WITH
MEMBER [Measures].[Yearly Reseller Sales Amount] AS
SUM
   (
   [Date].[Fiscal].[Fiscal Year].&[2008],
   Coalesceempty ([Measures].[Reseller Sales Amount], 0)
   )
MEMBER [Measures].[Running Total Reseller Sales Amount] AS
SUM
   (
   PeriodsToDate ([Date].[Fiscal].[Fiscal Year], [Date].[Fiscal].CurrentMember),
   Coalesceempty ([Measures].[Reseller Sales Amount], 0)
   )
MEMBER [Measures].[Running Total RSA String] AS
Generate
   (
   DESCENDANTS([Date].[Fiscal].[Fiscal Year].&[2008],[Date].[Fiscal].[Month]) AS curYear,
   CSTR([Measures].[Running Total Reseller Sales Amount])+'('+CSTR(curYear.CurrentOrdinal)+')',
   '-'
   )
SELECT
    {[Measures].[Running Total RSA String] } ON COLUMNS,
    {
    FILTER(
        NonEmpty
            (
            [Geography].[Geography].[Country].&[United States].Children,
            [Measures].[Reseller Sales Amount]
            ),
        [Measures].[Yearly Reseller Sales Amount] >500000
        )
    } ON ROWS
FROM
    [Adventure Works]
```

Name of named set

Result

	Running Total RSA String
Arizona	216303.1752(1)-226951.9276(2)-288518.784(3)-456012.6337(4)-462062.2177(5)-520734.4357(6)-
California	326144.3683(1)-656314.2274(2)-1051690.4[illegible]7(3)-1339[illegible]6.8454(4)-1609769.2318(5)-1925077.36
Colorado	64785.1614(1)-265027.4[illegible]8(2)-3[illegible]5551.[illegible]031(3)-346474.2567(4)-513466.0384(5)-574662.0124(6)-
Florida	128555.7901(1)-196250.8733(2)-2[illegible]0645.[illegible]799(3)-361209.7572(4)-418760.2343(5)-476758.2926(6)
Michigan	64718.4206(1)-122818.8882[illegible]160.9232(4)-277528.408(5)-347580.2959(6)-3
Missouri	76318.9816(1)-180201.4324[illegible]147.0028(4)-450464.5463(5)-525764.0543(6)-
New Hampshire	70004.8376(1)-77412.5336(2)-182917.9327(3)-251539.0709(4)-254107.9529(5)-324431.9084(6)-3
New York	0(1)-84683.4029(2)-204245.6036(3)-204245.6036(4)-262549.505(5)-354704.5507(6)-354704.5507(
North Carolina	0(1)-130258.099(2)-156519.8061(3)-156519.8061(4)-246272.3135(5)-273993.6815(6)-273993.681
Oregon	32901.6223(1)-113057.7694(2)-285308.4048(3)-332831.3868(4)-368168.0748(5)-507325.6788(6)-
Texas	160992.21(1)-490555.2394(2)-789583.999(3)-925781.691(4)-1217897.6558(5)-1399998.9747(6)-1
Utah	1037.154(1)-145848.249(2)-211119.671(3)-212888.549(4)-360831.2684(5)-418899.3493(6)-41957
Washington	236273.9271(1)-637499.437(2)-992460.1025(3)-1153777.0184(4)-1485222.2907(5)-1794701.118(

CurrentOrdinal

Step 5: Modify the last query to show CurrentOrdinal of the set "curYear" in parentheses if "Running Total Reseller Sales Amount" is less than $500K, otherwise show **zero.**

Strategy:

- This can be achieved by using IIF, in line if statement when displaying CurrentOrdinal in Generate function.
- In last query, update "Generate" function code as follows:

```
Generate
    (
    DESCENDANTS ([Date].[Fiscal].[Fiscal Year].&[2008], [Date].[Fiscal].[Month]) AS curYear,
    CSTR ([Measures].[Running Total Reseller Sales Amount] )+'('+
    IIF
      (
      [Measures].[Running Total Reseller Sales Amount]<500000,
      CSTR (curYear.CurrentOrdinal),
      '0'
      )
    +')',
    '-'
    )
```

- The result of the updated query will be as follows:

Result

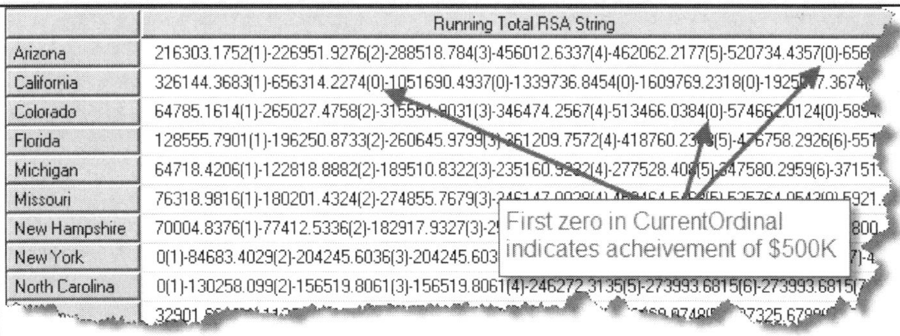

- Arrows identify the first zero in parentheses.
- For example, in the first line, zero in parentheses is in 6th position, as last CurrentOrdinal is 5. So, Arizona reached $500K sale in (5+1) = 6th month of fiscal year 2008 = December, 2007 (fiscal year 2008 starts in July, 2007 and 6th month is December, 2007).

Step 6: **(Final Goal)** For each state of "United States", find the number of months needed by resellers to sell $500K worth of products in fiscal year 2008

- Create a member [Running Total Reseller Sales Amount for next month] as follows:

```
MEMBER [Measures].[Running Total Reseller Sales Amount for next month] AS
SUM
    (
    PeriodsToDate ([Date].[Fiscal].[Fiscal Year],[Date].[Fiscal].CurrentMember.NextMember),
    CoalesceEmpty ([Measures].[Reseller Sales Amount],0)
    )
```

- Change code for Generate function as follows:

```
 MEMBER [Measures].[Month number reached $500K] AS
  GENERATE
    (
    DESCENDANTS ([Date].[Fiscal].[Fiscal Year].&[2008],[Date].[Fiscal].[Month]) AS curYear,
    CSTR
      (
      ------------------------------------------------------------------------------------------
      IIF ( [Measures].[Running Total Reseller Sales Amount]<500000,
        ----------------------------------------------------------------------------------------
        IIF ( [Measures].[Running Total Reseller Sales Amount for next month]>500000,
         CSTR (curYear.CurrentOrdinal+1), '0' )
        ----------------------------------------------------------------------------------------
      ,"0")
      ------------------------------------------------------------------------------------------
      ),'+')
```

- Display [Measures].[Month number reached $500K] in columns will return the following result:

Result

	Month number reached $500K
Arizona	0+0+0+0+6+0+0+0+0+0+0+0
California	2+0+0+0+0+0+0+0+0+0+0+0
Colorado	0+0+0+5+0+0+0+0+0+0+0+0
Florida	0+0+0+0+0+7+0+0+0+0+0+0
Michigan	0+0+0+0+0+0+0+0+10+0+0+0
Missouri	0+0+0+0+6+0+0+0+0+0+0+0
New Hampshire	0+0+0+0+0+0+0+0+10+0+0+0
New York	0+0+0+0+0+0+0+0+0+11+0+0
North Carolina	0+0+0+0+0+0+0+0+0+0+12+0
Oregon	0+0+0+0+6+0+0+0+0+0+0+0
Texas	0+3+0+0+0+0+0+0+0+0+0+0
Utah	0+0+0+0+0+0+8+0+0+0+0+0
Washington	2+0+0+0+0+0+0+0+0+0+0+0

- Adding values will give the required result, The final MDX query is as follows:

MDX

```
--Part 1 of 2
--------------------------------------------------------------------------------
WITH
MEMBER [Measures].[Yearly Reseller Sales Amount] AS
SUM
    (
    [Date].[Fiscal].[Fiscal Year].&[2008],
    Coalesceempty
        (
        [Measures].[Reseller Sales Amount],
        0
        )
    )
MEMBER [Measures].[Running Total Reseller Sales Amount] AS
SUM
    (
    PeriodsToDate
        (
        [Date].[Fiscal].[Fiscal Year],
        [Date].[Fiscal].CurrentMember
        ),
    Coalesceempty
        (
        [Measures].[Reseller Sales Amount],
        0
        )
    )

MEMBER [Measures].[Running Total Reseller Sales Amount for next month] AS
SUM
    (
    PeriodsToDate
        (
        [Date].[Fiscal].[Fiscal Year],
        [Date].[Fiscal].CurrentMember.NextMember
        ),
    Coalesceempty
        (
        [Measures].[Reseller Sales Amount],
        0
        )
    )

--------------------------------------------------------------------------------
```

MDX

```
--Part 2 of 2
--------------------------------------------------------------------------------
MEMBER [Measures].[Month number reached $500K] AS
StrToValue
(
    Generate
    (
    DESCENDANTS
        (
        [Date].[Fiscal].[Fiscal Year].&[2008],
        [Date].[Fiscal].[Month]
        ) AS curYear,
    CSTR
        (
        --------------------------------------------------------------------------
        IIF([Measures].[Running Total Reseller Sales Amount]<500000,
        --------------------------------------------------------------------------
        IIF ( [Measures].[Running Total Reseller Sales Amount for next month]>500000,
         CSTR(curYear.CurrentOrdinal+1),'0')
        --------------------------------------------------------------------------
        ,"0")
        --------------------------------------------------------------------------
        ),
    '+'
    )
)
SELECT
    {
    [Measures].[Month number reached $500K]
    } ON COLUMNS,
    {
    FILTER
        (
        NonEmpty
            (
            [Geography].[Geography].[Country].&[United States].Children,
            [Measures].[Reseller Sales Amount]
            ),
        [Measures].[Yearly Reseller Sales Amount] >500000
        )
    } ON ROWS
FROM
    [Adventure Works]
```

<Set>

<String>

The result is shown below:

Result

	Month number reached $500K
Arizona	6
California	2
Colorado	5
Florida	7
Michigan	10
Missouri	6
New Hampshire	10
New York	11
North Carolina	12
Oregon	6
Texas	3
Utah	8
Washington	2

To display the name of the month instead of the month number, modify calculated member as follows:

```
MEMBER [Measures].[Month Name] AS
[Date].[Fiscal].[Fiscal Year].&[2008].FirstChild.FirstChild.FirstChild.lead
([Measures].[Month number reached $500K]-1).Name
```

Result

	Month Name
Arizona	December 2007
California	August 2007
Colorado	November 2007
Florida	January 2008
Missouri	December 2007
Oregon	December 2007
Texas	September 2007
Utah	February 2008
Washington	August 2007

Query#3.14:

Goal: Find all cities of the state, which the city of Plano is in.

Solution 1: Using "Siblings" function.

MDX

```
SELECT
  {
  } ON COLUMNS,
  {
  [Geography].[Geography].[City].&[Plano]&[TX].Siblings
  } ON ROWS
FROM
  [Adventure Works]
```

Result

Solution 2: You can also get same result using "Parent" function and then display all children of the parent.

- Member.Siblings = Member.Parent.Children

MDX

```
SELECT
  {
  } ON COLUMNS,
  {
  [Geography].[Geography].[City].&[Plano]&[TX].Parent.Children
  } ON ROWS
FROM
  [Adventure Works]
```

Result

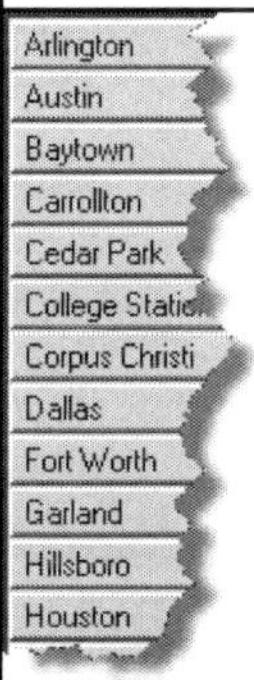

<Member>.Siblings

<Member>:

- Expression returns a valid member.

The Result:

- This returns a set of all siblings of the member <Member>; The result includes the <Member>.

Query#3.15:

Goal: From a given set of cities {Sydney, Calgary, Sacramento}, find cities that are in the same state as the city of San Francisco.

Strategy:

- Using "IsSibling" function, find cities are in the same state as the city of San Francisco.

MDX

Find if they are siblings or not ?

```
WITH
MEMBER [Measures].[IsSibling] AS
IsSibling
    (
    [Geography].[Geography].Currentmember,
    [Geography].[Geography].[City].&[San Francisco]&[CA]
    )

SELECT
    {
    [Measures].[IsSibling]
    }   ON COLUMNS,
    {
    [Geography].[Geography].[City].&[Sydney]&[NSW],
    [Geography].[Geography].[City].&[Calgary]&[AB],
    [Geography].[Geography].[City].&[Sacramento]&[CA]
    }    ON ROWS
FROM
    [Adventure Works]
```

Given set of cities

Result

	IsSibling
Sydney	False
Calgary	False
Sacramento	True

IsSibling (<Member1>, <Member2>)

<Member1>:

- Expression returns a valid member, e.g. [Geography].[Geography].[City].&[San Francisco]&[CA].

<Member2>:

- Expression returns a valid member, e.g. [Geography].[Geography].[City].&[Sacramento]&[CA].

The Result:

- This returns true if <Member1> and <Member2> are siblings else returns false.
- To return true, <Member1> and <Member2> should be from same dimension, same hierarchy, same level and have the same parent.

Query#3.16:

Goal: For a given date, find total "Reseller Sales Amount", and "Reseller Sales Amount" for the first and last day of the current month.

Strategy:

- In this example, let us assume the given date is Feb, 13, 2008.
- In "Fiscal" hierarchy of "Date" dimension, the month level is one level above the date level.
- All dates of a month are siblings.
- Using "FirstSibling" and "LastSibling" function, you can find the first day and the last day of a month.

MDX

```
SELECT
  {
  [Measures].[Reseller Sales Amount]
  } ON COLUMNS,
  {
  [Date].[Fiscal].[Date].&[20080213],
  [Date].[Fiscal].[Date].&[20080213].FirstSibling,
  [Date].[Fiscal].[Date].&[20080213].LastSibling
  } ON ROWS
FROM
  [Adventure Works]
```

Result

	Reseller Sales Amount
February 13, 2008	(null)
February 1, 2008	$2,699,300.79
February 29, 2008	$1,466.01

FirstSibling

<Member>.FirstSibling

<Member>:

- Expression returns a valid member.

The Result:

- If <Member> has sibling, it will return the first sibling of the member <Member>.

LastSibling

<Member>.LastSibling

<Member>:

- Expression returns a valid member.

The Result:

- If <Member> has sibling, it will return the last sibling of the member <Member>.

Query#3.17:

Goal: For a given month, find "Reseller Sales Amount" and also find:

- "Reseller Sales Amount" for a month, 3 months prior to the current month.
- "Reseller Sales Amount" for a month, 3 months past of the current month.

Strategy:

- For this example the given month is March, 2008.
- 3 months prior to March, 2008 is December, 2007 and can be found by using the "Lag" function.
- 3 months past of March, 2008 is June, 2008 and can be found by using the "Lead" function.

MDX

```
SELECT
  {
  [Measures].[Reseller Sales Amount]
  }  ON COLUMNS,
  {
  [Date].[Fiscal].[Month].&[2008]&[3],
  [Date].[Fiscal].[Month].&[2008]&[3].lag(3),
  [Date].[Fiscal].[Month].&[2008]&[3].lead(3)
  } ON ROWS
FROM    [Adventure Works]
```

Result

	Reseller Sales Amount
March 2008	$2,739,370.98
December 2007	$3,510,948.73
June 2008	$3,415,479.07

Lead

<Member>.Lead (<Index>)

<Member>:

- Expression returns a valid member, e.g. [Date].[Fiscal].[Month].&[2008]&[3].

<Index>:

- This is an integer, and is the number of positions ahead of the member <Member>.

The Result:

- This returns a member, which is <Index> positions ahead of the member <Member>.If <Index> is out of bounds, no member will be returned.

Lag

<Member>.Lag (<Index>)

<Member>:

- Expression returns a valid member, e.g. [Date].[Fiscal].[Month].&[2008]&[3].

<Index>:

- This is an integer, and is the number of positions behind of the member <Member>.

The Result:

- This returns a member, which is <Index> positions behind of the member <Member>.
- If <Index> is out of bounds, no member will be returned.

Query#3.18:

Goal: For a given month, find total "Reseller Sales Amount", and also find:

- "Reseller Sales Amount" for the previous month.
- "Reseller Sales Amount" for the next month.

Strategy:

- For this example the given month is "March, 2008".
- The previous month of "March, 2008" is "February, 2008" and can be found by using "PrevMember" function.
- The next month of "March, 2008" is "April, 2008" and can be found by using "NextMember" function.

MDX

```
SELECT
  {
  [Measures].[Reseller Sales Amount]
  } ON COLUMNS,
  {
  [Date].[Fiscal].[Month].&[2008]&[3],
  [Date].[Fiscal].[Month].&[2008]&[3].PrevMember,
  [Date].[Fiscal].[Month].&[2008]&[3].nextMember
  } ON ROWS
FROM
  [Adventure Works]
```

Result

	Reseller Sales Amount
March 2008	$2,739,370.98
February 2008	$2,700,766.80
April 2008	$2,204,623.41

PrevMember

<Member>.PrevMember

<Member>:

- Expression returns a valid member, e.g. [Date].[Fiscal].[Month].&[2008]&[3].

The Result:

- This returns the previous member of the member <Member>.
- If the previous member does not exist, no member will be returned.

NextMember

<Member>.NextMember

<Member>:

- Expression returns a valid member, e.g.[Date].[Fiscal].[Month].&[2008]&[3].

The Result:

- This returns the next member of the member <Member>.
- If the next member does not exist, no member will be returned.

Cousin

Cousin of a member is a member, which is in same position relative to another ancestor.

- Member and "Cousin of a member" are from same dimension, same hierarchy and same level.
- A Member is a cousin of itself.

Notes:

- Fiscal years start on July 1 of the previous year, means, "FY 2009" starts on July 1, 2008.
- "Q1 FY 2008" starts on July 1, 2007 and "Q4 FY 2008"starts on April 1, 2008 etc.
- "H1 FY 2008" starts on July 1, 2007 and "H2 FY 2008" starts on "January 1, 2008".

Example#	Member	Ancestor Expression	Cousin
#1	January 5, 2008	February, 2008	February 5, 2008
#2	January 5, 2008	Q4 FY 2008	April 5, 2008
#3	January 5, 2008	H1 FY 2009	July 5, 2008
#4	January 5, 2008	FY 2009	January 5, 2009

Detailed explanation of each example are listed below:

Example #1:

- Month level ancestor of member "January 5, 2008" is "January, 2008".
- January 5th is the fifth child of a month.
- "Ancestor Expression" is "February, 2008".
- So, Cousin is the fifth child of the month "February, 2008" or "February 5, 2008".

MDX	Result
SELECT { } ON COLUMNS, { Cousin ([Date].[Fiscal].[Date].&[20080105], [Date].[Fiscal].[Month].&[2008]&[2]) } ON ROWS FROM [Adventure Works]	February 5, 2008

Example #2:

- The quarter level ancestor of the member "January 5, 2008" is "Q3 FY 2008".
- January 5th is the fifth child of first month of a quarter.
- "Ancestor Expression" is "Q4 FY 2008".
- So, Cousin is the fifth child of first month of the quarter "Q4 FY 2008" or "April 5, 2008".

MDX	Result
SELECT { } ON COLUMNS, { Cousin ([Date].[Fiscal].[Date].&[20080105], [Date].[Fiscal].[Fiscal Quarter].&[2008]&[4]) } ON ROWS FROM [Adventure Works]	April 5, 2008

Example #3:

- The semester level ancestor of member "January 5, 2008" is "H2 FY 2008".
- January 5th is the fifth child of first month of first quarter of a semester.
- "Ancestor Expression" is "H1 FY 2009".
- So, Cousin is the fifth child of first month of first quarter of the semester "H1 FY 2009" or "July 5, 2008".

MDX	Result
SELECT { } ON COLUMNS, { Cousin ([Date].[Fiscal].[Date].&[20080105], [Date].[Fiscal].[Fiscal Semester].&[2009]&[1]) } ON ROWS FROM [Adventure Works]	July 5, 2008

Example #4:

- The year level ancestor of member "January 5, 2008" is "FY 2008".
- January 5th is the fifth child of first month of first quarter of second semester of the year.
- "Ancestor Expression" is "FY 2009".
- So, Cousin is the fifth child of first month of first quarter of second semester of the year "FY 2009" or "January 5, 2009".

MDX	Result
SELECT { } ON COLUMNS, { Cousin ([Date].[Fiscal].[Date].&[20080105], [Date].[Fiscal].[Fiscal Year].&[2009]) } ON ROWS FROM [Adventure Works]	January 5, 2009

Cousin (<Member> , <Ancestor>)

<Member>:

- Expression returns a valid member, e.g.[Date].[Fiscal].[Month].&[2008]&[3].

<Ancestor>:

- Typically, <Ancestor> is higher level than <Member>. For example, [Date].[Fiscal].[Fiscal Year].&[2009].

The Result:

- This returns a member, same position reference to <Ancestor>.
- If <Ancestor> is lower a level than <Member>, this function will return empty.

Steps to find Cousin of a member:

- Input: <Member> and <Ancestor>.
- Condition: <Member> and <Ancestor> should be in the same hierarchy.

1 Find the ancestor of <Member> that is in the same level of <Ancestor>, say it is <Ancestor1>.
2 Understand the relative position of <Member> respect to <Ancestor1>.
3 Find same relative position for <Ancestor>.

Figure 3-1: Example of cousins

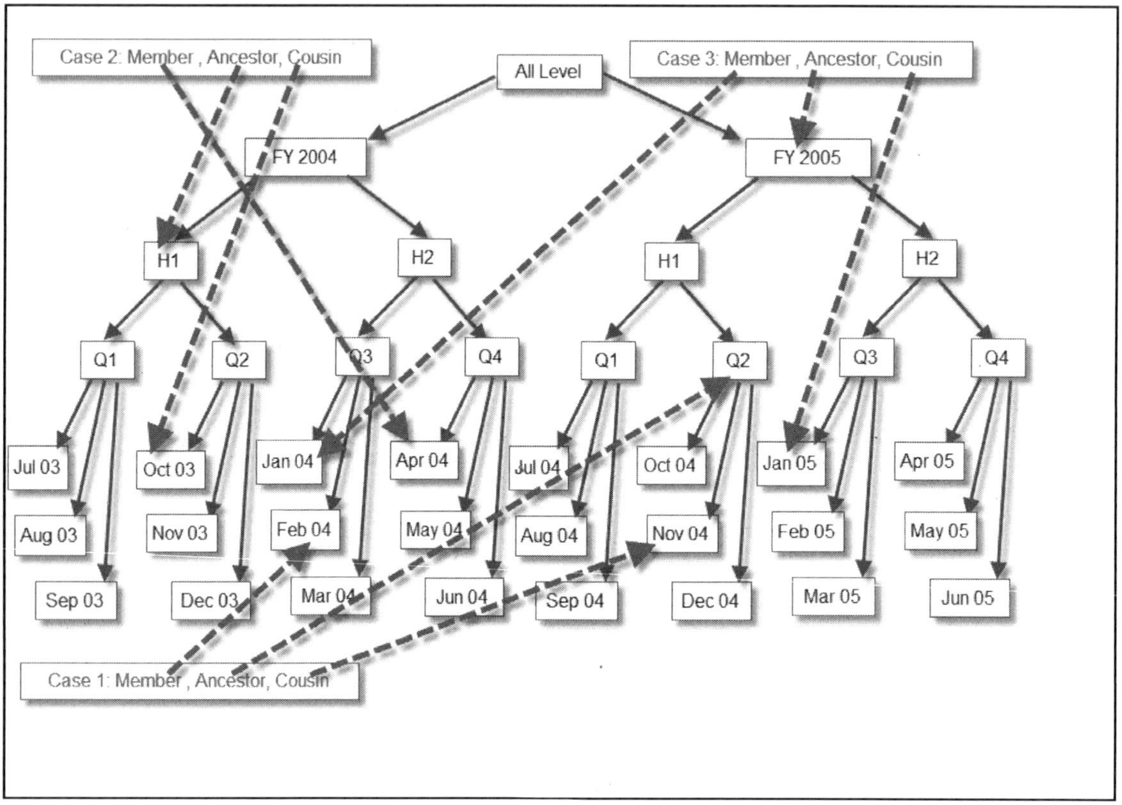

Case #1:

- Quarter level ancestor of the member "Feb, 2004" is "Q3 FY 2004". i.e. second child of the quarter.
- Given "Ancestor Expression" is "Q2 FY 2005", second child of the quarter is "Nov, 2004".
- The cousin of "Feb, 2004" is "Nov, 2004" for the ancestor "Q2 FY 2005".

Case #2:

- Semester level ancestor of member "April, 2004" is "H2 FY 2004".This is the first child of the second quarter of a semester.
- Given "Ancestor Expression" is "H1 FY 2004", the first child of the second quarter of the semester is "Oct, 2003".
- The cousin of "April, 2004" is "Oct, 2003" for the ancestor "H1 FY 2004".

Case #3:

- Year level ancestor of the member "Jan, 2004" is "FY 2004". This is the first child of the first quarter of the second semester of a fiscal year.
- Given "Ancestor Expression" is "FY 2005", the first child of the first quarter of the second semester of the fiscal year is "Jan, 2005".
- The cousin of "Jan, 2004" is "Jan, 2005" for the ancestor "FY 2005".

DefaultMember

There are three types of "Default Member" in SQL Server Analysis Services:

- **Default Measure** : Each cube has one default measure. You can set "Default Measure"of a cube using SQL Server Data Tools in properties of the cube.

- **Default Member of an Attribute Hierarchy**: Each attribute hierarchy has a default measure. You can set "Default Member"of an attribute hierarchy in properties of the attribute hierarchy using SQL Data Tools.

- **Default Member of an User Defined Hierarchy**: Each user defined hierarchy has a default member. You can set "Default Member"of an user defined hierarchy in "Calculations" of a cube using "Alter Cube" statement.

A hierarchy [Product].[Product Categories] have more than one level. "[Product].[Product Categories]" will return the default member of the hierarchy. You can use following MDX to find the name of the default member of the user defined hierarchy [Product].[Product Categories].

MDX	Result
WITH MEMBER [Measures].[Product Categories Default Member] AS [Product].[Product Categories].DefaultMember.Name SELECT { [Measures].[Product Categories Default Member] } ON COLUMNS FROM [Adventure Works]	Product Categories Default Member All Products

To find the default [Measures] of the cube, use following MDX:

MDX	Result
WITH MEMBER [Measures].[Default Member] AS [Measures].DefaultMember.Name SELECT { [Measures].[Default Member] } ON COLUMNS FROM [Adventure Works]	Default Member Reseller Sales Amount

To find the default member of an attribute hierarchy **Product.Product**, use the following MDX:

MDX	Result
WITH MEMBER [Measures].[Product Default Member] AS [Product].[Product].DefaultMember.Name SELECT { [Measures].[Product Default Member] } ON COLUMNS FROM [Adventure Works]	Product Default Member All Products

Notes:

- Though [Product].[Product Categories].DefaultMember.Name also returns the same value "All Products", these are two different values. One is the attribute hierarchy and the other is the user defined hierarchy.
- To see the difference, modify the name of "All Level" of the dimension "product" to "All Possible Products" and run the following query:

Attribute Hierarchy	User Defined Hierarchy
WITH MEMBER [Measures].[Product Default Member] AS [Product].[Product].DefaultMember.Name SELECT { [Measures].[Product Default Member] } ON COLUMNS FROM [Adventure Works]	WITH MEMBER [Measures].[Product Categories Default Member] AS [Product].[Product Categories].DefaultMember.Name SELECT { [Measures].[Product Categories Default Member] } ON COLUMNS FROM [Adventure Works]
Product Default Member All Possible Products	Product Categories Default Member All Products

Note: Modify "All Level" name of the dimension product back to "All Products"

Query#3.19:

Goal: For product [Product].[Product].[HL Headset], find "Reseller Sales Amount" for:

- Corresponding product subcategory
- Corresponding product category
- The "All Level"

Strategy:

- You can use "Ascendants" function for this product in hierarchy "Product Categories".
- [Product].[Product].[HL Headset] is not in hierarchy "Product Categories". It is in the attribute hierarchy "Product".
- "Ascendants" function will return only two levels for the attribute hierarchy [Product].[Product]:
    - "All Level"
    - "Individual level"
- To find corresponding member for "[Product].[Product].[HL Headset]" in hierarchy "Product Categories", use the "LinkMember" function.
- Then use "Ascendants" function to find all levels in the hierarchy "Product Categories".

Attribute Hierarchy

```
SELECT
  {
  [Measures].[Reseller Sales Amount]
  } ON COLUMNS,
  {
  Ascendants
    (
    [Product].[Product].[HL Headset]
    )
  } ON ROWS
FROM
  [Adventure Works]
```

	Reseller Sales Amount
HL Headset	$19,083.69
All Products	$71,513,036.12

Linked to User Defined Hierarchy

```
SELECT
  {
  [Measures].[Reseller Sales Amount]
  } ON COLUMNS,
  {
  Ascendants
    (
    LinkMember
      (
      [Product].[Product].[HL Headset],
      [Product].[Product Categories]
      )
    )
  } ON ROWS
FROM
  [Adventure Works]
```

	Reseller Sales Amount
HL Headset	$19,083.69
Headsets	$60,942.20
Components	$11,799,076.66
All Products	$80,450,596.98

LinkMember (<Member>, <Hierarchy>)

<Member>:

- Expression returns a valid member, e.g. [Product].[Product].[HL Headset].

<Hierarchy>:

- Expression returns a valid hierarchy. For example, [Product].[Product Categories].

The Result:

- This returns equivalent of the <Member> in <Hierarchy>.
- If the <Member> does not belong to <Hierarchy>, it will return null.

IsGeneration

IsGeneration returns true if a member has the given generation index.

What is a generation index?

- Leaf members have generation index 0.
- For non-leaf members:
  - Find the highest generation index from all child members.
  - Add 1 to the highest generation index.

Query#3.20:

Goal: Find all ancestors of [Product].[Product Categories].[Product].[HL Headset], and all members that have generation index 1.

MDX

```
WITH
MEMBER [Measures].[IsGeneration1] AS
IsGeneration
  (
  [Product].[Product Categories].CurrentMember,
  1
  )

SELECT
  {
  [Measures].[IsGeneration1]
  } ON COLUMNS,
  {
  Ascendants
    ([Product].[Product Categories].[Product].[HL Headset])
  } ON ROWS
FROM
  [Adventure Works]
```

Result

	IsGeneration1
HL Headset	False
Headsets	True
Components	False
All Products	False

Analysis of "Sales Territory" hierarchy of dimension "Sales Territory":

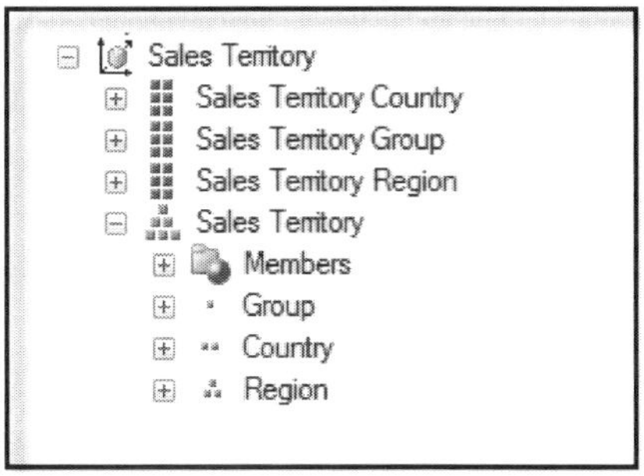

Figure 3-2 : Hierarchy "Sales Territory".

- This hierarchy has three levels, [Group], [Country] and [Region].
- [Region] rolls up to [Country].
- [Country] rolls up to [Group].
- [Group] rolls up to "All Level".

All regions are leafs, and all have generation index 0.

MDX

```
WITH
MEMBER [Measures].[IsGeneration0] AS
IsGeneration([Sales Territory].[Sales Territory].CurrentMember,0)
SELECT
  {
  [Measures].[IsGeneration0]
  } ON COLUMNS,
  {
  [Sales Territory].[Sales Territory].[Region]
  } ON ROWS
FROM
  [Adventure Works]
```

Result

	IsGeneration0
Central	True
Northeast	True
Northwest	True
Southeast	True
Southwest	True

In [Country] level, only "United States" has generation index 1.

MDX

```
WITH
MEMBER [Measures].[IsGeneration1] AS
IsGeneration([Sales Territory].[Sales Territory].CurrentMember,1)
SELECT
  {
  [Measures].[IsGeneration1]
  } ON COLUMNS,
  {
  [Sales Territory].[Sales Territory].[Country]
  } ON ROWS
FROM
  [Adventure Works]
```

Result

	IsGeneration1
France	False
Germany	False
United Kingdom	False
Canada	False
United States	True
Australia	False

Question: why do some countries have generation index 1, and some do not?

To find the answer, inspect the following query:

MDX

```
WITH
MEMBER [Measures].[IsGeneration0] AS
IsGeneration([Sales Territory].[Sales Territory].CurrentMember,0)
SELECT
  {
  [Measures].[IsGeneration0]
  } ON COLUMNS,
  {
  [Sales Territory].[Sales Territory].[Country]
  } ON ROWS
FROM
  [Adventure Works]
```

Result

	IsGeneration0
France	True
Germany	True
United Kingdom	True
Canada	True
United States	False
Australia	True

All countries except "United States" has generation index 0, because only United States has regions. Other countries do not have regions, so they are in leaf level and have generation index 0.

Let us find 0, 1, 2 generations for "Group" level.

MDX

```
WITH
MEMBER [Measures].[IsGeneration0] AS
IsGeneration([Sales Territory].[Sales Territory].CurrentMember,0)
MEMBER [Measures].[IsGeneration1] AS
IsGeneration([Sales Territory].[Sales Territory].CurrentMember,1)
MEMBER [Measures].[IsGeneration2] AS
IsGeneration([Sales Territory].[Sales Territory].CurrentMember,2)
SELECT
  {
  [Measures].[IsGeneration0],
  [Measures].[IsGeneration1],
  [Measures].[IsGeneration2]
  } ON COLUMNS,
  {
  [Sales Territory].[Sales Territory].[Group]
  } ON ROWS
FROM
  [Adventure Works]
```

Result

	IsGeneration0	IsGeneration1	IsGeneration2
Europe	False	True	False
NA	True	False	False
North America	False	True	True
Pacific	False	True	False

Analysis for the Groups:

- For Europe,
  - IsGeneration0 is false, because "Europe" is not in leaf level and has some children.
  - IsGeneration1 is true, because "Europe" has some children (countries), which are in leaf level.
  - IsGeneration2 is false, because "Europe" does not have any grand children (no country in "Europe" have regions).
- For NA:
  - IsGeneration0 is true, because this is unknown member and this is in leaf level.
  - IsGeneration1 and IsGeneration2 false as this is in leaf level and do not have any children.
- For North America:
  - IsGeneration0 is false, because "North America" is not in leaf level and has some children.
  - IsGeneration1 is true, because "North America" has some children (countries), which are in leaf level.
  - IsGeneration2 is true; because "North America" has at least one grand children. This also means, at least one country in "North America" has regions.
- For Pacific,
  - IsGeneration0 is false, because "Pacific" is not leaf level and has some children.
  - IsGeneration1 is true, because "Pacific" has some children (country), which are in leaf level.
  - IsGeneration2 is false, means "Pacific" does not have any grand-children. This also means that no country in "Pacific" has regions.

IsGeneration **(<Member>, <GenerationIndex>)**

<Member>:

- Expression returns a valid member, e.g. [Sales Territory].[Sales Territory].[Group].

<GenerationIndex>:

- This is an integer.
- Leaf members have generation index 0.
- For nonleaf members:
  - Find the highest generation index from all child members.
  - Then add 1 to that index.

The Result:

- This returns true if the generation index of <Member> is <GenerationIndex> else returns false.

DataMember

"DataMember" of a member returns a system-generated data member of a member and can be explained in following bullets:

- For leaf members, Member1 and Member1.DataMember will return same measure value.
- For non-leaf members, some cases Member1 and Member1.DataMember may return different measure values.

For example, in [Adventure Works] database, "Stephen Y. Jiang" is a sales manager:

- More than one sales persons report to him.
- All sales persons have "Sales Quota".
- This means, "Stephen Y. Jiang" also have "Sales Quota" which includes:
  - "Sales Quota" of "Stephen Y. Jiang".
  - "Sales Quota" of all sales persons report to him.

Following query differentiate between Member1 and Member1.DataMember:

Rollup Value	Non rollup value
WITH MEMBER [Measures].SalesQuota AS ([Employee].[Employees].CurrentMember, [Measures].[Sales Amount Quota]),FORMAT_STRING='Currency' SELECT { [Measures].SalesQuota } ON COLUMNS, { [Employee].[Employees].[Stephen Y. Jiang] } ON ROWS FROM [Adventure Works]	WITH MEMBER [Measures].SalesQuota AS ([Employee].[Employees].CurrentMember.DataMember, [Measures].[Sales Amount Quota]),FORMAT_STRING='Currency' SELECT { [Measures].SalesQuota } ON COLUMNS, { [Employee].[Employees].[Stephen Y. Jiang] } ON ROWS FROM [Adventure Works]
SalesQuota Stephen Y. Jiang $114,230,750.00	SalesQuota Stephen Y. Jiang $2,182,500.00

The different "Sales Quota" values for [Employee].[Employees].CurrentMember and [Employee].[Employees].CurrentMember.DataMember are because:

- [Employee].[Employees].CurrentMember means sum of "Sales Quota" of "Stephen Y. Jiang" and all sales people reporting to him.
- [Employee].[Employees].CurrentMember.DataMember means "Sales Quota" of "Stephen Y. Jiang" only.

Inspect the following query for individual sales quota and roll up sales quota:

MDX

```
WITH
MEMBER [Measures].[InvidualQuota] AS
  (
  [Employee].[Employees].CurrentMember.DataMember,
  [Measures].[Sales Amount Quota]
  ),FORMAT_STRING='Currency'
MEMBER [Measures].[RollupQuota] AS
  (
  [Employee].[Employees].CurrentMember,
  [Measures].[Sales Amount Quota]
  ),FORMAT_STRING='Currency'
SELECT
  {
  [Measures].[RollupQuota],
  [Measures].[InvidualQuota]
  } ON COLUMNS,
  {
  DESCENDANTS
    (
    [Employee].[Employees].[Stephen Y. Jiang],
    [Employee].[Employees].[Employee Level 05],
    SELF_BEFORE_AFTER
    )
  }  ON ROWS
FROM
  [Adventure Works]
```

Result

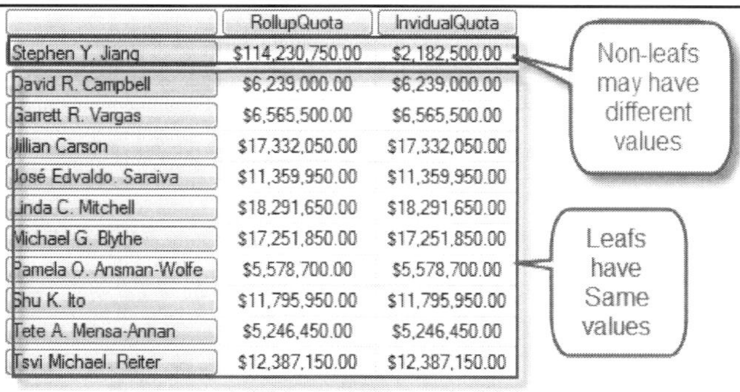

	RollupQuota	InvidualQuota
Stephen Y. Jiang	$114,230,750.00	$2,182,500.00
David R. Campbell	$6,239,000.00	$6,239,000.00
Garrett R. Vargas	$6,565,500.00	$6,565,500.00
Jillian Carson	$17,332,050.00	$17,332,050.00
José Edvaldo. Saraiva	$11,359,950.00	$11,359,950.00
Linda C. Mitchell	$18,291,650.00	$18,291,650.00
Michael G. Blythe	$17,251,850.00	$17,251,850.00
Pamela O. Ansman-Wolfe	$5,578,700.00	$5,578,700.00
Shu K. Ito	$11,795,950.00	$11,795,950.00
Tete A. Mensa-Annan	$5,246,450.00	$5,246,450.00
Tsvi Michael. Reiter	$12,387,150.00	$12,387,150.00

Analysis:

- For non-leaf members, a measure of Member1.DataMember means only for that member.
- Member1.DataMember applies to parent-child hierarchy.

> **<Member>.DataMember**
> <Member>:
> - Expression returns a valid member, e.g. [Employee].[Employees].[Stephen Y. Jiang].
>
> The Result:
> - This returns system generated data member.
> - DataMember returns measure for the **non-leaf member only and not a rollup value.**

UnknownMember

Unknown member is the unknown bucket. For example, if there is an entry in the fact table for "Reseller Sales" for product "ABC", and "ABC" product does not exist in the product dimension, then the "Reseller Sales" of product "ABC" goes to unknown bucket. Later in this chapter, unknown members will be created and different cases of unknown members will be analyzed.

There are two forms for unknown member:

- <Hierarchy>.UnknownMember
  This will return unknown member from top level.
  For example, [Product].[Product Categories].UnknownMember will return for unknown category.

MDX	Result
SELECT { [Measures].[Reseller Sales Amount] } ON COLUMNS, { [Product].[Product Categories].UnknownMember } On ROWS FROM [Adventure Works]	Reseller Sales Amount Unknown Products (null)

- In <Member>.UnknownMember, typically <Member> is the "All Level".
  [Product].[Product Categories].[All Products].UnknownMember will return unknown members of the individual level.
- You can also query unknown members for any level of a hierarchy

Following code returns nothing, which means, unknown member is not defined for Geography dimension.

MDX	Result
SELECT { [Measures].[Reseller Sales Amount] } ON COLUMNS, { [Geography].[Geography].UnknownMember } ON ROWS FROM [Adventure Works]	Reseller Sales Amount

Notes:

- Unknown member can be defined for a dimension.
- Unknown member cannot be defined for hierarchy or a level of a dimension.

Goal: Create unknown member for dimension "Geography".

Steps:

1 Open SQL Server Data Tools.

2 Open analysis services project "AdventureWorksDW2012Multidimensional-EE".

3 In solution explorer, double-click on dimension "Geography" in "Dimensions" folder.

4 In "Attributes" tab click on dimension "Geography".

5 In "Geography Dimension" properties, change "UnknownMemberName" as "Unknown Geography" and "UnknownMember" as "Visible".

Figure 3-3: Create unknown member for dimension Geography

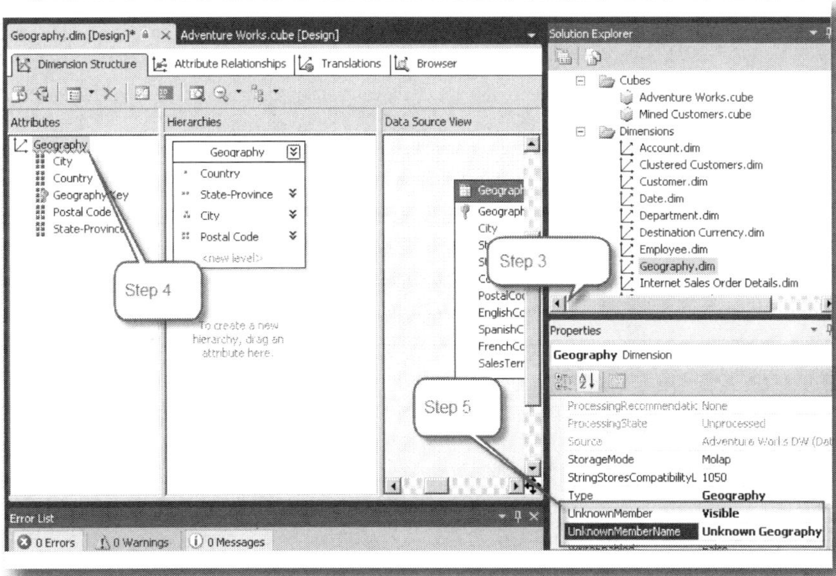

Save the configuration by clicking "Save" button.

7 Process the "Adventure Works" cube.

8 Run the last MDX query to verify the "UnknownMember" exists in Geography dimension.

<table>
<tr><th>MDX</th><th>Result</th></tr>
<tr><td>SELECT
{
[Measures].[Reseller Sales Amount]
} ON COLUMNS,
{
[Geography].[Geography].UnknownMember
} ON ROWS
FROM
[Adventure Works]</td><td>

	Reseller Sales Amount
Unknown Geography	(null)

</td></tr>
</table>

"UnknownMember" for Geography dimension is created but there are no data for "UnknownMember".

- FactResellerSales connected to Geography dimension via "DimReseller".
- Unknown geography means, the location of a reseller is not known.

To create data for Unknown geography, follow these steps:

1 Login to the **database engine**, go to the database "AdventureWorksDW2012".

2 Using following SQL statement, remove the foreign key constraint from the table "DimReseller", so you can add null Geography key in DimReseller table.

```
ALTER TABLE [dbo].[DimReseller]
DROP CONSTRAINT [FK_DimReseller_DimGeography]
```

3 For the reseller with ResellerKey 490, update GeographyKey to null

```
UPDATE dbo.DimReseller
SET GeographyKey=null
WHERE resellerkey = 490
```

4 Open SQL Server Data Tools and open project "AdventureWorksDW2012Multidimensional-EE".

5 In solution explorer, double-click on "Adventure works" in "Cubes" folder.

6 In Measures block, right click on "AdventureWorks" and select "properties".

7 In "Adventure Works Cube" properties, change following as shown in the Figure 3-4

- Change "ErrorConfiguration" to "custom".
- Change "KeyErrorLimitaction" to "StopLogging".
- Any other changes to match as in Figure 3-4.

Figure 3-4: Configuration in the cube to accommodate unknown member for dimension Geography.

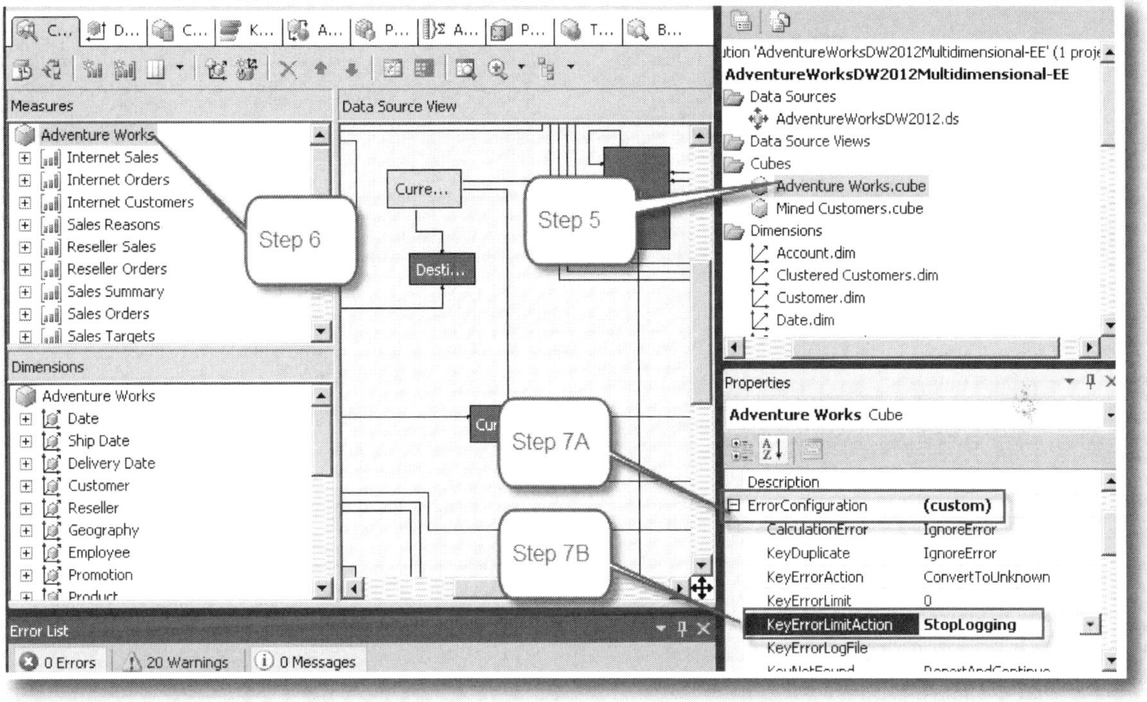

8 Save the configuration by clicking "Save" button.

9 Process the "Adventure Works" cube.

10 Run the last MDX query to verify the "UnknownMember" exists in Geography dimension.

MDX	Result
SELECT { [Measures].[Reseller Sales Amount] } ON COLUMNS, { [Geography].[Geography].UnknownMember } ON ROWS FROM [Adventure Works]	| | Reseller Sales Amount | | Unknown Geography | $418,436.53 |

The above Reseller Sales Amount belongs to the reseller with ResellerKey 490, for which GeographyKey modified to null.

Query#3.21:

Goal: Show top 5 products based on "Reseller Sales Amount", also show "Model Name" of each product.

Strategy:

- "Model Name" is an attribute hierarchy of product dimension.
- "Model Name" is not present in the hierarchy "Product Categories".
- For each product member, you can get "Model Name" by using "Properties" function.

MDX

```
WITH
MEMBER [Measures].[Model Name] AS
[Product].[Product Categories].CurrentMember.Properties("Model Name")
SELECT
  {
  [Measures].[Reseller Sales Amount],
  [Measures].[Model Name]
  } ON COLUMNS,
  {
  TOPCOUNT
    (
    [Product].[Product Categories].[Product],
    5,
    [Measures].[Reseller Sales Amount]
    )
  } ON ROWS
FROM
  [Adventure Works]
```

Result

	Reseller Sales Amount	Model Name
Mountain-200 Black, 38	$1,634,647.94	Mountain-200
Mountain-200 Black, 38	$1,471,078.72	Mountain-200
Road-350-W Yellow, 48	$1,380,253.88	Road-350-W
Touring-1000 Blue, 60	$1,370,784.22	Touring-1000
Mountain-200 Black, 42	$1,360,828.02	Mountain-200

Properties

<Member>.Properties (<Property> [, <TYPED>])

<Member>:

- Expression returns a valid member.
  For example, [Product].[Product Categories].[Product].&[447].

<Property>:

- This is the name of a property of <Member>. e.g. "Model Name".

The Result:

- This returns <Property> value of <Member>.
- TYPED will return strongly typed, explained below.

Inspect the following query to understand the difference between with and without TYPED parameter in "Properties" function.

Without TYPED

```
WITH
MEMBER [Measures].[EndDate] AS
[Employee].[Employee Department].CurrentMember.Properties("End Date")
SELECT
  {
  [Measures].[EndDate]
  } ON COLUMNS,
  {
  [Employee].[Employee Department].[Employee].&[4]
  } ON ROWS
FROM
  [Adventure Works]
```

	EndDate
Rob Walters	June 30, 2000

With TYPED

```
WITH
MEMBER [Measures].[EndDate] AS
[Employee].[Employee Department].CurrentMember.Properties("End Date",TYPED)
SELECT
  {
  [Measures].[EndDate]
  } ON COLUMNS,
  {
  [Employee].[Employee Department].[Employee].&[4]
  } ON ROWS
FROM
  [Adventure Works]
```

	EndDate
Rob Walters	6/30/2000

Analysis:

- The two queries return two different format of "End Date".
- With "TYPED" it returns SimpleEndDate, which is NameColumn of the attribute.
- Without "TYPED" it returns EndDate, which is ValueColumn of the attribute.

The following steps shows that NameColumn and ValueColumn are different for EndDate attribute of dimension date:

1 Open SQL Server Data Tools.
2 Open analysis services project "AdventureWorksDW2012Multidimensional-EE".
3 In solution explorer, double-click on dimension "Date" in "Dimensions" folder.
4 In "Attributes" block click on attribute "EndDate".
5 Verify the NameColumn and ValueColumn are different.

Figure 3-5: NameColumn and ValueColumn for attribute EndDate of dimension Date.

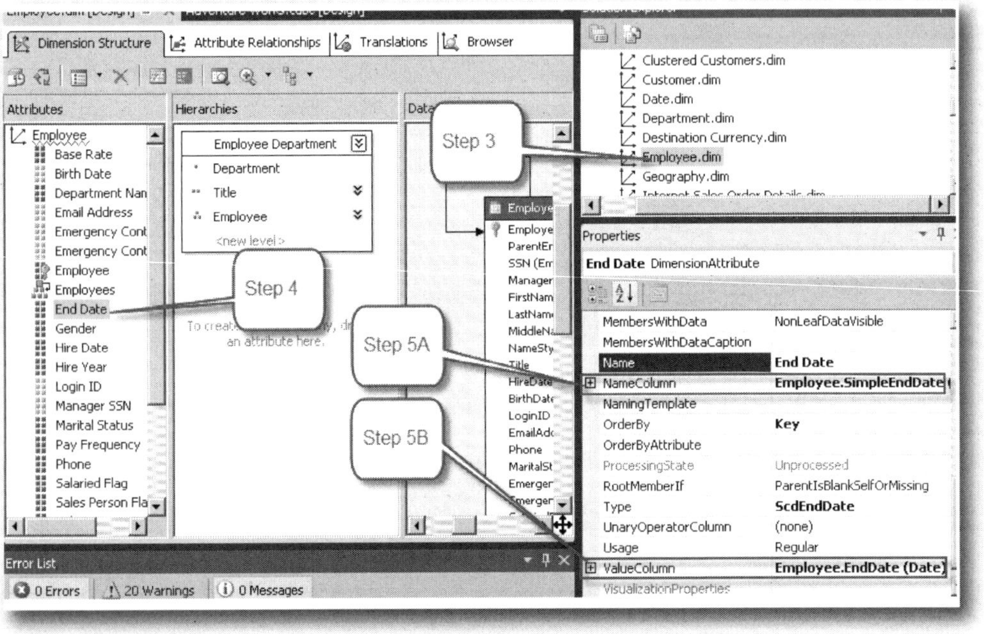

As NameColumn and ValueColumn are different:

- With "TYPED" it returns SimpleEndDate, which is NameColumn of the attribute.
- Without "TYPED" it returns EndDate, which is ValueColumn of the attribute.

EXERCISES

Exercise 3.1: Find "Reseller Sales Amount" for all non-empty calendar weeks of calendar year 2008. Also, show start date and end date of each week.

Exercise 3.2: Find the default member of attribute "Destination Currency" of dimension "Destination Currency".

Exercise 3.3: Find average list price of each product category.

Exercise 3.4: Find **"Reseller Sales Amount" for each product category** for the state of California for the fiscal year 2008 and compare with **total "Reseller Sales Amount"** for the state of California for fiscal year 2008.

Exercise 3.5: Find "Reseller Sales Amount", "Reseller Order Quantity" for states that contain following cities "Dallas" , "Austin", "Los Angeles", "Chicago" , "New York" , "Orlando", "Miami" for fiscal years 2007, 2008 for the product categories "Bikes" and "Clothing".

Chapter 4: Time Functions

This chapter explores and explains time functions in MDX with examples. One of the essential functions of this chapter is PeriodsToDate, which returns a set of time members from the start of a period to the current member. For example, "PeriodsToDate" function can be used to find all days from beginning of the year till July 1, 2012. Some derived functions of PeriodsToDate are YTD (**Y**ear **T**o Date), MTD (Month To Date), QTD (Quarter To Date) and WTD (Week To Date). SQL Server Analysis Services processes PeriodsToDate as a function applied to a regular hierarchy, and PeriodsToDate defined as "set of members range from first sibling to the current member".

Another important function is "ParallelPeriod", which returns a member that has the same relative position in the previous/later period. Other interesting functions are "LastPeriods", "OpeningPeriod","ClosingPeriod".

The most common question asked about Time Functions is how to find current time. There is no native MDX function to find the current time, but you can use VBA function "Now ()" in MDX to find current time. Note that, the current time does not have much use in SSAS cube. Since you need to convert data returned from "Now ()" to your corresponding date key. Another important point is that the date dimension needs to be pre-populated before the date can be used in a cube.

Agenda

Now (VBA)
OpeningPeriod
ClosingPeriod
PeriodsToDate
Ytd
Mtd
Qtd
Wtd
ParallelPeriod
LastPeriods

Exercises

OpeningPeriod

"OpeningPeriod" function returns the first member of a period, for example:

- Opening period of "Calendar year 2008" in "month level" is the first month of the calendar year, which is January, 2008.
- Opening period of "Calendar year 2008" in "day level" is the first day of the calendar year, which is January 1, 2008.
- Opening period of "March, 2008" in "day level" is the first day of the month, which is March 1, 2008.

Query#4.01:

Goal: Find "Reseller Sales Amount" for the first month of the second semester of fiscal year 2008 for state of Texas. Also display current date and time.

Strategy:

- Display "Reseller Sales Amount" in columns.
- Show the opening period of "second semester of fiscal year 2008" in the month level in rows.
- Use "Where" clause to limit the data to state of Texas only.
- Use VBA function Now() to display current date and time.

MDX

```
WITH
MEMBER [Measures].[CurrentDateTime] AS
Now()

SELECT
  {
  [Measures].[Reseller Sales Amount],
  [Measures].[CurrentDateTime]
  } ON COLUMNS,
  {
  OpeningPeriod
    (
    [Date].[Fiscal].[Month],
    [Date].[Fiscal].[Fiscal Semester].&[2008]&[2]
    )
  } ON ROWS
FROM
  [Adventure Works]
WHERE
  [Geography].[Geography].[State-Province].&[TX]&[US]
```

Result

	Reseller Sales Amount	CurrentDateTime
January 2008	$86,706.99	8/9/2012 11:57:29 AM

Query#4.02:

Goal: Find "Reseller Sales Amount" for the **first month** of **each fiscal semester** for the state of Texas.

Step 1: Find "Reseller Sales Amount" for each fiscal semester for the state of Texas.

Strategy:

- Show "Reseller Sales Amount" in columns.
- Show fiscal semesters in rows.
- Use the "Where" clause to limit "Reseller Sales Amount" for the state of Texas only.

MDX

```
SELECT
  {
  [Measures].[Reseller Sales Amount]
  } ON COLUMNS,
  {
  [Date].[Fiscal].[Fiscal Semester]
  } ON ROWS
FROM
  [Adventure Works]
WHERE
  [Geography].[Geography].[State-Province].&[TX]&[US]
```

Result

	Reseller Sales Amount
H2 FY 2005	(null)
H1 FY 2006	$550,963.32
H2 FY 2006	$717,745.68
H1 FY 2007	$1,603,955.98
H2 FY 2007	$1,223,699.97
H1 FY 2008	$1,224,429.29
H2 FY 2008	$915,388.12
H1 FY 2009	(null)
H2 FY 2009	(null)
H1 FY 2010	(null)
H2 FY 2010	(null)
H1 FY 2011	(null)

Step 2: Modify the last query to display name of the first month of each semester.

Strategy:

- Using OpeningPeriod, find the first month.

```
WITH
MEMBER [Measures].[FirstMonth] AS
OpeningPeriod
  (
  [Date].[Fiscal].[Month],
  [Date].[Fiscal].CurrentMember
  )
```

- To find the name of the month, use ".Name" for this member.

```
WITH
MEMBER [Measures].[FirstMonth] AS
OpeningPeriod
  (
  [Date].[Fiscal].[Month],
  [Date].[Fiscal].CurrentMember
  ).Name
```

MDX	Result
WITH MEMBER [Measures].[FirstMonth] AS OpeningPeriod ([Date].[Fiscal].[Month], [Date].[Fiscal].CurrentMember).Name SELECT { [Measures].[Reseller Sales Amount], [Measures].[FirstMonth] } ON COLUMNS, { [Date].[Fiscal].[Fiscal Semester] } ON ROWS FROM [Adventure Works] WHERE [Geography].[Geography].[State-Province].&[TX]&[US]	(see result grid below)

	Reseller Sales Amount	FirstMonth
H2 FY 2005	(null)	January 2005
H1 FY 2006	$550,963.32	July 2005
H2 FY 2006	$717,745.68	January 2006
H1 FY 2007	$1,603,955.98	July 2006
H2 FY 2007	$1,223,699.97	January 2007
H1 FY 2008	$1,224,429.29	July 2007
H2 FY 2008	$915,388.12	January 2008
H1 FY 2009	(null)	July 2008
H2 FY 2009	(null)	January 2009
H1 FY 2010	(null)	July 2009
H2 FY 2010	(null)	January 2010
H1 FY 2011	(null)	July 2010

Step 3: Modify the last query to display "Reseller Sales Amount" for the first month of each semester.

Strategy:

- To find "Reseller Sales Amount" for the first month of each semester, use the following code:

```
WITH
MEMBER [Measures].[RSAFirstMonth] AS
  (
  [Measures].[Reseller Sales Amount],
  OpeningPeriod
    (
    [Date].[Fiscal].[Month],
    [Date].[Fiscal].CurrentMember
    )
  )
```

Note: Following MDX code will give error:

```
WITH
MEMBER [Measures].[RSAFirstMonth] AS
  (
  [Measures].[Reseller Sales Amount],
  [Measures].[FirstMonth]
  )
```

Because, the tuple is not valid, since it has two members from the same dimension "Measures" and that breaks the rule of a tuple, **two members from same dimension ("Measures") is not allowed in a tuple**.

MDX

```
WITH
MEMBER [Measures].[FirstMonth] AS
OpeningPeriod
  (
  [Date].[Fiscal].[Month],
  [Date].[Fiscal].CurrentMember
  ).Name
MEMBER [Measures].[RSAFirstMonth] AS
  (
  [Measures].[Reseller Sales Amount],
  OpeningPeriod
    (
    [Date].[Fiscal].[Month],
    [Date].[Fiscal].CurrentMember
    )
  ),Format_string="Currency"
SELECT
  {
  [Measures].[Reseller Sales Amount],
  [Measures].[FirstMonth],
  [Measures].[RSAFirstMonth]
  } ON COLUMNS,
  {
  [Date].[Fiscal].[Fiscal Semester]
  } ON ROWS
FROM
  [Adventure Works]
WHERE
  [Geography].[Geography].[State-Province].&[TX]&[US]
```

Result

	Reseller Sales Amount	FirstMonth	RSAFirstMonth
H2 FY 2005	(null)	January 2005	(null)
H1 FY 2006	$550,963.32	July 2005	$34,872.16
H2 FY 2006	$717,745.68	January 2006	$30,188.71
H1 FY 2007	$1,603,955.98	July 2006	$282,309.58
H2 FY 2007	$1,223,699.97	January 2007	$140,419.53
H1 FY 2008	$1,224,429.29	July 2007	$160,992.21
H2 FY 2008	$915,388.12	January 2008	$86,706.99
H1 FY 2009	(null)	July 2008	(null)
H2 FY 2009	(null)	January 2009	(null)
H1 FY 2010	(null)	July 2009	(null)
H2 FY 2010	(null)	January 2010	(null)
H1 FY 2011	(null)	July 2010	(null)

OpeningPeriod (<Level> [, <Member>])

<Level>:

- A valid level. e.g [Date].[Fiscal].[Month].
- <Member> and <Level> should be from same the hierarchy.
- Typically, <Member> is ancestor of <Level>.

<Member>:

- This is an optional parameter.
- A valid member. e.g. [Date].[Fiscal].[Fiscal Semester].&[2008]&[2].

The Result:

- This returns first sibling of <Level> if <Member> is not passed.
- If <Member> is passed, it will only consider descendants of <Member> in <Level>.

Note: It will not return any error if the parameters of OpeningPeriod are not a Date/Time dimension, instead it will return the first sibling of the level. For example,

```
OpeningPeriod
  (
  [Product].[Product Categories].[Product],
  [Product].[Product Categories].[Category].[Bikes]
  ).Name
```

The above code will return the first product of the product category "Bikes".

MDX

```
WITH MEMBER [Measures].[FirstSibling] AS
OpeningPeriod
  (
  [Product].[Product Categories].[Product],
  [Product].[Product Categories].CurrentMember
  ).Name
SELECT
  {
  [Measures].[Reseller Sales Amount],
  [Measures].[FirstSibling]
  } ON COLUMNS,
  {
  [Product].[Product Categories].[Category]
  } ON ROWS
FROM
  [Adventure Works]
WHERE
  [Geography].[Geography].[State-Province].&[TX]&[US]
```

Result

	Reseller Sales Amount	FirstSibling
Accessories	$32,091.47	Hitch Rack - 4-Bike
Bikes	$5,176,738.21	Mountain-100 Black, 38
Clothing	$105,216.45	Men's Bib-Shorts, L
Components	$922,136.21	HL Bottom Bracket

ClosingPeriod

"ClosingPeriod" function returns the last member of a period, for example:

- Closing period of "Calendar year 2008" in "month level" is the last month of the calendar year, which is December, 2008.
- Closing period of "Calendar year 2008" in "day level" is the last day of the calendar year, which is December 31, 2008.
- Closing period of "March, 2008" in "day level" is the last day of the month, which is March 31, 2008.

Query#4.03:

Goal: Find "Reseller Sales Amount" for the first day of the last month of the second quarter of fiscal year 2008 for the state of Texas.

Strategy:

- Display "Reseller Sales Amount" in columns.
- Show opening period of "closing period of second quarter of fiscal year 2008".
- Use "Where" clause to limit to the state of Texas only.

<table>
<tr><td>MDX</td><td><pre>SELECT
  {
  [Measures].[Reseller Sales Amount]
  } ON COLUMNS,
  {
  OpeningPeriod
    (
    [Date].[Fiscal].[Date],
    ClosingPeriod
      (
      [Date].[Fiscal].[Month],
      [Date].[Fiscal].[Fiscal Quarter].&[2008]&[2]
)
)
  } ON ROWS
FROM
  [Adventure Works]
WHERE
  [Geography].[Geography].[State-Province].&[TX]&[US]</pre></td></tr>
<tr><td>Result</td><td><table><tr><th></th><th>Reseller Sales Amount</th></tr><tr><td>December 1, 2007</td><td>$113,461.18</td></tr></table></td></tr>
</table>

Note: It will not return an error if the parameters of ClosingPeriod are not a Date/Time dimension, instead it will return the last sibling of a level.

ClosingPeriod (<Level> [, <Member>])

<Level>:

- A valid level. e.g. [Date].[Fiscal].[Month].
- <Member> and <Level> should be from the same hierarchy.
- Typically, <Member> is ancestor of <Level>.

<Member>:

- This is an optional parameter.
- A valid member. e.g. [Date].[Fiscal].[Fiscal Semester].&[2004]&[2].

The Result:

- This returns last sibling of level <Level> if <Member> is not passed.
- If <Member> is passed, it will only consider descendants of <Member> in <Level>.

PeriodsToDate

"PeriodsToDate" function returns a "set of members" from "beginning of a period" to "a given date".

- PeriodsToDate ("Calendar Year", "March 15, 2009") means,
  A set of all days from beginning of the calendar year to March 15, 2009.
- "PeriodsToDate" function can be used also for months or quarters. For example,
  - PeriodsToDate ("Calendar Year", "May, 2009") will return all months of calendar year 2009 from January, 2009 to May, 2009.
  - PeriodsToDate ("Calendar Year", "Q3, 2009") will return all quarters of calendar year 2009 from Q1, 2009 to Q3, 2009.
  - PeriodsToDate ("Calendar Quarter", "May, 2009") will return all months of calendar quarter Q2, 2009 from April, 2009 to May, 2009.
  - PeriodsToDate ("Calendar Quarter", "May 12, 2009") will return all dates of calendar quarter Q2, 2009 from April 1, 2009 to May 12, 2009.

Example#1: Find all days of calendar year 2009 from beginning of the year until March 15, 2009.

MDX

```
SELECT
  { } ON COLUMNS,
  {
  PeriodsToDate
    (
    [Date].[Calendar].[Calendar Year],
    [Date].[Calendar].[Date].&[20090315]
    )
  } ON ROWS
FROM
  [Adventure Works]
```

Result

January 1, 2009
January 2, 2009
January 3, 2009
January 4, 2009
January 5, 2009
January 6, 2009
January 7, 2009
January 8, 2009
January 9, 2009
January 10, 2009
January 11, 2009
January 12, 2009
[illegible]

Example#2: Find all months of calendar year 2008 from beginning of the year until May, 2008.

<table>
<tr><th>MDX</th><th>Result</th></tr>
<tr><td>SELECT
{
} ON COLUMNS,
{
PeriodsToDate
(
[Date].[Calendar].[Calendar Year],
[Date].[Calendar].[Month].&[2008]&[5]
)
} ON ROWS
FROM
[Adventure Works]</td><td>January 2008
February 2008
March 2008
April 2008
May 2008</td></tr>
</table>

Analysis:

- In first parameter, a level("Calendar Year") is passed and not exact value of "Calendar Year 2008".
- The second parameter indicates that the member value is "May, 2008" and the current calendar year is 2008.
- The result will display all months from beginning of the calendar year 2008 until May, 2008.

Example#3: Modify the last query, change the year in the second parameter to 2009.

<table>
<tr><th>MDX</th><th>Result</th></tr>
<tr><td>SELECT
{
} ON COLUMNS,
{
PeriodsToDate
(
[Date].[Calendar].[Calendar Year],
[Date].[Calendar].[Month].&[2009]&[5]
)
} ON ROWS
FROM
[Adventure Works]</td><td>January 2009
February 2009
March 2009
April 2009
May 2009</td></tr>
</table>

Analysis:

- The second parameter indicates that the current calendar year is 2009 and current month is May, 2009.
- The result will display all months from beginning of the calendar year 2009 until May, 2009.

Example#4: Find all quarters of calendar year 2009 from beginning of the year until Q3, 2009.

MDX	Result
SELECT { } ON COLUMNS, { PeriodsToDate ([Date].[Calendar].[Calendar Year], [Date].[Calendar].[Calendar Quarter].&[2009]&[3]) } ON ROWS FROM [Adventure Works]	Q1 CY 2009 Q2 CY 2009 Q3 CY 2009

Example#5: Find all days of calendar quarter Q2, 2009 from beginning of the quarter until May12, 2009.

MDX	Result
SELECT { } ON COLUMNS, { PeriodsToDate ([Date].[Calendar].[Calendar Quarter], [Date].[Calendar].[Date].&[20090512]) } ON ROWS FROM [Adventure Works]	April 1, 2009 April 2, 2009 April 3, 2009 April 4, 2009 April 5, 2009 April 6, 2009 April 7, 2009 April 8, 2009 April 9, 2009 April 10, 2009 April 11, 2009 April 12, 2009 April 13, 2009 April 14, 2009 April 15, 2009 April 16, 2009

Analysis:

- The second parameter indicates that the member is "May 12, 2009" and current calendar quarter is "Q2 of 2009".
- The result will display all days from beginning of the calendar quarter Q2, 2009 until May 12, 2009.

Query#4.04:

Goal: Find "Reseller Sales Amount" for the first 4 months of each calendar year for the state of California.

Step 1: Find "Reseller Sales Amount" for each calendar year for the state California.

MDX

```
SELECT
  {
  [Measures].[Reseller Sales Amount]
  } ON COLUMNS,
  {
  [Date].[Calendar].[Calendar Year]
  } ON ROWS
FROM
  [Adventure Works]
WHERE
  [Geography].[Geography].[State-Province].&[CA]&[US]
```

Result

	Reseller Sales Amount
CY 2005	$1,172,119.07
CY 2006	$3,394,071.80
CY 2007	$3,558,441.96
CY 2008	$1,639,637.88
CY 2009	(null)
CY 2010	(null)

Step 2: Modify the last query and also show the name of the 4th-month name of each calendar year.

MDX

```
WITH
MEMBER [Measures].[4th Month] AS
Descendants
  (
  [Date].[Calendar].CurrentMember,
  [Date].[Calendar].[Month],  SELF
  ).Item(3).Name
SELECT
  {
  [Measures].[Reseller Sales Amount],
  [Measures].[4th Month]
  } ON COLUMNS,
  {
  [Date].[Calendar].[Calendar Year]
  } ON ROWS
FROM
  [Adventure Works]
WHERE
  [Geography].[Geography].[State-Province].&[CA]&[US]
```

Result

	Reseller Sales Amount	4th Month
CY 2005	$1,172,119.07	April 2005
CY 2006	$3,394,071.80	April 2006
CY 2007	$3,558,441.96	April 2007
CY 2008	$1,639,637.88	April 2008
CY 2009	(null)	April 2009
CY 2010	(null)	April 2010

Analysis:

- Following code will return the set of all months of the current calendar year.

```
Descendants
 (
 [Date].[Calendar].CurrentMember,
 [Date].[Calendar].[Month], SELF
 )
```

- "item(3)" returns the 4th month, since it is a zero based index.
- And item(3).Name will return the name of the 4th month.

Step 3: Modify the last query, show Reseller Sales Amount (RSA) for first 4 months of each calendar year.

MDX

```
WITH
MEMBER [Measures].[RSA for first 4 months] AS
SUM
  (
  PeriodsToDate
    (
    [Date].[Calendar].[Calendar Year],
    Descendants
      (
      [Date].[Calendar].CurrentMember,
      [Date].[Calendar].[Month],
      SELF
      ).Item(3)
    ),
  [Measures].[Reseller Sales Amount]
  )
SELECT
  {
  [Measures].[Reseller Sales Amount],
  [Measures].[RSA for first 4 months]
  } ON COLUMNS,
  {
  [Date].[Calendar].[Calendar Year]
  } ON ROWS
FROM
  [Adventure Works]
WHERE
  [Geography].[Geography].[State-Province].&[CA]&[US]
```

Result

	Reseller Sales Amount	RSA for first 4 months
CY 2005	$1,172,119.07	(null)
CY 2006	$3,394,071.80	$685,585.38
CY 2007	$3,558,441.96	$765,510.91
CY 2008	$1,639,637.88	$1,014,707.38
CY 2009	(null)	(null)
CY 2010	(null)	(null)

Analysis:

- The following pseudo code will return the set of the first four months of the current calendar year.

```
PeriodsToDate
  (
  [Date].[Calendar].[Calendar Year],
  "4th month of the year"
  )
```

- And the following pseudo code will return the sum of Reseller Sales Amount for the first four months of a calendar year.

```
Sum
  (
  "First four months of a calendar year",
   [Measures].[Reseller Sales Amount]
  )
```

PeriodsToDate **(<Level>, <Member>)**

<Level>:

- A valid level. For example, [Date].[Calendar].[Calendar Year].
- <Member> and <Level> should be from same hierarchy.
- Typically, <Level> is higher level than <Member>.

<Member>:

- A valid member. e.g. [Date].[Calendar].[Month].&[2009]&[5].

The Result:

- This returns a set of siblings of <Member>, starting from first member of <Level> till <Member>.

"PeriodsToDate" function will not give an error if <Level> and <Member> are not from a time dimension, but the result may not have much meaning.

For example,

```
PeriodsToDate
  (
  [Product].[Product Categories].[Category],
  [Product].[Product Categories].[Product].[Road Bottle Cage]
  )
```

- The product category for "Road Bottle Cage" is "Accessories".
- The result will display all products from first descendant of "Accessories" until "Road Bottle Cage".

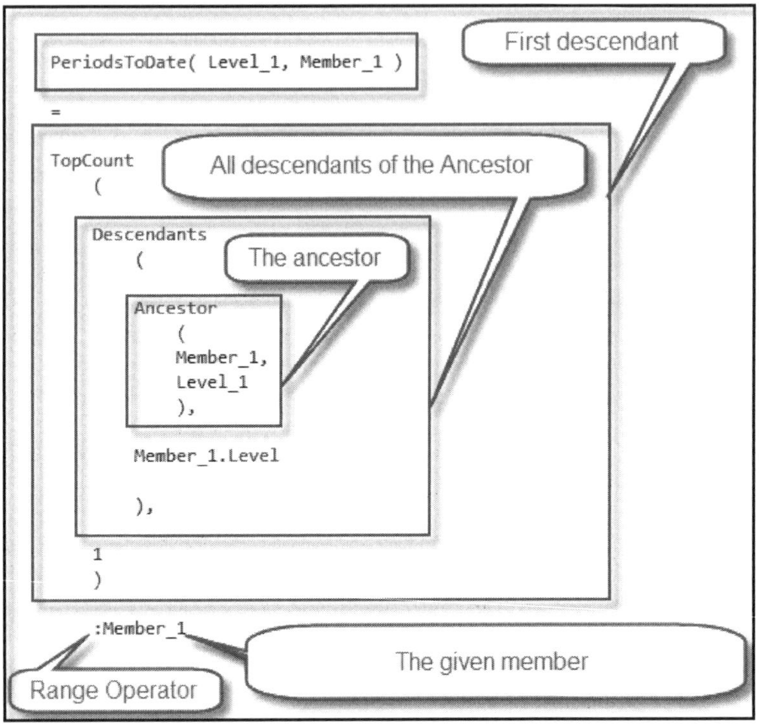

Figure 4-1: Equivalent of PeriodsToDate.

Though PeriodsToDate can be used for non-time dimension, but the result may not have much meaning.

Shortcut Functions of PeriodsToDate

Shortcut	Meaning	PeriodsToDate Equivalent
YTD	All days from beginning of the current year until the given date.	PeriodsToDate ("Year level", "A date")
QTD	All days from beginning of the current quarter until the given date.	PeriodsToDate ("Quarter level", "A date")
MTD	All days from beginning of the current month until the given date.	PeriodsToDate ("Month level", "A date")
WTD	All days from beginning of the current week until the given date.	PeriodsToDate ("Week level", "A date")

Query#4.05:

Goal: Find "Internet Sales Amount" for each day from beginning of the calendar year to January 20, 2008 for the state of New York.

Using PeriodsToDate

```
SELECT
  {
  [Measures].[Internet Sales Amount]
  } ON COLUMNS,
  {
  PeriodsToDate
    (
    [Date].[Calendar].[Calendar Year],
    [Date].[Calendar].[Date].&[20080120]
    )
  } ON ROWS
FROM
  [Adventure Works]
WHERE
  [Geography].[Geography].[State-Province].&[NY]&[US]
```

Result

	Internet Sales Amount
January 1, 2008	$26,394.20
January 2, 2008	$42,043.50
January 3, 2008	$46,519.08
January 4, 2008	$39,773.73
January 5, 2008	$38,727.37
January 6, 2008	$35,559.61
January 7, 2008	$53,206.93
January 8, 2008	$49,743.61
January 9, 2008	$35,343.95
January 10, 2008	$48,424.34
January 11, 2008	$48,800.98
January 12, 2008	$46,615.60
January 13, 2008	$41,774.31
January 14, 2008	$45,260.83
January 15, 2008	$50,908.56
January 16, 2008	$43,804.24
January 17, 2008	$30,545.37
January 18, 2008	$29,326.14
January 19, 2008	$34,962.34
January 20, 2008	$59,580.22

Using YTD

```
SELECT
  {
  [Measures].[Internet Sales Amount]
  } ON COLUMNS,
  {
  YTD
    (
    [Date].[Calendar].[Date].&[20040120]
    )
  } ON ROWS
FROM
  [Adventure Works]
WHERE
  [Geography].[Geography].[State-Province].&[NY]&[US]
```

Result

	Internet Sales Amount
January 1, 2008	$26,394.20
January 2, 2008	$42,043.50
January 3, 2008	$46,519.08
January 4, 2008	$39,773.73
January 5, 2008	$38,727.37
January 6, 2008	$35,559.61
January 7, 2008	$53,206.93
January 8, 2008	$49,743.61
January 9, 2008	$35,343.95
January 10, 2008	$48,424.34
January 11, 2008	$48,800.98
January 12, 2008	$46,615.60
January 13, 2008	$41,774.31
January 14, 2008	$45,260.83
January 15, 2008	$50,908.56
January 16, 2008	$43,804.24
January 17, 2008	$30,545.37
January 18, 2008	$29,326.14
January 19, 2008	$34,962.34
January 20, 2008	$59,580.22

Query#4.06:

Goal: Find "Internet Sales Amount" for each day from beginning of the calendar quarter to April 14, 2008 for the state of Maryland.

Using PeriodsToDate

```
SELECT
  {
  [Measures].[Internet Sales Amount]
  } ON COLUMNS,
  {
  PeriodsToDate
    (
    [Date].[Calendar].[Calendar Quarter],
    [Date].[Calendar].[Date].&[20080414]
    )
  } ON ROWS
FROM
  [Adventure Works]
WHERE
  [Geography].[Geography].[State-Province].&[MD]&[US]
```

Result

	Internet Sales Amount
April 1, 2008	$59,632.66
April 2, 2008	$53,368.64
April 3, 2008	$65,377.52
April 4, 2008	$59,039.03
April 5, 2008	$28,954.88
April 6, 2008	$62,806.51
April 7, 2008	$45,182.62
April 8, 2008	$47,996.28
April 9, 2008	$52,662.62
April 10, 2008	$49,820.65
April 11, 2008	$41,857.23
April 12, 2008	$48,461.70
April 13, 2008	$24,474.59
April 14, 2008	$52,127.74

Using QTD

```
SELECT
  {
  [Measures].[Internet Sales Amount]
  } ON COLUMNS,
  {
  QTD
    (
    [Date].[Calendar].[Date].&[20080414]
    )
  } ON ROWS
FROM
  [Adventure Works]
WHERE
  [Geography].[Geography].[State-Province].&[MD]&[US]
```

Result

	Internet Sales Amount
April 1, 2008	$59,632.66
April 2, 2008	$53,368.64
April 3, 2008	$65,377.52
April 4, 2008	$59,039.03
April 5, 2008	$28,954.88
April 6, 2008	$62,806.51
April 7, 2008	$45,182.62
April 8, 2008	$47,996.28
April 9, 2008	$52,662.62
April 10, 2008	$49,820.65
April 11, 2008	$41,857.23
April 12, 2008	$48,461.70
April 13, 2008	$24,474.59
April 14, 2008	$52,127.74

Query#4.07:

Goal: Find "Internet Sales Amount" for each day from beginning of the month to May 12, 2008 for the state of Florida.

Using PeriodsToDate

```
SELECT
  {
  [Measures].[Internet Sales Amount]
  } ON COLUMNS,
  {
  PeriodsToDate
    (
    [Date].[Calendar].[Month],
    [Date].[Calendar].[Date].&[20080512]
    )
  } ON ROWS
FROM
  [Adventure Works]
WHERE
  [Geography].[Geography].[State-Province].&[FL]&[US]
```

Result

	Internet Sales Amount
May 1, 2008	$82,428.38
May 2, 2008	$34,544.95
May 3, 2008	$60,570.85
May 4, 2008	$57,163.36
May 5, 2008	$70,674.10
May 6, 2008	$55,756.94
May 7, 2008	$70,209.73
May 8, 2008	$58,438.11
May 9, 2008	$69,079.22
May 10, 2008	$50,455.94
May 11, 2008	$60,258.98
May 12, 2008	$60,381.90

Using MTD

```
SELECT
  {
  [Measures].[Internet Sales Amount]
  } ON COLUMNS,
  {
  MTD
    (
    [Date].[Calendar].[Date].&[20080512]
    )
  } ON ROWS
FROM
  [Adventure Works]
WHERE
  [Geography].[Geography].[State-Province].&[FL]&[US]
```

Result

	Internet Sales Amount
May 1, 2008	$82,428.38
May 2, 2008	$34,544.95
May 3, 2008	$60,570.85
May 4, 2008	$57,163.36
May 5, 2008	$70,674.10
May 6, 2008	$55,756.94
May 7, 2008	$70,209.73
May 8, 2008	$58,438.11
May 9, 2008	$69,079.22
May 10, 2008	$50,455.94
May 11, 2008	$60,258.98
May 12, 2008	$60,381.90

Query#4.08:

Goal: Find "Internet Sales Amount" for each day from the beginning of the week to April 14, 2008 for the state of Florida.

Issue:

- There is no [Date] level defined in "Calendar Weeks" hierarchy.

Solution:

- To show dates, you need to add [Date] level in "Calendar Weeks" hierarchy.

Steps:

1 Open SQL Server Data Tools.
2 Open analysis services project "AdventureWorksDW2012Multidimensional-EE".
3 In solution explorer, double-click on dimension "Date" in "Dimensions" folder.
4 Drag "Date" from "Attributes" window to the hierarchy "Calendar Weeks", as shown in the figure below.
5 Go to "Attribute Relationship" tab and make sure
   - [Date] rolls up to [Calendar Week].
   - [Calendar Week] rolls up to [Calendar Year].
   - Attribute relationship will be look like, Date --> "Calendar Week" --> "Calendar Year".
6 Process the SSAS database.

Figure 4-2: Add [Date] level in hierarchy "Calendar Weeks".

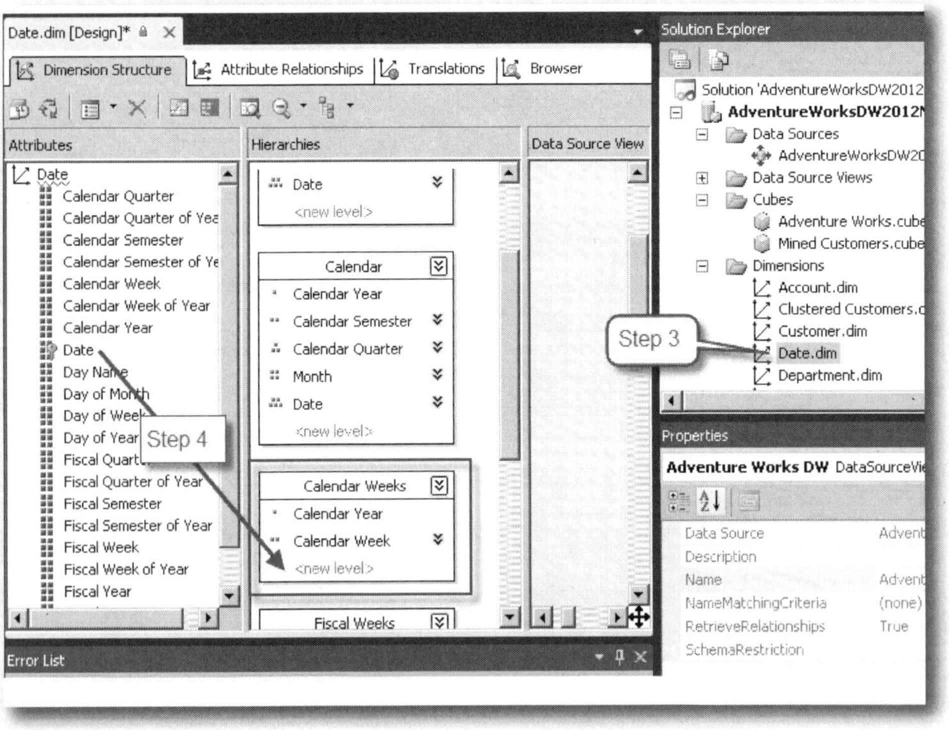

Now, you will able to find "Internet Sales Amount" for each day from the beginning of the week to April 14, 2008 for the state of Florida.

Using PeriodsToDate

```
SELECT
  {
  [Measures].[Internet Sales Amount]
  } ON COLUMNS,
  {
  PeriodsToDate
    (
    [Date].[Calendar Weeks].[Calendar Week],
    [Date].[Calendar Weeks].[Date].&[20080414]
    )
  } ON ROWS
FROM
  [Adventure Works]
WHERE
  [Geography].[Geography].[State-Province].&[FL]&[US]
```

Result

	Internet Sales Amount
April 13, 2008	$24,474.59
April 14, 2008	$52,127.74

Using WTD

```
SELECT
  {
  [Measures].[Internet Sales Amount]
  } ON COLUMNS,
  {
  WTD
    (
    [Date].[Calendar Weeks].[Date].&[20080414]
    )
  } ON ROWS
FROM
  [Adventure Works]
WHERE
  [Geography].[Geography].[State-Province].&[FL]&[US]
```

Result

	Internet Sales Amount
April 13, 2008	$24,474.59
April 14, 2008	$52,127.74

ParallelPeriod

ParallelPeriod of a "time member" is an equivalent "time member" in a prior/later period. For example,

- ParallelPeriod ("Year Level", 1, "May, 2009") = May, 2008.
  Member is "May, 2009" and Current Year is "2009", equivalent member of "May, 2009" in the previous year is May, 2008.
- ParallelPeriod ("Year Level", 1, "May12, 2009") = May12, 2008.
- ParallelPeriod ("Year Level", 2, "May12, 2009") = May12, 2007.
- ParallelPeriod ("Quarter Level", 1, "May 12, 2009") = February 12, 2009.
- ParallelPeriod ("Month Level", 1, "May 12, 2009") = April 12, 2009.

Query#4.09:

Goal: Find "Reseller Sales Amount" for each month of FY 2008 and compare with previous fiscal year for state of colorado.

MDX

```
WITH
MEMBER [Measures].[RSA Prior Data] AS
  (
  [Measures].[Reseller Sales Amount],
  ParallelPeriod
    (
    [Date].[Fiscal].[Fiscal Year],
    1,
    [Date].[Fiscal].CurrentMember
    )
  ), FORMAT_STRING="Currency"
SELECT
  {
  [Measures].[Reseller Sales Amount],
  [Measures].[RSA Prior Data]
  } ON COLUMNS,
  {
  DESCENDANTS
    (
    [Date].[Fiscal].[Fiscal Year].&[2008],
    [Date].[Fiscal].[Month]
    )
  } ON ROWS
FROM
  [Adventure Works]
WHERE
  [Geography].[Geography].[State-Province].&[CO]&[US]
```

Result

	Reseller Sales Amount	RSA Prior Data
July 2007	$64,785.16	$62,510.31
August 2007	$200,242.31	$193,123.20
September 2007	$50,524.43	$36,291.24
October 2007	$30,922.35	$48,434.27
November 2007	$166,991.78	$183,910.74
December 2007	$61,195.97	$35,418.13
January 2008	$14,805.52	$28,063.26
February 2008	$159,550.20	$179,735.50
March 2008	$52,975.79	$32,553.23
April 2008	$27,769.02	$31,787.52
May 2008	$144,785.65	$210,412.10
June 2008	$45,916.71	$29,514.12

Query#4.10:

Goal: Find "Internet Sales Amount" for each day from beginning of the month to May 12, 2008 and compare with **previous to previous** fiscal quarter, and display prior date.

MDX

```
WITH
MEMBER [Measures].[Prior Date] AS
ParallelPeriod
  (
  [Date].[Fiscal].[Fiscal Quarter],
  2,
  [Date].[Fiscal].CurrentMember
  ).Name
MEMBER [Measures].[ISA Prior Data] AS
  (
  [Measures].[Internet Sales Amount],
  ParallelPeriod
    (
    [Date].[Fiscal].[Fiscal Quarter],
    2,
    [Date].[Fiscal].CurrentMember
    )
  ), FORMAT_STRING="Currency"
SELECT
  {
  [Measures].[Internet Sales Amount],
  [Measures].[Prior Date],
  [Measures].[ISA Prior Data]
  } ON COLUMNS,
  {
  PeriodsToDate
    (
    [Date].[Fiscal].[Month],
    [Date].[Fiscal].[Date].&[20080512]
    )
  } ON ROWS
FROM
  [Adventure Works]
```

Result

	Internet Sales Amount	Prior Date	ISA Prior Data
May 1, 2008	$82,428.38	November 1, 2007	$27,392.37
May 2, 2008	$34,544.95	November 2, 2007	$38,023.42
May 3, 2008	$60,570.85	November 3, 2007	$49,081.40
May 4, 2008	$57,163.36	November 4, 2007	$28,476.54
May 5, 2008	$70,674.10	November 5, 2007	$32,476.96
May 6, 2008	$55,756.94	November 6, 2007	$38,762.57
May 7, 2008	$70,209.73	November 7, 2007	$39,303.62
May 8, 2008	$58,438.11	November 8, 2007	$28,390.22
May 9, 2008	$69,079.22	November 9, 2007	$46,553.41
May 10, 2008	$50,455.94	November 10, 2007	$52,843.56
May 11, 2008	$60,258.98	November 11, 2007	$18,442.19
May 12, 2008	$60,381.90	November 12, 2007	$36,868.67

ParallelPeriod **(<Level>, <Index>, <Member>)**

<Level>:

- A valid level in time hierarchy. For example, [Date].[Calendar].[Calendar Year].

<Index>:

- Integer indicates the number of past period.
  - For <Level> as year,
    - 1 means one year prior.
    - 2 means two years prior.
    - Similarly, (-1) means 1 year later.
  - For <Level> as month,
    - 1 means one month prior.
    - (-2) means two months later.

<Member>:

- A valid member. e.g. [Date].[Calendar].[Month].&[2009]&[5].

The Result:

- This returns an equivalent of the <Member> in a prior/later period.

LastPeriods

"LastPeriods" function returns a set of previous siblings, **including** the member.

For example

- LastPeriods (2, "March, 2009") = {"February, 2009", "March, 2009"}
- LastPeriods (3, "March 12, 2009") = {"March 10, 2009", "March 11, 2009", "March 12, 2009"}
- LastPeriods (2, "Q3, 2009") = {"Q2, 2009", "Q3, 2009"}

LastPeriods **(<Count>, <Member>)**

<Member>:

- A valid member from time dimension.
  For example, [Date].[Calendar].[Month].&[2009]&[5].

<Count>:

- A positive Integer indicates the distance of prior period.
- A negative integer indicates the distance of later period.

The Result:

- This returns a set of prior siblings of member <Member>, number of siblings determined by <Count>, <Count> includes the member <Member>.

Query#4.11:

Goal: Find "Internet Sales Amount" for each day from beginning of the calendar quarter to April 14, 2008. Also display sum of "Internet Sales Amount" for 10 previous days for each day.

MDX

```
WITH
MEMBER [Measures].[ISA Last 10 days] AS
SUM
  (
  LastPeriods
    (
    10,
    [Date].[Fiscal].CurrentMember
    ),
  [Measures].[Internet Sales Amount]
  ), FORMAT_STRING="Currency"
SELECT
  {
  [Measures].[Internet Sales Amount],
  [Measures].[ISA Last 10 days]
  } ON COLUMNS,
  {
  PeriodsToDate
    (
    [Date].[Calendar].[Calendar Quarter],
    [Date].[Calendar].[Date].&[20080414]
    )
  } ON ROWS
FROM
  [Adventure Works]
```

Result

	Internet Sales Amount	ISA Last 10 days
April 1, 2008	$59,632.66	$481,525.80
April 2, 2008	$53,368.64	$483,553.33
April 3, 2008	$65,377.52	$500,562.95
April 4, 2008	$59,039.03	$525,521.27
April 5, 2008	$28,954.88	$510,772.31
April 6, 2008	$62,806.51	$511,743.27
April 7, 2008	$45,182.62	$511,366.15
April 8, 2008	$47,996.28	$526,734.99
April 9, 2008	$52,662.62	$526,419.78
April 10, 2008	$49,820.65	$524,841.41
April 11, 2008	$41,857.23	$507,065.98
April 12, 2008	$48,461.70	$502,159.04
April 13, 2008	$24,474.59	$461,256.11
April 14, 2008	$52,127.74	$454,344.82

EXERCISES

Exercise 4.1: Find:

a. [Internet Order Quantity] for all products sold in June, 2008.

b. [Internet Order Quantity] for all products shipped in June, 2008.

c. [Internet Order Quantity] for all products sold in June 2008 and shipped in June, 2008.

Exercise 4.2: Find [Reseller Sales Amount] for each month of calendar year 2008, and show the sum of [Reseller Sales Amount] for prior 12 months for each month.

Exercise 4.3:

a. Find [Internet Sales Amount] for the current year for the state of Texas.

b. Find [Internet Sales Amount] for the current month for the state of Texas.

c. Find [Internet Sales Amount] for today for the state of Texas.

Exercise 4.4: Find the first and last year, which have non-empty "Reseller Sales Amount" in [Adventure Works] cube.

Chapter 5: String Functions

This chapter explores string functions in MDX. MDX does not have all possible string functions, but does have functions needed specifically for SSAS. The chapter is divided into two major parts, native MDX string functions and VBA string functions, which can be used along with native MDX code.

The first part of this chapter explains native MDX string functions. There are two types of string functions in native MDX. The first type converts a member, a set or a tuple to a string and the second type converts a string to a member, a set or a tuple. In both cases members need to be in a fully qualified name. Most of these functions are used for communication between external interfaces, for example, SQL Server Reporting Services (SSRS).

The second part of this chapter explains VBA string functions. Not all VBA functions can be used in MDX; this section covers VBA functions that can be used in MDX.Since you may already be familiar with these VBA functions, they described briefly. Please note that, VBA functions are not native to MDX and performance of these VBA functions is slower than native MDX functions. So, if possible, avoid using VBA functions in MDX. It is a good idea to implement common string manipulation function and modules in ETL (Extract Transfer & Load) or as a named query in data source view (DSV). Last, but not least, "Exercises" will help you practice some MDX queries.

Agenda

MemberToStr, StrToMember, SetToStr, StrToSet, TupleToStr, StrToTuple, StrToValue, Members(String)

VBA functions
Len, Left, Right, Ltrim, Rtrim, InStr, Chr, ChrW, Cstr, Mid, Space ,Str, StrCmp, UCase, LCase

Exercises

MemberToStr

- "MemberToStr" function converts a member to a formatted string that represents the member. MemberToStr (<Member>) = <Member>.UniqueName
- The most common use of MemberToStr is in dropdown list in a report as value of a member.

Query#5.01:

Goal: Display "Reseller Order Quantity" in parentheses for city of "San Francisco" and all of its ancestors. Also show a formatted string that represents members.

MDX

```
WITH
MEMBER [Measures].[TheOrderCount] AS
  (
  [Measures].[Reseller Order Quantity],
  [Geography].[Geography].CurrentMember
  )
MEMBER [Measures].[TheGeoMemberName] AS
[Geography].[Geography].CurrentMember.Name+
"("+ cstr([Measures].[TheOrderCount]) +")"

MEMBER [Measures].[TheGeoMemberValue] AS
MemberToStr ([Geography].[Geography].CurrentMember)

SELECT
  {
  [Measures].[TheGeoMemberName],
  [Measures].[TheGeoMemberValue]
  } ON COLUMNS,
  {
  ASCENDANTS
    (
    [Geography].[Geography].[City].&[San Francisco]&[CA]
    )
  } ON ROWS
FROM
  [Adventure Works]
```

Result

	TheGeoMemberName	TheGeoMemberValue
San Francisco	San Francisco(52)	[Geography].[Geography].[City].&[San Francisco]&[CA]
California	California(24302)	[Geography].[Geography].[State-Province].&[CA]&[US]
United States	United States(131633)	[Geography].[Geography].[Country].&[United States]
All Geographies	All Geographies(214378)	[Geography].[Geography].[All Geographies]

Analysis:

- [Measures].[Reseller Order Quantity] is total order quantity.
- Order quantity for current geographical location is
  (
  [Measures].[Reseller Order Quantity],
  [Geography].[Geography].CurrentMember
)
- MemberToStr ([Geography].[Geography].CurrentMember) is equal to [Geography].[Geography].CurrentMember.UniqueName
- Values for
  [Geography].[Geography].CurrentMember.UniqueName
  And
  [Geography].[Geography].CurrentMember.Name are different.

For example,
If the CurrentMember of [Geography].[Geography] is [Geography].[Geography].[City].&[San Francisco]&[CA]
Then,

[Geography].[Geography].CurrentMember.UniqueName
= [Geography].[Geography].[City].&[San Francisco]&[CA]
And
[Geography].[Geography].CurrentMember.Name = San Francisco

Query#5.02:

Goal: Display "Reseller Count" in parentheses for city of "San Francisco" and all of its ancestors. Also show a formatted string that represents members.

Step 1: Find reseller count for each country.

Current cube does not have "Reseller Count" as a measure. Following steps create a measure group "Reseller", which will have "Reseller Count" as a measure.

1 Open SQL Server Data Tools.
2 Open SSAS database "AdventureWorksDW2012Multidimensional-EE".
3 In solution explorer, double-click on cube "Adventure Works" in "Cubes" folder.
4 Right click on "Adventure Works" in Measures tab, select "**New Measure Group**", third in the list.
5 Select the table "Reseller"
6 Click OK
7 Deploy and process the cube.

Figure 5-1: Create new measure group.

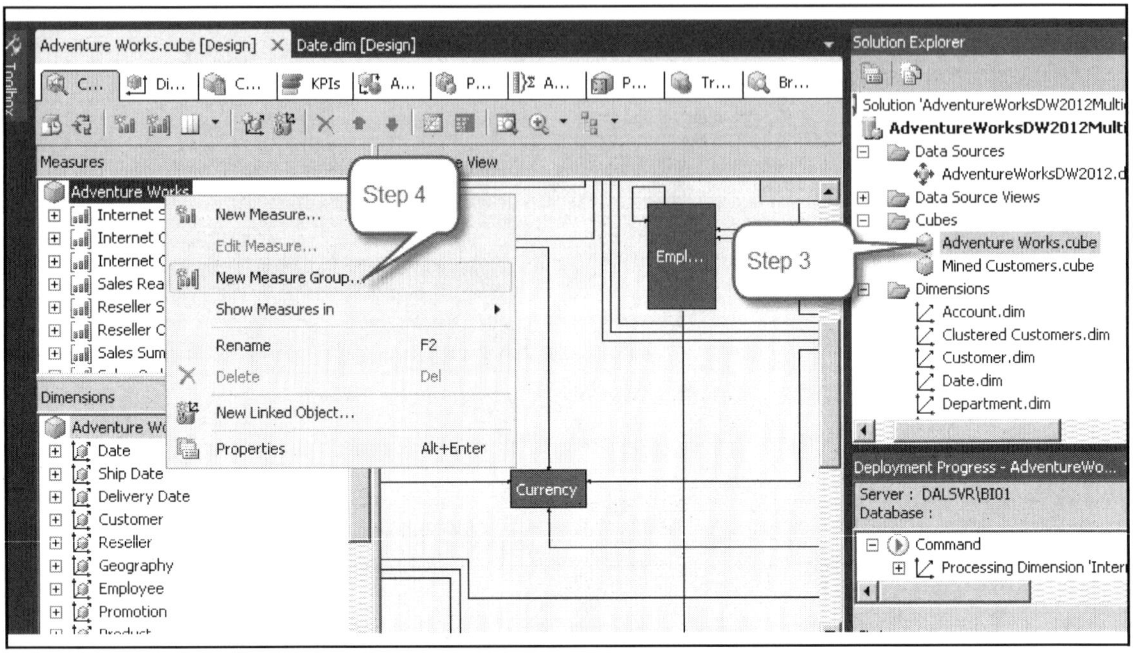

Now, you will be able to find “Reseller Count” for each country, as follows:

MDX

```
WITH
MEMBER [Measures].[The Reseller Count] AS
[Measures].[Reseller Count]

SELECT
  {
  [Measures].[The Reseller Count]
  } ON COLUMNS,
  {
  [Geography].[Geography].[Country]
  } ON ROWS
FROM
  [Adventure Works]
```

Result

	The Reseller Count
Australia	40
Canada	114
France	40
Germany	40
United Kingdom	40
United States	426
Unknown Geography	1

Step 2: Display "Reseller Count" in parentheses for city of "San Francisco" and all of its ancestors. Also show formatted string that represents members.

MDX

```
WITH
MEMBER [Measures].[TheResellerCount] AS
  (
  [Measures].[Reseller Count],
  [Geography].[Geography].CurrentMember
  )
MEMBER [Measures].[TheGeoMemberName] AS
[Geography].[Geography].CurrentMember.Name+
"("+CSTR ([Measures].[TheResellerCount]) +")"
MEMBER [Measures].[TheGeoMemberValue] AS
MemberToStr ([Geography].[Geography].CurrentMember)

SELECT
  {
  [Measures].[TheGeoMemberName],
  [Measures].[TheGeoMemberValue]
  } ON COLUMNS,
  {
  ASCENDANTS
    (
    [Geography].[Geography].[City].&[San Francisco]&[CA]
    )
  } ON ROWS
FROM
  [Adventure Works]
```

Result

	TheGeoMemberName	TheGeoMemberValue
San Francisco	San Francisco(1)	[Geography].[Geography].[City].&[San Francisco]&[CA]
California	California(78)	[Geography].[Geography].[State-Province].&[CA]&[US]
United States	United States(426)	[Geography].[Geography].[Country].&[United States]
All Geographies	All Geographies(701)	[Geography].[Geography].[All Geographies]

MemberToStr (<Member>)

<Member>:

- A valid member, e.g. [Geography].[Geography].[City].&[San Francisco]&[CA].

The Result:

- Returns a formatted string, which represents the member, <Member>.

StrToMember

- StrToMember converts a formatted string to a member.
- The most common use is a parameter from an external source.

Query#5.03:

Goal: Display "Reseller Sales Amount" for each product category for a given country. Country name passed as a formatted string.

MDX

```
WITH
MEMBER Measures.[Given String] AS
"[Geography].[Geography].[Country].&[Canada]"

SELECT
  {
  [Measures].[Reseller Sales Amount]
  } ON COLUMNS,
  {
  [Product].[Product Categories].[Category]
  } ON ROWS
FROM
  [Adventure Works]
WHERE
  StrToMember(Measures.[Given String])
```

Result

	Reseller Sales Amount
Accessories	$118,127.35
Bikes	$11,636,380.59
Clothing	$378,947.63
Components	$2,244,470.02

Analysis:

- "[Geography].[Geography].[Country].&[Canada]" is the value of the string.
- The string value can be passed from an external system, e.g. SSRS report.

Notes:

- StrToMember function has an optional flag CONSTRAINED.
- If CONSTRAINED is passed, the string passed should be a valid member and resolvable. Otherwise, it will return an error string.
- The CONSTRAINED flag is used to prevent SQL injection.

Following example demonstrates a use of CONSTRAINED flag.

Example:

- [Geography].[Geography].[Country].&[Japan] is not a valid member.
- Following queries demonstrates the difference between with and without CONSTRAINED flag:

WITHOUT CONSTRAINED

```
WITH
MEMBER Measures.[Given String] AS
"[Geography].[Geography].[Country].&[Japan]"

SELECT
  {
  [Measures].[Reseller Sales Amount]
  } ON COLUMNS,
  {
  [Product].[Product Categories].[Category]
  } ON ROWS
FROM
  [Adventure Works]
WHERE
  StrToMember (Measures.[Given String])
```

	Reseller Sales Amount
Accessories	(null)
Bikes	(null)
Clothing	(null)
Components	(null)

WITH CONSTRAINED

```
WITH
MEMBER Measures.[Given String] AS
"[Geography].[Geography].[Country].&[Japan]"

SELECT
  {
  [Measures].[Reseller Sales Amount]
  } ON COLUMNS,
  {
  [Product].[Product Categories].[Category]
  } ON ROWS
FROM
  [Adventure Works]
WHERE
  StrToMember (Measures.[Given String],CONSTRAINED)
```

Executing the query ...
Query (14, 1) The restrictions imposed by the CONSTRAINED flag in the STRTOMEMBER function were violated.
Execution complete

StringToMember **(<String> [,CONSTRAINED])**

<String>:

- A string that represents a valid member, e.g. "[Geography].[Geography].[Country].&[Canada]"

CONSTRAINED:

- This is an optional flag.
- If CONSTRAINED is passed, the string passed should be a valid member and resolvable. Otherwise it will return an error string.
- This flag is also present in other functions like StrToSet, StrToTuple and StrToValue.
- The CONSTRAINED flag is used to prevent SQL injection.

The Result:

- Returns a member, which represents the string, <String>.

SetToStr

- SetToStr converts a set to a formatted string that represents the set.
- All members of the set will be represented by <Member>.UniqueName.

Usage:

- SetToStr function can be used to capture multiple selections from the list of parameters.
- This function is used in conversion of data from mdx to external function.

Query#5.04:

Goal: Create a string that represents a set of two countries "United States", "Canada".

Strategy:

- Create a calculated measure that holds the string.
- Use SetToStr to convert the MDX set to string format.

MDX	WITH
	MEMBER Measures.[Countries Str] AS
	SetToStr
	(
	{
	[Geography].[Geography].[Country].&[United States],
	[Geography].[Geography].[Country].&[Canada]
	}
	)
	SELECT
	{
	Measures.[Countries Str]
	} ON COLUMNS
	FROM
	[Adventure Works]

Result	Countries Str {[Geography].[Geography].[Country].&[United States],[Geography].[Geography].[Country].&[Canada]}

To simplify your code, you can also create a named set as follows:

```
WITH
SET MySet AS
    {
    [Geography].[Geography].[Country].&[United States],
    [Geography].[Geography].[Country].&[Canada]
    }
```

SetToStr (MySet) will return same result.

MDX	WITH
	SET MySet AS
	{
	[Geography].[Geography].[Country].&[United States],
	[Geography].[Geography].[Country].&[Canada]
	}
	
	MEMBER Measures.[Countries Str] AS
	SetToStr (MySet)
	
	SELECT
	{
	Measures.[Countries Str]
	} ON COLUMNS
	FROM
	[Adventure Works]

Result	Countries Str {[Geography].[Geography].[Country].&[United States],[Geography].[Geography].[Country].&[Canada]}

Notes:

If a member is passed to the function SetToStr, it will convert the member to a tuple and then the tuple to a set and then finally the set to a string. For example, if you pass the member [Geography].[Geography].[Country].&[Canada], "SetToStr" function will return the string "{[Geography].[Geography].[Country].&[Canada]}", as shown below:

MDX	WITH MEMBER Measures.[Countries Str] AS SetToStr ([Geography].[Geography].[Country].&[Canada]) SELECT { Measures.[Countries Str] } ON COLUMNS FROM [Adventure Works]
Result	Countries Str {[Geography].[Geography].[Country].&[Canada]}

Similarly, if a tuple is passed to the function SetToStr, it will convert the tuple to a set and then the set to a string. For example, if you pass the tuple:

```
(
[Product].[Product Categories].[Category].[Bikes],
[Geography].[Geography].[Country].&[Canada]
)
```

It will return the set,

```
{
  (
  [Product].[Product Categories].[Category].&[1],
  [Geography].[Geography].[Country].&[Canada]
  )
}
```

MDX

```
WITH
MEMBER Measures.[TheString] AS
SetToStr
  (
    (
    [Product].[Product Categories].[Category].[Bikes],
    [Geography].[Geography].[Country].&[Canada]
    )
  )

SELECT
  {
  Measures.[TheString]
  } ON COLUMNS
FROM
  [Adventure Works]
```

Result

TheString
{([Product].[Product Categories].[Category].&[1],[Geography].[Geography].[Country].&[Canada])}

SetToStr (<Set>)

<Set>:

- A valid set or a named set or a member or a tuple.

The Result:

- Returns a formatted string, which represents the set, <Set>.
- If a member is passed instead of a set, member will be converted to a tuple and then the tuple will be converted to a set.
- If a tuple is passed instead of a set, the tuple will be converted to a set.

StrToSet

- StrToSet converts a formatted string to a set.
- Each member of the set will be represented by an UniqueName.

Query#5.05:

Goal: You received a string from an external function, and the expected value of the string is a set of countries and can be represented by:

```
WITH
MEMBER [Measures].[Given String] AS
    "
     {
     ([Geography].[Geography].[Country].&[United States]),
     ([Geography].[Geography].[Country].&[Canada])
    }
    "
```

Find "Reseller Sales Amount" for each member of the above set defined in the "Given String".

Note:

- Convert the "Given String" to set using the function "StrToSet".

MDX

```
WITH
MEMBER [Measures].[Given String] AS
"
{
([Geography].[Geography].[Country].&[United States]),
([Geography].[Geography].[Country].&[Canada])
}
"
SELECT
  {
  [Measures].[Reseller Sales Amount]
  } ON COLUMNS,
  {
  StrToSet ([Measures].[Given String])
  } ON ROWS
FROM
      [Adventure Works]
```

Result

	Reseller Sales Amount
United States	$53,189,364.68
Canada	$14,377,925.60

If a member is stored in "Given String",

- StrToSet will convert "Given String" to a member.
- Then convert from the member to a tuple.
- Then convert from the tuple to a set.

For example, for "[Geography].[Geography].[Country].&[Canada]", StrToSet will return the set {([Geography].[Geography].[Country].&[Canada])}.

MDX	Result
WITH MEMBER [Measures].[Given String] AS "[Geography].[Geography].[Country].&[Canada]" SELECT { [Measures].[Reseller Sales Amount] } ON COLUMNS, { StrToSet ([Measures].[Given String]) } ON ROWS FROM [Adventure Works]	Reseller Sales Amount Canada $14,377,925.60

If a tuple is stored in "Given String",

- StrToSet will convert "Given String" to a tuple.
- Then convert the tuple to a set.

For example,

```
"
 (
 [Geography].[Geography].[Country].&[Canada],
 [Product].[Product Categories].[Category].[Bikes]
 )
"
```

StrToSet will return the set

```
{
 (
 [Geography].[Geography].[Country].&[Canada],
 [Product].[Product Categories].[Category].&[1]
 )
}
```

as shown below:

MDX

```
WITH MEMBER [Measures].[Given String] AS
" (
  [Geography].[Geography].[Country].&[Canada],
  [Product].[Product Categories].[Category].[Bikes]
  )"
SELECT
  {
  [Measures].[Reseller Sales Amount]
  } ON COLUMNS,
  {
  StrToSet([Measures].[Given String])
  } ON ROWS
FROM
  [Adventure Works]
```

Result

		Reseller Sales Amount
Canada	Bikes	$11,636,380.59

Notes:

- StrToSet function has an optional flag CONSTRAINED.
- If CONSTRAINED is passed, the string passed should be a valid member, tuple or set and resolvable. Otherwise, it will return an error string.
- The CONSTRAINED flag is used to prevent SQL injection.

Following example demonstrates the use of CONSTRAINED flag for the invalid country:

WITHOUT CONSTRAINED

```
WITH
MEMBER [Measures].[Given String] AS
"[Geography].[Geography].[Country].&[Japan]"
SELECT
  {
  [Measures].[Reseller Sales Amount]
  } ON COLUMNS,
  {
  StrToSet ([Measures].[Given String])
  } ON ROWS
FROM
  [Adventure Works]
```

Reseller Sales Amount

WITH CONSTRAINED

```
WITH
MEMBER [Measures].[Given String] AS
"[Geography].[Geography].[Country].&[Japan]"
SELECT
  {
  [Measures].[Reseller Sales Amount]
  } ON COLUMNS,
  {
  StrToSet ([Measures].[Given String],CONSTRAINED)
  } ON ROWS
FROM
  [Adventure Works]
```

Executing the query ...
Query (9, 2) The restrictions imposed by the CONSTRAINED flag in the STRTOSET function were violated.
Execution complete

Analysis:

- In the above example, [Geography].[Geography].[Country].&[Japan] is not a valid member.
- Without CONSTRAINED flag, MDX query will return nothing as the member [Geography].[Geography].[Country].&[Japan] does not exist in the cube.
- With CONSTRAINED flag the MDX query will return an error.

For valid members, tuples or a set, with CONSTRAINED and without CONSTRAINED will return same result.

WITHOUT CONSTRAINED

```
WITH
MEMBER [Measures].[Given String] AS
"[Geography].[Geography].[Country].&[Canada]"
SELECT
  {
  [Measures].[Reseller Sales Amount]
  } ON COLUMNS,
  {
  StrToSet ([Measures].[Given String])
  } ON ROWS
FROM
  [Adventure Works]
```

	Reseller Sales Amount
Canada	$14,377,925.60

WITH CONSTRAINED

```
WITH
MEMBER [Measures].[Given String] AS
"[Geography].[Geography].[Country].&[Canada]"
SELECT
  {
  [Measures].[Reseller Sales Amount]
  } ON COLUMNS,
  {
  StrToSet
    (
    [Measures].[Given String],
    CONSTRAINED
    )
  } ON ROWS
FROM
  [Adventure Works]
```

	Reseller Sales Amount
Canada	$14,377,925.60

StrToSet **(<String> [,CONSTRAINED])**

<String>:

- A string that represents a set.
- If a member is passed, the member will be converted to a tuple and then the tuple will be converted to a set.
- If a tuple passed, the tuple will be converted to a set.

CONSTRAINED:

- This is an optional flag, if passed, members, tuples or a set passed to the function should be valid and resolvable. Otherwise, it will return an error string.
- This flag is also present in other functions like StrToMember, StrToTuple and StrToValue.

The Result:

- Returns a set which represents the string, <String>.

TupleToStr

- "TupleToStr" function converts a tuple to a formatted string that represents the tuple.
- Most common use of TupleToStr is to send the string form of a tuple to an external function.

Query#5.06:

Goal: Return following tuple as a string:

```
(
[Product].[Product Categories].[Category].&[4],
[Geography].[Geography].[City].&[Seattle]&[WA]
)
```

Strategy:

- Create a calculated member.
- Convert the given tuple to string using TupleToStr function.

MDX

```
WITH
MEMBER Measures.[The Output String] AS
TupleToStr
  (
    (
    [Product].[Product Categories].[Category].&[4],
    [Geography].[Geography].[City].&[Seattle]&[WA]
    )
  )
SELECT
  {
  Measures.[The Output String]
  } ON COLUMNS
FROM
  [Adventure Works]
```

Result

The Output String
([Product].[Product Categories].[Category].&[4],[Geography].[Geography].[City].&[Seattle]&[WA])

TupleToStr **(<Tuple>)**

<Tuple>:

- A valid tuple.

The Result:

- This returns a formatted string, which represents the tuple, <Tuple>.

StrToTuple

- "StrToTuple" function converts a formatted string to a tuple.
- All members of the tuple should be represented by UniqueName.

Query#5.07:

Goal: You received a string from an external function:

```
"
(
[Product].[Product Categories].[Category].&[4],
[Geography].[Geography].[City].&[Seattle]&[WA],
[Date].[Fiscal].[Fiscal Year].&[2007]
)
"
```

Find "Reseller Sales Amount" for the above tuple stored in the string.

MDX	WITH MEMBER [Measures].[Given String] AS " ([Product].[Product Categories].[Category].&[4], [Geography].[Geography].[City].&[Seattle]&[WA], [Date].[Fiscal].[Fiscal Year].&[2007]) " SELECT { [Measures].[Reseller Sales Amount] } ON COLUMNS, { StrToTuple ([Measures].[Given String]) } ON ROWS FROM [Adventure Works]
Result	(see result grid below)

			Reseller Sales Amount
Accessories	Seattle	FY 2007	$3,032.90

If you remove the parentheses from last string, the string will not represent a tuple anymore , so if you pass

```
"
[Product].[Product Categories].[Category].&[4],
[Geography].[Geography].[City].&[Seattle]&[WA],
[Date].[Fiscal].[Fiscal Year].&[2007]
"
```

to StrToTuple , it will return an error.

- The string is in the form of "a,b,c", MDX expects tuple in this form "(a,b,c)".
- If a string is in the form of "a", MDX converts it to "(a)" and treats as a tuple.

Note: Assume a, b and c are members.

MDX	WITH MEMBER [Measures].[Given String] AS " [Product].[Product Categories].[Category].&[4], [Geography].[Geography].[City].&[Seattle]&[WA], [Date].[Fiscal].[Fiscal Year].&[2007] " SELECT { [Measures].[Reseller Sales Amount] } ON COLUMNS, { StrToTuple([Measures].[Given String]) } ON ROWS FROM [Adventure Works]
Result	Executing the query ... Parser: The syntax for ',' is incorrect. Execution complete

If a member is passed to the function "StrToTuple",

- It will convert the string to a member.
- Then converts the member to a tuple.

For example, if you pass " [Product].[Product Categories].[Category].&[4]" to the function "StrToTuple", following steps will occur:

- Convert the string "[Product].[Product Categories].[Category].&[4]" to member [Product].[Product Categories].[Category].&[4].
- Convert the member [Product].[Product Categories].[Category].&[4] to tuple "([Product].[Product Categories].[Category].&[4])".

MDX

```
WITH
MEMBER [Measures].[Given String] AS
"[Product].[Product Categories].[Category].&[4]"
SELECT
  {
  [Measures].[Reseller Sales Amount]
  } ON COLUMNS,
  {
  StrToTuple ([Measures].[Given String])
  } ON ROWS
FROM
  [Adventure Works]
```

Result

	Reseller Sales Amount
Accessories	$571,257.55

StrToTuple function has an optional flag CONSTRAINED,

- String passed should have a valid member or tuple and resolvable. Otherwise, it will return an error.
- The CONSTRAINED flag is used to prevent SQL injection.

In following example, [Geography].[Geography].[City].&[Seattle]&[ZZ] is not a valid member.

WITHOUT CONSTRAINED

```
WITH
MEMBER [Measures].[Given String] AS
"
  (
  [Product].[Product Categories].[Category].&[4],
  [Geography].[Geography].[City].&[Seattle]&[ZZ]
  )
"
SELECT
  {
  StrToTuple([Measures].[Given String])
  } ON COLUMNS
FROM
  [Adventure Works]
```

WITH CONSTRAINED

```
WITH
MEMBER [Measures].[Given String] AS
"
  (
  [Product].[Product Categories].[Category].&[4],
  [Geography].[Geography].[City].&[Seattle]&[ZZ]
  )
"
SELECT
  {
  StrToTuple([Measures].[Given String],CONSTRAINED)
  } ON COLUMNS
FROM
  [Adventure Works]
```

Executing the query ...
Query (11, 2) The restrictions imposed by the CONSTRAINED flag in the STRTOTUPLE function were violated.
Execution complete

StrToTuple (<String>[,CONSTRAINED])

<String>:

- A string represents a tuple.
- If a member is passed, the member will be converted to tuple.

CONSTRAINED:

- This is an optional flag, if passed, a member or a tuple passed should be valid and resolvable. Otherwise, it will return an error string.
- This flag is also present in other functions like StrToMember, StrToSet and StrToValue.

The Result:

- This returns a tuple for the string, <String>.

StrToValue

- StrToValue converts a formatted string to a numeric value.

Query#5.08:

Goal: For a given string "(1000+2000)/15+178", find the numeric value of the given string.

MDX	Result

WITH
MEMBER [Measures].[Given String] AS
"(1000+2000)/15+178"
 	
MEMBER [Measures].[Given Value] AS
StrToValue ([Measures].[Given String])
 	
SELECT
  {
  [Measures].[Given Value]
  } ON COLUMNS
FROM
  [Adventure Works]
	Given Value
	378

"StrToValue" function has an optional flag CONSTRAINED, if passed:

- The string should contain only scalar value and needs to be **directly resolvable** to a scalar value. Otherwise, it will return an error.

For example,

- StrToValue ("200",CONSTRAINED) will not return any error because the string directly resolvable to a scalar value.
- But StrToValue ("(1000+2000)/15+178",CONSTRAINED) will return error because the string directly not resolvable to a scalar value.

- Similarly, StrToValue ("[Measures].[Reseller Sales Amount]",CONSTRAINED) will return error because the string is not directly resolvable to a scalar value.

WITHOUT CONSTRAINED	WITH CONSTRAINED
WITH MEMBER [Measures].[Given String] AS "200" MEMBER [Measures].[Given Value] AS StrToValue ([Measures].[Given String]) SELECT { [Measures].[Given Value] } ON COLUMNS FROM [Adventure Works]	WITH MEMBER [Measures].[Given String] AS "200" MEMBER [Measures].[Given Value] AS StrToValue ([Measures].[Given String], CONSTRAINED) SELECT { [Measures].[Given Value] } ON COLUMNS FROM [Adventure Works]
Given Value 200	Given Value 200

- The above StrToValue does not return an error because the string is directly resolvable to a scalar value.

WITHOUT CONSTRAINED	WITH CONSTRAINED
WITH MEMBER [Measures].[Given String] AS "(1000+2000)/15+178" MEMBER [Measures].[Given Value] AS StrToValue ([Measures].[Given String]) SELECT { [Measures].[Given Value] } ON COLUMNS FROM [Adventure Works]	WITH MEMBER [Measures].[Given String] AS "(1000+2000)/15+178" MEMBER [Measures].[Given Value] AS StrToValue ([Measures].[Given String],CONSTRAINED) SELECT { [Measures].[Given Value] } ON COLUMNS FROM [Adventure Works]
Given Value 378	Given Value #Error

- The above StrToValue returns an error because the string is not **directly** resolvable to a scalar value, as the string "(1000+2000)/15+178" is not a scalar value.

StrToValue (<String> [, CONSTRAINED])

<String>:

- A string represents a numeric expression or MDX expression, for example, "[Measures].[Reseller Sales Amount]".

CONSTRAINED:

- This is an optional flag, if passed, the string must be resolvable to a scalar value, or it will return an error string.
- This flag is also present in other functions like StrToMember, StrToSet and StrToTuple.

The Result:

- This returns numerical value of the string, <String>.

Members (<String>)

- "Members" function converts a formatted string to a member.
- This function is equivalent to StrToMember but without the CONSTRAINED flag.

Query#5.09:

Goal: Display "Reseller Sales Amount" for each product category for a given fiscal year. The fiscal year is passed as a string.

MDX

```
WITH
MEMBER Measures.[Given String] AS
"[Date].[Fiscal].[Fiscal Year].&[2007]"

SELECT
  {
  [Measures].[Reseller Sales Amount]
  } ON COLUMNS,
  {
  [Product].[Product Categories].[Category]
  } ON ROWS
FROM
  [Adventure Works]
WHERE
  Members
    (
    Measures.[Given String]
    )
```

Result

	Reseller Sales Amount
Accessories	$124,392.98
Bikes	$22,318,453.80
Clothing	$749,409.98
Components	$4,592,821.98

VBA Functions

VBA stands for **V**isual **B**asic for **A**pplications functions. MDX expressions can use any supported VBA and Excel functions in addition to MDX functions, but these functions are slow compared to native MDX functions.

VBA Functions	Description
Len (<string>)	Returns length of a given string.
Right (<string>, <count>)	Returns a substring starting from rightmost character.
Left (<string>, <count>)	Returns a substring starting from leftmost character.
InStr ([start], <string1>, <string2>)	Returns the position of the first occurance of <string2> in <string1>. Optionally you can supply start position.
Trim (<string>)	Returns a string with leading and trailing spaces removed.
Ltrim (<string>)	Returns a string with leading spaces removed.
Rtrim (<string>)	Returns a string with trailing spaces removed.
Chr (<AsciiCode>)	Returns a character based on the <AsciiCode>.
Cstr (<value>)	Converts a value to a string.
Lcase (<string>)	Converts a string to lower case.
Ucase (<string>)	Converts a string to upper case.
Space (<count>)	Returns a string consists of specified number of spaces.
StrComp (<string1>, <string2>)	• string1 > string2 then 1 • string1 < string2 then -1 • string1 = string2 then 0
Format (<string>, <format>)	Formats a string , common formats are: "Percent", "Currency", "Short Date", "Standard" etc.
Mid (<string>, <start>, <count>)	Returns a substring starting from <start> position and specified characters.
Str (<number>)	Converts a number to string.
Val (<string>)	Returns a number found in a specified string, and stops reading after first non-numeric character.

Len (<string>): Returns the length of a given string.

Query#5.10: List name of all products and also display length of each "product name" string.

MDX

```
WITH
MEMBER [Measures].[StrLength] AS
LEN ([Product].[Product Categories].CurrentMember.Name)
SELECT
  {
  [Measures].[StrLength]
  } ON COLUMNS,
  {
  [Product].[Product Categories].[Product]
  } ON ROWS
FROM
  [Adventure Works]
```

Result

	StrLength
Hitch Rack - 4-Bike	19
All-Purpose Bike Stand	22
Mountain Bottle Cage	20
Road Bottle Cage	16
Water Bottle - 30 oz.	21
Bike Wash - Dissolver	21
Fender Set - Mountain	21
Sport-100 Helmet, Black	23
Sport-100 Helmet, Black	23
Sport-100 Helmet, Black	23
Sport-100 Helmet, Blue	22
Sport-100 Helmet, Blue	22
Sport-100 Helmet, Blue	22

Left (<string>): Returns a substring of a given string starting from leftmost character.

Query#5.11: Display "Reseller Sales Amount" for all products which name starts with "Road-650".

MDX

```
SELECT
  {
  [Measures].[Reseller Sales Amount]
  }ON COLUMNS,
  {
  FILTER
    (
    [Product].[Product Categories].[Product],
    LEFT
      (
      [Product].[Product Categories].CurrentMember.Name,
      8
      )= "Road-650"
    )
  } ON ROWS
FROM
      [Adventure Works]
```

Result

	Reseller Sales Amount
Road-650 Black, 44	$131,710.09
Road-650 Black, 44	$329,968.27
Road-650 Black, 48	$75,502.60
Road-650 Black, 48	$189,326.98
Road-650 Black, 52	$293,841.03
Road-650 Black, 52	$679,332.30
Road-650 Black, 58	$234,896.98
Road-650 Black, 58	$573,356.09
Road-650 Black, 60	$133,807.39
Road-650 Black, 60	$330,932.60
Road-650 Black, 62	$73,405.31
Road-650 Black, 62	$189,796.78
Road-650 Red, 44	$295,718.52
Road-650 Red, 44	$587,454.85
Road-650 Red, 48	$235,316.44

Right (<string>): Returns a substring starting of a given string from rightmost character.

Query#5.12: Display "Reseller Sales Amount" for all products which name ends with "58".

MDX

```
SELECT
  {
  [Measures].[Reseller Sales Amount]
  } ON COLUMNS,
  {
  FILTER
    (
    [Product].[Product Categories].[Product],
    RIGHT
      (
      [Product].[Product Categories].CurrentMember.Name,
      2
      )= "58"
    )
  } ON ROWS
FROM
    [Adventure Works]
```

Result

	Reseller Sales Amount
Road-250 Black, 58	$448,965.56
Road-250 Black, 58	$435,404.97
Road-250 Red, 58	$448,965.56
Road-250 Red, 58	$435,404.97
Road-450 Red, 58	$507,978.30
Road-650 Black, 58	$234,896.98
Road-650 Black, 58	$573,356.09
Road-650 Red, 58	$65,855.05
Road-650 Red, 58	$181,810.28
Road-750 Black, 58	$180,788.65
Touring-3000 Blue, 58	$168,632.23
Touring-3000 Yellow, 58	$96,008.13
HL Road Frame - Blac	(null)

InStr (<string1>, <string2>): Returns the position of the first occurrence of <string2> in <string1>.

Query#5.13: Display "Reseller Sales Amount" for all products which have "Bike" in the name of the product.

MDX

```
SELECT
  {
  [Measures].[Reseller Sales Amount]
  } ON COLUMNS,
  {
  FILTER
    (
    [Product].[Product Categories].[Product],
    InStr
      (
      [Product].[Product Categories].CurrentMember.Name,
      "Bike"
      )>0
    )
  } ON ROWS
FROM
    [Adventure Works]
```

Result

	Reseller Sales Amount
Hitch Rack - 4-Bike	$197,736.16
All-Purpose Bike Stand	(null)
Bike Wash - Dissolver	$11,188.37
Mountain Bike Socks, L	$513.00
Mountain Bike Socks, M	$6,060.39

Ltrim (<string>): Returns a string with trailing spaces removed.
Rtrim (<string>): Returns a string with leading spaces removed.
Trim (<string>): Returns a string with leading and trailing spaces removed.

Query#5.14: For a given string "   This is a test string   ", show the string along with result string from Ltrim, Rtrim and Trim.

MDX

```
WITH
MEMBER Measures.[Given String] AS
"        This is a test string    "

MEMBER Measures.[Ltrim applied] AS
Ltrim(Measures.[Given String])

MEMBER Measures.[Rtrim applied] AS
Rtrim(Measures.[Given String])

MEMBER Measures.[Trim applied] AS
Trim(Measures.[Given String])

SELECT
  {
  Measures.[Given String],
  Measures.[Ltrim applied],
  Measures.[Rtrim applied],
  Measures.[Trim applied]
  } ON COLUMNS
FROM
  [Adventure Works]
```

Result

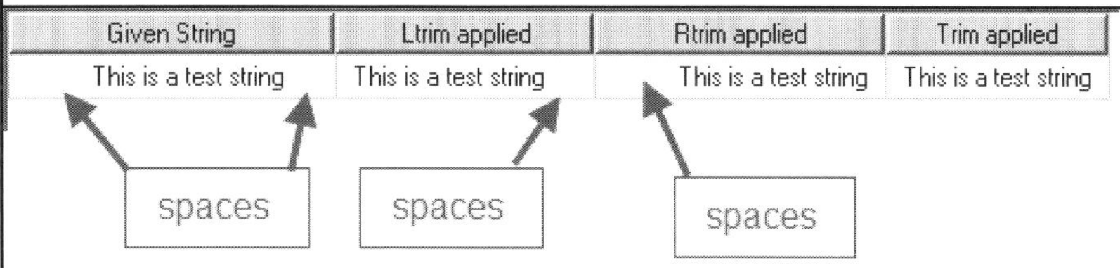

Chr (<AsciiCode>): Returns a character based on the <AsciiCode>.
Cstr (<value>): Converts a value to a string.
Str (<value>): Converts a value to a string.
Lcase (<string>): Converts a string to lower case.
Ucase (<string>): Converts a string to upper case.
Space (<count>): Returns a string consists of the specified number of spaces.

Query#5.15: For a given values
Country name = "fRAnce"
Sales Amount = 33456.78 dollar
Using those two values, Create output as "The sales amount for France is $33456.78".

Strategy:

- Ucase("f")+ Lcase("RAnce")= France
- Mid ("fRAnce",2) = "RAnce", substring starts from second character till end of the string.
- 36 is ascii code for dollar, so Chr(36) = $.
- To convert 33456.78 to string, cstr(33456.78) = "33456.78", you can also use str(33456.78) = "33456.78".

MDX

```
WITH
MEMBER [Measures].[The Country] AS
"fRAnce"
MEMBER [Measures].[The Sales Amount] AS
33456.78
MEMBER [Measures].[The Output] AS
"The Sales Amount for"+ space(1)+
Ucase(Left([Measures].[The Country],1))+
Lcase(Mid([Measures].[The Country],2))+
space(1)+"is" +space(1)+
chr(36)+
cstr([Measures].[The Sales Amount])

SELECT
  {
  [Measures].[The Output]
  } ON COLUMNS
FROM
  [Adventure Works]
```

Result

The Output
The Sales Amount for France is $33456.78

StrComp (<string1>, <string2>): Compares two strings.

Query#5.16: Compare strings string1 and string2 for following cases:

- Case #1: string1 <string2 (assume string1 = "abc"and string2="bcd")
- Case #2: string1 >string2 (assume string1 = "bcd"and string2="abc")
- Case #3: string1 =string2 (assume string1 = "abc"and string2="abc")

string1 < string2	string1 > string2	string1 = string2
WITH MEMBER [Measures].[String1] AS "abc" MEMBER [Measures].[String2] AS "bcd" MEMBER [Measures].[The Result] AS StrComp ([Measures].[String1], [Measures].[String2]) SELECT { [Measures].[The Result] } ON COLUMNS FROM [Adventure Works]	WITH MEMBER [Measures].[String1] AS "bcd" MEMBER [Measures].[String2] AS "abc" MEMBER [Measures].[The Result] AS StrComp ([Measures].[String1], [Measures].[String2]) SELECT { [Measures].[The Result] } ON COLUMNS FROM [Adventure Works]	WITH MEMBER [Measures].[String1] AS "abc" MEMBER [Measures].[String2] AS "abc" MEMBER [Measures].[The Result] AS StrComp ([Measures].[String1], [Measures].[String2]) SELECT { [Measures].[The Result] } ON COLUMNS FROM [Adventure Works]
The Result -1	The Result 1	The Result 0

Val (<string>): Returns a number found in a specified string, and stops reading after first non-numeric character.

For example:

- val("123 abc") = 123
- val("12abc3") = 12
- val("abc123") = 0

Format (<string | Numeric>, <format>): Formats specified string in a specified format.

For example:

- Format (0.56, "percent") = 56.00%, displays the percent.
- Format ("0.56", "percent") = 56.00%, converts a string to numeric and then find the percent.
- Format ("2.56", "percent") = 256.00%.
- Format ("aa2.56", "percent") = aa2.56, this does not return any error, as the string cannot return percent it returns the input string.
- Format ("123456.789", "General Number") = 123456.789, displays a number without thousand separators.
- Format ("123456.789", "Standard") = 123,456.789, displays a number with thousand separators.
- Format (".789", "Fixed") = 0.79, displays at least one digit to the left of the decimal place and two digits to the right of the decimal place.
- Format ("123456.789", "currency") = $123,456.79, displays a currency symbol, thousand separators as well as two decimal places.
- Format ("ss123456.789", "currency") = ss123456.789, if it cannot format the input data, it will return unchanged data.
- Format ("123456.789", "scientific") = 1.23E+05.
- Format ("123", "On/Off") = On, displays Off if the number is 0 else On.
- Format ("0", "On/Off") = Off, displays Off if the number is 0 else On.
- Format ("123", "Yes/No") = Yes, displays No if the number is 0 else Yes.
- Format ("0", "Yes/No") = No, displays No if the number is 0 else Yes.
- Format ("123" , "True/False") = True, displays False if the number is 0 else True.
- Format ("0", "True/False") = False, displays False if the number is 0 else True.
- Format ("2012-03-02", "Short Date") = 3/2/2012, format date based on your system's short date setting.
- Format ("2012-03-02", "Medium Date") = Friday, March 02, 2012, format date based on your system's medium date setting.
- Format ("2012-03-02", "Long Date") = Friday, March 02, 2012, format date based on your system's long date setting.
- Format (now (), "Short time") = 10:51 AM, format time based on your system's short time setting.
- Format (now (), "Medium time") = 10:53:39 AM, Format time based on your system's medium time setting.
- Format (now (), "Long time") = 10:54:26 AM, format time based on your system's long time setting.

EXERCISES

Exercise 5.1: Find "Reseller Sales Amount" for all products for calendar year 2008 which have string "Pedal" in the model name.

Exercise 5.2: Find "Reseller Sales Amount" for all non-empty weeks for calendar year 2007. Week names are "Week 1 CY 2007", "Week 2 CY 2007" etc. Modify week names with two digits, padded with zero in the left, for example, "Week 01 CY 2007", "Week 02 CY 2007" etc.

Exercise 5.3: Display non empty "Reseller Sales Amount" for cities in the state of Texas.
a. Sort the list by "Reseller Sales Amount".
b. Sort the list by "City Name".

Exercise 5.4: For a given year and a state, both passed as string parameters, find "Reseller Sales Amount".

Exercise 5.5: Display all states of United States and also display string length of each state name.

Chapter 6: Numeric Functions

Like any other language, numeric functions are an integral part of MDX. Native MDX does not have an extensive list of numeric functions, because, most of the numeric calculations are located in "ETL module", "ETL post processing module" or in data source view. If you still need some more numeric functions, VBA numeric functions can be used along with native MDX functions. Please note that, VBA functions are not native to MDX and performance of these VBA functions are slower than native MDX functions.

The first section of this chapter explores some common numeric functions as well as some functions unique to MDX. For example, Aggregate function calculates the value of a measure depend on the "AggregateFunction" property configured for the measure. "Rank" function ranks a list of dimension members depending on a measure, for example, rank all states of "United States" by the "Reseller Sales Amount". The "VisualTotals" function used for changing the grand total depends on the members selected. Another important function is "RollupChildren", which calculates a measure of a non-leaf member by rolling up children.

The second section of this chapter explores some common numeric VBA functions that can be used in MDX. Since you may already be familiar with these VBA functions, they described briefly. Last but not least, "Exercises" will help you to practice some MDX queries.

Agenda

Sum, Max, Min, Avg, Aggregate, CoalesceEmpty, Rank,VisualTotals, RollupChildren

VBA Functions
Abs, Atn, Cos, Exp, Fix, Format, Int, Log, Rnd, Round, Sgn, Sin, Tan

Exercises

Query#6.01:

Goal: Display "Reseller Order Quantity" for first six months of fiscal year 2008 for each product category for the state of California. Also display:

- Total sales, maximum sales, minimum sales and average sales for each **product category**.
- Total sales, maximum sales, minimum sales and average sales for each **month.**

Step 1:

- Display all product categories in rows.
- In Columns, use "PeriodsToDate" function to find first six months of fiscal year 2008.
  Note: Fiscal year 2008 starts from July, 2007 and ends in June, 2008.
- Use "Where" clause to limit all measures to the state of California
  [Geography].[Geography].[State-Province].&[CA]&[US]

MDX

```
SELECT
  {
  PeriodsToDate
    (
    [Date].[Fiscal].[Fiscal Year],
    [Date].[Fiscal].[Month].&[2007]&[12]
    )
  } ON COLUMNS,
  {
  [Product].[Product Categories].[Category]
  } ON ROWS
FROM
  [Adventure Works]
WHERE
  [Geography].[Geography].[State-Province].&[CA]&[US]
```

Result

	July 2007	August 2007	September 2007	October 2007	November 2007	December 2007
Accessories	$2,889.15	$4,105.24	$5,691.67	$3,220.23	$2,339.78	$3,789.18
Bikes	$243,384.65	$257,687.43	$276,519.63	$255,756.06	$228,966.73	$254,793.79
Clothing	$5,871.50	$9,925.10	$14,113.51	$4,201.33	$6,437.31	$9,604.91
Components	$73,999.06	$58,452.10	$99,051.44	$24,868.73	$32,288.56	$47,120.26

Analysis:

- The values displayed above are not "Reseller Order Quantity" (since values are formatted as currency).
- The values displayed are the default measure of the cube, which is "Reseller Sales Amount".

Step 2:

- To display "Reseller Order Quantity" instead of "Reseller Sales Amount", add [Measures].[Reseller Order Quantity] in "Where" clause, as follows:

```
(
[Geography].[Geography].[State-Province].&[CA]&[US],
[Measures].[Reseller Order Quantity]
)
```

<table>
<tr><td>MDX</td><td><pre>SELECT
  {
  PeriodsToDate
    (
    [Date].[Fiscal].[Fiscal Year],
    [Date].[Fiscal].[Month].&[2007]&[12]
)
  } ON COLUMNS,
  {
  [Product].[Product Categories].[Category]
  } ON ROWS
FROM
  [Adventure Works]
WHERE
  (
  [Geography].[Geography].[State-Province].&[CA]&[US],
  [Measures].[Reseller Order Quantity]
)</pre></td></tr>
<tr><td>Result</td><td>
<table>
<tr><th></th><th>July 2007</th><th>August 2007</th><th>September 2007</th><th>October 2007</th><th>November 2007</th><th>December 2007</th></tr>
<tr><td>Accessories</td><td>153</td><td>149</td><td>210</td><td>117</td><td>87</td><td>139</td></tr>
<tr><td>Bikes</td><td>323</td><td>296</td><td>380</td><td>281</td><td>276</td><td>305</td></tr>
<tr><td>Clothing</td><td>259</td><td>392</td><td>534</td><td>206</td><td>280</td><td>354</td></tr>
<tr><td>Components</td><td>253</td><td>256</td><td>420</td><td>112</td><td>149</td><td>225</td></tr>
</table>
</td></tr>
</table>

Step 3:

- Find sum of "Reseller Order Quantity" for all 6 months for each product category.

```
SUM
  (
  PeriodsToDate
    (
    [Date].[Fiscal].[Fiscal Year],
    [Date].[Fiscal].[Month].&[2007]&[12]
    ),
  [Measures].[Reseller Order Quantity]
  )
```

- Currently, columns contain members of hierarchy "[Date].[Fiscal]"
- To display "The Sum" in columns, create a calculated member "The Sum" **in hierarchy**, [Date].[Fiscal].
- Note: Most of the time calculated members are created for [Measures], but this example shows that you can create calculated members in any hierarchy.

MDX

```
WITH
MEMBER [Date].[Fiscal].[The Sum] AS
SUM
   (
   PeriodsToDate
      (
      [Date].[Fiscal].[Fiscal Year],
      [Date].[Fiscal].[Month].&[2007]&[12]
      )
   )
SELECT
   {
   PeriodsToDate
      (
      [Date].[Fiscal].[Fiscal Year],
      [Date].[Fiscal].[Month].&[2007]&[12]
      ),
   [Date].[Fiscal].[The Sum]
   } ON COLUMNS,
   {
   [Product].[Product Categories].[Category]
   } ON ROWS
FROM
   [Adventure Works]
WHERE
   (
   [Geography].[Geography].[State-Province].&[CA]&[US],
   [Measures].[Reseller Order Quantity]
   )
```

Result

	July 2007	August 2007	September 2007	October 2007	November 2007	December 2007	The Sum
Accessories	153	149	210	117	87	139	855
Bikes	323	296	380	281	276	305	1,861
Clothing	259	392	534	206	280	354	2,025
Components	253	256	420	112	149	225	1,415

Step 4:

- Create a named set "The Months" for
  PeriodsToDate
  (
  [Date].[Fiscal].[Fiscal Year],
  [Date].[Fiscal].[Month].&[2007]&[12]
)
- Also create calculated members, "The Sum", "The Max", "The Min" and "The Avg".

MDX

```
WITH
SET [The Months] AS
PeriodsToDate
  (
  [Date].[Fiscal].[Fiscal Year],
  [Date].[Fiscal].[Month].&[2007]&[12]
  )
MEMBER [Date].[Fiscal].[The Sum] AS SUM ([The Months],[Measures].[Reseller Order Quantity])
MEMBER [Date].[Fiscal].[The Max] AS MAX ([The Months],[Measures].[Reseller Order Quantity])
MEMBER [Date].[Fiscal].[The Min] AS MIN ([The Months],[Measures].[Reseller Order Quantity])
MEMBER [Date].[Fiscal].[The Avg] AS AVG ([The Months],[Measures].[Reseller Order Quantity])
SELECT
  {
  [The Months],
  [Date].[Fiscal].[The Sum],
  [Date].[Fiscal].[The Max],
  [Date].[Fiscal].[The Min],
  [Date].[Fiscal].[The Avg]
  } ON COLUMNS,
  {
  [Product].[Product Categories].[Category]
  } ON ROWS
FROM
  [Adventure Works]
WHERE
  (
  [Geography].[Geography].[State-Province].&[CA]&[US],
  [Measures].[Reseller Order Quantity]
  )
```

Result

	July 2007	August 2007	September 2007	October 2007	November 2007	December 2007	The Sum	The Max	The Min	The Avg
Accessories	153	149	210	117	87	139	855	210	87	143
Bikes	323	296	380	281	276	305	1,861	380	276	310
Clothing	259	392	534	206	280	354	2,025	534	206	338
Components	253	256	420	112	149	225	1,415	420	112	236

Step 5:

- This step is an improvement of the query and result remains same as the last result.
- SUM ([The Months],[Measures].[Reseller Order Quantity]) can be modified to SUM ([The Months]), and will return the same result because "Where" clause set the current [Measures] context as "Reseller Order Quantity".
- Similarly, you can modify to MAX ([The Months]), MIN ([The Months]) and AVG ([The Months]).

MDX

```
WITH
SET [The Months] AS
PeriodsToDate
  (
  [Date].[Fiscal].[Fiscal Year],
  [Date].[Fiscal].[Month].&[2007]&[12]
  )
MEMBER [Date].[Fiscal].[The Sum] AS SUM ([The Months])
MEMBER [Date].[Fiscal].[The Max] AS MAX ([The Months])
MEMBER [Date].[Fiscal].[The Min] AS MIN ([The Months])
MEMBER [Date].[Fiscal].[The Avg] AS AVG ([The Months])
SELECT
  {
  [The Months],
  [Date].[Fiscal].[The Sum],
  [Date].[Fiscal].[The Max],
  [Date].[Fiscal].[The Min],
  [Date].[Fiscal].[The Avg]
  } ON COLUMNS,
  {
  [Product].[Product Categories].[Category]
  } ON ROWS
FROM
  [Adventure Works]
WHERE
  (
  [Geography].[Geography].[State-Province].&[CA]&[US],
  [Measures].[Reseller Order Quantity]
  )
```

Result

	July 2007	August 2007	September 2007	October 2007	November 2007	December 2007	The Sum	The Max	The Min	The Avg
Accessories	153	149	210	117	87	139	855	210	87	143
Bikes	323	296	380	281	276	305	1,861	380	276	310
Clothing	259	392	534	206	280	354	2,025	534	206	338
Components	253	256	420	112	149	225	1,415	420	112	236

Step 6:

- Find total sales, maximum sales, minimum sales and average sales for each **month**.
- Create calculated members in hierarchy "[Product].[Product Categories]" and apply aggregate function over all members of "[Product].[Product Categories]".

MDX

```
WITH
SET [The Months] AS
PeriodsToDate
  (
  [Date].[Fiscal].[Fiscal Year],
  [Date].[Fiscal].[Month].&[2007]&[12]
  )
MEMBER [Date].[Fiscal].[The Sum] AS SUM ([The Months])
MEMBER [Date].[Fiscal].[The Max] AS MAX ([The Months])
MEMBER [Date].[Fiscal].[The Min] AS MIN ([The Months])
MEMBER [Date].[Fiscal].[The Avg] AS AVG ([The Months])

MEMBER [Product].[Product Categories].[The Sum] AS SUM ([Product].[Product Categories].[Category])
MEMBER [Product].[Product Categories].[The Max] AS MAX ([Product].[Product Categories].[Category])
MEMBER [Product].[Product Categories].[The Min] AS MIN ([Product].[Product Categories].[Category])
MEMBER [Product].[Product Categories].[The Avg] AS AVG ([Product].[Product Categories].[Category])

SELECT
  {
  [The Months],
  [Date].[Fiscal].[The Sum], [Date].[Fiscal].[The Max],
  [Date].[Fiscal].[The Min], [Date].[Fiscal].[The Avg]
  } ON COLUMNS,
  {
  [Product].[Product Categories].[Category],
  [Product].[Product Categories].[The Sum], [Product].[Product Categories].[The Max],
  [Product].[Product Categories].[The Min],  [Product].[Product Categories].[The Avg]
    } ON ROWS
FROM
  [Adventure Works]
WHERE
  (
  [Geography].[Geography].[State-Province].&[CA]&[US],
  [Measures].[Reseller Order Quantity]
  )
```

The final result:

	July 2007	August 2007	September 2007	October 2007	November 2007	December 2007	The Sum	The Max	The Min	The Avg
Accessories	153	149	210	117	87	139	855	210	87	143
Bikes	323	296	380	281	276	305	1,861	380	276	310
Clothing	259	392	534	206	280	354	2,025	534	206	338
Components	253	256	420	112	149	225	1,415	420	112	236
The Sum	988	1,093	1,544	716	792	1,023	6,156	1,544	716	1,026
The Max	323	392	534	281	280	354	2,164	534	280	361
The Min	153	149	210	112	87	139	850	210	87	142
The Avg	247	273	386	179	198	256	1,539	386	179	257

Sum (<Set>, <Numeric Expression>)
Max (<Set>, <Numeric Expression>)
Min (<Set>, <Numeric Expression>)
Avg (<Set>, <Numeric Expression>)

All these aggregate functions have the same parameters:
<Set>:

- A valid set.
  For example, [Product].[Product Categories].[Category].

<Numeric Expression>:

- This is an optional parameter.
- If passed, aggregate function will apply for this value.
  For example, [Measures].[Reseller Order Quantity].
- If this parameter is not passed, the aggregate function will apply for current [Measures] context.

The Result (Sum):

- Returns total sum of <Numeric Expression> or current [Measures] over the set <Set>.

The Result (Max):

- Returns maximum of <Numeric Expression> or current [Measures] over the set <Set>.

The Result (Min):

- Returns minimum of <Numeric Expression> or current [Measures] over the set <Set>.

The Result (Avg):

- Returns average of <Numeric Expression> or current [Measures] over the set <Set>.

Aggregate

- An aggregation function returns a value that is calculated by aggregating over a set.
- Different aggregate functions are:
    - Sum
    - Max
    - Min
    - Avg
    - Count
    - DistinctCount
    - FirstChild
    - LastChild
    - FirstNonEmpty
    - LastNonEmpty
    - By Account
- Every **Measure** of a cube has a default aggregation function.

Use following steps to see “aggregation function” assigned for measure [Measures].[Reseller Sales Amount]:

1 Open SQL Data Tools and open SSAS database “AdventureWorksDW2012Multidimensional-EE”.

2 In solution explorer, double-click on the cube, “Adventure Works” in “Cubes” folder.

3 Expand measure group “Reseller Sales” and right click on measure “Reseller Sales Amount” and select “Properties”.

4 In properties window, “AggregateFunction” property value is “Sum” and can be selected from the drop-down list as shown below.

Note: To set "AggregateFunction" as none, cube should have atleast one time dimension and the feature is available to SQL Server Enterprise edition only.

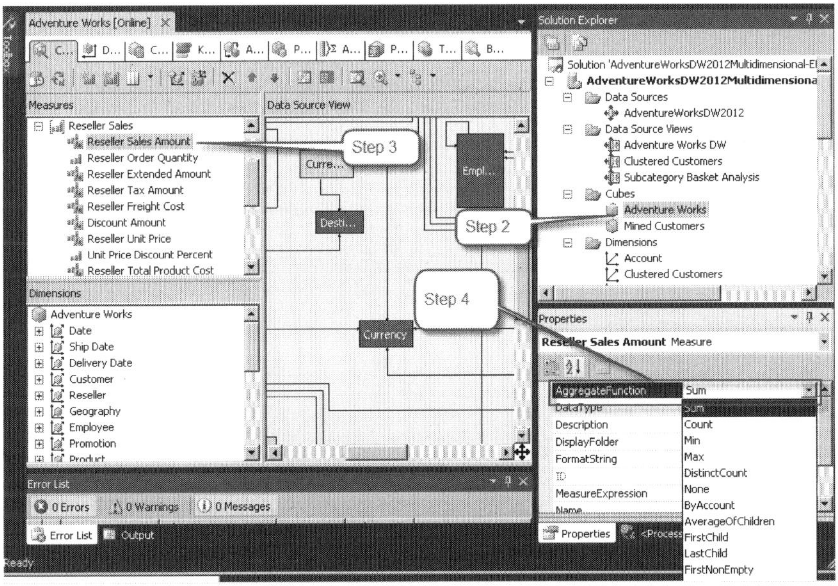

Figure 6-1: Set “AggregateFunction” property for measure “Reseller Sales Amount”.

Query#6.02:

Goal: Display sum of "Reseller Sales Amount" for first four months of fiscal year 2008 for each product category for United States.

Solution 1: Using "Sum" function

- Display each product category in rows.
- Create a calculated member [Measures].[The Sum] , which calculates the sum of "Reseller Sales Amount" over a four month period using "Sum" function.

MDX

```
WITH
MEMBER [Measures].[The Sum] AS
Sum
  (
  PeriodsToDate
    (
    [Date].[Fiscal].[Fiscal Year],
    [Date].[Fiscal].[Month].&[2007]&[10]
    ),
  [Measures].[Reseller Sales Amount]
  )

SELECT
  {
  [Measures].[The Sum]
  } ON COLUMNS,
  {
  [Product].[Product Categories].[Category]
  } ON ROWS
FROM
  [Adventure Works]
WHERE
  [Geography].[Geography].[Country].&[United States]
```

Result

	The Sum
Accessories	$86,304.70
Bikes	$5,840,803.43
Clothing	$212,225.26
Components	$1,566,654.94

Alternatively, you can use the aggregate function to display the same, because the AggregateFunction for measure "Reseller Sales Amount" is "Sum".
So, in this case
Sum (<set>, [Measures].[Reseller Sales Amount]) = Aggregate (<set>, [Measures].[Reseller Sales Amount]).
The following query demonstrated the use of "Aggregate" function instead of "Sum".

Solution 2: Using "Aggregate" function

- Display each product category in rows.
- Create a calculated member [Measures].[The Sum], which calculates sum of "Reseller Sales Amount" over four months period using "Aggregate" function.
- As "AggregateFunction" property of measure "Reseller Sales Amount" is "Sum", both "Sum" and "Aggregate" function will return the same result.

MDX	Result

WITH
MEMBER [Measures].[The Sum] AS
Aggregate
  (
  PeriodsToDate
    (
    [Date].[Fiscal].[Fiscal Year],
    [Date].[Fiscal].[Month].&[2007]&[10]
    ),
  [Measures].[Reseller Sales Amount]
)
 	
SELECT
  {
  [Measures].[The Sum]
  } ON COLUMNS,
  {
  [Product].[Product Categories].[Category]
  } ON ROWS
FROM
  [Adventure Works]
WHERE
  [Geography].[Geography].[Country].&[United States]
	| | The Sum |
	|---|---|
	| Accessories | $86,304.70 |
	| Bikes | $5,840,803.43 |
	| Clothing | $212,225.26 |
	| Components | $1,566,654.94 |

Goal: Change AggregateFunction property of measure "Reseller Sales Amount" from "Sum" to "Max".

Steps:

1 Open SQL Server Data Tools. Open SSAS project "AdventureWorksDW2012Multidimensional-EE".
2 In solution explorer, double-click on the cube, "Adventure Works" in "Cubes" folder.
3 Expand measure group "Reseller Sales" and right click on measure "Reseller Sales Amount" and select "Properties".
4 In properties window, "AggregateFunction" property value is "Sum", change to "Max".
5 Process the cube and re-run the last query, "The Sum" will show **maximum** "Reseller Sales Amount" for

the period instead of the sum of "Reseller Sales Amount" for the period.

MDX

```
WITH
MEMBER [Measures].[The Sum] AS
Aggregate
  (
  PeriodsToDate
    (
    [Date].[Fiscal].[Fiscal Year],
    [Date].[Fiscal].[Month].&[2007]&[10]
    ),
  [Measures].[Reseller Sales Amount]
  )
SELECT
  {
  [Measures].[The Sum]
  } ON COLUMNS,
  {
  [Product].[Product Categories].[Category]
  } ON ROWS
FROM
  [Adventure Works]
WHERE
  [Geography].[Geography].[Country].&[United States]
```

Result

	The Sum
Accessories	$1,504.80
Bikes	$27,893.62
Clothing	$1,259.82
Components	$12,064.49

Note: Change AggregateFunction property of measure "Reseller Sales Amount" back to "Sum".

Aggregate **(<Set>, <Numeric Expression>)**

<Set>:

- A valid set. For example, [Product].[Product Categories].[Category].

<Numeric Expression>:

- This is an optional parameter.
- If a value is passed, "AggregateFunction" property of given [Measures] will be applied. For example, [Measures].[Reseller Order Quantity].
- If this parameter is not passed, "AggregateFunction" is applied to current [Measures] context.

The Result:

- First finds the aggegate function from "AggregateFunction" property of the given measure.
- Then return aggegate of current [Measures] over the set <Set>.

CoalesceEmpty

- If a "numeric value" is null, CoalesceEmpty will return an alternate "numeric value".
- Similarly, if a string value is null, CoalesceEmpty will return an alternate "string value".

For example, CoalesceEmpty(X, Y) means:

- If X is null then CoalesceEmpty(X, Y) will return Y.

Query#6.03:

Goal: Display "Reseller Sales Amount" for each product category for each calendar year.

MDX

```
SELECT
  {
  [Product].[Product Categories].[Category]
  } ON COLUMNS,
  {
  [Date].[Calendar].[Calendar Year]
  } ON ROWS
FROM
  [Adventure Works]
WHERE
  [Measures].[Reseller Sales Amount]
```

Result

	Accessories	Bikes	Clothing	Components
CY 2005	$20,235.36	$7,395,348.63	$34,376.34	$615,474.98
CY 2006	$92,735.35	$19,956,014.67	$485,587.15	$3,610,092.47
CY 2007	$296,532.88	$25,551,775.07	$871,864.19	$5,482,497.29
CY 2008	$161,794.33	$13,399,243.18	$386,013.16	$2,091,011.92
CY 2009	(null)	(null)	(null)	(null)
CY 2010	(null)	(null)	(null)	(null)

Goal: Modify the last query, show $0.00, if "Reseller Sales Amount" is null.

- To show $0.00, if "Reseller Sales Amount" is null, you can use following expression: CoalesceEmpty([Measures].[Reseller Sales Amount], 0)
- But unlike SQL "Coalesce" function, you cannot just replace "Reseller Sales Amount" with CoalesceEmpty([Measures].[Reseller Sales Amount], 0), or you will get following error:

MDX

```
SELECT
  {
  [Product].[Product Categories].[Category]
  } ON COLUMNS,
  {
  [Date].[Calendar].[Calendar Year]
  } ON ROWS
FROM
  [Adventure Works]
WHERE
  CoalesceEmpty ( [Measures].[Reseller Sales Amount], 0 )
```

Result

Executing the query ...
The WHERE clause function expects a tuple set expression for the argument. A string or numeric expression was used.
Execution complete

Analysis:

- The error message means, the "Where" clause expects a tuple not a numeric value.
- To fix ths, you can create a calculated member "The RSA"

```
WITH
MEMBER [Measures].[The RSA] AS
CoalesceEmpty
  (
  [Measures].[Reseller Sales Amount],
  0
  )
```

- Replacing [Measures].[Reseller Sales Amount] with [Measures].[The RSA] in "Where" clause will fix the issue because [Measures].[The RSA] is a member, not a numeric or a string.

MDX

```
WITH
MEMBER [Measures].[The RSA] AS
CoalesceEmpty
  (
  [Measures].[Reseller Sales Amount],
  0
  ), FORMAT_STRING="Currency"
SELECT
  {
  [Product].[Product Categories].[Category]
  } ON COLUMNS,
  {
  [Date].[Calendar].[Calendar Year]
  } ON ROWS
FROM
  [Adventure Works]
WHERE
  [Measures].[The RSA]
```

Result

	Accessories	Bikes	Clothing	Components
CY 2005	$20,235.36	$7,395,348.63	$34,376.34	$615,474.98
CY 2006	$92,735.35	$19,956,014.67	$485,587.15	$3,610,092.47
CY 2007	$296,532.88	$25,551,775.07	$871,864.19	$5,482,497.29
CY 2008	$161,794.33	$13,399,243.18	$386,013.16	$2,091,011.92
CY 2009	$0.00	$0.00	$0.00	$0.00
CY 2010	$0.00	$0.00	$0.00	$0.00

FORM-1

CoalesceEmpty (<Numeric Expression 1>, <Numeric Expression 2>, ...])

<Numeric Expression 1>, <Numeric Expression 2>,...:

- Valid numeric expressions.

The Result:

- If <Numeric Expression 1> is null then the function will return <Numeric Expression 2> and so on.

FORM-2

CoalesceEmpty (<String Expression 1>, <String Expression 2>,...])

<String Expression 1>, <String Expression 2>,...:

- Valid string expressions.

The Result:

- If <String Expression 1> is null then the function will return <String Expression 2> and so on.

Rank

- "Rank" function returns the rank of a tuple or a member in a set, based on a numeric expression.
- "Rank" function does not sort the set based on the rank of tuple.

Query#6.04:

Goal-1: Display "Reseller Sales Amount" for each state of "United States" for fiscal year 2007.

MDX

```
SELECT
  {
  [Measures].[Reseller Sales Amount]
  } ON COLUMNS,
  {
  [Geography].[Geography].[Country].&[United States].Children
  } ON ROWS
FROM
  [Adventure Works]
WHERE
    [Date].[Fiscal].[Fiscal Year].&[2007]
```

Result

	Reseller Sales Amou
Alabama	$15,497.20
Arizona	$448,353.42
California	$3,860,128.46
Colorado	$1,071,753.62
Connecticut	$498,866.74
Florida	$515,173.61
Georgia	$345,141.06
Idaho	$8,724.01
Illinois	$103,451.65
Indiana	$671,294.92
Kentucky	$16,857.89
Maine	$388,169.48
...land	(null)

Goal-2: Modify the last query to show position of each state among all states of "United States" based on "Reseller Sales Amount".

Strategy:

- Use "Rank" function to find the position of each state among all states of "United States" based on "Reseller Sales Amount" for fiscal year 2007.
- Create a calculated member [Measures].[The Rank] to show the position.

MDX

```
WITH
MEMBER [Measures].[The Rank] AS
Rank
 (
 [Geography].[Geography].CurrentMember,
 [Geography].[Geography].[Country].&[United States].Children,
 [Measures].[Reseller Sales Amount]
 )
SELECT
 {
 [Measures].[Reseller Sales Amount],
 [Measures].[The Rank]
 } ON COLUMNS,
 {
 [Geography].[Geography].[Country].&[United States].Children
 } ON ROWS
FROM
 [Adventure Works]
WHERE
 [Date].[Fiscal].[Fiscal Year].&[2007]
```

Result

	Reseller Sales Amount	The Rank
Alabama	$15,497.20	30
Arizona	$448,353.42	14
California	$3,860,128.46	1
Colorado	$1,071,753.62	4
Connecticut	$498,866.74	12
Florida	$515,173.61	11
Georgia	$345,141.06	16
Idaho	$8,724.01	32
Illinois	$103,451.65	27
Indiana	$671,294.92	7
Kentucky	$16,857.89	29
Maine	$388,169.48	15
Maryland	(null)	36
Massachusetts	$12,826.06	31
Michigan	$590,727.99	9
Minnesota	$216,514.67	22
Mississippi	$145,196.69	26
Missouri	$641,459.81	8
Montana	$5,309.34	34
Nevada	$205,796.56	23

Goal-3: Modify the last query to sort the list of states based on rank in ascending order.

Strategy:

- To sort states, you can use "Order" function in rows as follows:

```
Order
 (
 [Geography].[Geography].[Country].&[United States].Children,
 [Measures].[The Rank],
 ASC
 )
```

- As all members are from same level, hence, ASC and BASC will return same result.

MDX

```
WITH
MEMBER [Measures].[The Rank] AS
Rank
  (
  [Geography].[Geography].CurrentMember,
  [Geography].[Geography].[Country].&[United States].Children,
  [Measures].[Reseller Sales Amount]
  )

SELECT
  {
  [Measures].[Reseller Sales Amount],
  [Measures].[The Rank]
  } ON COLUMNS,
  {
  Order
    (
    [Geography].[Geography].[Country].&[United States].Children,
    [Measures].[The Rank],
    ASC
    )
  } ON ROWS
FROM
  [Adventure Works]
WHERE
  [Date].[Fiscal].[Fiscal Year].&[2007]
```

Result

	Reseller Sales Amount	The Rank
California	$3,860,128.46	1
Texas	$2,827,655.94	2
Washington	$2,032,833.85	3
Colorado	$1,071,753.62	4
New Hampshire	$1,040,864.22	5
Tennessee	$900,332.75	6
Indiana	$671,294.92	7
Missouri	$641,459.81	8
Michigan	$590,727.99	9
Utah	$559,546.19	10
Florida	$515,173.61	11
Connecticut	$498,866.74	12
New York	$488,777.96	13
Arizona	$448,353.42	14
Maine	$388,169.48	15
Georgia	$345,141.06	16
Wyoming	$306,506.49	17
Virginia	$268,340.99	18
Oregon	$268,243.36	19

Rank (<Tuple>, <Set>,[<Numeric Expression>])

<Tuple>:

- A valid tuple. For example, [Geography].[Geography].CurrentMember.
- Both <Tuple> and <Set> should refer to same hierarchy.

<Set>:

- A valid set. For example, [Geography].[Geography].[Country].&[United States].Children.

<Numeric Expression>:

- Valid numeric expression. For example, [Measures].[Reseller Sales Amount].

The Result:

- This returns the rank of a tuple in a set, based on a numeric expression.

VisualTotals

- VisualTotals applies to a set.
- If the given set consists of parents, children and grand-children, etc., "VisualTotals" function will convert the measures of **parents** such that, it will look like as if parents only have children that present in the current set only.

Query#6.05:

Goal-1: Display "Reseller Sales Amount" for "United States" and three states "New York", "California" and "Virginia" for fiscal year 2007.

MDX

```
SELECT
  {
  [Measures].[Reseller Sales Amount]
  } ON COLUMNS,
  {
  [Geography].[Geography].[Country].&[United States],
  [Geography].[Geography].[State-Province].&[NY]&[US],
  [Geography].[Geography].[State-Province].&[CA]&[US],
  [Geography].[Geography].[State-Province].&[VA]&[US]
  } ON ROWS
FROM
  [Adventure Works]
WHERE
  [Date].[Fiscal].[Fiscal Year].&[2007]
```

Result

	Reseller Sales Amount
United States	$19,335,397.26
New York	$488,777.96
California	$3,860,128.46
Virginia	$268,340.99

Analysis:

- United States has states other than NY, CA and VA.
- Hence,
  "Sum of Reseller Sales Amount of (NY+CA+VA)" = $4,617,247.41
  "Reseller Sales Amount of United States" = $19,335,397.26

But,

- You may be interested only these three states of United States and want to show sum of Reseller Sales Amount of (NY+CA+VA) as total Reseller Sales Amount of United States.
- These can be achieved by using "VisualTotals" function,
  VisualTotals ("United States", NY, CA, VA)
  will modify "Reseller Sales Amount of United States" as "Sum of Reseller Sales Amount of (NY+CA+VA)".

Goal-2: Display "Reseller Sales Amount" for "United States" and three states "New York", "California" and "Virginia" for fiscal year 2007. Also show "Reseller Sales Amount of United States" as equal to sum of Reseller Sales Amount of (NY+CA+VA).

MDX

```
SELECT
 {
 [Measures].[Reseller Sales Amount]
 } ON COLUMNS,
 {
 VisualTotals
  (
   {
   [Geography].[Geography].[Country].&[United States],
   [Geography].[Geography].[State-Province].&[NY]&[US],
   [Geography].[Geography].[State-Province].&[CA]&[US],
   [Geography].[Geography].[State-Province].&[VA]&[US]
   }
  )
 } ON ROWS
FROM
 [Adventure Works]
WHERE
 [Date].[Fiscal].[Fiscal Year].&[2007]
```

Result

	Reseller Sales Amount
United States	$4,617,247.42
New York	$488,777.96
California	$3,860,128.46
Virginia	$268,340.99

Analysis:

- Modified "Reseller Sales Amount of United States" = "Sum of Reseller Sales Amount of (NY+CA+VA)".

- If you move [Geography].[Geography].[Country].&[United States] from first position to second position, the set will be:

  ```
  {
  [Geography].[Geography].[State-Province].&[NY]&[US],
  [Geography].[Geography].[Country].&[United States],
  [Geography].[Geography].[State-Province].&[CA]&[US],
  [Geography].[Geography].[State-Province].&[VA]&[US]
  }
  ```

  The modified "Reseller Sales Amount of United States" will be changed to sum of CA and VA only.

MDX	Result

SELECT
{
[Measures].[Reseller Sales Amount]
} ON COLUMNS,
{
VisualTotals
(
{
[Geography].[Geography].[State-Province].&[NY]&[US],
[Geography].[Geography].[Country].&[United States],
[Geography].[Geography].[State-Province].&[CA]&[US],
[Geography].[Geography].[State-Province].&[VA]&[US]
}
)
} ON ROWS
FROM
[Adventure Works]
WHERE
[Date].[Fiscal].[Fiscal Year].&[2007]
	| | Reseller Sales Amount |
	| New York | $488,777.96 |
	| United States | $4,128,469.46 |
	| California | $3,860,128.46 |
	| Virginia | $268,340.99 |

Analysis:

- The above result is not correct.
  As
  Modified Reseller Sales Amount of United States = $4,128,469.46
  and
  Sum of Reseller Sales Amount of (NY+CA+VA) = $4,617,247.41
  doesnot match.
- Why Reseller Sales Amount of United States = $4,128,469.46?
- Modified "Reseller Sales Amount of United States" = "Sum of Reseller Sales Amount of (CA+VA)"
  = $3,860,128.46 + $268,340.99 = $4,128,469.46
- This means, it sums **all children after the parent** location in the set.
- If [Geography].[Geography].[Country].&[United States] is moved from second position to third position, the set will be:

```
{
[Geography].[Geography].[State-Province].&[NY]&[US],
[Geography].[Geography].[State-Province].&[CA]&[US],
[Geography].[Geography].[Country].&[United States],
[Geography].[Geography].[State-Province].&[VA]&[US]
}
```

"Modified Reseller Sales Amount of United States" will be changed to Reseller Sales Amount for VA only.

MDX

```
SELECT
 {
 [Measures].[Reseller Sales Amount]
 } ON COLUMNS,
 {
 VisualTotals
  (
   {
   [Geography].[Geography].[State-Province].&[NY]&[US],
   [Geography].[Geography].[State-Province].&[CA]&[US],
   [Geography].[Geography].[Country].&[United States],
   [Geography].[Geography].[State-Province].&[VA]&[US]
   }
  )
 } ON ROWS
FROM
 [Adventure Works]
WHERE
 [Date].[Fiscal].[Fiscal Year].&[2007]
```

Result

	Reseller Sales Amount
New York	$488,777.96
California	$3,860,128.46
United States	$268,340.99
Virginia	$268,340.99

If you move "[Geography].[Geography].[Country].&[United States]" from third position to fourth position, the set will be:

```
{
[Geography].[Geography].[State-Province].&[NY]&[US],
[Geography].[Geography].[State-Province].&[CA]&[US],
[Geography].[Geography].[State-Province].&[VA]&[US],
[Geography].[Geography].[Country].&[United States]
}
```

The modified "Reseller Sales Amount of United States" will be changed to sum of Reseller Sales Amount of all states of United States.

This case is equivalent to not using the "VisualTotals" function as there is no member after [Geography].[Geography].[Country].&[United States].

MDX	Result

SELECT
{
[Measures].[Reseller Sales Amount]
} ON COLUMNS,
{
VisualTotals
(
{
[Geography].[Geography].[State-Province].&[NY]&[US],
[Geography].[Geography].[State-Province].&[CA]&[US],
[Geography].[Geography].[State-Province].&[VA]&[US],
[Geography].[Geography].[Country].&[United States]
}
)
} ON ROWS
FROM
[Adventure Works]
WHERE
[Date].[Fiscal].[Fiscal Year].&[2007]
	<table><tr><th></th><th>Reseller Sales Amount</th></tr><tr><td>New York</td><td>$488,777.96</td></tr><tr><td>California</td><td>$3,860,128.46</td></tr><tr><td>Virginia</td><td>$268,340.99</td></tr><tr><td>United States</td><td>$19,335,397.26</td></tr></table>

Analysis:

- For "VisualTotals" function, parents should be located before children.
- If you have multiple levels, all parents should be located immediately before children. For example, following query has three levels:

```
{
[Geography].[Geography].[All Geographies],
[Geography].[Geography].[Country].&[France],
[Geography].[Geography].[State-Province].&[45]&[FR],
[Geography].[Geography].[State-Province].&[91]&[FR],
[Geography].[Geography].[Country].&[United States],
[Geography].[Geography].[State-Province].&[NY]&[US],
[Geography].[Geography].[State-Province].&[CA]&[US],
[Geography].[Geography].[State-Province].&[VA]&[US]
}
```

- This means that, [Geography].[Geography].[Country].&[United States] should immediately precede all states of United States.
- Similarly, [Geography].[Geography].[Country].&[France] should immediately precede all states of France.

Solution:

- Arrange the input set according to hierarchy.
- Easiest way to arrange the set according to hierarchy is to use "Hierarchize" function.

MDX

```
SELECT
   {
   [Measures].[Reseller Sales Amount]
   } ON COLUMNS,
   {
   VisualTotals
      (
      Hierarchize
         (
         {
         [Geography].[Geography].[All Geographies],
         [Geography].[Geography].[Country].&[France],
         [Geography].[Geography].[State-Province].&[45]&[FR],
         [Geography].[Geography].[State-Province].&[91]&[FR],
         [Geography].[Geography].[Country].&[United States],
         [Geography].[Geography].[State-Province].&[NY]&[US],
         [Geography].[Geography].[State-Province].&[CA]&[US],
         [Geography].[Geography].[State-Province].&[VA]&[US]
         }
         )
      )
   } ON ROWS
FROM
   [Adventure Works]
WHERE
   [Date].[Fiscal].[Fiscal Year].&[2007]
```

Result

	Reseller Sales Amount
All Geographies	$5,060,627.65
France	$443,380.23
Essonne	$2,342.53
Loiret	$441,037.70
United States	$4,617,247.42
California	$3,860,128.46
New York	$488,777.96
Virginia	$268,340.99

Analysis:

- Using "Hierarchize" function will resolve the position issue for "VisualTotals" function.
- In the above result, you do not know which parents have modified value.

To identify the parents which have modified value, you can use the second parameter "Pattern" of VisualTotals function.

- If second parameter is "* - VT", all parents that have modified value, the name of the parent will be changed.
  - [Geography].[Geography].[All Geographies] will be changed to [Geography].[Geography].[All Geographies -VT].
  - [Geography].[Geography].[Country].&[France] will be changed to [Geography].[Geography].[Country].&[France - VT].

- [Geography].[Geography].[Country].&[United States] will be changed to [Geography].[Geography].[Country].&[United States - VT].

MDX

```
SELECT
   {
   [Measures].[Reseller Sales Amount]
   } ON COLUMNS,
   {
   VisualTotals
      (
      Hierarchize
         (
         {
         [Geography].[Geography].[All Geographies],
         [Geography].[Geography].[Country].&[France],
         [Geography].[Geography].[State-Province].&[45]&[FR],
         [Geography].[Geography].[State-Province].&[91]&[FR],
         [Geography].[Geography].[Country].&[United States],
         [Geography].[Geography].[State-Province].&[NY]&[US],
         [Geography].[Geography].[State-Province].&[CA]&[US],
         [Geography].[Geography].[State-Province].&[VA]&[US]
         }
         ),"*-VT"
      )
   } ON ROWS
FROM
   [Adventure Works]
WHERE
   [Date].[Fiscal].[Fiscal Year].&[2007]
```

Result

	Reseller Sales Amount
All Geographies - VT	$5,060,627.65
France - VT	$443,380.23
Essonne	$2,342.53
Loiret	$441,037.70
United States - VT	$4,617,247.42
California	$3,860,128.46
New York	$488,777.96
Virginia	$268,340.99

VisualTotals (<Set>, [<Pattern>])

<Set>:

- A valid set. The set should be arranged according to hierarchy.

  {
  [Geography].[Geography].[Country].&[United States],
  [Geography].[Geography].[State-Province].&[NY]&[US],
  [Geography].[Geography].[State-Province].&[CA]&[US],
  [Geography].[Geography].[State-Province].&[VA]&[US]
  }

<Pattern>:

- This is an optional parameter. e.g. "* -VT". If passed, all parents that have modified value, the name of the parent will be changed, * will be replaced by the parent name.

The Result:

- This returns measures for parents generated by dynamically totaling child members in the specified set <Set>.

RollupChildren

- RollupChildren returns measures of a member of a hierarchy by rolling up children.
- This means that, each measure will be generated by rolling up the values of the children of a specified member of a Hierarchy using the specified unary operator.

Goal: Change "AggregateFunction" property of measure "Reseller Sales Amount" from "Sum" to "Max".

Steps:

1 Open SQL Server Data Tools. Open SSAS project "AdventureWorksDW2012Multidimensional-EE".
2 In solution explorer, double-click on the cube, "Adventure Works" in "Cubes" folder.
3 Expand measure group "Reseller Sales" and right click on measure "Reseller Sales Amount"and select "Properties".
4 In properties window, change "AggregateFunction" property value from "Sum" to "Max".
5 Process the cube.

Query#6.06:

Goal: Display "Reseller Sales Amount" for "United States" for fiscal year 2007 and compare the result with calculating "Reseller Sales Amount" by rolling up children using the unary operator "+".

MDX

```
WITH
MEMBER [Geography].[Geography].[United States RollUp] AS
RollUpChildren
 (
 [Geography].[Geography].[Country].&[United States],
 "+"
 )
SELECT
 {
 [Measures].[Reseller Sales Amount]
 } ON COLUMNS,
 {
 [Geography].[Geography].[Country].&[United States],
 [Geography].[Geography].[United States RollUp]
 } ON ROWS
FROM
 [Adventure Works]
WHERE
 [Date].[Fiscal].[Fiscal Year].&[2007]
```

Result

	Reseller Sales Amount
United States	$16,665.60
United States RollUp	$313,078.87

Analysis:

- As "AggregateFunction" property of "Reseller Sales Amount" changed to "Max", "Reseller Sales Amount" for "United States" means maximum "Reseller Sales Amount" among all children of "United States" and so on.
- Using "RollupChildren" function, "Reseller Sales Amount" for "United States" calculated as the sum of "Reseller Sales Amount" of all children of "United States".

Goal: Change "AggregateFunction" property of measure "Reseller Sales Amount" from "Max" to "Sum".

Steps:

1 Open SQL Server Data Tools.
2 Open SSAS project "AdventureWorksDW2012Multidimensional-EE".
3 In solution explorer, double-click on the cube, "Adventure Works" in "Cubes" folder.
4 Expand measure group "Reseller Sales" and right click on measure "Reseller Sales Amount" and select "Properties".
5 In properties window, change "AggregateFunction" property value from "Max" to "Sum".
6 Process the cube.

RollupChildren **(<Member>, <Unary Operator>)**

<Member>:

- A valid member. For example, [Geography].[Geography].[Country].&[United States].

<Unary Operator>:

- + : Total = Total + Children.
- - : Total = Total - Children.
- * : Total = Total * Children.
- / : Total = Total / Children.
- % : Total = Total % Children.
- ~ : Total = Do not use any rollup.

The Result:

- Returns measure by rolling up children using unary operator <Unary Operator>.

VBA Functions

VBA stands for **V**isual **B**asic for **A**pplications functions. MDX expressions can use any supported VBA and Excel function but these functions are slow compared to native MDX functions.

VBA Functions	Description
Abs (<number>)	Returns absolute value of a number. Abs (-65.58) = 65.58
Atn (<number>)	Returns arctangent value of a number.
Cos (<angle>)	Return the cosine of an angle. Angle is in radians.
Exp (<number>)	e raised to the power of <number>. where e = 2.71828183
Fix (<number>)	Returns integer part of a decimal number. For negative number it returns the greater or equal number. Fix (-55.89) = -55
Int (<number>)	Returns integer part of a decimal number. For negative number it returns the lower or equal number. Int (-55.89) = -56
Log (<number>, <base>)	Returns logarithm of a number, <number> to a specified base <base>.
Rnd()	Returns a random number between 0 and 1.
Round (<number>, <digit count>)	Returns the specified number rounded to the number decimal places of <digit count>. If <digit count> is not specified, the function will round with no decimal points. For example, Round (663.43) = 663 Round (663.56) = 664 Round (663.56,1) = 663.6
Sin (<angle>)	Returns the sine of an angle. Angle is in radians.
Sgn (<number>)	Returns sign of a number, for positive numbers Sgn returns 1 and for negative numbers it returns -1. Sgn (663.58) = 1 Sgn (-663.58) = -1

VBA Functions	Description
Tan (<angle>)	Returns the tangent of an angle. Angle is in radians.
Format (<number>, <format>)	For example: • Format (0.56, "percent") = 56.00% • Format (2.56, "percent") = 256.00%. • Format (123456.789, "General Number") = 123456.789. Displays a number without thousands separator. • Format (123456.789, "Standard") = 123,456.789. Displays a number with thousand separators. • Format (.789, "Fixed") = 0.79. Displays at least one digit to the left of the decimal place and two digits to the right of the decimal place. • Format (123456.789, "currency"). Displays a currency symbol, thousand separators as well as two decimal places. • Format (123456.789, "scientific") = 1.23E+05. • Format (123, "On/Off") = On. Displays Off if the number is 0 else On. • Format (0, "On/Off") = Off. Displays Off if the number is 0 else On. • Format(123,"Yes/No") = Yes. Displays No if the number is 0 else Yes. • Format (0, "Yes/No") = No. Displays No if the number is 0 else Yes. • Format (123, "True/False") = True. Displays False if the number is 0 else True. • Format (0, "True/False") = False. Displays False if the number is 0 else True.

EXERCISES

Exercise 6.1: Find the monthly average of "Reseller Sales Amount" for fiscal year 2007 for the state of New York for following cases:

A. Include months with no sales.

B. Exclude months with no sales.

Exercise 6.2: Rank products based on "Reseller Sales Amount" for the state of Florida for fiscal year 2008. Do not show products that have no sales.

Exercise 6.3: The following result shows "Reseller Sales Amount" for "Bikes", "Clothing" and "All Products" for the state of Texas with "Reseller Sales Amount" of "All Products" as sum of all product categories. Modify the query to show "Reseller Sales Amount" of "All Products" as sum of product categories Bikes and Clothing.

MDX

```
SELECT
  {
  [Measures].[Reseller Sales Amount]
  } ON COLUMNS,
  {
  VisualTotals
    (
      {
      [Product].[Product Categories].[Category].[Bikes],
      [Product].[Product Categories].[Category].[Clothing],
      [Product].[Product Categories].[All Products]
      }
    )
  } ON ROWS
FROM
  [Adventure Works]
WHERE
  [Geography].[Geography].[State-Province].&[TX]&[US]
```

Result

	Reseller Sales Amount
Bikes	$5,176,738.21
Clothing	$105,216.45
All Products	$6,236,182.34

Chapter 7: Statistical Functions

MDX provides numerous statistical functions. This chapter explores them in detail with examples and graphical presentation of data. The chapter is divided into two major sections.

The first section explores some common statistical functions like Median, Standard Deviation (Stdev), Variance, Correlation and Covariance. It also explains the meaning of these functions with very simple examples, interpretation of these functions and differences with other similar functions. Standard Deviation (stdev) of a measure for a set is the measurement of the variation of the "Measure" from average value of the "Measure" for the set. Low Standard Deviation means the measure is close to the mean value. High Standard Deviation means the measure is far from the mean value. Unit of Variance is different from data. So, value of Variance may not be directly associate with data. Square root of Variance is the Standard Deviation, and Standard Deviation has same units as of data.

The second section explains functions of linear regression equation and how they can be used to analyze data. This section also explains graphical representation of data. For example, from set of points, "LinRegIntercept" function returns the intercept of the regression line and "LinRegSlope" function returns the slope of the regression line.

Last but not least, "Exercises" will help you to practice some MDX queries.

Agenda

Median

Median of a set of numerical data is a numerical value that divides lower half and upper half of the data.

Goal: From a set of numerical data {87, 45, 90, 44, 65, 21, 34}, find the median of the set.

Step 1: Sort the set in ascending order

Position	Numerical Data
1	21
2	34
3	44
4	45
5	65
6	87
7	90

Step 2: Total number of items in the set = 7.
So, middle position is 4. So Median = 45

Note: If there is an even number of members and if M1 and M2 are two values in two middle values, then median is the mean of M1 and M2 = (M1 + M2)/2.

Query#7.01:

Goal: Find the **monthly median** of "Reseller Sales Amount" for United States for fiscal year 2007.

Strategy:

- To find median of all months of fiscal year 2007, two parameters needed as follows:
  - The Set = All months of FY 2007.
  - The Measure = "Reseller Sales Amount".

Following code will return monthly median:

```
Median
 (
 Descendants
  (
  [Date].[Fiscal].[Fiscal Year].&[2007],
  [Date].[Fiscal].[Month]
  ),
 [Measures].[Reseller Sales Amount]
 )
```

MDX	Result
WITH MEMBER [Measures].[The Median] AS Median (Descendants ([Date].[Fiscal].[Fiscal Year].&[2007], [Date].[Fiscal].[Month]), [Measures].[Reseller Sales Amount]), FORMAT_STRING="Currency" SELECT { [Measures].[The Median] } ON COLUMNS FROM [Adventure Works] WHERE [Geography].[Geography].[Country].&[United States]	The Median $1,493,904.70

You can also manually calculate the median with the following steps:

Step 1: Display "Reseller Sales Amount" for the United States for all months of fiscal year 2007.

```
SELECT
  {
  [Measures].[Reseller Sales Amount]
  } ON COLUMNS,
  {
  Descendants
    (
    [Date].[Fiscal].[Fiscal Year].&[2007],
    [Date].[Fiscal].[Month]
    )
  } On ROWS
FROM
  [Adventure Works]
WHERE
  [Geography].[Geography].[Country].&[United States]
```

Result

	Reseller Sales Amount
July 2006	$1,577,391.34
August 2006	$2,497,472.65
September 2006	$1,900,990.51
October 2006	$1,286,450.90
November 2006	$2,213,450.70
December 2006	$1,410,418.06
January 2007	$985,745.10
February 2007	$1,766,608.89
March 2007	$963,022.31
April 2007	$1,321,439.56
May 2007	$2,112,720.38
June 2007	$1,299,686.86

Step 2: Modify the last query to sort the months based on "Reseller Sales Amount".

MDX

```
SELECT
 {
 [Measures].[Reseller Sales Amount]
 } ON COLUMNS,
 {
 Order
  (
  Descendants
   (
   [Date].[Fiscal].[Fiscal Year].&[2007],
   [Date].[Fiscal].[Month]
   ),
  [Measures].[Reseller Sales Amount],
  BASC
  )
 } On ROWS
FROM
 [Adventure Works]
WHERE
 [Geography].[Geography].[Country].&[United States]
```

Result

	Reseller Sales Amount
March 2007	$963,022.31
January 2007	$985,745.10
October 2006	$1,286,450.90
June 2007	$1,299,686.86
April 2007	$1,321,439.56
December 2006	$1,410,418.06
July 2006	$1,577,391.34
February 2007	$1,766,608.89
September 2006	$1,900,990.51
May 2007	$2,112,720.38
November 2006	$2,213,450.70
August 2006	$2,497,472.65

As the total number of months is an even number, there two middle values "December, 2006" and "July, 2006".

The median = (M1+M2)/2 = (1,410,418.06+1,577,391.34)/2 = 1,493,904.70.

Median (<Set>, [<Numeric Expression>])

<Set>:

- A valid set. For example, all months of fiscal year 2007.

```
Descendants
 (
 [Date].[Fiscal].[Fiscal Year].&[2007],
 [Date].[Fiscal].[Month]
 )
```

<Numeric Expression>:

- A valid numeric expression. This is an optional parameter. If it is not passed the current measure context will be processed as the value.

The Result:

- Returns median of <numeric expression> over the set <Set>.

Stdev/StdevP

- The Standard Deviation shows how much variation the data has from the mean value.
- Low Standard Deviation means, close to the mean value.
- High Standard Deviation means, far from the mean value.
- The difference between Stdev and StdevP are:
  - Stdev is calculated using the unbiased population formula (dividing by n-1).
  - StdevP is calculated using the biased population formula (dividing by n).

Query#7.02:

Goal: Display "Reseller Sales Amount" for United States for each month of fiscal year 2007. Also show the Standard Deviation.

MDX

```
WITH
MEMBER [Measures].[The Stdev] AS
Stdev
  (
  Descendants
    (
    [Date].[Fiscal].[Fiscal Year].&[2007],
    [Date].[Fiscal].[Month]
    ),
  [Measures].[Reseller Sales Amount]
  ), FORMAT_STRING="Currency"
SELECT
  {
  [Measures].[Reseller Sales Amount],
  [Measures].[The Stdev]
  } ON COLUMNS,
  {
  Descendants
    (
    [Date].[Fiscal].[Fiscal Year].&[2007],
    [Date].[Fiscal].[Month]
    )
} ON ROWS
FROM
  [Adventure Works]
WHERE
  [Geography].[Geography].[Country].&[United States]
```

Result

	Reseller Sales Amount	The Stdev
July 2006	$1,577,391.34	$490,555.00
August 2006	$2,497,472.65	$490,555.00
September 2006	$1,900,990.51	$490,555.00
October 2006	$1,286,450.90	$490,555.00
November 2006	$2,213,450.70	$490,555.00
December 2006	$1,410,418.06	$490,555.00
January 2007	$985,745.10	$490,555.00
February 2007	$1,766,608.89	$490,555.00
March 2007	$963,022.31	$490,555.00
April 2007	$1,321,439.56	$490,555.00
May 2007	$2,112,720.38	$490,555.00
June 2007	$1,299,686.86	$490,555.00

Stdev (<Set>,[<Numeric Expression>])
StdevP (<Set>,[<Numeric Expression>])

<Set>:

- A valid set. For example, all months of fiscal year 2007.
  Descendants ([Date].[Fiscal].[Fiscal Year].&[2007], [Date].[Fiscal].[Month])

<Numeric Expression>:

- A valid numeric expression.
- This is an optional parameter, if it is not passed, the current measure context will be processed as the value.

The Result:

- Returns standard deviation of <numeric expression> over the set <Set>.
- Stdev is calculated using the unbiased population formula (dividing by n-1).
- StdevP is calculated using the biased population formula (dividing by n).

Variance/Var/VarianceP/VarP

- The variance is a measure of how far a set of numbers are spread out from each other.
- Variance is an alias of Var. Similarly, VarianceP is an alias of VarP.
- The difference between Var and VarP are:
  - Var is calculated using the unbiased population formula (dividing by n-1).
  - VarP is calculated using the biased population formula (dividing by n).
- The unit of variance is different from the unit of data. Unit of variance is square of unit of data. So, the value of variance may not be directly associate with data.
- The square root of variance is Stdev, which has the same unit as of data.

Query#7.03:

Goal: Display "Reseller Sales Amount" for United States for each month of fiscal year 2007. Also show variance of Reseller Sales Amount over the months of fiscal year 2007.

MDX

```
WITH
MEMBER [Measures].[The Var] AS
Var
  (
  Descendants
    (
    [Date].[Fiscal].[Fiscal Year].&[2007],
    [Date].[Fiscal].[Month]
    ),
  [Measures].[Reseller Sales Amount]
  )
-- Continue to the next page
```

Result

	Reseller Sales Amount	The Var	The VarP
July 2006	$1,577,391.34	237309547270.018	217533751664.183
August 2006	$2,497,472.65	237309547270.018	217533751664.183
September 2006	$1,949,258.12	237309547270.018	217533751664.183
October 2006	$1,286,450.90	237309547270.018	217533751664.183
November 2006	$2,213,450.70	237309547270.018	217533751664.183
December 2006	$1,441,966.71	237309547270.018	217533751664.183
January 2007	$985,745.10	237309547270.018	217533751664.183
February 2007	$1,766,608.89	237309547270.018	217533751664.183
March 2007	$992,691.91	237309547270.018	217533751664.183
April 2007	$1,321,439.56	237309547270.018	217533751664.183
May 2007	$2,112,720.38	237309547270.018	217533751664.183
June 2007	$1,326,792.78	237309547270.018	217533751664.183

MDX	Result
MEMBER [Measures].[The VarP] AS VarP (Descendants ([Date].[Fiscal].[Fiscal Year].&[2007], [Date].[Fiscal].[Month]), [Measures].[Reseller Sales Amount]) SELECT { [Measures].[Reseller Sales Amount], [Measures].[The Var], [Measures].[The VarP] } ON COLUMNS, { Descendants ([Date].[Fiscal].[Fiscal Year].&[2007], [Date].[Fiscal].[Month]) } ON ROWS FROM [Adventure Works] WHERE [Geography].[Geography].[Country].&[United States]	

Var **(<Set>, [<Numeric Expression>])**
VarP **(<Set>, [<Numeric Expression>])**

<Set>:

- A valid set. For example, all months of fiscal year 2007.
  Descendants ([Date].[Fiscal].[Fiscal Year].&[2007], [Date].[Fiscal].[Month])

<Numeric Expression>:

- A valid numeric expression.
- This is an optional parameter, if it is not passed, the current measure context will be processed as the value.

The Result:

- Returns variance of <numeric expression> over the set <Set>.
- Var is calculated using the unbiased population formula (dividing by n-1).
- VarP is calculated using the biased population formula (dividing by n).

Correlation

- The "Correlation" function calculates the correlation coefficient of a pair of values (x, y).
- The correlation coefficient ranges from −1 to 1.

Interpretation:

- A value "1" implies that a linear equation describes the relationship between X and Y perfectly, with all data points lying on a line for which Y increases as X increases.
- A value of −1 implies that all data points lie on a line for which Y decreases as X increases.
- A value of 0 implies that there is no linear correlation between the variables.

Query#7.04:

Goal: Display correlation co-efficient for following combination for fiscal year 2007:

- Case #1: "Reseller Sales Amount" and "Reseller Tax Amount".
- Case #2: "Reseller Sales Amount" and "Customer Count".
- Case #3: "Internet Sales Amount" and "Customer Count".

Analysis:

Case#	X Value	Y Value	Descriptions
1	Reseller Sales Amount	Reseller Tax Amount	• In most cases, as X increases, Y value will increase. • Estimated value of the Correlation co-efficient will be close to 1. • Which means, X value is dependent on Y value.
2	Reseller Sales Amount	Customer Count	• "Customer Count" is the count for internet customers and is not related to "Reseller Sales Amount". • Estimated value of the Correlation co-efficient will be close to 0. • Which means, X value is independent on Y value.
3	Internet Sales Amount	Customer Count	• "Customer Count" is the count for internet customers and in most cases, "Internet Sales Amount" will increases as "Customer Count" increase. • Estimated value of the Correlation co-efficient will be close to 1.

Case#1: Correlation co-efficient between "Reseller Sales Amount" and "Reseller Tax Amount".

MDX

```
WITH
MEMBER [Measures].[The Correlation] AS
Correlation
  (
  DESCENDANTS
    (
    [Date].[Fiscal].[Fiscal Year].&[2007],
    [Date].[Fiscal].[Month]
    ),
  [Measures].[Reseller Sales Amount],
  [Measures].[Reseller Tax Amount]
  )
SELECT
  {
  [Measures].[Reseller Sales Amount],
  [Measures].[Reseller Tax Amount],
  [Measures].[The Correlation]
  } ON COLUMNS,
  {
  DESCENDANTS
    (
    [Date].[Fiscal].[Fiscal Year].&[2007],
    [Date].[Fiscal].[Month]
    )
  } ON ROWS
FROM
  [Adventure Works]
```

Result

	Reseller Sales Amount	Reseller Tax Amount	The Correlation
July 2006	$2,393,689.53	$191,495.16	1
August 2006	$3,601,190.71	$288,095.26	1
September 2006	$2,885,359.20	$230,828.74	1
October 2006	$1,802,154.21	$144,172.33	1
November 2006	$3,053,816.33	$244,305.30	1
December 2006	$2,185,213.21	$174,817.06	1
January 2007	$1,317,541.83	$105,403.34	1
February 2007	$2,384,846.59	$190,787.72	1
March 2007	$1,563,955.08	$125,116.40	1
April 2007	$1,865,278.43	$149,222.27	1
May 2007	$2,880,752.68	$230,460.21	1
June 2007	$1,987,872.71	$159,029.81	1

Case#2: Correlation co-efficient between "Reseller Sales Amount" and "Customer Count".

MDX

```
WITH
MEMBER [Measures].[The Correlation] AS
Correlation
  (
  DESCENDANTS
    (
    [Date].[Fiscal].[Fiscal Year].&[2007],
    [Date].[Fiscal].[Month]
    ),
  [Measures].[Reseller Sales Amount],
  [Measures].[Customer Count]
  )
SELECT
  {
  [Measures].[Reseller Sales Amount],
  [Measures].[Customer Count],
  [Measures].[The Correlation]
  } ON COLUMNS,
  {
  DESCENDANTS
    (
    [Date].[Fiscal].[Fiscal Year].&[2007],
    [Date].[Fiscal].[Month]
    )
  } ON ROWS
FROM
  [Adventure Works]
```

Result

	Reseller Sales Amount	Customer Count	The Correlation
July 2006	$2,393,689.53	253	-0.107243552764414
August 2006	$3,601,190.71	281	-0.107243552764414
September 2006	$2,885,359.20	198	-0.107243552764414
October 2006	$1,802,154.21	229	-0.107243552764414
November 2006	$3,053,816.33	193	-0.107243552764414
December 2006	$2,185,213.21	330	-0.107243552764414
January 2007	$1,317,541.83	244	-0.107243552764414
February 2007	$2,384,846.59	272	-0.107243552764414
March 2007	$1,563,955.08	272	-0.107243552764414
April 2007	$1,865,278.43	294	-0.107243552764414
May 2007	$2,880,752.68	335	-0.107243552764414
June 2007	$1,987,872.71	321	-0.107243552764414

Case#3: Correlation co-efficient between "Internet Sales Amount" and "Customer Count".

MDX

```
WITH
MEMBER [Measures].[The Correlation] AS
Correlation
  (
  DESCENDANTS
    (
    [Date].[Fiscal].[Fiscal Year].&[2007],
    [Date].[Fiscal].[Month]
    ),
  [Measures].[Internet Sales Amount],
  [Measures].[Customer Count]
  )
SELECT
  {
  [Measures].[Internet Sales Amount],
  [Measures].[Customer Count],
  [Measures].[The Correlation]
  } ON COLUMNS,
  {
  DESCENDANTS
    (
    [Date].[Fiscal].[Fiscal Year].&[2007],
    [Date].[Fiscal].[Month]
    )
  } ON ROWS
FROM
  [Adventure Works]
```

Result

	Internet Sales Amount	Customer Count	The Correlation
July 2006	$500,365.16	253	0.957811619811356
August 2006	$546,001.47	281	0.957811619811356
September 2006	$350,466.99	198	0.957811619811356
October 2006	$415,390.23	229	0.957811619811356
November 2006	$335,095.09	193	0.957811619811356
December 2006	$577,314.00	330	0.957811619811356
January 2007	$438,865.17	244	0.957811619811356
February 2007	$489,090.34	272	0.957811619811356
March 2007	$485,574.79	272	0.957811619811356
April 2007	$506,399.27	294	0.957811619811356
May 2007	$562,772.56	335	0.957811619811356
June 2007	$554,799.23	321	0.957811619811356

Correlation (<Set>, <Number1> [, <Number2>])

<Set>:

- A valid set. For example, all months of fiscal year 2007.
  Descendants ([Date].[Fiscal].[Fiscal Year].&[2007], [Date].[Fiscal].[Month])

<Number1>:

- A valid numeric expression.

<Number2>:

- A valid numeric expression.
- This is an optional parameter, if it is not passed, the current measure context will be processed as the value.

The Result:

- Returns Correlation co-efficient of the pair (<Number1>,<Number2>) over the set <Set>.

Covariance/CovarianceN

- Covariance is a measure of how much two variables x and y change together.
- The unit of covariance is different from the unit of data, so magnitude of covariance may not have an obvious interpretation.
- The difference between Covariance and CovarianceN are:
  - Covariance is calculated using the unbiased population formula (dividing by the number of x-y pairs, then subtracting 1).
  - CovarianceN is calculated using the biased population formula (dividing by the number of x-y pairs).

Interpretation:

- A positive value means, X is directly proportionate to Y.
- A negative value means, X is inversely proportional to Y.

Query#7.05:

Goal:

Case # 1:

Display covariance between "Reseller Sales Amount" and "Reseller Tax Amount" for each month of fiscal year 2007

Case # 2:

Display covariance between "Reseller Sales Amount" and "Reseller Average Unit Price" for each month of fiscal year 2007

Case#1: Covariance between "Reseller Sales Amount" and "Reseller Tax Amount".

Strategy:

- Display "Reseller Sales Amount" and "Reseller Tax Amount" for each month of fiscal year 2007. This data may not be required for the query, but will help us to compare the values.
- Create a calculated member [Measures].[The Covariance] to show the covariance. The value will be repeated for all rows.

MDX

```
WITH
MEMBER [Measures].[The Covariance] AS
Covariance
  (
  DESCENDANTS
    (
    [Date].[Fiscal].[Fiscal Year].&[2007],
    [Date].[Fiscal].[Month]
    ),
  [Measures].[Reseller Sales Amount],
  [Measures].[Reseller Tax Amount]
  )
SELECT
  {
  [Measures].[Reseller Sales Amount],
  [Measures].[Reseller Tax Amount],
  [Measures].[The Covariance]
  } ON COLUMNS,
  {
  ORDER
    (
    DESCENDANTS
      (
      [Date].[Fiscal].[Fiscal Year].&[2007],
      [Date].[Fiscal].[Month]
      ),
    [Measures].[Reseller Sales Amount],
    BASC
    )
  } ON ROWS
FROM
  [Adventure Works]
```

Result

	Reseller Sales Amount	Reseller Tax Amount	The Covariance
January 2007	$1,317,541.83	$105,403.34	33353522484.6274
March 2007	$1,563,955.08	$125,116.40	33353522484.6274
October 2006	$1,802,154.21	$144,172.33	33353522484.6274
April 2007	$1,865,278.43	$149,222.27	33353522484.6274
June 2007	$1,987,872.71	$159,029.81	33353522484.6274
December 2006	$2,185,213.21	$174,817.06	33353522484.6274
February 2007	$2,384,846.59	$190,787.72	33353522484.6274
July 2006	$2,393,689.53	$191,495.16	33353522484.6274
May 2007	$2,880,752.68	$230,460.21	33353522484.6274
September 2006	$2,885,359.20	$230,828.74	33353522484.6274
November 2006	$3,053,816.33	$244,305.30	33353522484.6274
August 2006	$3,601,190.71	$288,095.26	33353522484.6274

Case#2: Covariance between "Reseller Sales Amount" and "Reseller Average Unit Price".

Strategy:

- Display "Reseller Sales Amount" and "Reseller Average Unit Price" for all months of fiscal year 2007.
- Create a calculated member [Measures].[The Covariance] to show the covariance. The value will be repeated for all rows.

MDX

```
WITH
MEMBER [Measures].[The Covariance] AS
Covariance
  (
  DESCENDANTS
    (
    [Date].[Fiscal].[Fiscal Year].&[2007],
    [Date].[Fiscal].[Month]
    ),
  [Measures].[Reseller Sales Amount],
  [Measures].[Reseller Average Unit Price]
  )

SELECT
  {
  [Measures].[Reseller Sales Amount],
  [Measures].[Reseller Average Unit Price],
  [Measures].[The Covariance]
  } ON COLUMNS,
  {
  ORDER
    (
    DESCENDANTS
      (
      [Date].[Fiscal].[Fiscal Year].&[2007],
      [Date].[Fiscal].[Month]
      ),
    [Measures].[Reseller Sales Amount],
    BASC
    )
  } ON ROWS
FROM
  [Adventure Works]
```

Result

	Reseller Sales Amount	Reseller Average Unit Price	The Covariance
January 2007	$1,317,541.83	$428.87	-7044459.20523894
March 2007	$1,563,955.08	$450.03	-7044459.20523894
October 2006	$1,802,154.21	$382.00	-7044459.20523894
April 2007	$1,865,278.43	$369.78	-7044459.20523894
June 2007	$1,987,872.71	$390.32	-7044459.20523894
December 2006	$2,185,213.21	$407.08	-7044459.20523894
February 2007	$2,384,846.59	$488.76	-7044459.20523894
July 2006	$2,393,689.53	$350.74	-7044459.20523894
May 2007	$2,880,752.68	$400.51	-7044459.20523894
September 2006	$2,885,359.20	$365.30	-7044459.20523894
November 2006	$3,053,816.33	$412.48	-7044459.20523894
August 2006	$3,601,190.71	$372.75	-7044459.20523894

Analysis:

Case#	X Value	Y Value	Descriptions
1	Reseller Sales Amount	Reseller Tax Amount	• In most cases, as "Reseller Sales Amount" increases, "Reseller Tax Amount" value will increase. • Expected value for Covariance will be a positive number. • Which means, X value is directly proportional to Y value.
2	Reseller Sales Amount	Reseller Average Unit Price	• In most cases, "Reseller Average Unit Price" decreases as "Reseller Sales Amount" increases. • Expected value for covariance will be a negative number. • Which means, X value is inversely proportional to Y value.

Covariance (<Set>, <Number_y> [, <Number_x>])
CovarianceN (<Set>, <Number_y> [, <Number_x>])

<Set>:

- A valid set. For example, all months of fiscal year 2007.
  Descendants ([Date].[Fiscal].[Fiscal Year].&[2007], [Date].[Fiscal].[Month])

<Number_y>:

- Valid numeric expression, represents y-axis.

<Number_x>:

- A valid numeric expression, represents the x-axis.
- This is an optional parameter, if it is not passed, the current measure context will be processed as the value.

The Result:

- Returns covariance of the pair (<Number_x>, <Number_y>) over the set <Set>.
- **Covariance** is calculated using the unbiased population formula (dividing the number of x-y pairs, then subtracting 1).
- **CovarianceN** is calculated using the biased population formula (dividing by the number of x-y pairs).

LinRegIntercept and LinRegSlope

- Linear regression calculates the equation of a regression line, y = ax + b, "a" is the slope and "b" is the intercept of the straight line.
- From a set of points, the **LinRegIntercept** function returns the intercept of the regression line (b in the previous equation).
  Set of points means, values of x and y i.e. (x1, y1), (x2, y2), (x3, y3) etc.
- From a set of points, the **LinRegSlope** function returns the slope of the regression line ("a" in the previous equation). Means, a = tan (angle between the line and x-axis)

Goal: Display "Sales Amount Quota" and "Reseller Sales Amount" for each month of fiscal year 2007 and create a graph by plotting "Sales Amount Quota" in x-axis and "Reseller Sales Amount" on y-axis.

MDX

```
SELECT
  {
  [Measures].[Sales Amount Quota],
  [Measures].[Reseller Sales Amount]
  } ON COLUMNS,
  {
  DESCENDANTS
    (
    [Date].[Fiscal].[Fiscal Year].&[2007],
    [Date].[Fiscal].[Month]
    )
  } ON ROWS
FROM
  [Adventure Works]
```

Result

	Sales Amount Quota	Reseller Sales Amount
July 2006	1614479.08066331	$2,393,689.53
August 2006	5075787.81554917	$3,601,190.71
September 2006	3846733.10378752	$2,885,359.20
October 2006	1500515.92766341	$1,802,154.21
November 2006	4128467.02932304	$3,053,816.33
December 2006	3025017.04301355	$2,185,213.21
January 2007	1036241.394153	$1,317,541.83
February 2007	2762067.11604435	$2,384,846.59
March 2007	2114691.48980266	$1,563,955.08
April 2007	1708699.92263403	$1,865,278.43
May 2007	4391482.39081395	$2,880,752.68
June 2007	1938817.68655201	$1,987,872.71

Before plotting this data, scale down all data by dividing by 100000 and create two calculated members:

- [Measures].[The RSA] for [Measures].[Reseller Sales Amount].
- [Measures].[The SAQ] for [Measures].[Sales Amount Quota].

MDX

```
WITH
MEMBER [Measures].[The SAQ] AS
Int ([Measures].[Sales Amount Quota]/100000)
MEMBER [Measures].[The RSA] AS
Int ([Measures].[Reseller Sales Amount]/100000)
SELECT
  {
  [Measures].[The SAQ],
  [Measures].[The RSA]
  } ON COLUMNS,
  {
  ORDER
    (
    DESCENDANTS
      (
      [Date].[Fiscal].[Fiscal Year].&[2007],
      [Date].[Fiscal].[Month]
      ),
    [Measures].[The SAQ]
    )
  } ON ROWS
FROM
  [Adventure Works]
```

Result

	The SAQ	The RSA
January 2007	10	13
March 2007	21	15
February 2007	27	23
April 2007	17	18
June 2007	19	19
May 2007	43	28
October 2006	15	18
December 2006	30	21
November 2006	41	30
July 2006	16	23
September 2006	38	28
August 2006	50	36

Notes:

- Please note that "The RSA" increases as "The SAQ" increases.
- Plot "The SAQ" on x-axis and "The RSA" on y-axis using SQL Server Reporting Services.

Figure 7-1: "Reseller Sales Amount" versus "Sales Amount Quota" graph.

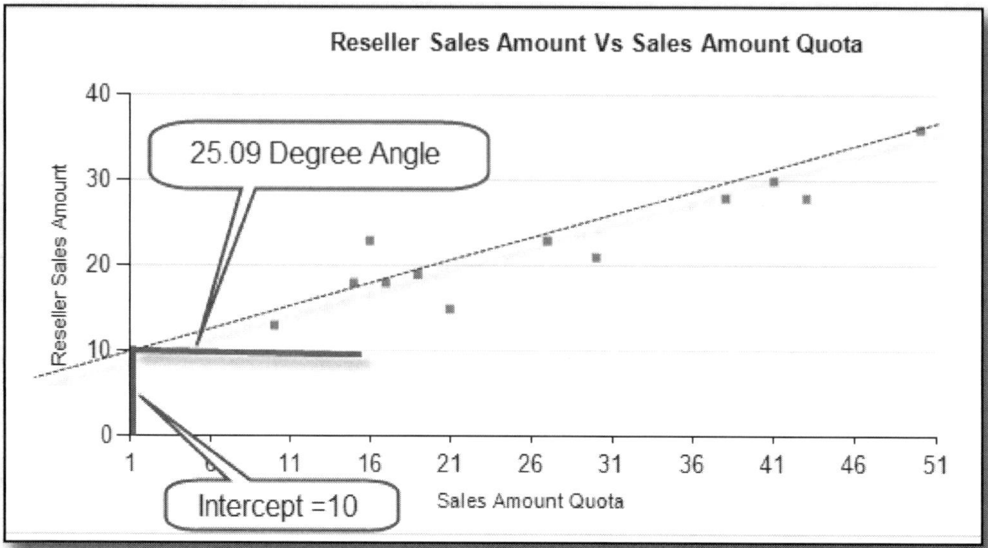

After plotting the graph, you can find "intercept" and "slope" of the line. You can also find slope and intercept using LinRegslope and LinRegIntercept function, as follows:

MDX	WITH
	MEMBER [Measures].[The Intercept] AS
	Int
	  (
	  LinRegIntercept
	    (
	    DESCENDANTS
	      (
	      [Date].[Fiscal].[Fiscal Year].&[2007],
	      [Date].[Fiscal].[Month]
	      ),
	    [Measures].[Reseller Sales Amount],
	    [Measures].[Sales Amount Quota]
	    )/100000
	  )
	-- continued in next page..

MDX

```
MEMBER [Measures].[The Slope] AS
LinRegSlope
  (
  DESCENDANTS
    (
    [Date].[Fiscal].[Fiscal Year].&[2007],
    [Date].[Fiscal].[Month]
    ),
  [Measures].[Reseller Sales Amount],
  [Measures].[Sales Amount Quota]
  )
SELECT
  {
  [Measures].[The Intercept],
  [Measures].[The Slope]
  } ON COLUMNS
FROM
  [Adventure Works]
```

Result

The Intercept	The Slope
10	0.467359027644877

Notes:

- "The intercept" is the intercept on the y-axis as shown in the Figure 7-1.
- "The slope" = 0.47 = tan(25.09), means the line makes approximately 25.09 degree with x-axis.

LinRegIntercept (<Set>, <Number_y> [, <Number_x>])
LinRegSlope (<Set>, <Number_y> [, <Number_x>])

<Set>:

- A valid set. For example, all months of fiscal year 2007.

  Descendants ([Date].[Fiscal].[Fiscal Year].&[2007], [Date].[Fiscal].[Month])

<Number_y>:

- A valid numeric expression.

<Number_x>:

- A valid numeric expression.
- This is an optional parameter, if it is not passed, the current measure context will be processed as the value.

The Result:

For the regression line, y = ax + b

- LinRegIntercept function returns the intercept of the regression line ("b" from above equation).
- LinRegSlope function returns the slope of the regression line ("a" from above equation).

LinRegPoint

- Linear regression calculates the equation of a regression line y = ax + b, "a" is slope and "b" is the intercept.
- LinRegPoint predicts the linear regression of a set, and returns the variance associated with the regression line, y = ax + b.

Query#7.06:

Goal: Given

- "Sales Amount Quota" and "Reseller Sales Amount" for each month of fiscal year 2007.
- "Sales Amount Quota" for each month of fiscal year 2008.

Predict "Reseller Sales Amount" for each month of fiscal year 2008.

Strategy:

- Create a calculated member [Measures].[The Predicted RSA] using LinRegPoint function.
- There are four parameters in LinRegPoint function:
  - <new_x>: Sales Amount Quota for 2008.
  - <set>: All months of fiscal year 2007.
  - <old_y>: Reseller Sales Amount for 2007.
  - <old_x>: Sales Amount Quota for 2007.
- The output will be new_y, which is the predicted value for Reseller Sales Amount for 2008.

MDX	Result

WITH
MEMBER [Measures].[The Predicted RSA] AS
LinRegPoint
  (
  [Measures].[Sales Amount Quota],
  DESCENDANTS
    (
    [Date].[Fiscal].[Fiscal Year].&[2007],
    [Date].[Fiscal].[Month]
    ),
  [Measures].[Reseller Sales Amount],
  [Measures].[Sales Amount Quota]
  ), FORMAT_STRING="Currency"
 	
MEMBER [Measures].[The SAQ] AS
[Measures].[Sales Amount Quota],
FORMAT_STRING="Currency"
-- Continued to the next page	

MDX

```
SELECT
  {
  [Measures].[The SAQ],
  [Measures].[The Predicted RSA]
  } ON COLUMNS,
  {
  DESCENDANTS
    (
    [Date].[Fiscal].[Fiscal Year].&[2008],
    [Date].[Fiscal].[Month]
    )
  } ON ROWS
FROM
  [Adventure Works]
```

Result

	The SAQ	The Predicted RSA
July 2007	$3,701,762.60	$2,766,987.97
August 2007	$5,569,123.72	$3,641,576.97
September 2007	$4,462,113.68	$3,123,102.64
October 2007	$2,840,219.20	$2,363,479.31
November 2007	$4,812,855.47	$3,287,374.52
December 2007	$3,443,925.32	$2,646,228.44
January 2008	$2,014,211.43	$1,976,613.96
February 2008	$3,645,869.26	$2,740,810.01
March 2008	$2,390,919.31	$2,153,047.19
April 2008	$2,869,423.12	$2,377,157.12
May 2008	$4,431,562.70	$3,108,793.92
June 2008	$3,058,014.18	$2,465,484.80

Analysis:

- In LinRegPoint function:
  - <New_x> = "Sales Amount Quota" for each month of fiscal year 2008, because the rows of the main MDX query list all months of fiscal year 2008.
  - <Old_y> = "Reseller Sales Amount" for 2007, because second parameter <Set> is all months of fiscal year 2007.
  - <Old_x> = "Sales Amount Quota" for 2007, because second parameter <Set> is all months of fiscal year 2007.
- <New_y> is calculated for each value of <New_x>.
- Means, [Measures].[The Predicted RSA] is calculated for each value of "Sales Amount Quota" for each month of fiscal year 2008.

LinRegPoint (<New_x>, <Set>, <Old_y> [,<Old_x>])

<New_x>:

- A valid numeric expression.

<Set>:

- A valid set, for which <New_x> will be calculated. For example, all months of fiscal year 2008.

  Descendants ([Date].[Fiscal].[Fiscal Year].&[2008], [Date].[Fiscal].[Month])

<Old_y>:

- A valid numeric expression applied to set <Set>.

<Old_x>:

- A valid numeric expression applied to set <Set>. This is an optional parameter, if it is not passed, the current measure context will be processed as the value.

The Result :

- LinRegPoint function predicts <New_y> based on <Set>, <Old_x> and <Old_y>.

LinRegR2

- Linear regression calculates the equation of a regression line.
  y = ax + b, "a" is slope and "b" is the intercept.
- LinRegR2 function returns the statistical R2 (co-efficient of determination)that describes the fit of the linear equation to the points.

Query#7.07:

Goal: Find statistical R2 associated with the regression line represented by for "Sales Amount Quota" and "Reseller Sales Amount" for each month of fiscal year 2007.

MDX

```
WITH
MEMBER [Measures].[The R2] AS
LinRegR2
 (
 DESCENDANTS
  (
  [Date].[Fiscal].[Fiscal Year].&[2007],
  [Date].[Fiscal].[Month]
  ),
 [Measures].[Reseller Sales Amount],
 [Measures].[Sales Amount Quota]
 )
SELECT
  {
  [Measures].[The R2]
  } ON COLUMNS
FROM
        [Adventure Works]
```

Result

The R2
0.842450032943276

LinRegR2 **(<Set>, <Number_y> [, <Number_x>])**

<Set>:

- A valid set. For example, all months of fiscal year 2007.
  Descendants ([Date].[Fiscal].[Fiscal Year].&[2007], [Date].[Fiscal].[Month])

<Number_y>:

- A valid numeric expression.

<Number_x>:

- A valid numeric expression. This is an optional parameter, if it is not passed, the current measure context will be processed as the value.

The Result:

- LinRegR2 function returns statistical R2 of the regression line.

LinRegVariance

- Linear regression calculates the equation of a regression line
  y = ax + b, "a" is slope and "b" is the intercept.
- LinRegVariance function returns the variance associated with the linear equation.

Query#7.08:

Goal: Find variance associated with the regression line represented by for "Sales Amount Quota" and "Reseller Sales Amount" for all months of fiscal year 2007.

MDX

```
WITH
MEMBER [Measures].[The Variance] AS
LinRegVariance
  (
  DESCENDANTS
    (
    [Date].[Fiscal].[Fiscal Year].&[2007],
    [Date].[Fiscal].[Month]
    ),
  [Measures].[Reseller Sales Amount],
  [Measures].[Sales Amount Quota]
  )
SELECT
  {
  [Measures].[The Variance]
  } ON COLUMNS
FROM
  [Adventure Works]
```

Result

The Variance
78822694368.5186

LinRegVariance (<Set>, <Number_y> [, <Number_x>])

<Set>:

- A valid set. For example, all months of fiscal year 2007.
  Descendants ([Date].[Fiscal].[Fiscal Year].&[2003], [Date].[Fiscal].[Month])

<Number_y>:

- A valid numeric expression.

<Number_x>:

- A valid numeric expression.This is an optional parameter, if it is not passed, the current measure context will be proccessed.

The Result:

- LinRegVariance function returns variance associated with the regression line.

EXERCISES

Exercise 7.1: Find the weekly median of "Internet Order Quantity" for fiscal year 2008.

Exercise 7.2: Find weekly covariance of "Internet Sales Amount" and "Internet Tax Amount" for fiscal year 2008.

Exercise 7.3: Assume "Internet Sales Amount" is directy proportional to "Internet Tax Amount"and form linear regression equation y = mx + c, Given

- "Internet Sales Amount" and "Internet Tax Amount" for each week of fiscal year 2007.
- "Internet Sales Amount" for each week of fiscal year 2008.

Predict "Internet Tax Amount" for each week of fiscal year 2008.

Chapter 8: MDX Scripting Statements

Agenda

Calculate
Scope
This
Freeze
If

Exercises

MDX scripting statements are used in "Calculations" of a cube or in a user session. Though there are only five functions in this chapter, these functions are frequently used and very important for cube development.

"Calculations" of a cube can only be edited by using "SQL Server Data Tools" (formerly known as "Business Intelligence Development Studio") in either online or offline mode. To edit calculations of a cube, open the cube in SQL Server Data Tools and go to the "Calculations" tab. You can view calculations of a cube in either "Form View" or "Script View".

Calculated members and named sets that are defined in "Calculations" of a cube are in global scope of the cube and can be accessed by any session connected to the cube. Re-usability of global calculated members qualified them to be a part of global cache and improve performance of MDX queries.

"Calculate" is the first statement in the "Calculations" of a cube and enables calculations. Without the "Calculate" statement, all measures of the cube will return null.

The "Scope" statement limits MDX code applied to a subcube instead of applying to the whole cube. "This" statement represents current subcube within a scope statement and is normally used in the left side of a statement. "Freeze" statement locks cell values of a specified subcube to their current values.

Calculate

- "Calculate" is the first statement in "Calculations" of a cube.
- "Calculate" tells each cell in the cube to aggregate from lower granularity cells.
- You should not remove the "Calculate;" statement from the first line of "Calculations" of a cube. If you remove, all measures will return as null.

Goal: Open "Calculations" of the cube [Adventure Works].

Steps:

1 Open SQL Server Data Tools.
2 Open SSAS database "AdventureWorksDW2012Multidimensional-EE".
3 In solution explorer, double-click on cube "Adventure Works" in "Cubes" folder.
4 Click on "Calculations" tab.
5 Click on "Script View" button.

Figure 8-1: Open "Calculations" tab of the cube "Adventure Works".

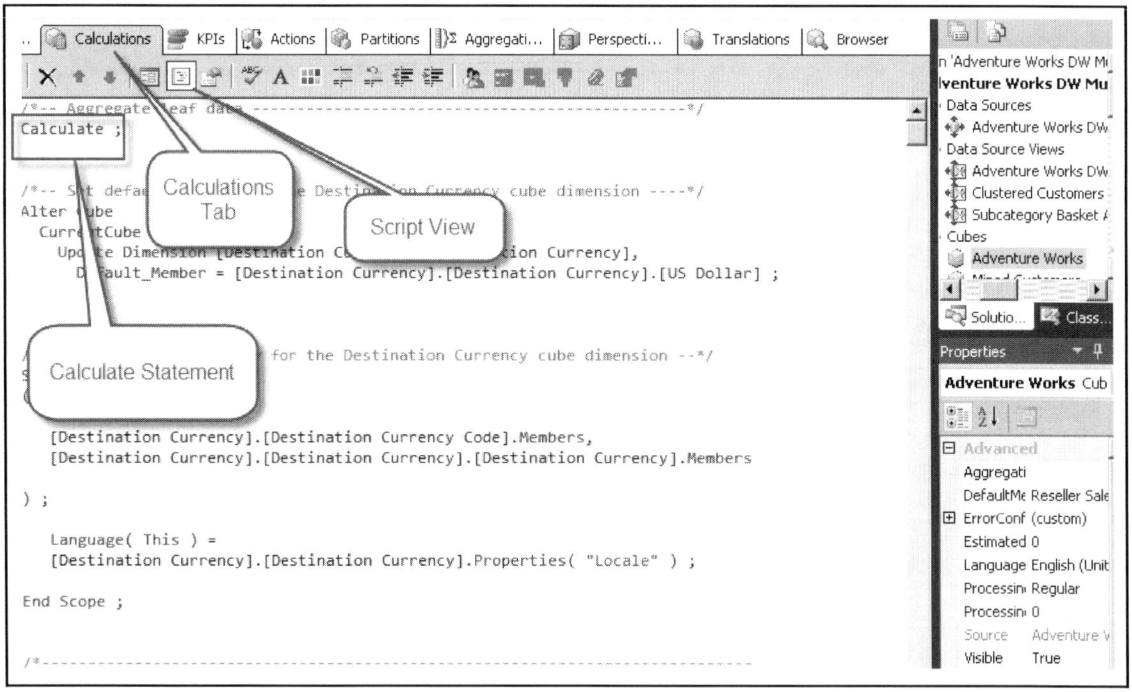

Goal: Demonstrate the result of removing "Calculate" statement from "Calculations" of the cube "Adventure Works".

Steps:

1 Open SQL Server Management Studio and find "Reseller Sales Amount" for all product categories.

MDX

```
SELECT
  {
  [Measures].[Reseller Sales Amount]
  } ON COLUMNS,
  {
  [Product].[Product Categories].[Category]
  } ON ROWS
FROM
  [Adventure Works]
```

Result

	Reseller Sales Amount
Accessories	$571,257.55
Bikes	$66,012,957.84
Clothing	$1,772,148.94
Components	$11,675,796.11

2 Open SQL Server Data Tools.

3 Open SSAS database "AdventureWorksDW2012Multidimensional-EE".

4 Click on "Calculations" tab.

5 Click on "Script View" button.

6 Comment the first line with two dashes:
--Calculate;

7 Save the project which will save the "Calculations of the cube" in the server.
Note: for calculations, **you do not need to process the cube** if you open cube online.

8 Re-run the last MDX query.

MDX

```
SELECT
  {
  [Measures].[Reseller Sales Amount]
  } ON COLUMNS,
  {
  [Product].[Product Categories].[Category]
  } ON ROWS
FROM
  [Adventure Works]
```

Result

	Reseller Sales Amount
Accessories	(null)
Bikes	(null)
Clothing	(null)
Components	(null)

This demonstrates that, you should not remove "Calculate" statement from the first line of a cube's MDX script. If you remove, all aggregations will show as null.

9 Now, un-comment the first line:
Calculate;

10 Save the project and that will save the project in the server.

Scope

- If you want to run an MDX statement to a part of a cube and not the whole cube, you can use "Scope" statement to define your scope.

Goal: Find "Reseller Sales Amount" for each product category and for each year.

MDX

```
SELECT
  {
  [Product].[Product Categories].[Category]
  } ON COLUMNS,
  {
  [Date].[Fiscal].[Fiscal Year]
  } ON ROWS
FROM
  [Adventure Works]
WHERE
  [Measures].[Reseller Sales Amount]
```

Result

	Accessories	Bikes	Clothing	Components
FY 2005	(null)	(null)	(null)	(null)
FY 2006	$36,814.85	$15,018,534.07	$66,327.53	$1,166,765.32
FY 2007	$124,433.35	$22,417,419.69	$750,716.33	$4,629,101.14
FY 2008	$410,049.73	$28,866,427.79	$960,796.98	$6,003,210.20
FY 2009	(null)	(null)	(null)	(null)
FY 2010	(null)	(null)	(null)	(null)
FY 2011	(null)	(null)	(null)	(null)

Query#8.01:

Goal: In the last query, there is no "Reseller Sales Amount" for fiscal year 2009. Create MDX statements in "Calculations" of the cube such that, "Reseller Sales Amount" for fiscal year 2009 is 110% of "Reseller Sales Amount" for fiscal year 2008.

To identify "Reseller Sales Amount" for fiscal year 2009, you can use following scope statement:

```
SCOPE
  (
  [Measures].[Reseller Sales Amount],
  [Date].[Fiscal].[Fiscal Year].&[2009]
  );
```

And the action,

```
([Measures].[Reseller Sales Amount], [Date].[Fiscal].[Fiscal Year].&[2009])
  = ([Measures].[Reseller Sales Amount], [Date].[Fiscal].[Fiscal Year].&[2008] ) *1.10
```

This means,
[Reseller Sales Amount] of FY 2009 = 110% of [Reseller Sales Amount] of FY 2008.

Steps:

1 Open SQL Server Data Tools.
2 Open SSAS database "AdventureWorksDW2012Multidimensional-EE".
3 Click on "Calculations" tab and click on "Script View" button.
4 Add following script at the end of MDX script and save.

MDX SCRIPT

```
-- Scope
----------------------------------------------------------------
SCOPE
  (
  [Measures].[Reseller Sales Amount],
  [Date].[Fiscal].[Fiscal Year].&[2009]
  );
-- Action
----------------------------------------------------------------
 (
 [Measures].[Reseller Sales Amount],
 [Date].[Fiscal].[Fiscal Year].&[2009]
 ) =
 (
 [Measures].[Reseller Sales Amount],
 [Date].[Fiscal].[Fiscal Year].&[2008]
 ) *1.10;
----------------------------------------------------------------
END SCOPE;
```

The last query will now show "Reseller Sales Amount" for FY 2009 as 110% of "Reseller Sales Amount" for FY 2008 .

MDX

```
SELECT
  {
  [Product].[Product Categories].[Category]
  } ON COLUMNS,
  {
  [Date].[Fiscal].[Fiscal Year]
  } ON ROWS
FROM
  [Adventure Works]
WHERE
  [Measures].[Reseller Sales Amount]
```

Result

	Accessories	Bikes	Clothing	Components
FY 2005	(null)	(null)	(null)	(null)
FY 2006	$36,814.85	$15,018,534.07	$66,327.53	$1,166,765.32
FY 2007	$124,433.35	$22,417,419.69	$750,716.33	$4,629,101.14
FY 2008	$410,049.73	$28,866,427.79	$960,796.98	$6,003,210.20
FY 2009	$451,054.70	$31,753,070.57	$1,056,876.67	$6,603,531.22
FY 2010	(null)	(null)	(null)	(null)
FY 2011	(null)	(null)	(null)	(null)

Scope (<SubCube>);
<Mdx Statements>;
End Scope;

<SubCube>:

- A valid subcube. For example, ([Date].[Fiscal].[Fiscal Year].&[2009]).

<Mdx Statements>:

- Valid mdx statements.

The Result:

- Limit the <Mdx Statements> to the <SubCube>.

This

- "This" represents current subcube.
- This function must be used in the left side of an assignment.

In the last MDX script, the left side of "Action" of the last MDX script, represents subcube of the Scope statement, and can be replaced by "This":

"This" equals

```
(
[Measures].[Reseller Sales Amount],
[Date].[Fiscal].[Fiscal Year].&[2009]
)
```

MDX SCRIPT

```
-- Scope
-------------------------------------------------------------
SCOPE
  (
  [Measures].[Reseller Sales Amount],
  [Date].[Fiscal].[Fiscal Year].&[2009]
  );
-- Action
-----------------------------------------------------------
THIS =
  (
  [Measures].[Reseller Sales Amount],
  [Date].[Fiscal].[Fiscal Year].&[2008]
  ) * 1.10;
-----------------------------------------------------------
END SCOPE;
```

In the above statement,

```
This =
    (
    [Measures].[Reseller Sales Amount],
    [Date].[Fiscal].[Fiscal Year].&[2008]
    ) *1.10;
```

You can remove [Measures].[Reseller Sales Amount] from above expression,
This = ([Date].[Fiscal].[Fiscal Year].&[2008]) * 1.10;

This means, in the above expression that the current measure will be evaluated. The measure in the scope statement is [Measures].[Reseller Sales Amount] and will be treated as the current measure.

The final MDX script is:

MDX SCRIPT

```
-- Scope
----------------------------------------------------------------------
SCOPE
  (
  [Measures].[Reseller Sales Amount],
  [Date].[Fiscal].[Fiscal Year].&[2009]
  );
-- Action
----------------------------------------------------------------------
THIS = ([Date].[Fiscal].[Fiscal Year].&[2008]) * 1.10;
----------------------------------------------------------------------
END SCOPE;
```

It is a good practice to always use "This" to avoid "out of context change". For example, following scope statement is for FY 2009:

```
Scope
    (
    [Measures].[Reseller Sales Amount],
    [Date].[Fiscal].[Fiscal Year].&[2009]
    );
```

The "Scope" statement is used to update "Members" which are in scope. If you do not use "This" statement, you should be able to change members in "out of context change".

This MDX script modifies data out of context:

MDX SCRIPT

```
-- Scope
----------------------------------------------------------------------
SCOPE
   (
   [Measures].[Reseller Sales Amount],
   [Date].[Fiscal].[Fiscal Year].&[2009]
   );
-- Action
----------------------------------------------------------------------
  (
  [Measures].[Reseller Sales Amount],
  [Date].[Fiscal].[Fiscal Year].&[2010]
  ) = ([Date].[Fiscal].[Fiscal Year].&[2008]) *1.10;
----------------------------------------------------------------------
END SCOPE;
```

Inspect the following query to see what has been changed,

MDX

```
SELECT
   {
   [Product].[Product Categories].[Category]
   } ON COLUMNS,
   {
   [Date].[Fiscal].[Fiscal Year]
   } ON ROWS
FROM
   [Adventure Works]
WHERE
   [Measures].[Reseller Sales Amount]
```

Result

	Accessories	Bikes	Clothing	Components
FY 2005	(null)	(null)	(null)	(null)
FY 2006	$36,814.85	$15,018,534.07	$66,327.53	$1,166,765.32
FY 2007	$124,433.35	$22,417,419.69	$750,716.33	$4,629,101.14
FY 2008	$410,049.73	$28,866,427.79	$960,796.98	$6,003,210.20
FY 2009	(null)	(null)	(null)	(null)
FY 2010	$451,054.70	$31,753,070.57	$1,056,876.67	$6,603,531.22
FY 2011	(null)	(null)	(null)	(null)

Notes:

- All "Reseller Sales Amount" values for fiscal year 2009 are null.
- All "Reseller Sales Amount" values for fiscal year 2010 are 110% of corresponding values in fiscal year 2008.
- Though the scope is defined for "Reseller Sales Amount of FY 2009" ,the assignment within "Scope" was an "out of context" change of "Reseller Sales Amount" for FY 2010.
- To avoid out of context changes, use "This".

Query#8.02:

Goal: Modify the last scope statement to create all measures for fiscal year 2009 as 110% of corresponding measure for fiscal year 2008.

Modify the last scope statement and use "This", as follows:

MDX SCRIPT

```
-- Scope
------------------------------------------------------------------------
SCOPE
  (
  [Measures].[Reseller Sales Amount],
  [Date].[Fiscal].[Fiscal Year].&[2009]
  );
-- Action
------------------------------------------------------------------------
THIS = ([Date].[Fiscal].[Fiscal Year].&[2008] ) *1.10;
------------------------------------------------------------------------
END SCOPE;
```

Inspect the following query and note that:

- Only one measure "Reseller Sales Amount" has value for FY 2009.
- The other two measures, "Reseller Order Quantity" and "Reseller Tax Amount" is null for FY 2009.

MDX

```
SELECT
  {
  [Measures].[Reseller Sales Amount],
  [Measures].[Reseller Order Quantity],
  [Measures].[Reseller Tax Amount]
  } ON COLUMNS,
  {
  [Date].[Fiscal].[Fiscal Year]
  } ON ROWS
FROM
  [Adventure Works]
```

Result

	Reseller Sales Amount	Reseller Order Quantity	Reseller Tax Amount
FY 2005	(null)	(null)	(null)
FY 2006	$16,288,441.77	21,890	$1,303,075.29
FY 2007	$27,921,670.52	78,959	$2,233,733.61
FY 2008	$36,240,484.70	113,529	$2,899,238.71
FY 2009	$39,864,533.17	(null)	(null)
FY 2010	(null)	(null)	(null)
FY 2011	(null)	(null)	(null)

To implement all measures for fiscal year 2009 as 110% of corresponding measure for fiscal year 2008, remove [Measures].[Reseller Sales Amount] from the scope statement, as shown below:

MDX SCRIPT

```
-- Scope
-----------------------------------------------------------------------
SCOPE
  (
  [Date].[Fiscal].[Fiscal Year].&[2009]
  );
-- Action
-----------------------------------------------------------------------
THIS = ([Date].[Fiscal].[Fiscal Year].&[2008]) *1.10;
-----------------------------------------------------------------------
END SCOPE;
```

Notes:

- ([Measures].[Reseller Sales Amount], [Date].[Fiscal].[Fiscal Year].&[2009]) means "Reseller Sales Amount" of FY 2009.
- ([Date].[Fiscal].[Fiscal Year].&[2009]) means all measures of FY 2009.

The result of the last query will now show all other measures:

MDX

```
SELECT
  {
  [Measures].[Reseller Sales Amount],
  [Measures].[Reseller Order Quantity],
  [Measures].[Reseller Tax Amount]
  } ON COLUMNS,
  {
  [Date].[Fiscal].[Fiscal Year]
  } ON ROWS
FROM
  [Adventure Works]
```

Result

	Reseller Sales Amount	Reseller Order Quantity	Reseller Tax Amount
FY 2005	(null)	(null)	(null)
FY 2006	$16,288,441.77	21,890	$1,303,075.29
FY 2007	$27,921,670.52	78,959	$2,233,733.61
FY 2008	$36,240,484.70	113,529	$2,899,238.71
FY 2009	$39,864,533.17	124,882	$3,189,162.58
FY 2010	(null)	(null)	(null)
FY 2011	(null)	(null)	(null)

Query#8.03:

Goal: Remove the last scope statement from calculations of the cube; create MDX statements to create all measures for fiscal year 2009 to be 110% of corresponding measure for fiscal year 2008 without using any scope statement.

Steps:

1. Remove the last scope statement from mdx script.
2. Add following statements in the mdx script of the cube:

MDX SCRIPT

```
([Date].[Fiscal].[Fiscal Year].&[2009]) = ([Date].[Fiscal].[Fiscal Year].&[2008] ) * 1.10;
```

3 Verify the result by running last query:

MDX

```
SELECT
  {
  [Measures].[Reseller Sales Amount],
  [Measures].[Reseller Order Quantity],
  [Measures].[Reseller Tax Amount]
  } ON COLUMNS,
  {
  [Date].[Fiscal].[Fiscal Year]
  } ON ROWS
FROM
  [Adventure Works]
```

Result

	Reseller Sales Amount	Reseller Order Quantity	Reseller Tax Amount
FY 2005	(null)	(null)	(null)
FY 2006	$16,288,441.77	21,890	$1,303,075.29
FY 2007	$27,921,670.52	78,959	$2,233,733.61
FY 2008	$36,240,484.70	113,529	$2,899,238.71
FY 2009	$39,864,533.17	124,882	$3,189,162.58
FY 2010	(null)	(null)	(null)
FY 2011	(null)	(null)	(null)

Analysis:

- The left side of the assignment is all measures of fiscal year 2009.
- The above MDX script is equivalent to following scope statement.

MDX SCRIPT

```
-- Scope
------------------------------------------------------------------------
SCOPE
  (
  [Date].[Fiscal].[Fiscal Year].&[2009]
  );
-- Action
------------------------------------------------------------------------
THIS = ([Date].[Fiscal].[Fiscal Year].&[2008]) * 1.10;
------------------------------------------------------------------------
END SCOPE;
```

The scope statement,

```
SCOPE
    (
    [Date].[Fiscal].[Fiscal Year].&[2009]
    );
```

Means the subcube includes all members for fiscal year 2009 in "Year" level but not in "Semester" level or any other lower level. Inspect following queries:

For Year level

```
SELECT
  {
  [Measures].[Reseller Sales Amount],
  [Measures].[Reseller Order Quantity],
  [Measures].[Reseller Tax Amount]
  } ON COLUMNS,
  {
  [Date].[Fiscal].[Fiscal Year]
  } ON ROWS
FROM
  [Adventure Works]
```

	Reseller Sales Amount	Reseller Order Quantity	Reseller Tax Amount
FY 2005	(null)	(null)	(null)
FY 2006	$16,288,441.77	21,890	$1,303,075.29
FY 2007	$27,921,670.52	78,959	$2,233,733.61
FY 2008	$36,240,484.70	113,529	$2,899,238.71
FY 2009	$39,864,533.17	124,882	$3,189,162.58
FY 2010	(null)	(null)	(null)
FY 2011	(null)	(null)	(null)

For Quarter level

```
SELECT
  {
  [Measures].[Reseller Sales Amount],
  [Measures].[Reseller Order Quantity],
  [Measures].[Reseller Tax Amount]
  } ON COLUMNS,
  {
  [Date].[Fiscal].[Fiscal Quarter]
  } ON ROWS
FROM
  [Adventure Works]
```

	Reseller Sales Amount	Reseller Order Quantity	Reseller Tax Amount
Q3 FY 2005	(null)	(null)	(null)
Q4 FY 2005	(null)	(null)	(null)
Q1 FY 2006	$3,193,633.97	4,385	$255,490.70
Q2 FY 2006	$4,871,801.34	6,450	$389,744.10
Q3 FY 2006	$4,069,186.04	4,626	$325,534.87
Q4 FY 2006	$4,153,820.42	6,429	$332,305.62
Q1 FY 2007	$8,880,239.44	27,414	$710,419.16
Q2 FY 2007	$7,041,183.75	19,772	$563,294.69
Q3 FY 2007	$5,266,343.51	12,307	$421,307.47
Q4 FY 2007	$6,733,903.82	19,466	$538,712.29
Q1 FY 2008	$10,926,196.09	39,784	$874,095.67
Q2 FY 2008	$9,276,226.01	28,615	$742,098.07
Q3 FY 2008	$7,102,685.11	17,609	$568,214.79
Q4 FY 2008	$8,935,377.49	27,521	$714,830.18
Q1 FY 2009	(null)	(null)	(null)
Q2 FY 2009	(null)	(null)	(null)
Q3 FY 2009	(null)	(null)	(null)
Q4 FY 2009	(null)	(null)	(null)

Above queries show the difference between the query in "Year" level and "Quarter" level:

- The last scope statement modified the measures for [Date].[Fiscal].[Fiscal Year].&[2009] to 110% of [Date].[Fiscal].[Fiscal Year].&[2008].
- But the last scope statement does not modify measures for: [Date].[Fiscal].[Fiscal Quarter].&[2009]&[1] or any other children of FY 2009.
- Measures for all children of [Date].[Fiscal].[Fiscal Year].&[2009] will show as null because last scope statement does not apply to any children of [Date].[Fiscal].[Fiscal Year].&[2009].

- **However, if your scope statement modifies in "Quarter" level, you will see the effect on "Year" level. This is because "Year" level is dependent on "Quarter" level but "Quarter" level is not dependent on "Year" level.**

Query#8.04:

Goal: Modify the last scope statement, such that, all measures for all fiscal quarters of 2009 are 110% of the corresponding quarter of previous fiscal year.

Strategy:

- To update measures for each quarter of fiscal year 2009 as the corresponding quarter of the previous year, use "ParallelPeriod" function as follows:

```
ParallelPeriod
      (
      [Date].[Fiscal].[Fiscal Year],
      1,
      [Date].[Fiscal].CurrentMember
      )
```

The scope statement will look like this:

MDX SCRIPT

```
-- Scope
----------------------------------------------------------------------
SCOPE
  (
  Descendants
    (
    [Date].[Fiscal].[Fiscal Year].&[2009],
    [Date].[Fiscal].[Fiscal Quarter]
    )
  );
-- Action
----------------------------------------------------------------------
THIS =
  (
  ParallelPeriod
    (
    [Date].[Fiscal].[Fiscal Year],
    1,
    [Date].[Fiscal].CurrentMember
    )
  ) *1.10;
----------------------------------------------------------------------
END SCOPE;
```

The following queries compare "Year" level and "Quarter" level:

For Year level

```
SELECT
  {
  [Measures].[Reseller Sales Amount],
  [Measures].[Reseller Order Quantity],
  [Measures].[Reseller Tax Amount]
  } ON COLUMNS,
  {
  [Date].[Fiscal].[Fiscal Year]
  } ON ROWS
FROM
  [Adventure Works]
```

	Reseller Sales Amount	Reseller Order Quantity	Reseller Tax Amount
FY 2005	(null)	(null)	(null)
FY 2006	$16,288,441.77	21,890	$1,303,075.29
FY 2007	$27,921,670.52	78,959	$2,233,733.61
FY 2008	$36,240,484.70	113,529	$2,899,238.71
FY 2009	$39,864,533.17	124,882	$3,189,162.58
FY 2010	(null)	(null)	(null)
FY 2011	(null)	(null)	(null)

For Quarter level

```
SELECT
  {
  [Measures].[Reseller Sales Amount],
  [Measures].[Reseller Order Quantity],
  [Measures].[Reseller Tax Amount]
  } ON COLUMNS,
  {
  [Date].[Fiscal].[Fiscal Quarter]
  } ON ROWS
FROM
  [Adventure Works]
```

Q2 FY 2008	$9,276,226.01	28,615	$742,098.07
Q3 FY 2008	$7,102,685.11	17,609	$568,214.79
Q4 FY 2008	$8,935,377.49	27,521	$714,830.18
Q1 FY 2009	$12,018,815.70	43,762	$961,505.24
Q2 FY 2009	$10,203,848.61	31,477	$816,307.88
Q3 FY 2009	$7,812,953.62	19,370	$625,036.27
Q4 FY 2009	$9,828,915.24	30,273	$786,313.20
Q1 FY 2010	(null)	(null)	(null)

The following queries compare "Quarter" level and "Month" level:

For Quarter level

```
SELECT
  {
  [Measures].[Reseller Sales Amount],
  [Measures].[Reseller Order Quantity],
  [Measures].[Reseller Tax Amount]
  } ON COLUMNS,
  {
  [Date].[Fiscal].[Fiscal Quarter]
  } ON ROWS
FROM
  [Adventure Works]
```

Q2 FY 2008	$9,276,226.01	28,615	$742,098.07
Q3 FY 2008	$7,102,685.11	17,609	$568,214.79
Q4 FY 2008	$8,935,377.49	27,521	$714,830.18
Q1 FY 2009	$12,018,815.70	43,762	$961,505.24
Q2 FY 2009	$10,203,848.61	31,477	$816,307.88
Q3 FY 2009	$7,812,953.62	19,370	$625,036.27
Q4 FY 2009	$9,828,915.24	30,273	$786,313.20
Q1 FY 2010	(null)	(null)	(null)

For Month level

```
SELECT
  {
  [Measures].[Reseller Sales Amount],
  [Measures].[Reseller Order Quantity],
  [Measures].[Reseller Tax Amount]
  } ON COLUMNS,
  {
  [Date].[Fiscal].[Month]
  } ON ROWS
FROM
  [Adventure Works]
```

	Reseller Sales Amount	Reseller Order Quantity	Reseller Tax Amou...
June 2008	$3,415,479.07	10,260	$273,238.32
July 2008	(null)	(null)	(null)
August 2008	(null)	(null)	(null)
September 2008	(null)	(null)	(null)
October 2008	(null)	(null)	(null)
November 2008	(null)	(null)	(null)

Analysis:

- "Quarter" level measures of fiscal year 2009 modified.
- "Year" level measures depend on "Quarter" level measures. So, "Year" level measures are 110% of the previous year.
- "Month" level measures do not depend on "Quarter" level measures. So, "Month" level measures for fiscal year 2009 are not changed.
- So, if you modify measures for a level,
  - All levels below this level will remain unaffected by the "Scope" statement.
  - All levels above this level will reflect the update.

Freeze

- Some cells in a cube may be dependent on other cells of the cube.
  For example,
  - Measures of fiscal years are dependent on measures of fiscal semesters.
  - Measures of fiscal semesters are dependent on measures of fiscal quarters.
- "Freeze" statement can lock cell values of a specified subcube to their current values.

Following pseudo code represents behavior of "Freeze" statement.

Statements	X Value	Y Value
INTEGER X,Y;	Null	Null
X=101;	101	Null
Y=X;	101	101
X=102;	102	102
FREEZE(Y)	102	102
X=103;	103	102

Query#8.05:

Goal: Modify the last scope statement, such that,

- All measures for the fiscal quarter of 2009 are 110% of corresponding measure for the fiscal quarter of fiscal year 2008.
- However, do not update measures for the fiscal year 2009 in "Year" level.

Strategy:

- Freeze "Year" Level.
- Modify "Quarter" Level.

MDX SCRIPT

```
-- Freeze
----------------------------------------------------------------------
FREEZE ([Date].[Fiscal].[Fiscal Year].&[2009]);
-- Scope
----------------------------------------------------------------------
SCOPE
  (
  Descendants
    (
    [Date].[Fiscal].[Fiscal Year].&[2009],
    [Date].[Fiscal].[Fiscal Quarter]
    )
  );
-- Action
----------------------------------------------------------------------
THIS =
  (
  ParallelPeriod
    (
    [Date].[Fiscal].[Fiscal Year],
    1,
    [Date].[Fiscal].CurrentMember
    )
  ) * 1.10;
----------------------------------------------------------------------
END SCOPE;
```

Analysis:

- The measures for all quarters of fiscal year 2009 will be calculated to be 110% of corresponding quarters in fiscal year 2008. This means
  [Date].[Fiscal].[Fiscal Quarter].&[2009]&[1] = 110 % of [Date].[Fiscal].[Fiscal Quarter].&[2008]&[1]
  [Date].[Fiscal].[Fiscal Quarter].&[2009]&[2] = 110 % of [Date].[Fiscal].[Fiscal Quarter].&[2008]&[2]
  [Date].[Fiscal].[Fiscal Quarter].&[2009]&[3] = 110 % of [Date].[Fiscal].[Fiscal Quarter].&[2008]&[3]
  [Date].[Fiscal].[Fiscal Quarter].&[2009]&[4] = 110 % of [Date].[Fiscal].[Fiscal Quarter].&[2008]&[4]
- All measures of "Semester" level, [Date].[Fiscal].[Fiscal Semester].&[2009]&[1] and [Date].[Fiscal].[Fiscal Semester].&[2009]&[2] will be calculated as the summation of corresponding quarters.
- Because of the "Freeze" statement, all measures of [Date].[Fiscal].[Fiscal Year].&[2009] will not be calculated as sum of all semesters of fiscal year 2009.

The following queries compare "Year" level and "Quarter" level:

For Year level

```
SELECT
  {
  [Measures].[Reseller Sales Amount],
  [Measures].[Reseller Order Quantity],
  [Measures].[Reseller Tax Amount]
  } ON COLUMNS,
  {
  [Date].[Fiscal].[Fiscal Year]
  } ON ROWS
FROM
  [Adventure Works]
```

	Reseller Sales Amount	Reseller Order Quantity	Reseller Tax Amount
FY 2005	(null)	(null)	(null)
FY 2006	$16,288,441.77	21,890	$1,303,075.29
FY 2007	$27,921,670.52	78,959	$2,233,733.61
FY 2008	$36,240,484.70	113,529	$2,899,238.71
FY 2009	(null)	(null)	(null)
FY 2010	(null)	(null)	(null)
FY 2011	(null)	(null)	(null)

For Quarter level

```
SELECT
  {
  [Measures].[Reseller Sales Amount],
  [Measures].[Reseller Order Quantity],
  [Measures].[Reseller Tax Amount]
  } ON COLUMNS,
  {
  [Date].[Fiscal].[Fiscal Quarter]
  } ON ROWS
FROM
  [Adventure Works]
```

	Reseller Sales Amount	Reseller Order Quantity	Reseller Tax Amount
Q3 FY 2005	(null)	(null)	(null)
Q4 FY 2005	(null)	(null)	(null)
Q1 FY 2006	$3,193,633.97	4,385	$255,490.70
Q2 FY 2006	$4,871,801.34	6,450	$389,744.10
Q3 FY 2006	$4,069,186.04	4,626	$325,534.87
Q4 FY 2006	$4,153,820.42	6,429	$332,305.62
Q1 FY 2007	$8,880,239.44	27,414	$710,419.16
Q2 FY 2007	$7,041,183.75	19,772	$563,294.69
Q3 FY 2007	$5,266,343.51	12,307	$421,307.47
Q4 FY 2007	$6,733,903.82	19,466	$538,712.29
Q1 FY 2008	$10,926,196.09	39,784	$874,095.67
Q2 FY 2008	$9,276,226.01	28,615	$742,098.07
Q3 FY 2008	$7,102,685.11	17,609	$568,214.79
Q4 FY 2008	$8,935,377.49	27,521	$714,830.18
Q1 FY 2009	$12,018,815.70	43,762	$961,505.24
Q2 FY 2009	$10,203,848.61	31,477	$816,307.88
Q3 FY 2009	$7,812,953.62	19,370	$625,036.27
Q4 FY 2009	$9,828,915.24	30,273	$786,313.20
Q1 FY 2010	(null)	(null)	(null)
Q2 FY 2010	(null)	(null)	(null)
Q3 FY 2010	(null)	(null)	(null)
Q4 FY 2010	(null)	(null)	(null)
Q1 FY 2011	(null)	(null)	(null)
Q2 FY 2011	(null)	(null)	(null)

Analysis:

- The [Reseller Sales Amount] for fiscal year 2009 is null because of the "Freeze" statement before the scope statement.
  Freeze ([Date].[Fiscal].[Fiscal Year].&[2009]);
- The "Reseller Sales Amount" for all quarters of fiscal year 2009 is 110% of the corresponding quarter of fiscal year 2008, because of the "Scope" statement.

The following queries display results of "Semester" level and "Month" level query:

For Semester level

```
SELECT
  {
  [Measures].[Reseller Sales Amount],
  [Measures].[Reseller Order Quantity],
  [Measures].[Reseller Tax Amount]
  } ON COLUMNS,
  {
  [Date].[Fiscal].[Fiscal Semester]
  } ON ROWS
FROM
  [Adventure Works]
```

	Reseller Sales Amount	Reseller Order Quantity	Reseller Tax Amount
H2 FY 2005	(null)	(null)	(null)
H1 FY 2006	$8,065,435.31	10,835	$645,234.80
H2 FY 2006	$8,223,006.46	11,055	$657,840.49
H1 FY 2007	$15,921,423.19	47,186	$1,273,713.85
H2 FY 2007	$12,000,247.33	31,773	$960,019.76
H1 FY 2008	$20,202,422.10	68,399	$1,616,193.74
H2 FY 2008	$16,038,062.60	45,130	$1,283,044.97
H1 FY 2009	$22,222,664.31	75,239	$1,777,813.11
H2 FY 2009	$17,641,868.86	49,643	$1,411,349.47
H1 FY 2010	(null)	(null)	(null)
H2 FY 2010	(null)	(null)	(null)
H1 FY 2011	(null)	(null)	(null)

For Month level

```
SELECT
  {
  [Measures].[Reseller Sales Amount],
  [Measures].[Reseller Order Quantity],
  [Measures].[Reseller Tax Amount]
  } ON COLUMNS,
  {
  [Date].[Fiscal].[Month]
  } ON ROWS
FROM
  [Adventure Works]
```

	Reseller Sales Amount	Reseller Order Quantity	Reseller Tax Amo
May 2008	$3,315,275.00	10,127	$265,221.99
June 2008	$3,415,479.07	10,260	$273,238.32
July 2008	(null)	(null)	(null)
August 2008	(null)	(null)	(null)
September 2008	(null)	(null)	(null)
October 2008	(null)	(null)	(null)
November 2008	(null)	(null)	(null)
December 2008	(null)	(null)	(null)
January 2009	(null)	(null)	(null)
February 2009	(null)	(null)	(null)
March 2009	(null)	(null)	(null)
April 2009	(null)	(null)	(null)
May 2009	(null)	(null)	(null)
June 2009	(null)	(null)	(null)
July 2009	(null)	(null)	(null)
August 2009	(null)	(null)	(null)

Analysis:

For semester level:

- "Reseller Sales Amount" is sum of corresponding quarters.
- "Freeze" statement only freezes "Year" level and does not have any effect on "Semester" level.

For month level:

- "Reseller Sales Amount" shows no value in "Month" level, because, Month level does not depend on "Quarter' level.
- "Freeze" statement only freezes "Year" level and does not have any effect on "Month" level.

Query#8.06:

Goal: Modify the last scope statement so all measures for all fiscal quarters of 2009 are 110% of corresponding quarters of the fiscal year 2008. But do not update measures for upper levels, "Semester" and "Year".

MDX SCRIPT

```
-- Freeze
---------------------------------------------------------------------
FREEZE ([Date].[Fiscal].[Fiscal Year].&[2009]);
FREEZE
  (
  Descendants
    (
    [Date].[Fiscal].[Fiscal Year].&[2009],
    [Date].[Fiscal].[Fiscal Semester]
    )
  );
-- Scope
---------------------------------------------------------------------
SCOPE
  (
  Descendants
    (
    [Date].[Fiscal].[Fiscal Year].&[2009],
    [Date].[Fiscal].[Fiscal Quarter]
    )
   );
-- Action
---------------------------------------------------------------------
THIS =
  (
  ParallelPeriod
    (
    [Date].[Fiscal].[Fiscal Year],
    1,
    [Date].[Fiscal].CurrentMember
    )
  ) * 1.10;
---------------------------------------------------------------------
END SCOPE;
```

Freeze (<SubCube>);

<SubCube>:

- A valid subcube. For example, ([Date].[Fiscal].[Fiscal Year].&[2009]).

The Result:

- Lock cell values of a specified <SubCube> to their current values.

IF ..THEN .. END IF

- Executes if given condition is true.
- Note: There is no **else** part.

Query#8.07:

Goal: Modify the last scope statement such that:

- All measures for fiscal year 2009 are 110% of corresponding measure for fiscal year 2008.
- Except for "Reseller Freight Cost" for fiscal year 2009 is 115% of "Reseller Freight Cost" for fiscal year 2008.

MDX SCRIPT

```
------------------------------------------------------------------------------------------------
SCOPE
  (
  [Date].[Fiscal].[Fiscal Year].&[2009]
  );
------------------------------------------------------------------------------------------------
IF ([Measures].CurrentMember IS [Measures].[Reseller Freight Cost])
THEN
This = ([Date].[Fiscal].[Fiscal Year].&[2008] ) * 1.15
END IF;
------------------------------------------------------------------------------------------------
IF NOT ([Measures].CurrentMember IS [Measures].[Reseller Freight Cost])
THEN
THIS = ([Date].[Fiscal].[Fiscal Year].&[2008] ) * 1.10
END IF;
------------------------------------------------------------------------------------------------
END SCOPE;
```

The following MDX query shows:

- All measures for fiscal years 2009 are 110% of corresponding measure for fiscal year 2008, except for "Reseller Freight Cost" for fiscal year 2009 which is 115% of "Reseller Freight Cost" for fiscal year 2008.
- Only "Reseller Sales Amount" and "Reseller Order Quantity" is shown, but all measures for fiscal 2009 are 110% of corresponding measure for fiscal year 2008 except "Reseller Freight Cost".

MDX

```
SELECT
  {
  [Measures].[Reseller Sales Amount],
  [Measures].[Reseller Order Quantity],
  [Measures].[Reseller Freight Cost]
  } ON COLUMNS,
  {
  [Date].[Fiscal].[Fiscal Year]
  } ON ROWS
FROM
  [Adventure Works]
```

Result

	Reseller Sales Amount	Reseller Order Quantity	Reseller Freight Cost
FY 2005	(null)	(null)	(null)
FY 2006	$16,288,441.77	21,890	$407,211.12
FY 2007	$27,921,670.52	78,959	$698,042.05
FY 2008	$36,240,484.70	113,529	$906,012.74
FY 2009	$39,864,533.17	124,882	$1,041,914.65
FY 2010	(null)	(null)	(null)
FY 2011	(null)	(null)	(null)

115%

110%

IF <Condition> THEN <Assignment> END IF;

<Condition>:

- A valid Boolean expression returns true or false.
  For example,
  [Measures].CurrentMember IS [Measures].[Reseller Freight Cost]
  Returns true if current measure is [Measures].[Reseller Freight Cost] else returns false.

<Assignment>:

- A valid MDX assignment statement.

The Result:

- Executes the <Assignment> statement when <Condition> is true.

EXERCISES

Exercise 8.1: Write a scope statement to set "Reseller Sales Amount" to null for all products which have string "Pedal" in the product name for fiscal year 2008.

Exercise 8.2: Write scope statements for "Internet Sales Amount" for year 2008 to:

a. Set Memorial Day weekend as tax free weekend.

b. Set 4th July weekend as tax free weekend for clothing.

Exercise 8.3: Write a scope statement to set following for the state of California:

a. Set "Reseller Sales Amount" to null for any dates before December 17, 2007.

b. Modify the last scope statement to set "Reseller Sales Amount" to null for all dates between December 17, 2007 and March 5, 2008.

c. Modify the last scope statement to set "Reseller Sales Amount" to null for any date after March 5, 2008.

Exercise 8.4: Create an MDX scope statement to set "Reseller Tax Amount" for the month of March of each year to null.

Exercise 8.5: Create a calculated measure [Measures].[Management Bonus Pct]. Write scope statement to set:

a. [Measures].[Management Bonus Pct] for leaf level to zero.

b. [Measures].[Management Bonus Pct] for first level to 0.05%.

c. [Measures].[Management Bonus Pct] for each level to 0.03% more than the lower level.

Chapter 9: MDX Data Definition And Manipulation Statements

MDX is typically used for querying a cube but can be used for data definition and manipulation. This chapter explains some common data definition and manipulation statements used in MDX. An alternate way to implement data definition and manipulation functions is to use XMLA and SQL Server Data Tools.

The first section explains data definition statements for Member, Set and Cell calculations. These DDL or DML functions can be used in "Calculations" of a cube or in a session. This means that the scope of DDL or DML statements can be the whole cube or the current session. "Member" and "Set" in this section are calculated member and named set.

The second section explores data definition statements for cube and subcube. For example, the **Alter Cube...Create Dimension Member...** statement can be used to write back data to the cube and underlying table in the relational data warehouse. "Create SubCube" statement creates a cube in the scope of the current session with the same name as the original cube, but "Create Session Cube" creates a temporary subcube in the current session with a different name than the original cube. Another interesting statement is "Create Global Cube", which creates a persistent cube locally and saves in a ".cub" file.

The third section explains some interesting data manipulation statements.

Agenda

Create Member, Update Member, Drop Member, Create Set, Drop Set, Create Cell Calculation

Alter Cube, Refresh Cube, Create Subcube, Drop Subcube, Create session Cube, Create Global Cube, Create Action, Drop Action

Drillthrough, Clear Calculations, Call, Update Cube

Exercises

Create Member

- Creates a **calculated member**.
- Typically, a calculated member is created in "Calculations" of a cube.
- Different **scopes of a calculated member**:
  - **Cube:** If a calculated member is defined in "Calculations" of a cube, the scope is the cube. This means that the calculated member will be available to any session connected to the cube.
  - **Session:** If a calculated member is defined in a session, the scope is limited to that session only.
  - **Query:** If a calculated member is defined in an MDX query using "WITH MEMBER", the scope is limited to the current query only.

Query#9.01:

Goal:

- Create a global calculated member for "Reseller Sales Amount for last 12 months Running Total", including the current month.
- Write an MDX query to display [Reseller Sales Amount] for each month of fiscal year 2008 for the state of California and also show the member "Reseller Sales Amount for last 12 months Running Total".

Strategy:

- Create a member [Measures].[RSA 12 Months Running Total] in **cube's calculation** as a sum of the last 12 months reseller sales amount.
- In the MDX query, display all months for fiscal year 2008 on rows.
- To show the reseller sales amount for the state of California, add the condition in "Where" clause.

MDX SCRIPT

```
CREATE MEMBER CurrentCube.[Measures].[RSA 12 Months Running Total] AS
SUM
  (
  ParallelPeriod
    (
    [Date].[Fiscal].[Fiscal Year],
    1,
    [Date].[Fiscal].Currentmember
    ).lead(1)
  :
  [Date].[Fiscal].Currentmember,
  [Measures].[Reseller Sales Amount]
  );
```

Analysis:

- Unlike "WITH MEMBER", member name in "Calculations" of a cube needs to be fully qualified member name. This means, cube name or CurrentCube in the prefix of the member name.
- Unlike "WITH MEMBER", create member in calculations of a cube has a semicolon (";") at the end of the statement.

- "ParallelPeriod" function is used to find the corresponding member in the prior year and lead(1) is used to move one position ahead.
  For example, if the current month is "March, 2008".
  Corresponding month in the prior year = "March, 2007".
  Last 12 months including the current month = "April, 2007" to "March, 2008".
- Another important point is that the new measure [Measures].[RSA 12 Months Running Total] is in global scope, which means, any session that connects to the cube will be able to see this calculated member.

The following query shows "Reseller Sales Amount" and the new measure [Measures].[RSA 12 Months Running Total] for each month of fiscal year 2008.

MDX

```
SELECT
  {
  [Measures].[Reseller Sales Amount],
  [Measures].[RSA 12 Months Running Total]
  } ON COLUMNS,
  {
  DESCENDANTS
    (
    [Date].[Fiscal].[Fiscal Year].&[2008],
    [Date].[Fiscal].[Month]
    )
  } ON ROWS
FROM
  [Adventure Works]
```

Result

	Reseller Sales Amount	RSA 12 Months Running Total
July 2007	$2,665,650.54	$28,193,631.53
August 2007	$4,212,971.51	$28,805,412.33
September 2007	$4,047,574.04	$29,967,627.17
October 2007	$2,282,115.88	$30,447,588.83
November 2007	$3,483,161.40	$30,876,933.91
December 2007	$3,510,948.73	$32,202,669.43
January 2008	$1,662,547.32	$32,547,674.92
February 2008	$2,700,766.80	$32,863,595.13
March 2008	$2,739,370.98	$34,039,011.03
April 2008	$2,204,623.41	$34,378,356.01
May 2008	$3,315,275.00	$34,812,878.33
June 2008	$3,415,479.07	$36,240,484.70

The new measure is not associated with any measure group. To verify use following steps:

1 Open "SQL Server Management Studio".
2 Connect "Analysis Services" of the database server.
3 Expand the "Databases" node and click on database "AdventureWorksDW2012Multidimensional-EE" and click on "New Query".
4 Expand the "Measures" of "Adventure Works" cube.

Figure 9-1 : The new measure is not associated with a measure group.

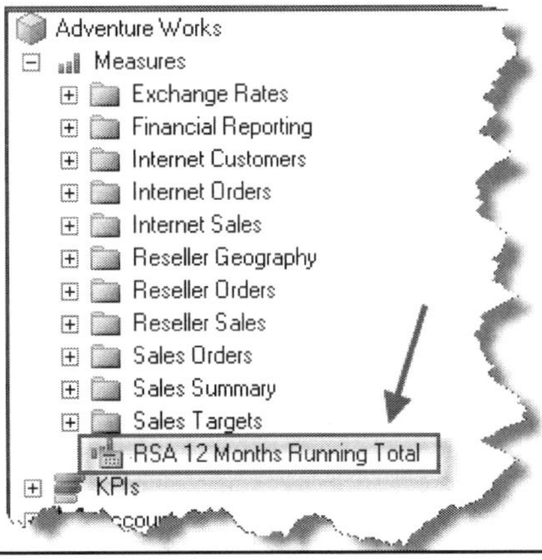

To move the measure [Measures].[RSA 12 Months Running Total] to measure group "Reseller Sales", set the ASSOCIATED_MEASURE_GROUP property in the last CREATE MEMBER command.

MDX SCRIPT

```
CREATE MEMBER CurrentCube.[Measures].[RSA 12 Months Running Total] AS
SUM
  (
  [Date].[Fiscal].Currentmember.lag(1)
  :
  [Date].[Fiscal].Currentmember,
  [Measures].[Reseller Sales Amount]
  ),
FORMAT_STRING="Currency",
NON_EMPTY_BEHAVIOR =
  {
  [Measures].[Reseller Sales Amount]
  },
VISIBLE = 1 ,
ASSOCIATED_MEASURE_GROUP = 'Reseller Sales';
```

Other common properties in CREATE MEMBER command are:

- FORMAT_STRING = "Currency" , will format the measure as currency.
- NON_EMPTY_BEHAVIOR = {[Measures].[Reseller Sales Amount]}, can be described as:
  - The member [Measures].[RSA 12 Months Running Total] is non-empty if [Measures].[Reseller Sales Amount] is non-empty.
  - This means that if [Measures].[Reseller Sales Amount] is empty then [Measures].[RSA 12 Months Running Total] will be empty.
  - Also, if [Measures].[Reseller Sales Amount] is empty there is **no need to calculate** [Measures].[RSA 12 Months Running Total] and this will **save system resources**.
- VISIBLE = 1, makes a measure visible.
- ASSOCIATED_MEASURE_GROUP = 'Reseller Sales', will display this measure in [Reseller Sales] measure group.

The new measure is now associated with "Reseller Sales" measure group. To verify use following steps:

1 Open "SQL Server Management Studio".
2 Connect to "Analysis Services" of the database server.
3 Expand the "Databases" node and click on database "AdventureWorksDW2012Multidimensional-EE".
4 Click on "New Query" button.
5 Expand "Measures" of "Adventure Works" cube.
6 Expand the measure group "Reseller Sales". You will see the new measure [Measures].[RSA 12 Months Running Total].

Figure 9-2: The new measure is now associated with the measure group "Reseller Sales".

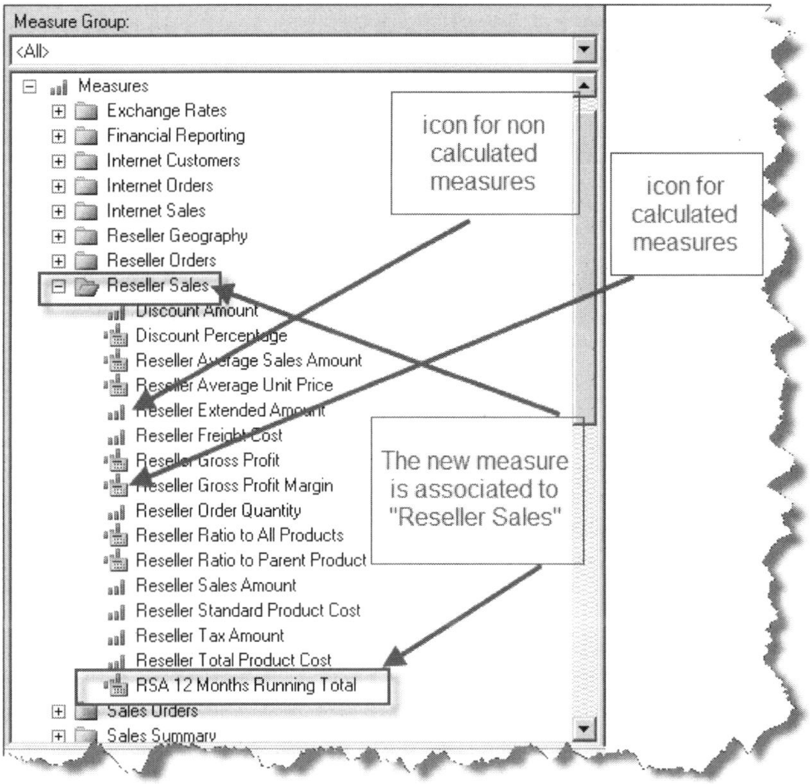

Query#9.02:

Goal: Modify the last query such that the calculated member "RSA 12 Months Running Total" is null if any "Reseller Sales Amount" of last 12 months is null.

Strategy:

- Create a calculated member [Measures].[RSA 12 Months Running Min] in cube's calculation as the minimum of last 12 months Reseller Sales Amount.
- Using the "Case" statement, modify the logic of [Measures].[RSA 12 Months Running Total]:
  - If [Measures].[RSA 12 Months Running Min] is null then return null.
  - If [Measures].[RSA 12 Months Running Min] is not null , then return the sum of last 12 months "Reseller Sales Amount".
- Set Visible = 0 for the member [Measures].[RSA 12 Months Running Min] .
  - This will not show [Measures].[RSA 12 Months Running Min] in the list of measures for measure group "Reseller Sales".
  - This will not prohibit you from using [Measures].[RSA 12 Months Running Min] in your MDX query.

MDX SCRIPT

```
CREATE
MEMBER CurrentCube.[Measures].[RSA 12 Months Running Min] AS
MIN
    (
    ParallelPeriod
        (
        [Date].[Fiscal].[Fiscal Year],
        1,
        [Date].[Fiscal].CurrentMember
        ).lead(1):
        [Date].[Fiscal].CurrentMember,
    CoalesceEmpty([Measures].[Reseller Sales Amount],-1)
    ),
FORMAT_STRING="Currency",
NON_EMPTY_BEHAVIOR = { [Measures].[Reseller Sales Amount] },
VISIBLE = 0,
ASSOCIATED_MEASURE_GROUP = 'Reseller Sales';

CREATE MEMBER CurrentCube.[Measures].[RSA 12 Months Running Total] AS
CASE
    WHEN [Measures].[RSA 12 Months Running Min] =-1 THEN
    NULL
    ELSE
    SUM
        (
        ParallelPeriod
            (
            [Date].[Fiscal].[Fiscal Year],
            1,
            [Date].[Fiscal].CurrentMember
            ).lead(1):
            [Date].[Fiscal].CurrentMember,
        [Measures].[Reseller Sales Amount]
        )
    END,
FORMAT_STRING="Currency",
NON_EMPTY_BEHAVIOR = { [Measures].[Reseller Sales Amount] },
VISIBLE = 1 ,
ASSOCIATED_MEASURE_GROUP = 'Reseller Sales';
```

To verify the [Measures].[RSA 12 Months Running Total] returns null if any value is null , let us display the "Reseller Sales Amount" and [Measures].[RSA 12 Months Running Total] for each month of fiscal year 2006.

MDX

```
SELECT
  {
  [Measures].[Reseller Sales Amount],
  [Measures].[RSA 12 Months Running Total]
  } ON COLUMNS,
  {
  DESCENDANTS
    (
    [Date].[Fiscal].[Fiscal Year].&[2006],
    [Date].[Fiscal].[Month]
    )
  } ON ROWS
FROM
  [Adventure Works]
```

Result

	Reseller Sales Amount	RSA 12 Months Running Total
July 2005	$489,328.58	(null)
August 2005	$1,538,408.31	(null)
September 2005	$1,165,897.08	(null)
October 2005	$844,721.00	(null)
November 2005	$2,324,135.80	(null)
December 2005	$1,702,944.54	(null)
January 2006	$713,116.69	(null)
February 2006	$1,900,788.93	(null)
March 2006	$1,455,280.41	(null)
April 2006	$882,899.94	(null)
May 2006	$2,269,116.71	(null)
June 2006	$1,001,803.77	$16,288,441.77

Analysis:

- Only June, 2006 shows value for [Measures].[RSA 12 Months Running Total], because there is no "Reseller Sales Amount" available prior to July, 2005.
- The following query shows [Measures].[RSA 12 Months Running Total] for all months of fiscal year 2007 and there are no null values during this period.

MDX

```
SELECT
  {
  [Measures].[Reseller Sales Amount],
  [Measures].[RSA 12 Months Running Total]
  } ON COLUMNS,
  {
  DESCENDANTS
    (
    [Date].[Fiscal].[Fiscal Year].&[2007],
    [Date].[Fiscal].[Month]
    )
  } ON ROWS
FROM
    [Adventure Works]
```

Result

	Reseller Sales Amount	RSA 12 Months Running Total
July 2006	$2,393,689.53	$18,192,802.71
August 2006	$3,601,190.71	$20,255,585.12
September 2006	$2,885,359.20	$21,975,047.24
October 2006	$1,802,154.21	$22,932,480.45
November 2006	$3,053,816.33	$23,662,160.98
December 2006	$2,185,213.21	$24,144,429.65
January 2007	$1,317,541.83	$24,748,854.79
February 2007	$2,384,846.59	$25,232,912.45
March 2007	$1,563,955.08	$25,341,587.12
April 2007	$1,865,278.43	$26,323,965.61
May 2007	$2,880,752.68	$26,935,601.58
June 2007	$1,987,872.71	$27,921,670.52

Create [SESSION | HIDDEN | CALCULATED] Member <Member Name> AS
<Mdx Expression>
[,<Property Name> = <Property Value> .. n]
[, SCOPE_ISOLATION = CUBE] ;

[SESSION | HIDDEN | CALCULATED]:

- This is an optional flag.
- SESSION: Scope of the member is limited to the current session only.
- HIDDEN: The member is hidden.
- CALCULATED: This is default value and means this member is a calculated member.

<Member Name>:

- If the name of the member is "Member1", then the member can be expressed as one of the two ways:
  - CurrentCube.Member1.
  - <Cube Name>.Member1.

<Mdx Expression>:

- A valid MDX expression that creates the member.

<Property Name>:

Following are standard properties:

- ASSOCIATED_MEASURE_GROUP: You can associate a member with a measure group. For example, ASSOCIATED_MEASURE_GROUP = 'Reseller Sales'.
- FORMAT_STRING: Format your member. For example, FORMAT_STRING = "Percent".
- VISIBLE: You can hide or show your member with this flag. For example, VISIBLE = 1.
- NON_EMPTY_BEHAVIOR: The calculated member will be empty if any of the listed members are empty. For example, NON_EMPTY_BEHAVIOR = {[Measures].[Reseller Sales Amount]}
- SOLVE_ORDER: If a member depends on another calculated member, SOLVE_ORDER determines the calculation order of these members.
- DISPLAY_FOLDER: A string that is the path of the display folder of the client application.
- CAPTION: A user defined string for a caption for this member.

SCOPE_ISOLATION:

- By default, cube calculations are evaluated before any session members.
- If you want to calculate a session member before "cube calculation", you can set SCOPE_ISOLATION = TRUE for session members.

The Result:

- Creates a calculated member <Member Name>.

Query#9.03:

Goal:

- Create a calculated member in **current session** for average "Reseller Sales Amount" of last 12 months.
- Write an MDX query to display "Reseller Sales Amount" for each month of fiscal year 2008 for the state of California and also show average "Reseller Sales Amount" for last 12 months.

Strategy:

- Create a calculated member in SQL Server management Studio (SSMS) query session.
- In SSMS, you can have only one MDX statement at a time. Multiple MDX statements are not allowed. Means,
    - "Create member statement" and "MDX query" cannot be run at the same time, because multiple MDX statements are not allowed in SSMS session.
    - You need to create member statement first and then run MDX query in the same session.

Step 1: Open SSMS and execute following MDX statement to create a **session** member.

MDX

```
CREATE MEMBER [Adventure Works].[Measures].[RSA Monthly Average -12] AS
AVG
    (
    [Date].[Fiscal].Currentmember.lag(11)
    :
    [Date].[Fiscal].Currentmember,
    [Measures].[Reseller Sales Amount]
    ),
FORMAT_STRING="Currency",
ASSOCIATED_MEASURE_GROUP = 'Reseller Sales';
```

Complete cube name is needed. You cannot use "CurrentCube".

Result

```
Executing the query ...
Execution complete
```

Analysis:

- The above MDX statement creates a calculated member [Adventure Works].[Measures].[RSA Monthly Average -12] in the current session. This means this member will not be available to other sessions connected to the cube.
- Once this session is closed, the member will be removed.
- After executing the above MDX statement, comment out the above code and run following MDX query.

Step 2: In the same session execute the following MDX query to display the reseller sales amount for each month of fiscal year 2008 for the state of California and average reseller sales amount for the last 12 months.

MDX

```
SELECT
  {
  [Measures].[Reseller Sales Amount],
  [Measures].[RSA Monthly Average-12]
  } ON COLUMNS,
  {
  DESCENDANTS
    (
    [Date].[Fiscal].[Fiscal Year].&[2008],
    [Date].[Fiscal].[Month]
    )
  } ON ROWS
FROM
  [Adventure Works]
WHERE
  [Geography].[Geography].[State-Province].&[CA]&[US]
```

Result

	Reseller Sales Amount	RSA Monthly Average -12
July 2007	$326,144.37	$342,853.80
August 2007	$330,169.86	$326,387.03
September 2007	$395,376.27	$302,846.90
October 2007	$288,046.35	$322,507.02
November 2007	$270,032.39	$306,822.69
December 2007	$315,308.14	$296,536.83
January 2008	$234,951.07	$312,427.58
February 2008	$250,028.71	$302,231.07
March 2008	$273,972.63	$300,304.70
April 2008	$255,754.98	$317,303.20
May 2008	$281,730.44	$303,531.71
June 2008	$343,200.05	$297,059.60

Analysis:

- [Measures].[RSA Monthly Average-12] is running average of 12 previous months .
- If you create a member using "WITH MEMBER", it will return the same result, but the scope of the member will be "current query" instead of "current session".

Update Member

- Updates a **calculated member**.
- "Update Member" **cannot** be used in "Calculations" of a **cube**.
- "Update Member" **can** only be used in scope of a **session**.
- You cannot modify "SOLVE_ORDER" property of a member using "Update Member" statement, because, members always preserve the relative precedence.
- As "Update Member" cannot be used in calculations of a cube, you cannot use "CurrentCube" in Member name. Instead you need to use the complete cube name in the prefix of the member name.

Query#9.04:

Goal: In the last session of SSMS, modify member [Measures].[RSA Monthly Average -12], add an additional property NON_EMPTY_BEHAVIOR = { [Measures].[Reseller Sales Amount] }.

Strategy:

- Write "Update Member" statement for [Measures].[RSA Monthly Average -12] in the same SSMS session.

<table>
<tr><td>MDX</td><td><pre>UPDATE MEMBER [Adventure Works].[Measures].[RSA Monthly Average -12] AS
AVG
   (
   [Date].[Fiscal].Currentmember.lag(11)
   :
   [Date].[Fiscal].Currentmember,
   [Measures].[Reseller Sales Amount]
   ),
FORMAT_STRING="Currency",
ASSOCIATED_MEASURE_GROUP = 'Reseller Sales',
NON_EMPTY_BEHAVIOR = { [Measures].[Reseller Sales Amount] };</pre></td></tr>
<tr><td>Result</td><td><pre>Executing the query ...
Execution complete</pre></td></tr>
</table>

Analysis:

- The above MDX statement will update the member [Measures].[RSA Monthly Average -12].
- Note that properties are separated by a comma (",").
- Each MDX statement ends with a semicolon (";").

Update Member <Member Name> AS
<Mdx Expression>
[, <Property Name> = <Property Value> .. n]
[, SCOPE_ISOLATION = CUBE] ;

<Member Name>:

- If the name of the member is Member1.
  then the member is expressed as <cube name>.Member1.

<Mdx Expression>:

- A valid MDX expression that creates the member.

<Property Name>:

Followings are standard properties:

- ASSOCIATED_MEASURE_GROUP: You can associate your member to a measure group. For example, ASSOCIATED_MEASURE_GROUP = "Reseller Sales".
- FORMAT_STRING: Format the member. For example, FORMAT_STRING = "Percent".
- VISIBLE: You can hide or show a member by using this flag. For example, VISIBLE = 1.
- NON_EMPTY_BEHAVIOR: The member will be empty if any of the listed members are empty. For example
  NON_EMPTY_BEHAVIOR = {[Measures].[Reseller Sales Amount]}, this hint improves the performace of a query.
- DISPLAY_FOLDER: A string that is the path of the display folder of the client application.

SCOPE_ISOLATION:

- By default, cube calculations are evaluated before any session members.
- If you want to calculate a session member before cube calculation, you can use this flag as SCOPE_ISOLATION = TRUE for the session member.

The Result:

- Updates a calculated member <Member Name>.

Drop Member

- Drops a **calculated member**.
- This function cannot be used in calculations of a **cube**.
- Like "Update Member", "Drop Member" can only be used within the scope of a session.
- As Drop Member cannot be used in "Calculations" of a cube, you cannot use "CurrentCube" in the member name. Instead you need to use the complete cube name in prefix to the member name.

Query#9.05:

Goal: In the last working session, drop the member [Measures].[RSA Monthly Average -12].

Strategy:

- Drop Member statement for [Measures].[RSA Monthly Average -12] in the same SSMS session.
- Verify the member [Measures].[RSA Monthly Average -12] dropped using the last MDX query.

Step 1: Drop the calculated member.

MDX	DROP MEMBER [Adventure Works].[Measures].[RSA Monthly Average -12];
Result	Executing the query ... Execution complete

Step 2: Verify the calculated member is dropped.

MDX	SELECT { [Measures].[Reseller Sales Amount], [Measures].[RSA Monthly Average -12] } ON COLUMNS, { DESCENDANTS ([Date].[Fiscal].[Fiscal Year].&[2008], [Date].[Fiscal].[Month]) } ON ROWS FROM [Adventure Works] WHERE [Geography].[Geography].[State-Province].&[CA]&[US]
	Executing the query ... Query (52, 4) The '[RSA Monthly Average -12]' member was not found in the cube when the string, [Measures].[RSA Monthly Average -12], was parsed. Execution complete

Drop Member <member>[..n] ;

<Member>:

- This is the name of a calculated member in a session.

The Result:

- Drops a calculated member <Member> from a session.
- You can drop more than one member at a time by listing member names separated by commas.

Create Set

- Creates a named set.
- Typically a named set is created in "Calculations" of a cube.
- Different scopes of a named set:
    - **Cube:** If a named set is defined in "Calculations" of a cube, then scope is the whole cube. This means, the named set will be available to any session connected to the cube.
    - **Session:** If a named set is defined in a session, the scope is limited to that session only.
    - **Query:** If a named set is defined in an MDX query using "WITH SET", then scope is limited to that query only.
- Two types of set evaluation:
    - STATIC: The set is evaluated at the time of execution of "Create Set" statement, if any member added or removed from the set, the named set will not be modified.
    - DYNAMIC: In this case, the named set will be evaluated every time query executes.
- Set visibility:
    - HIDDEN: This makes the set hidden from users.
- Before creating a set, you need to know:
    - Member type of this set. For example, set of products, set of dates, set of cities etc.
    - A set can only have one type of objects.
    - A set can have members from more than one level within a hierarchy, e.g. city, state, country.
    - Named sets are located in corresponding dimension.
    - While creating named sets, you can specify name of a folder within the dimension. In [Adventure Works] named sets located in folder "Sets" in each dimension.

Query#9.06:

Goal: Create a named set "Top 10 Cities of USA" based on Reseller Sales Amount which has most reseller sales in global scope of the cube .

Strategy:

- The type of objects in named set is "City".
- Dimension is Geography.
- Create the named set in "Calculations" of the cube.

MDX SCRIPT

```
CREATE DYNAMIC SET CURRENTCUBE.[Top 10 Cities of USA] AS
TopCount
    (
    DESCENDANTS
        (
        [Geography].[Geography].[Country].&[United States],
        [Geography].[Geography].[City],
        SELF
        ),
    10,
    [Measures].[Reseller Sales Amount]
    ),
DISPLAY_FOLDER = 'Sets';
```

Analysis:

- To find "All cities of United States", use "Descendants" function.
- Use "TopCount" function to find top 10 cities of United States based on "Reseller Sales Amount".

To locate the newly created named set "Top 10 Cities of USA":

1. Open "SQL Server Management Studio".
2. Connect "Analysis Services" of the database server.
3. Expand the "Databases" node.
4. Click on database "Adventure-WorksDW2012Multidimensional-EE" and click on "New Query".
5. Expand the dimension Geography.
6. Expand the folder "Sets".

Figure 9-3 : The location of the named set.

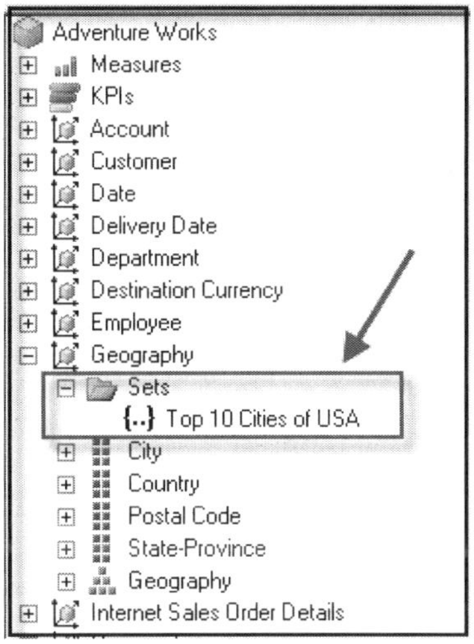

To verify the named set is working properly, display

- "Reseller Sales Amount" for each member of set "Top 10 Cities of USA".

MDX

```
SELECT
  {
  [Measures].[Reseller Sales Amount]
  } ON COLUMNS,
  {
  [Top 10 Cities of USA]
  } On ROWS
FROM
  [Adventure Works]
```

Result

	Reseller Sales Amount
Seattle	$2,070,007.39
Nashua	$1,585,740.11
Garland	$1,526,739.08
Memphis	$1,409,370.77
Tooele	$1,314,068.16
Loveland	$1,291,408.50
Houston	$1,266,287.90
Bellingham	$1,248,138.17
Miami	$1,202,924.80
San Antonio	$1,198,138.20

Query#9.07:

Goal: Hide the named set "Top 10 Cities of USA" from users.

Strategy:

- Open the "Calculations' tab of the cube in "Script View" mode.
- Modify the last "Create Set" statement, and use "HIDDEN" keyword to hide the set from users.

MDX SCRIPT	

```
CREATE HIDDEN DYNAMIC SET CURRENTCUBE.[Top 10 Cities of USA] AS
TopCount
    (
    DESCENDANTS
        (
        [Geography].[Geography].[Country].&[United States],
        [Geography].[Geography].[City],
        SELF
        ),
    10,
    [Measures].[Reseller Sales Amount]
    ),
DISPLAY_FOLDER = 'Sets';
```

To verify the newly created named set "Top 10 Cities of USA"is hidden from user:

1 Open a new session of "SQL Server Management Studio".
2 Connect "Analysis Services" of the database server.
3 Expand the "Databases" node.
4 Click on database "Adventure-WorksDW2012Multidimensional-EE" and click on "New Query".
5 Expand the dimension Geography.
6 You will see there is no folder named "Sets".

Figure 9-4: Named set "Top 10 Cities of USA"is hidden from user.

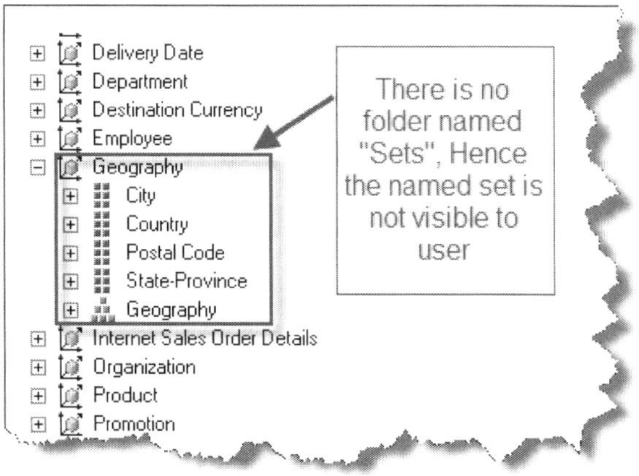

Analysis:

- The named set is now hidden from users.
- The named set "Top 10 Cities of USA" still exists in the cube but is hidden from users.
- You can display the named set "Top 10 Cities of USA" using MDX query as shown in the following query.

MDX

```
SELECT
  {
  [Measures].[Reseller Sales Amount]
  } ON COLUMNS,
  {
  [Top 10 Cities of USA]
  } On ROWS
FROM
  [Adventure Works]
```

Result

	Reseller Sales Amount
Seattle	$2,070,007.39
Nashua	$1,585,740.11
Garland	$1,526,739.08
Memphis	$1,409,370.77
Tooele	$1,314,068.16
Loveland	$1,291,408.50
Houston	$1,266,287.90
Bellingham	$1,248,138.17
Miami	$1,202,924.80
San Antonio	$1,198,138.20

Query#9.08:
Goal:

- Create a named set,"10 Least Profitable Products" in scope of a session.
- Write an MDX query to display "Reseller Sales Amount" and "Gross Profit Margin" for each member of [10 Least Profitable Products].

Strategy:

- Create named set,"10 Least Profitable Products" in SQL Server management Studio (SSMS) query session.
- In SSMS, you can have only one MDX statement at a time as multiple statements are not allowed. This means,
  - "Create Set" statement and "MDX query" cannot run at the same time.
  - Run "Create Set" statement first and then run MDX query in the same session.

Step 1: Open SSMS and execute following MDX statement to create a named set in current session.

MDX

```
CREATE DYNAMIC SET
[Adventure Works].[10 Least Profitable Products]
AS
BOTTOMCOUNT
  (
  FILTER
    (
    [Product].[Product Categories].[Product],
    [Measures].[Gross Profit Margin] < 0
    ),
  10,
  [Measures].[Gross Profit Margin]
  );
```

Step 2: In the same session execute the following MDX query to display the measures for the named set.

MDX

```
SELECT
  {
  [Measures].[Reseller Sales Amount],
  [Measures].[Gross Profit Margin]
  } ON COLUMNS,
  {
  [10 Least Profitable Products]
  } On ROWS
FROM   [Adventure Works]
```

Result

	Reseller Sales Amount	Gross Profit Margin
Short-Sleeve Classic Jersey, XL	$224,833.69	-24.76%
Long-Sleeve Logo Jersey, L	$171,347.14	-20.67%
Short-Sleeve Classic Jersey, L	$164,388.96	-20.42%
Road-650 Red, 44	$587,454.85	-17.83%
Short-Sleeve Classic Jersey, S	$104,272.85	-13.81%
Long-Sleeve Logo Jersey, M	$94,603.97	-13.06%
Touring-3000 Blue, 50	$657,192.28	-11.33%
Touring-3000 Yellow, 62	$660,303.45	-10.78%
Long-Sleeve Logo Jersey, L	$28,399.49	-10.70%
AWC Logo Cap	$5,081.05	-10.60%

Create [SESSION] [STATIC | DYNAMIC] [HIDDEN] Set <Set Name> As <Set Expression> [, <Property Name> = <Property Value> ... n]

[SESSION]:

- You can use this to create a named set which has a scope limited to the current session only.
- If not used,
  - For session, the scope of the named set of a session will be limited to current session only.
  - For "Calculations" of a cube, the scope will be the cube.

[STATIC | DYNAMIC]

- STATIC: The set is evaluated at the time of execution of "Create Set" statement. If any member is added or removed from the set, the named set will not have any effect.
- DYNAMIC: In this case, the named set will be evaluated every time query executes.

[HIDDEN]

- This flag hides the set from users.

<Set Name>:

- If the name of the set is Set1, then the set name can be expressed as one of the two ways:
  - CurrentCube.Set1.
  - <Cube Name>.Set1.

<Set Expression>:

- A valid MDX expression that creates the named set <Set Name>.

<Property Name>:

Followings are standard properties:

- DISPLAY_FOLDER: A string that is the path of the display folder of the client application.
- CAPTION: A user defined string of a caption for this member.

The Result:

- Creates a named set <Set Name>.

Drop Set

- Drops a named set.
- This function cannot be used in "Calculations" of a cube.
- Like "Update Member" and "Drop Member", "Drop Set" can only be used within the scope of a **session**.

Query#9.09:

Goal: In the last working session, drop the named set [Adventure Works].[10 Least Profitable Products].

MDX	DROP SET [Adventure Works].[10 Least Profitable Products];
Result	Executing the query ... Execution complete

Verify the named set [Adventure Works].[10 Most Loss Products] dropped using the last MDX statement.

MDX	Result
SELECT { [Measures].[Reseller Sales Amount], [Measures].[Gross Profit Margin] } ON COLUMNS, { [10 Least Profitable Products] } On ROWS FROM [Adventure Works]	Executing the query ... Query (7, 4) The dimension '[10 Least Profitable Products]' was not found in the cube when the string, [10 Least Profitable Products], was parsed. Execution complete

Drop Set <Set>[..n];

<Set>:

- A valid named set.

The Result:

- Drops a named set <Set>.
- You can drop more than one named set at a time by listing named set names separated by commas.

With/Create Cell Calculation

- This command is deprecated; you should use MDX assignments instead. But you may be need to know the basic concepts to understand any legacy code.
- This MDX statement modifies some cell values in a cube.
  For example,
  Let us assume, "Reseller Sales Amount" for fiscal year 2009 is not correct and was entered 8.25% too high.
  To correct temporarily, you can calculate "Reseller Sales Amount" for fiscal year 2009 as [Reseller Sales Amount]/1.0825.
- Different scopes of a cell calculation:
  - **Query:** If a cell calculation is defined in an MDX query using "WITH CELL CALCULATION", the scope is limited to that query only.
  - **Session:** If a cell calculation is defined in a session, the scope is limited to that session only.
  - **Cube:** If a cell calculation is defined in calculation of a cube, the scope is the cube. This means the cell calculation is available to any session connected to the cube.

Query#9.10:

Goal: [Reseller Sales Amount] for fiscal year 2009 is not correct and 8.25% too high. Create a cell calculation in scope of MDX query to modify [Reseller Sales Amount] for fiscal year 2009 as [Reseller Sales Amount]/1.0825.

Step 1: Execute following MDX query to display "Reseller Sales Amount" for each fiscal year.

MDX

```
SELECT
  {
  [Measures].[Reseller Sales Amount]
  } ON COLUMNS,
  {
  [Date].[Fiscal].[Fiscal Year]
  } ON ROWS
FROM
  [Adventure Works]
```

Result

	Reseller Sales Amount
FY 2005	(null)
FY 2006	$16,288,441.77
FY 2007	$27,921,670.52
FY 2008	$36,240,484.70
FY 2009	$39,864,533.17
FY 2010	(null)
FY 2011	(null)

Step 2: Create a Cell Calculation in query scope using WITH CELL CALCULATION.
Strategy:

- The following expression returns all cells you want to modify:

```
(
[Measures].[Reseller Sales Amount],
[Date].[Fiscal].[Fiscal Year].&[2009]
)
```

- Modified value will be, [Measures].[Reseller Sales Amount]/1.0825.

MDX

```
WITH CELL CALCULATION [Fix RSA]
FOR
  '
  (
  [Measures].[Reseller Sales Amount],
  [Date].[Fiscal].[Fiscal Year].&[2009]
  )
  '
AS
  [Measures].[Reseller Sales Amount]/1.0825

SELECT
  {
  [Measures].[Reseller Sales Amount]
  } ON COLUMNS,
  {
  [Date].[Fiscal].[Fiscal Year]
  } ON ROWS
FROM
  [Adventure Works]
```

Result

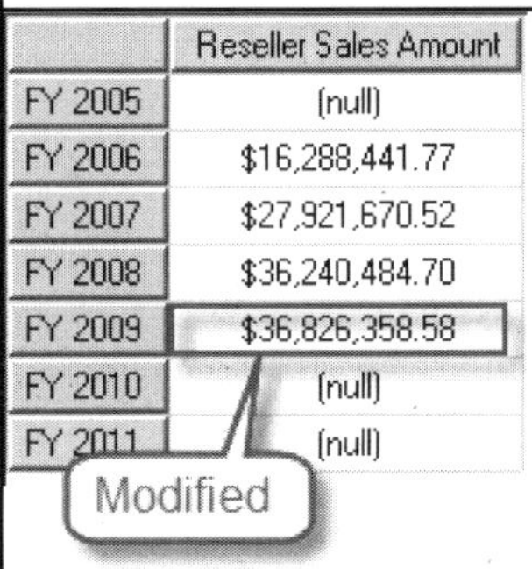

	Reseller Sales Amount
FY 2005	(null)
FY 2006	$16,288,441.77
FY 2007	$27,921,670.52
FY 2008	$36,240,484.70
FY 2009	$36,826,358.58
FY 2010	(null)
FY 2011	(null)

Query#9.11:

Goal: [Reseller Sales Amount] for fiscal year 2009 is not correct and is 8.25% too high. Create a cell calculation in scope of a **session** to modify "Reseller Sales Amount" for fiscal year 2009 as "Reseller Sales Amount"/1.0825.

Step 1: In SSMS and execute following MDX query to display [Reseller Sales Amount] for each fiscal year.

MDX

```
SELECT
  {
  [Measures].[Reseller Sales Amount]
  } ON COLUMNS,
  {
  [Date].[Fiscal].[Fiscal Year]
  } ON ROWS
FROM
  [Adventure Works]
```

Result

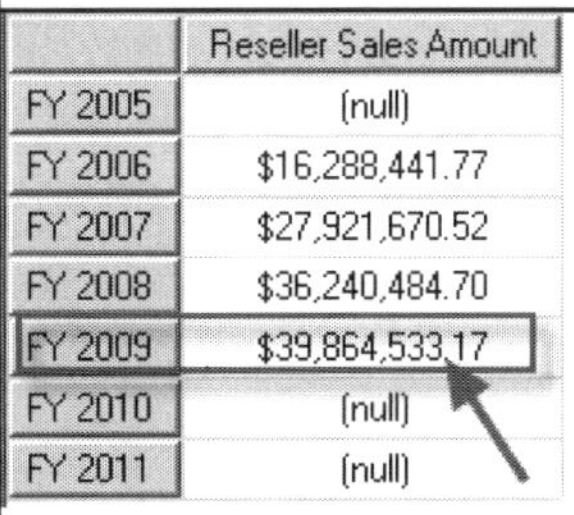

	Reseller Sales Amount
FY 2005	(null)
FY 2006	$16,288,441.77
FY 2007	$27,921,670.52
FY 2008	$36,240,484.70
FY 2009	$39,864,533.17
FY 2010	(null)
FY 2011	(null)

Step 2: In the same session, execute the following MDX statement to create cell calculation.

MDX

```
CREATE CELL CALCULATION
[Adventure Works].[Fix RSA]
FOR
  '
  (
  [Measures].[Reseller Sales Amount],
  [Date].[Fiscal].[Fiscal Year].&[2009]
  )
  '
AS
  [Measures].[Reseller Sales Amount]/1.0825;
```

Result

```
Executing the query ...
Execution complete
```

Step 3: In the same working session of SSMS execute last MDX query to display [Reseller Sales Amount] for each fiscal year.

MDX

```
SELECT
  {
  [Measures].[Reseller Sales Amount]
  } ON COLUMNS,
  {
  [Date].[Fiscal].[Fiscal Year]
  } ON ROWS
FROM
  [Adventure Works]
```

Result

	Reseller Sales Amount
FY 2005	(null)
FY 2006	$16,288,441.77
FY 2007	$27,921,670.52
FY 2008	$36,240,484.70
FY 2009	$36,826,358.58
FY 2010	(null)
FY 2011	(null)

Value changed

Step 4: To drop Cell Calculation from the session, use Drop Cell Calculation MDX statement.

MDX

```
DROP CELL CALCULATION
 [Adventure Works].[Fix RSA];
```

Result

```
Executing the query ...
Execution complete
```

Alter Cube

- Modifies the structure of a cube.
- This means you can add, delete or update a dimension member.
- Create/Update/Drop/Move dimension members of a cube and the corresponding table in relational data warehouse. This is also known as dimension write back.Write back means:
  - It updates data in a cube.
  - Write back to underlying relational table.
  - Process the cube dimension.

- **Create** a dimension member means:
  - Insert a new member in dimension.
  - Insert a new row in the underlying relational table.
  - Process the cube dimension.

- **Update** a dimension member means:
  - Update properties of a member in dimension.
  - Update the row in underlying relational table.
  - Process the cube dimension.

- **Drop** a dimension member means:
  - Delete the dimension member from dimension.
  - Delete the row from underlying relational table.
  - Process the cube dimension.

- **Move** a dimension member means:
  - Move the dimension member from one parent to other in the dimension.
  - Update parent key for the related row of underlying relational table.
  - Process the cube dimension.

- There are **restrictions/ conditions** for **write back**. These are:
  - To enable write back, go to properties of a dimension, set property "Write Enabled" as "True".
  - The dimension should be in the pure star schema, which means the dimension should be based on **only one** underlying table.
  - To do write back using MDX, the dimension should be in **parent-child** relationship.

Query#9.12:

Goal: Using "Alter Cube" statement set [United States] as the default member of Geography hierarchy in Geography dimension.

Step 1: Find default member of Geography hierarchy in Geography dimension.

MDX	Result
SELECT { [Geography].[Geography].DefaultMember } ON COLUMNS FROM [Adventure Works]	All Geographies $120,315,130.15

Step 2: Add following code at the end of "Calculations" of the cube and save.

MDX Script

```
ALTER CUBE [Adventure Works]
UPDATE DIMENSION [Geography].[Geography],
DEFAULT_MEMBER = [Geography].[Geography].[Country].&[United States];
```

Step 3: Verify that the default member of "Geography" hierarchy of "Geography" dimension is changed to "United States".

MDX	Result
SELECT { [Geography].[Geography].DefaultMember } ON COLUMNS FROM [Adventure Works]	United States $75,899,230.39

Query#9.13:

Goal: Using MDX, create a member in dimension "Account".

Account Number = 4500213

Account Type = 'Revenue'

Parent of this Account = "Intercompany Sales"

Account Description = "Financial Consultancy"

Parent Account Code Alternate Key = 5000

Operator = '+'
Value Type = 'Currency'
Note: Dimension Account has parent-child relationship

Step 1:

- Open the SSAS project in SQL Server Data Tools.
- Open the dimension "Account".
- Add following attributes to the dimension, by dragging these attributes from "Data Source View" of the table to attribute area of the dimension "Account":
    - Parent Account Code Alternate Key
    - Operator
    - Value Type
- Go to the properties of attribute "Account", set "Attribute HierarchyVisible" property as "True".
- Go to properties of dimension "Account", set "Write Enabled" property as "True".
- Process the SSAS database.

Step 2:

- Open SQL Server Management Studio.
- Select the SSAS database "AdventureWorksDW2012Multidimensional-EE".
- Execute following MDX to create a member in dimension "Account".

MDX	Result
ALTER CUBE [Adventure Works] CREATE DIMENSION MEMBER [Account].[Accounts].&[52].[Financial Consultancy], [Account Type]='Revenue', [Account Number]=4500213, [Operator]='+', [Value Type]='Currency', [Parent Account Code Alternate Key] =5000;	Executing the query ... Execution complete

Step 3:

To verify the dimension member is created in the cube:

- In SQL Server Management Studio, Expand the Dimension "Account".
- Expand the hierarchy "Accounts".
- Expand the level "Account Level 07".
- You will see a node for "Financial Consultancy". This is the account created using above Alter Cube...Create Dimension Member statement.

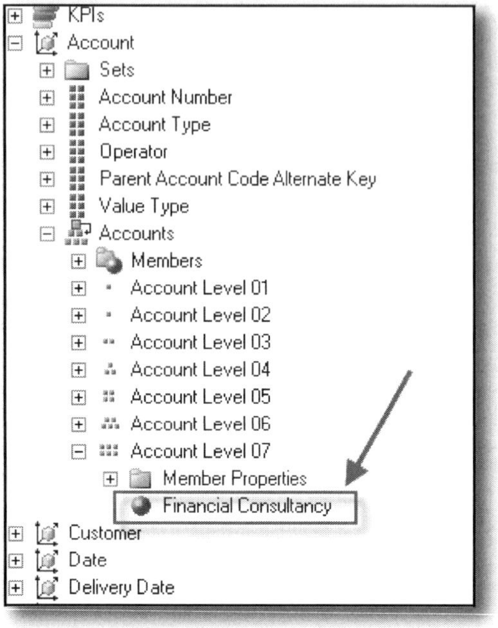

Step 4:

To verify data for the dimension member is written into the underlying table DimAccount.

- Open SQL Server Management Studio, connect to the database engine.
- Run the following Query.

SQL

```
Use [AdventureWorksDW2012];

SELECT TOP 5 *
FROM dbo.DimAccount
ORDER BY AccountKey DESC
```

Result

	AccountKey	ParentAccountKey	AccountCodeAlternateKey	ParentAccountCodeAlternateKey	AccountDescription	AccountTy
1	116	52	4500213	5000	Financial Consultancy	Revenue
2	101	51	4200	4110	Trade Sales	Revenue
3	100	27	2220	2200	Current Installments of Long-term Debt	Liabilities
4	99	95	9540	9500	Square Footage	Balances
5	98	95	9530	9500	Average Unit Price	Balances

Query#9.14:

Goal: Using MDX, update member in dimension Account created in the last query from existing Operator '+' to '~'.

Step 1:

- Open SQL Server Management Studio.
- Select the SSAS database "AdventureWorksDW2012Multidimensional-EE".
- Execute following MDX to update the member in dimension "Account"

MDX	Result
ALTER CUBE [Adventure Works] UPDATE DIMENSION MEMBER [Account].[Accounts].&[52].[Financial Consultancy], [Operator]='~';	Executing the query ... Execution complete

Step 2:

- Verify the dimension member data is updated in underlying table DimAccount.
- Open SQL Server Management Studio, connect to the database engine.
- Run the following Query.

SQL

```
Use [AdventureWorksDW2012];

SELECT TOP 5 *
FROM dbo.DimAccount
ORDER BY AccountKey DESC
```

Result

AccountKey	ParentAccountKey	AccountCodeAlternateKey	ParentAccountCodeAlternateKey	AccountDescription	AccountType	Operator
116	52	4500213	5000	Financial Consultancy	Revenue	~
101	51	4200	4110	Trade Sales	Revenue	+
100	27	2220	2200	Current Installments of Long-term Debt	Liabilities	+
99	95	9540	9500	Square Footage	Balances	~
98	95	9530	9500	Average Unit Price	Balances	~

Refresh Cube

- This MDX statement refreshes the client cache of a cube.
- This means, the client application will be synchronized with the server.

  For example,
  REFRESH CUBE [Adventure Works]

- If there is a local cube, local cube will be rebuilt.
- All data will be refreshed from server to client but refresh does not mean data will be refreshed from

the relational data warehouse to the SSAS cube.

- Typically, this MDX statement is issued by a client.

Create SubCube

- Creates a SubCube, which is a subset of the base cube.
- Syntax for Create SubCube is:
  Create SubCube <sub cube name> AS <mdx select>
- The scope of the subcube is the current session. This means, you can create a subcube in one SSMS session and use the subcube throughout the session.
- The name of the subcube must **always be the same as the name of the base cube**.
  For example,
  - For [Adventure Works] cube, you can only create a subcube with the same base cube name, which is "[Adventure Works]".
  - After creation of the subcube for the session, [Adventure Works] will refer to the subcube and not the base cube.
- Until now, in all MDX queries, only two axes are used, "Columns" and "Rows". In the select statement of a subcube, you can have more than two axes.
- The <mdx select> should not have:
  - "With Member" or "With Set" clause.
  - "Non Empty" clause.
- Optionally, you can use the "Non Visual" clause for <mdx select> to keep the true totals of the base cube.

Query#9.15:

Goal:

- Create a subcube for "Bike" sales in United States for fiscal year 2008 for all reseller business types.
- Write an MDX query to display "Reseller Sales Amount" for each state of United States for all reseller business types.

Strategy:

- You cannot run "Create SubCube" and an MDX query at the same time in a session.
- Create SubCube first and then run the MDX query.

Step 1:

Run following MDX statements to create subcube [Adventure Works]:

```
CREATE SUBCUBE [Adventure Works] AS
SELECT
  {
  [Product].[Product Categories].[Category].[Bikes]
  } ON 0,
  {
  [Geography].[Geography].[Country].&[United States]
```

```
  } ON 1,
  {
  [Reseller].[Reseller Type].[Business Type]
  } ON 2,
  {
  [Date].[Fiscal].[Fiscal Year].&[2008]
  } ON 3,
  {
  [Measures].[Reseller Sales Amount],
  [Measures].[Reseller Tax Amount]
  } ON 4
FROM
  [Adventure Works];
```

Step 2:

Run following MDX query to display "Reseller Sales Amount" for each state of United States for all reseller business types.

MDX

```
SELECT
  {
  [Reseller].[Reseller Type].[Business Type]
  } ON COLUMNS,
  {
  [Geography].[Geography].[Country].&[United States].Children
  } ON ROWS
FROM
  [Adventure Works]
WHERE
  [Measures].[Reseller Sales Amount]
```

Result

	Specialty Bike Shop	Value Added Reseller	Warehouse
Alabama	$18,031.10	(null)	$9,740.29
Arizona	$1,208.31	$301,169.21	$472,741.20
California	$294,564.13	$1,595,625.66	$1,079,481.72
Colorado	$55,704.21	$696,936.06	$107,744.20
Connecticut	$37,137.97	$229,839.24	$104,941.22
Florida	$94,165.29	$194,906.66	$386,848.40
Georgia	$36,433.57	$258,745.64	$5,021.39
Idaho	$4,730.36	$192,471.77	(null)
Illinois	$37,381.25	$20,971.84	$323.99
Indiana	(null)	(null)	$102,349.86
Kentucky	$18,646.07	$96,551.58	(null)
Maine	(null)	(null)	$68,946.20
Maryland	(null)	(null)	(null)
Massachusetts	$27,554.98	(null)	$4,698.18
Michigan	$68,063.50	$221,884.59	$175,977.04

Analysis:

- The complete description of the above query is:
  "Reseller Sales Amount" for each state of United States for all reseller business types for product category "Bikes" for fiscal year 2008.
- You can only see the members that are defined in the subcube.
  For example, "Internet Sales Amount" will not have any value.
- By default, Create SubCube has "Visual Totals" active. This means "All Level" will show the total of members in the subcube (not total from the base cube).

Step 3:

Modify last query to show "All Level".

MDX

```
SELECT
  {
  [Reseller].[Reseller Type].[All Resellers],
  [Reseller].[Reseller Type].[Business Type].Members
  } ON COLUMNS,
  {
  [Geography].[Geography].[All Geographies],
  [Geography].[Geography].[Country].&[United States].Children
  } ON ROWS
FROM
  [Adventure Works]
WHERE
  [Measures].[Reseller Sales Amount]
```

Result

	All Resellers	Specialty Bike Shop	Value Added Reseller	Warehouse
All Geographies	$16,694,041.63	$1,309,954.18	$8,720,196.14	$6,663,891.31
Alabama	$27,771.39	$18,031.10	(null)	$9,740.29
Arizona	$775,118.73	$1,208.31	$301,169.21	$472,741.20
California	$2,969,671.51	$294,564.13	$1,595,625.66	$1,079,481.72
Colorado	$860,384.47	$55,704.21	$696,936.06	$107,744.20
Connecticut	$371,918.43	$37,137.97	$229,839.24	$104,941.22
Florida	$675,920.35	$94,165.29	$194,906.66	$386,848.40
Georgia	$300,200.59	$36,433.57	$258,745.64	$5,021.39
Idaho	$197,202.13	$4,730.36	$192,471.77	(null)
Illinois	$58,677.09	$37,381.25	$20,971.84	$323.99
Indiana	$102,349.86	(null)	(null)	$102,349.86
Kentucky	$115,197.65	$18,646.07	$96,551.58	(null)
Maine	$68,946.20	(null)	(null)	$68,946.20
Maryland	(null)	(null)	(null)	(null)
Massachusetts	$32,253.16	$27,554.98	(null)	$4,698.18
Michigan	$465,925.12	$68,063.50	$221,884.59	$175,977.04

Analysis:

- "Reseller Sales Amount" for "All Geographies" shows as $16,694,041.63, which is equal to "Reseller Sales Amount" for "United States" for product category "Bikes" for fiscal year 2008. This shows that, "All Geographies" only looks in the subcube not the base cube.
- To show "All Levels" as the base cube, you should use the NON VISUAL the <mdx select> of the subcube definition.

Step 4:

- Open a new session of SQL Server Management Studio connected to your analysis services database.
- Modify the last MDX statement for create subcube, add NON VISUAL before the <mdx select>.
- Run the MDX to create subcube.

MDX

```
CREATE SUBCUBE [Adventure Works] AS
NON VISUAL
  (
  SELECT
     {
     [Product].[Product Categories].[Category].[Bikes]
     } ON 0,
     {
     [Geography].[Geography].[Country].&[United States]
     } ON 1,
     {
     [Reseller].[Reseller Type].[Business Type]
     } ON 2,
     {
     [Date].[Fiscal].[Fiscal Year].&[2008]
     } ON 3,
     {
     [Measures].[Reseller Sales Amount],
     [Measures].[Reseller Tax Amount]
     } ON 4
  FROM
     [Adventure Works]
  );
```

Analysis:

- For the above subcube, "Reseller Sales Amount" for "All Geographies" will be equal to "All Geographies" of the base cube.

Step 5:

- In the same session of SSMS, run the same query as step 3.
- But this time there will be a different result because "NON VISUAL" function added in <mdx select> of subcube definition. "Reseller Sales Amount" for "All Geographies" is total "Reseller Sales Amount" from the base cube.

MDX

```
SELECT
  {
  [Reseller].[Reseller Type].[All Resellers],
  [Reseller].[Reseller Type].[Business Type].Members
  } ON COLUMNS,
  {
  [Geography].[Geography].[All Geographies],
  [Geography].[Geography].[Country].&[United States].Children
  } ON ROWS
FROM
  [Adventure Works]
WHERE
  [Measures].[Reseller Sales Amount]
```

Result

	All Resellers	Specialty Bike Shop	Value Added Reseller	Warehouse
All Geographies	$80,032,160.45	$6,756,166.18	$34,967,517.33	$38,308,476.95
Alabama	$45,429.03	$18,055.39	(null)	$27,373.64
Arizona	$1,432,585.57	$13,899.92	$520,779.78	$897,905.86
California	$9,764,270.71	$754,050.04	$4,694,531.15	$4,315,689.52
Colorado	$2,395,913.84	$58,775.07	$1,883,326.14	$453,812.63
Connecticut	$1,125,700.41	$107,591.67	$621,954.55	$396,154.19
Florida	$2,299,888.87	$192,969.53	$792,949.11	$1,313,970.23
Georgia	$1,044,577.80	$172,820.83	$726,740.28	$145,016.68
Idaho	$227,301.75	$6,962.38	$220,339.37	(null)
Illinois	$607,939.97	$148,853.97	$306,948.57	$152,137.43
Indiana	$1,073,388.59	(null)	$452,027.95	$621,360.64
Kentucky	$163,713.84	$36,463.26	$114,906.76	$12,343.82
Mai[illegible]	$47[illegible]	[illegible]ull)	[illegible]6.68	$220,888.85

Drop SubCube

- Drops a subcube from the current session.
- Syntax for Drop SubCube is "**Drop SubCube <sub cube name>**".
- For example, you can use following code to drop the subcube from the current session:
  DROP SUBCUBE [Adventure Works]

Create Session Cube

- Creates and populates a temporary cube in the current session.
- Unlike Subcube, session cube can have a different cube name than the base cube.

In "Create Session Cube" command:

- "Measures" need to be defined before "Dimensions".
- "Measures" are defined by using keyword MEASURE.
- Dimensions and Hierarchies are defined by keyword DIMENSION.
- To create levels and members in a dimension, use keyword LEVEL and MEMBER.
  For example,
  ```
  DIMENSION [Adventure Works].[Geography].[Geography]
    (
    LEVEL     [Country],
    MEMBER    [Geography].[Geography].[Country].&[United States]
    )
  ```
- Levels need to be defined before members.
- You can create groups with some restrictions.
  For example, create group of months called "Holiday season FY 2008", which consists of two months "November, 2007" and "December, 2007".
  1. Create the level for group, using following statement:
     ```
     LEVEL   [Seasons] GROUPING
     ```
  2. Create the group with members, using following statements:
     ```
     GROUP   [Seasons].[Holiday season FY 2008]
        (
        MEMBER [Date].[Fiscal].[Month].&[2007]&[11],
        MEMBER [Date].[Fiscal].[Month].&[2007]&[12]
        )
     ```
- Restrictions of grouping:
  - Groups are based on the same dimension only.
  - Groups not allowed for:
    - Unnatural hierarchies.
    - Discretized attribute hierarchies.
    - Parent-Child hierarchies.
    - Linked dimensions.
    - ROLAP dimensions.

Query#9.16:

Goal: Create a session cube for "Bike" sales for product categories for countries for fiscal data. Also create following groups:

- "Holiday season FY 2008" = "Nov, 2007" and "Dec, 2007".
- "North American Countries" = "United States" and "Canada".

MDX

Level then Member

Measure then Dimension

```
CREATE SESSION CUBE [Reseller Cube]
FROM    [Adventure Works]
    (
    MEASURE     [Adventure Works].[Reseller Sales Amount],
    MEASURE     [Adventure Works].[Reseller Tax Amount],

    DIMENSION   [Adventure Works].[Product].[Product Categories]
        (
        LEVEL   [Category],
        MEMBER  [Product].[Product Categories].[Category].[Bikes]
        ),

    DIMENSION   [Adventure Works].[Geography].[Geography]
        (
        LEVEL   [Country],
        LEVEL   [CountryGroups] GROUPING,
        MEMBER  [Geography].[Geography].[Country].&[United States],
        GROUP   [CountryGroups].[North American Countries]
            (
            MEMBER [Geography].[Geography].[Country].&[United States],
            MEMBER [Geography].[Geography].[Country].&[Canada]
            )
        ),

    DIMENSION   [Adventure Works].[Date].[Fiscal]
        (
        LEVEL   [Seasons] GROUPING,
        GROUP   [Seasons].[Holiday season FY 2008]
            (
            MEMBER [Date].[Fiscal].[Month].&[2007]&[11],
            MEMBER [Date].[Fiscal].[Month].&[2007]&[12]
            )
        )
    )
```

Level for Group

Group Definition

Create Global Cube

- Creates a persistent cube locally, by retrieving data from analysis server and save in a **.cub** file.
- You need to define a storage location to store the .cub file locally.
- The result of "Create Global Cube" is a **.cub file**, which can be accessed by various applications, (for example Microsoft Excel).

Query#9.17:

Goal:

- Create a global cube for product categories, geography, customers and fiscal data for measures [Reseller Sales Amount], [Reseller Tax Amount], [Sales Amount], [Total Product Cost] & [Internet Sales Amount].
- Open the file using Microsoft Excel application.

Step 1:

- Create a directory "C:\ResellerAnalysis".Execute following MDX statement in SSMS.

MDX	CREATE GLOBAL CUBE [ResellerAnalysis] Storage 'C:\ResellerAnalysis\ResellerAnalysis.cub' FROM [Adventure Works] (MEASURE [Adventure Works].[Reseller Sales Amount], MEASURE [Adventure Works].[Reseller Tax Amount], MEASURE [Adventure Works].[Sales Amount], MEASURE [Adventure Works].[Total Product Cost], MEASURE [Adventure Works].[Internet Sales Amount], DIMENSION [Adventure Works].[Product].[Product Categories], DIMENSION [Adventure Works].[Geography].[Geography], DIMENSION [Adventure Works].[Date].[Fiscal], DIMENSION [Adventure Works].[Customer])

Step 2:

- Open "Microsoft Excel 2010", go to "Data" tab.
- Click on "existing connections".
- Click on "Browse for more..." and select C:\ResellerAnalysis\ResellerAnalysis.cub".

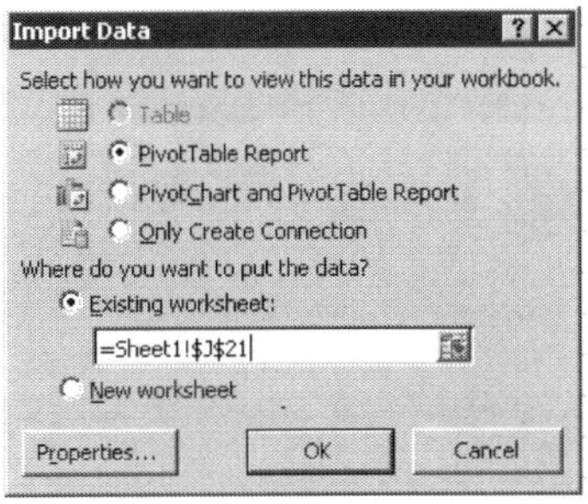

Figure 9-5 : Import Data dialog.

- Click "OK" on Import Data dialog.

- You will be able to see data in an Excel Pivot table.
- Select following fields from the Pivot table field list
    - Reseller Sales Amount.
    - Fiscal Year
    - Geography
- Select the view of the Pivot table field list as "Fields section Only".

Figure 9-6: Open locally persistent cube from Microsoft Excel 2010.

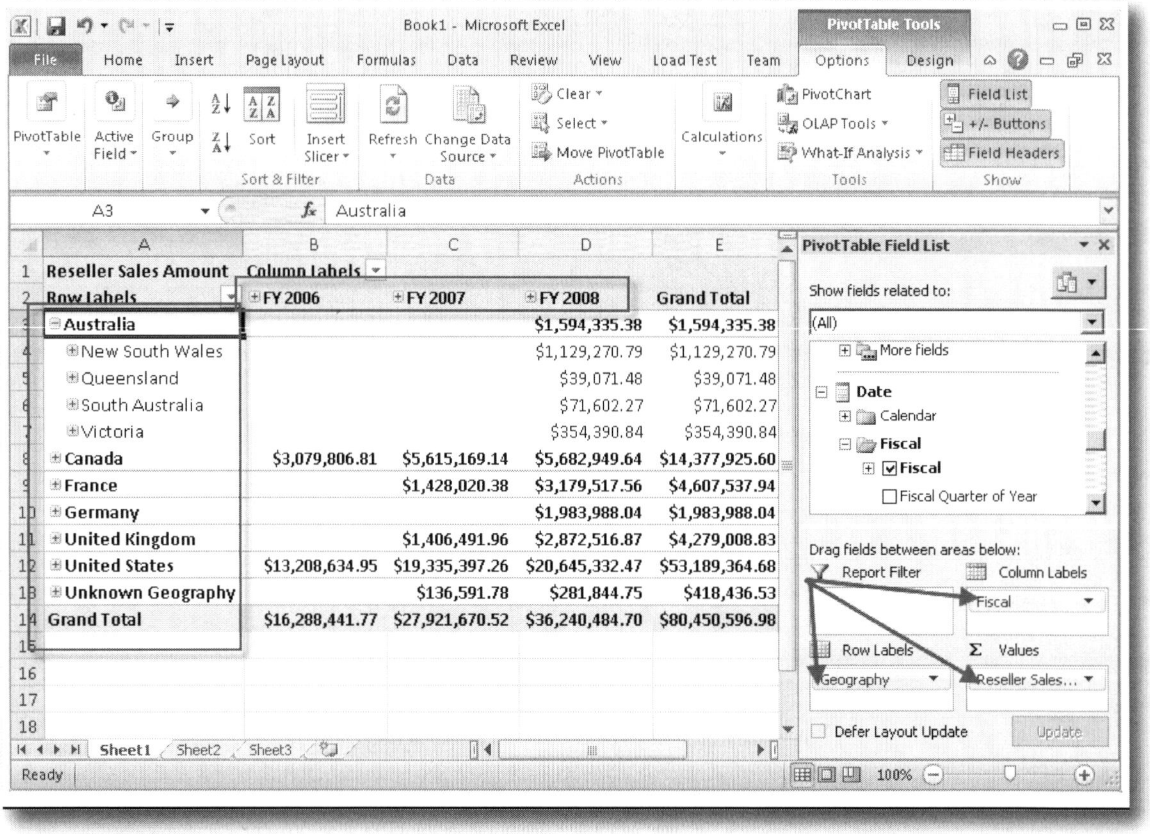

Create Action

- This creates an action for a cube, dimension, hierarchy or set. Different types of standard actions are:
    - URL
    - HTML
    - Command Line
    - Dataset
    - Rowset
    - Statement
    - Proprietary

Query#9.18:

Goal: Create an URL action for states in Geography dimension to show the map in maps.google.com.

MDX	
	CREATE ACTION [Adventure Works].[Show State Map] FOR [Geography].[Geography].[State-Province] AS "http://maps.google.com?q="+ [Geography].[State-Province].CurrentMember.Name, TYPE=URL, CAPTION="State Map..";

Drop Action

- Drops an action.

To drop previous action, execute following query:

MDX	
	DROP ACTION [Adventure Works].[Show State Map]

DrillThrough

- Returns detail data from underlying table.
- The MDX query should return **only one cell**; Drillthrough will return a detail of one cell only.

For example,

```
DRILLTHROUGH
SELECT
  {
  [Measures].[Reseller Sales Amount]
  } ON COLUMNS,
  {
  [Product].[Product Categories].[Category]
  } ON ROWS
FROM
  [Adventure Works]
```

This MDX query will return an error, because if returns **more than one cell**. Instead you can display "Reseller Sales Amount" for Bikes which will return one cell instead of all product categories.

```
DRILLTHROUGH
SELECT
  {
  [Measures].[Reseller Sales Amount]
  } ON COLUMNS
FROM
  [Adventure Works]
WHERE
  [Product].[Product Categories].[Category].&[1]
```

- You can optionally define the maximum number of rows you want to display.
- By default, **Drillthrough** will return all columns from the underlying tables. You can also optionally define which columns of underlying table you want to display.
  - Column names for the dimension have $ in front of dimension name. For example, city of Geography dimension can be expressed as [$Geography].[City].
  - Column names for measures name is expressed as "Measure Group Name"."Measure Name". For example "Reseller Sales Amount" of "Reseller Sales" measure group can be expressed as [Reseller Sales].[Reseller Sales Amount].
- Drillthrough function does not need any additional security. This means that if a user has access to execute the MDX that returns the cell, the user should be able to see the Drillthrough data.

Query#9.18:

Goal: Find details for "Reseller Sales Amount" for Bike sales for the state of Texas for fiscal year 2008. Also show maximum 200 rows. Include the following fields from underlying data: Delivery date, Product name, "Reseller Sales Amount" and "Reseller Order Quantity".

Step 1: Find "Reseller Sales Amount" for Bike sales for the state of Texas for fiscal year 2008.

MDX	Result
SELECT { [Measures].[Reseller Sales Amount] } ON COLUMNS FROM [Adventure Works] WHERE ([Geography].[Geography].[State-Province].&[TX]&[US], [Product].[Product Categories].[Category].[Bikes], [Date].[Fiscal].[Fiscal Year].&[2008])	Reseller Sales Amount $1,735,299.03

Step 2: Modify last query, add DRILLTHROUGH to see all columns in underlying data.

MDX

```
DRILLTHROUGH
SELECT
  {
  [Measures].[Reseller Sales Amount]
  } ON COLUMNS
FROM
  [Adventure Works]
WHERE
  (
  [Geography].[Geography].[State-Province].&[TX]&[US],
  [Product].[Product Categories].[Category].[Bikes],
  [Date].[Fiscal].[Fiscal Year].&[2008]
  )
```

Result

[Reseller Sales].[Reseller Sales Amount]	[Reseller Sales].[...	[Reseller Sales].[...	[Reseller Sales].[...	[Reseller Sales].[...	[Reseller S
3061.782	3	3061.782	244.9426	76.5446	0
1295.976	4	1295.976	103.6781	32.3994	0
1619.97	5	1619.97	129.5976	40.4993	0
2689.176	4	2689.176	215.1341	67.2294	0
672.294	1	672.294	53.7835	16.8074	0
4082.376	4	4082.376	326.5901	102.0594	0
3061.782	3	3061.782	244.9426	76.5446	0
4398.03	3	4398.03	351.8424	109.9508	0
4398.03	3	4398.03	351.8424	109.9508	0
2932.02	2	2932.02	234.5616	73.3005	0
5864.04	4	5864.04	469.1232	146.601	0
971.982	3	971.982	77.7586	24.2996	0
2689.176	4	2689.176	215.1341	67.2294	0
1466.0[illegible]	[illegible]	[illegible]	[illegible]	36.6[illegible]	[illegible]

Step 3: Modify the last query, add "MaxRows"clause immediately after "Drillthrough" to limit number of rows to 200 and "Return" clause at the end end of the query to display only selected columns.

MDX

```
DRILLTHROUGH
MAXROWS 200
SELECT
  {
  [Measures].[Reseller Sales Amount]
  } ON COLUMNS
FROM
  [Adventure Works]
WHERE
  (
  [Geography].[Geography].[State-Province].&[TX]&[US],
  [Product].[Product Categories].[Category].[Bikes],
  [Date].[Fiscal].[Fiscal Year].&[2008]
  )
RETURN
  [$Delivery Date].[Date] AS DeliveryDate,
  [$Product].[Product] AS  ProductName,
  [Reseller Sales].[Reseller Sales Amount] AS SalesAmount,
  [Reseller Sales].[Reseller Order Quantity] AS SalesQuantity
```

Result

DeliveryDate	ProductName	SalesAmount	SalesQuantity
July 13, 2007	Road-350-W Ye...	3061.782	3
July 13, 2007	Road-750 Black...	1295.976	4
July 13, 2007	Road-750 Black...	1619.97	5
July 13, 2007	Road-550-W Ye...	2689.176	4
July 13, 2007	Road-550-W Ye...	672.294	1
July 13, 2007	Road-350-W Ye...	4082.376	4
July 13, 2007	Road-350-W Ye...	3061.782	3
July 13, 2007	Road-250 Black...	4398.03	3
July 13, 2007	Road-250 Black...	4398.03	3
July 13, 2007	Road-250 Red, ...	2932.02	2
July 13, 2007	Road-250 Black...	5864.04	4
July 13, 2007	Road-750 Black...	971.982	3
July 13, 2007	Road-550-W Ye...	2689.176	4
July 13, 2007	Road-250 Black...	1466.01	1
July 13, 2007	Road-350-W Ye...	3061.782	3
July 13, 2007	Road-550-W Ye...	2016.882	3

Clear Calculations

- Removes calculations from a cube.
- You cannot use this statement in "Calculations" of a cube as it will give an error "Script contains statement, which is not allowed".
- You can use "Clear Calculations" in a session. It will remove all calculations for the scope of the session. However, it will not remove from "Calculations" of the cube.

Query#9.19:

Goal: Remove all calculations of a cube in a session.

Step 1: Open SQL Server Management Studio and connect to analysis services. Show "Reseller Sales Amount" and "Reseller Gross Profit" for all product categories.

MDX

```
SELECT
  {
  [Measures].[Reseller Sales Amount],
  [Measures].[Reseller Gross Profit]
  } ON COLUMNS,
  {
  [Product].[Product Categories].[Category]
  } ON ROWS
FROM
  [Adventure Works];
```

Result

	Reseller Sales Amount	Reseller Gross Profit
Accessories	$571,257.55	$195,779.98
Bikes	$66,012,957.84	($1,015,531.18)
Clothing	$1,772,148.94	$230,754.18
Components	$11,675,796.11	$1,017,085.96

Note: "Reseller Sales Amount" is not a calculated member but "Reseller Gross Profit" is a calculated member and this calculated member is defined in calculations of the cube.

Step 2:

- In the same SQL Server Management Studio session, execute Clear Calculations.
- This should remove calculations. This means, "Reseller Gross Profit" will not exist anymore.

MDX

```
CLEAR CALCULATIONS FROM [Adventure Works];
```

Result

```
Executing the query ...
Execution complete
```

Step 3:

- In the same SQL Server Management Studio session, execute the query from step 1 to display "Reseller Sales Amount" and "Reseller Gross Profit" for all product categories.
- As calculated members from this session is removed , the query will return an error.

MDX	Result
SELECT { [Measures].[Reseller Sales Amount], [Measures].[Reseller Gross Profit] } ON COLUMNS, { [Product].[Product Categories].[Category] } ON ROWS FROM [Adventure Works];	Executing the query ... Query (4, 2) The '[Reseller Gross Profit]' member was not found in the cube when the string, [Measures].[Reseller Gross Profit], was parsed. Execution complete

Call

- "Call" statement executes a registered stored procedure.
- A stored procedure in SSAS means **.Net assembly functions** and is called from MDX.
- Steps for implementing stored procedure or .net assembly:
  - Create a .Net library to create your .net method, which may return a value or void.
  - Build the .net library, the output will be .dll file.
  - Register the above mentioned .dll in SQL Server Analysis Services.
  - Now you can use the above functions in MDX.

Query#9.20:

Goal: Write a HelloWorld() function in .Net and call the function from MDX.

Steps:

1 Create a c# .net library in "Visual Studio", name of the library: MyLib.
2 Rename the class1 to "Message".
3 Add a method "HelloWorld" in class "Message", which returns the string "Hello World"

```
MyLib.Message
using System;
using System.Collections.Generic;
using System.Linq;
using System.Text;

namespace MyLib
{
    public class Message
    {
        public string HelloWorld()
        {
            return "Hello World";
        }
    }
}
```

Figure 9-6 : C# code for HelloWorld().

4 Compile the project.
5 MyLib.dll will be generated in the "bin" directory of the project.
6 Open the SSAS database [Adventure Works] in SSMS.
7 Right click on Assemblies and add new assembly MyLib.dll.
8 Permission: Unrestricted.
9 Impersonation: Service Account.
10 Now following MDX will display the string:

MDX	Result
WITH MEMBER [Measures].[HelloWorld] AS MyLib.HelloWorld() SELECT { [Measures].[HelloWorld] } ON COLUMNS FROM [Adventure Works];	HelloWorld Hello World

Query#9.21:

Goal: Write a "CreateDirectory (string <directory name>)" function in .Net, which creates a directory in C:\Workspace. Call this function from MDX using "Call" statement.

Steps:

1 Create a directory "C:\Workspace" in your machine.
2 Open the library MyLib in Visual Studio.
3 Add a method "CreateDirectory (string <directory name>)" in class "Message", which creates directory <directory name> in "C:\Workspace".

Note: This function creates a directory.

4 Open the SSAS database [Adventure Works] in SSMS.
5 Expand "Assembles" and delete MyLib.dll.
6 Right click on "Assemblies" and add MyLib.dll.
7 Permission: Unrestricted.
8 Impersonation: Service Account.

Figure 9-7: C# code for CreateDirectory().

```
using System;
using System.Collections.Generic;
using System.Linq;
using System.Text;
using System.IO;

namespace MyLib
{
    public class Message
    {
        public string HelloWorld()
        {
            return "Hello World";
        }

        public void CreateDirectory(string directory_name)
        {
            string path = @"c:\Workspace\" + directory_name;
            try
            {
                DirectoryInfo di = Directory.CreateDirectory(path);
            }
            catch (Exception e)
            {
            }
            finally { }
        }

    }
}
```

9 Run the following MDX.

MDX	Result
CALL MyLib.CreateDirectory("test1");	Executing the query ... Execution complete

10 Verify the directory "test1" is created in directory "C:\workspace".

Update Cube

- **Update Cube** assigns a value to a tuple.
- Update cube cannot be used in "Calculations" of a cube.
- When update cube is executed in **session** of SQL Server Management Studio, the scope of the change is **limited to that session only**.
- This means that if a value is assigned to a tuple, the value will not be visible to other sessions.

Query#9.22:

Goal: There are no sales for fiscal year 2009. Write back some sample sales in the cube only for this session.

Step 1:

- Open a SQL Server Management Studio session
- Find "Reseller Sales Amount" for each fiscal year.

MDX

```
SELECT
  {
  [Measures].[Reseller Sales Amount]
  } ON COLUMNS,
  {
  [Date].[Fiscal].[Fiscal Year]
  } ON ROWS
FROM
  [Adventure Works]
```

Result

	Reseller Sales Amount
FY 2005	(null)
FY 2006	$16,288,441.77
FY 2007	$27,921,670.52
FY 2008	$36,240,484.70
FY 2009	(null)
FY 2010	(null)
FY 2011	(null)

Analysis:

- There are no sales for fiscal year 2009.

Step 2: Add some sample sales for fiscal year 2009 using Update cube statement.

Strategy:

- You cannot just write for tuple
  ([Measures].[Reseller Sales Amount], [Date].[Fiscal].[Fiscal Year].&[2009])
  This will give memory error, because there are too many combinations that need to be updated.
- To create more precise sample data for 2009, execute following MDX in current session of SSMS:

```
UPDATE CUBE
  [Adventure Works]
SET
  (
  [Measures].[Reseller Sales Amount],
```

```
[Date].[Fiscal].[Date].&[20090116],
[Geography].[Geography].[Postal Code].&[75074]&[Plano]&[TX],
[Product].[Product Categories].[Product].&[447],
[Reseller].[Reseller Type].[Reseller].&[347],
[Delivery Date].[Fiscal].[Date].&[20090116],
[Ship Date].[Fiscal].[Date].&[20090116],
[Employee].[Employees].&[114],
[Promotion].[Promotions].[Category].&[Reseller].&[Seasonal Discount].&[11],
[Sales Territory].[Sales Territory].[Region].&[3],
[Source Currency].[Source Currency].&[US Dollar]
) = 1000;
```

Step 3: In the same session of SSMS, find "Reseller Sales Amount" for each fiscal year.

MDX

```
SELECT
  {
  [Measures].[Reseller Sales Amount]
  } ON COLUMNS,
  {
  [Date].[Fiscal].[Fiscal Year]
  } ON ROWS
FROM
  [Adventure Works]
```

Result

	Reseller Sales Amount
FY 2005	(null)
FY 2006	$16,288,441.77
FY 2007	$27,921,670.52
FY 2008	$36,240,484.70
FY 2009	$1,000.00
FY 2010	(null)
FY 2011	(null)

Note: Sales added for FY 2009. The scope of the update cube statement is the **current session only**.

EXERCISES

Exercise 9.1: Using Alter Cube statement in calculation of cube, change default destination currency to Euro.

Exercise 9.2: Find "Reseller Sales Amount" in GBP for "United Kingdom" for March, 2008.

Exercise 9.3: Find "Customer Name", "Source Currency" and "Sales Order Number" for all internet sales for product "Water Bottle - 30 oz." in June 1, 2008.

Chapter 10: MDX Performance Tuning And Best Practices

This chapter explores some common performance issues and best practices in MDX. The tuning process needs to be part of all major phases of software development cycle, viz.

- Design phase
- Development phase
- Production phase

Early detection of performance issues saves time and money. Fixing a design issue in "Production phase" will cost exponential amount of time and money. In this chapter, some of the most important topics of each phase explained.

The first section explains "MDX Query Processing Architecture", which is necessary to understand the tuning process. Designers, developers and administrators of the system must understand the architecture of MDX processing to design an optimize system and write effective MDX queries.

The second section explain and explores tuning tips in design, development and production phases. Tuning also depends on real data from production. For example, "Usage Based Aggregation" is a design of aggregation based on the production data. There are total fifteen tips included in this chapter. These tips do not cover all possible tuning issues but provide a good overview of common tuning issues and solutions. Another important point is, always avoid over design a system. Most commercial systems are tuned for most common issues and events.

Agenda

- *MDX Query Processing Architecture*
- ***Design Phase Tuning***:
  Dimension Design
  Aggregation Design
  Partition Design
- ***Development Phase Tuning***:
  MDX Tuning
- ***Production Phase Tuning***:
  Disable Query Logging
  Usage Based Aggregation
  Configure Parallelism

MDX Query Processing Architecture

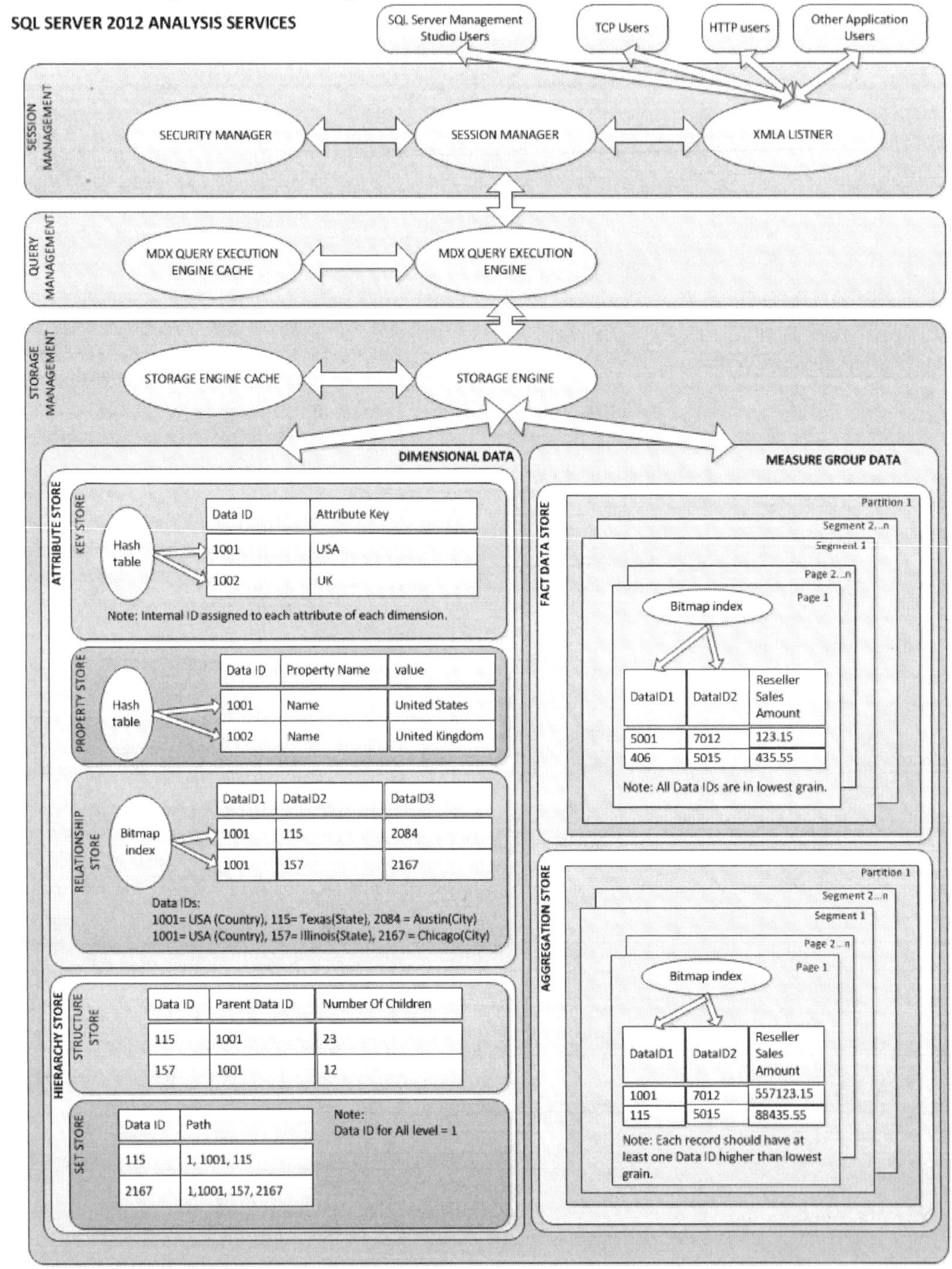

Figure 10-1: MDX Query Processing Architecture.

Three Layers

The architecture is divided into three layers:

- **Session Management**: This is the topmost layer and is responsible for managing user sessions and user authentication.
- **Query Management:** This layer is responsible for executing MDX queries, retrieving data from storage and returning results to the user.
- **Storage Management**:
  - Retrieval orders of locations are:
    - Storage Engine Cache.
    - If data is not present in "Storage Engine Cache", look for data in Aggregations.
    - If data is not present in "Aggregations", look for data in appropriate partition or dimension where data is physically stored.

Session Management

The Session Management layer has three main components:

- **XMLA Listener**: XMLA stands for XML for Analysis. XMLA Listener waits for user requests. Once user session request is received, it passes session request to "Session Manager".
- **Session Manager**: Session manager manages activities of user sessions as well as role-based permissions with the help of "Security Manager".
- **Security Manager**: The security manager identifies the user and retrieves permissions based the user's role.

Query Management

The Query Management layer has two main components:

- **MDX Query Execution Engine**: The MDX query execution engine is responsible for:
  - Parsing MDX code
  - Generating execution plan
  - Requesting data from storage
  - Caching the execution plan and data in "MDX Query Execution Cache"
  - Returning data to the user
- **MDX Query Execution Engine Cache**: The MDX query execution engine caches "storage execution plan" and data for recent queries and can be accessed by future requests depending on the scope of a query. There are three scopes of cache:
  - **Cube**: For global MDX queries, the execution plan and data for a query can be used by any other query. For example, when a calculated member defined in "Calculations" of a cube, the scope of the MDX is global and cache can be used by any other query connected to the cube with the same security context.
  - **Session**: When a query has a session scope, the execution plan and data can be used by that session only.
  - **Query**: Any execution plan within a query can be used in that query. For example, "With Member" in a query will be cached throughout the query.

Storage Management

The Storage Management layer has three main components:

- **Storage Engine**: The Storage Engine retrieves data from data stores for dimensions and partitions. It also co-ordinates the data merging from multiple partitions/segments.
- **Storage Engine Cache**: The "Storage Engine Cache" stores data for future use.
- **Data Stores**: This is the most important part of "MDX Query Architecture". All dimension and fact data stored in "Data Stores". Two types of "Data Stores":
  - **Dimensional Data Store**: "Dimension Data Store" stores dimension data of the cube and can be categorized into two groups:
    - Attribute Store
    - Hierarchy Store
  - **Measure Group Data Store**: "Measure Group Data Store" stores measure data of the cube and can be categorized two groups:
    - Fact Data Store
    - Aggregation Store

Attribute Store

"Attribute Store" stores all attributes of all dimensions. There are three types of attribute stores, "Key Store", "Property Store" and "Relationship Store", as described below.

- **Key Store**: For each attribute of each dimension, "SQL Server Analysis Services" assign an internal ID called DataID for each key values. For example, "Geography" dimension has five attributes:
  - [Geography Key]
  - Country
  - State-Province
  - City
  - [Postal Code]

  For [Geography Key] attribute,

    - [Geography Key] is not visible to users as "AttributeHierarchyVisible" property is false for this attribute.
    - "Key Columns" have only one column, which is GeographyKey. DataID will be assigned to each attribute key. Let us assume following Data IDs for some of the attribute keys:

Data ID	[Geography Key] Attribute Key
1001	432
1002	360
1003	578
1004	522
1005	409

Above table consists of [Geography Key] for postal codes 94109, 33127, 60610, 10007, 75201 and later used in "Relationship Store".

For Country attribute,

- "Key Columns" have only one column, which is EnglishCountryRegionName. A DataID will be assigned to each attribute key. Let us assume following Data IDs for some attribute keys:

Data ID	Country Attribute Key
2001	Australia
2002	United States
2003	United Kingdom
2004	Germany
2005	Canada
2006	France

For State-Province attribute,

- "Key Columns" is a collection of StateProvinceCode and CountryRegion code. A DataID will be assigned to each attribute key. Let us assume following Data IDs for some attribute keys:

Data ID	State-Province Attribute Key
3001	IL,US
3002	CA,US
3003	TX,US
3004	NY,US
3005	FL,US

- "Name Column" is StateProvince name and treated as properties of the attribute and discuss in the "Property Store" bullet.

For City attribute,

- "Key Columns" is a collection of City and StateProvinceCode. A DataID will be assigned to each attribute key. Let us assume following Data IDs for some attribute keys:

Data ID	City Attribute Key
4001	Chicago,IL
4002	San Francisco, CA
4003	Dallas, TX
4004	New York, NY
4005	Miami, FL

For Postal-Code attribute,

- "Key Columns" is a collection of City and StateProvinceCode. A DataID will be assigned to each attribute key. Let us assume following Data IDs for some attribute keys:

Data ID	Postal-Code Attribute Key
5001	60610, Chicago,IL
5002	94109, San Francisco, CA
5003	75201, Dallas, TX
5004	10007, New York, NY
5005	33127, Miami, FL

Hash tables for "Attribute Store" will ensure faster access.

- **Property Store**: The "Property Store" stores properties of attributes, for example, name of an attribute, translation etc.

Data ID	Name	Description
3001	Illinois	IL,US
3002	California	CA,US
3003	Texas	TX,US
3004	New York	NY,US
3005	Florida	FL,US

Hash tables for "Property Store" will ensure faster access.

- **Relationship Store**: The "Relationship store" contains relationship among attributes of a dimension. Some sample relationship store entries are shown below:

Data ID Geography Key	Data ID Country	Data ID State-Province	Data ID City	Data ID Postal-Code	Description
1001	2002	3001	4001	5001	60610, Chicago,IL, US
1002	2002	3002	4002	5002	94109, San Francisco, CA,US
1003	2002	3003	4003	5003	75201, Dallas, TX,US
1004	2002	3004	4004	5004	10007, New York, NY,US
1005	2002	3005	4004	5005	33127, Miami, FL,US

Bitmap index for "Relationship Store" ensures faster access.

Hierarchy Store

The "Hierarchy Store" stores all hierarchies of all dimensions and has two types of stores "Set Store" and "Structure Store" as described below:

- **Set Store**: This store has one entry for each member of the hierarchy, and it stores the complete path from first level (All Level) to the current member. The path of a member is defined by using Data IDs.
  For example, following are some entries for "Geography" hierarchy:

Data ID	Path	Description
101	101	All level of the hierarchy
2002	101,2002	United States, Level: Country
2006	101,2006	France, Level: Country
3005	101,2002,3005	Florida, Level: State-Province
3003	101,2002,3003	Texas, Level: State-Province
4003	101,2002,3003, 4003	Dallas, Level: City
4005	101,2002,3005, 4005	Maimi, Level: City
5003	101,2002,3003, 4003,5003	75201, Level: Postal-Code
5005	101,2002,3005, 4005,5005	33127, Level: State-Province

- **Structure Store**: The "Structure Store" stores the hierarchy structure. It stores Data ID, Parent Data ID and number of children. Below is the representation of the "Structure Store" for above "Set Store" entries for "Geography" hierarchy:

Data ID	Parent Data ID	Number Of Children	Description
101	0	1320	All level of the hierarchy
2002	101	788	United States, Level: Country
2006	101	102	France, Level: Country
3005	2002	15	Florida, Level: State-Province
3003	2002	23	Texas, Level: State-Province
4003	3003	1	Dallas, Level: City
4005	3005	1	Maimi, Level: City
5003	4003	0	75201, Level: Postal-Code
5005	4005	0	33127, Level: State-Province

The data structure of "Fact Data Store" and "Aggregation Store" is the same for MOLAP storage:

- The store is divided into one or more partitions.
- Each partition consists of one or more Segments.
- Each Segment is divided into 256 pages.
- Each page contains 256 records.
- Typically, the size of each segment is 64 KB.

Fact Data Store

The "Fact Data Store" stores all fact data at the lowest level (lowest grain). This store does not store any aggregation data. All Data IDs are at the lowest level. "Reseller Sales Amount" in following table is an example (although these are not real values).

Data ID Geography Key	Data ID Product Key	Data ID Date Key	...	Reseller Sales Amount
1001	12001	23001	...	$123.15
1002	12002	23002	...	$435.55
1003	12003	23003	...	$565.55
1004	12004	23004	...	$434.77
1005	12005	23005	...	$414.22

Aggregation Store

"Aggregation Store" stores all aggregated fact data of the cube. Means, this store does not store any lowest grain fact data.

- At least, one Data ID of each record must be higher than the lowest grain.
- In the following example, State-Province and Month are higher than the lowest grain level.
- You can have more than one Data IDs from level higher than the lowest grain level.

Data ID State-Province	Data ID Product Key	Data ID Month	...	Reseller Sales Amount
3001	12001	23001	...	$21123.15
3002	12002	23002	...	$12435.55
3003	12003	23003	...	$13565.55
3004	12004	23004	...	$21434.77
3005	12005	23005	...	$12414.22

Design Phase Tuning

As the name suggests, these tuning tips are for design issues of the application and typically resolved during design phase of the application.

Tip #1: Design Your Dimension Efficiently

- **Hierarchies**:

  There are two types of hierarchies, "Attribute Hierarchies" and "User Defined Hierarchies":

  - Attribute Hierarchies: These are default hierarchies for each attribute, and typically have two levels
    (a) "All Level"
    (b) "Individual Level"

    Tip #1.1: Do not disable "All Level" for Attribute Hierarchies.

    - Disabling "All Level" means queries must slice the data on an attribute value, always slicing of data will slow down the performance of a MDX query.
    - Enable "All Level" of an attribute by setting "IsAggregatable" property to "true".

    Tip #1.2: Attribute Hierarchies are slower than corresponding User Defined Hierarchies.

    - Aggregation does not include "Attribute Hierarchies" and hence MDX queries using "Attribute Hierarchies" is slower than corresponding queries on "User Defined Hierarchies".

  - User Defined Hierarchies: There are two different types of "User Defined Hierarchies", "Natural Hierarchies" and "Unnatural Hierarchies":
    - Natural Hierarchies: These are hierarchies "Naturally" exist within the data. For example, for "Geography" dimension, the following levels create a natural hierarchy:
      - All Level
      - Country
      - State-Province
      - City
      - Postal-Code

    - Unnatural Hierarchies: These hierarchies may not "Naturally" exist within the data. For example, Product has "color" and "size" properties but these may not be related to each other:
      - All Level
      - Color
      - Size
      - Product

    Tip #1.3: Natural Hierarchies are faster than Unnatural Hierarchies.

    Aggregation does not include "Unnatural Hierarchies" and hence MDX queries using "Unnatural Hierarchies" are slower than the corresponding queries on "Natural Hierarchies".

- **Attribute Relationships**:
  All levels of a natural hierarchy should have attribute relationships defined.

Tip #1.4: Do not forget to define attribute relationships for Natural Hierarchies. Natural Hierarchy without an Attribute Relationship = Unnatural Hierarchy.

Once all the attributes of a hierarchy have been identified, the next step is to identify each value of attributes uniquely. That means, identify "Key Columns" of each attribute. For example, attributes of "Geography" hierarchy of the "Geography" dimension can be described as follows:

Attribute Name	Key Columns	Description
Country	EnglishCountryRegionName	EnglishCountryRegionName is unique in the cube.
State-Province	CountryRegionCode, StateProvinceCode	Same state may exist in another country.
City	StateProvinceCode, City	Same city may exist in another state.
Postal-Code	StateProvinceCode, City, Postal-Code	Same Postal-Cod may exist in another city of another state.

- Duplicate keys: Duplicate keys always create rollup issues in a hierarchy. You need to select the action for detection of duplicate keys, which can be:
  - IgnoreError
  - ReportAndContinue
  - ReportAndStop

Tip #1.5: Avoid Duplicate Keys.

- Flexible versus Rigid attribute relationships: A "Flexible" relationship means that a member can change parent and "Rigid" relationship means that a member cannot change its parent.
  For example,
  - The relationship between "City" and "State-Province" is "Flexible", if "City" can be moved from one state to another state.
  - The relationship between "City" and "State-Province" is "Rigid" if "City" cannot be moved from one state to another state.

Tip #1.6: "Rigid" Relationship needs "Process Full" for dimension and fact. Try to avoid "Rigid" relationships, unless it is necessary.

Tip #2: Partition Your Measure Data Efficiently

- Partition means, partition of "Measure Groups" of a cube.
- Partitions are mutually exclusive sets, but not necessarily uniform sets. For example, very common criteria for partitions are "Time". You can have partitions for
  - FY 2007, FY 2008, FY 2009, FY 2010 and FY 2011.
  - For the current year, you can have monthly partitions.
- Each partition is bound to a query, a view or a source table.

Tip #2.1: Query gives flexibility to define partition criteria.

Using a query for partition gives flexibility to select wide range of data based on query criteria.

Tip #2.2: Size of a partition should not exceed 250MB or 20 million records.

If the partition size exceeds any of these limits, It should be broken into smaller partitions.

Tip #2.3: Too many small partitions will have negative effect on performance.

Partition size should not be less than 4096 records. Consider merging small partitions into a bigger partition.

Tip #3: Design Your Aggregation Efficiently

The design of aggregation depends on the design of hierarchies and attribute relationships. Some check points about aggregation:

- Aggregation is defined for each partition of a measure group.
- Aggregation means summarized value of a "Measure Group" for different levels of a hierarchy.
- Hierarchy is defined for dimensions.
- Attribute relationship is defined for hierarchies.

For example,

- "Geography" is a dimension.
- "Geography" is also a name of a hierarchy in the dimension "Geography".
  This hierarchy has five levels:
    - "All Level".
    - Country: "Country" rolls up to "All Level".
    - State-Province: "State-Province" rolls up to "Country".
    - City: "City" rolls up to "State-Province".
    - Postal-Code: "Postal-Code" rolls up to "City".

- There are three attribute relationships in this hierarchy
  - "Postal-Code" and "City".
  - "City" and "State-Province'.
  - "State-Province' and "Country".

Aggregations can be created in two different phases:

- **Design Phase**: This is the initial design of aggregations and can be created using the tool "Aggregation Design Wizard".
- **Production Phase**: This is the re-design of aggregations, depends on the real data and can be created using the tool "Usage Based Aggregation". This topic is discussed in the production phase tuning.

Tip #3.1: To include an attribute for aggregation, set "Aggregation Usage" of cube attribute.
If an attribute participated in more than one "Measure Groups", setting "Aggregation Usage" property of a cube attribute will enable or disable participation in all Aggregations of all "Measure Groups".

Aggregation Usage Property	Description
DEFAULT	This is the default value. Aggregation or not, depends on type of attribute and dimension.
FULL	Every aggregation of every related "Measures Group" of this cube must include this attribute.
UNRESTRICTED	Attribute will be evaluated if it is a valuable aggregation.
NONE	This attribute will not be added to any aggregation of the cube.

Tip #3.2: The One-Third Rule
Analysis services only builds those aggregations that have aggregation size of less than one third of the size of the fact table counts.

Tip #3.3: In Aggregation Wizard, use production object counts.
You cannot build accurate aggregations using non-production data. Use production statistics in aggregation wizard for cost analysis. This will generate a more accurate estimation of the analysis.

Tip #3.4: More Aggregations means longer processing time of the cube.
Each aggregation of data needs additional time to process. That means more time will be needed during processing of the cube. So, do not add unnecessary aggregations.

Development Phase Tuning

Tuning MDX is very important to get best performance of queries. Before writing MDX, you need to understand the design of the cube and data relationships to write efficient queries.

Tip #4: Smaller Space Is Always Faster Than Bigger Space

- Always try to work with the smallest possible space.
- For example, remove empty tuples, to reduce the space size.

The following example shows using "NON EMPTY" keyword or NonEmpty function to speed up the query.

Query: Find "Reseller Sales Amount" for each product for each fiscal year for each [State-Province].

WITHOUT NON EMPTY	WITH NON EMPTY

SELECT
{
[Measures].[Reseller Sales Amount]
} ON COLUMNS,
{
[Date].[Fiscal].[Fiscal Year]
*
[Product].[Product Categories].[Product]
*
[Geography].[Geography].[State-Province]
}
ON ROWS
FROM
[Adventure Works]
	SELECT
	{
	[Measures].[Reseller Sales Amount]
	} ON COLUMNS,
	NON EMPTY
	{
	[Date].[Fiscal].[Fiscal Year]
	*
	[Product].[Product Categories].[Product]
	*
	[Geography].[Geography].[State-Province]
	} ON ROWS
	FROM
	[Adventure Works]

Response time= 18440 mili seconds.	**Response time=** 872 mili seconds.

Notes: Response time improved by using "NON EMPTY" keyword for rows.

- "NonEmpty" function instead of "NON EMPTY" will return similar result.

SELECT
{
[Measures].[Reseller Sales Amount]
} ON COLUMNS,
{
NonEmpty
(
[Date].[Fiscal].[Fiscal Year]
*
[Product].[Product Categories].[Product]
*
[Geography].[Geography].[State-Province]
)
}
ON ROWS
FROM
[Adventure Works]
	Response time
	= 949 mili seconds.

Tip #5: Subspace Is Faster Than Cell-By-Cell

Instead of applying a calculation to each member of a set, apply calculation to the entire set.

For example,

You can find "Reseller Sales Amount" for "Canada", in two ways:

- **Calculating Cell-By-Cell**:

```
MEMBER [Measures].[RSA-Canada] AS
SUM
  (
  FILTER
    (
    [Geography].[Geography].[Country].Members,
    [Geography].[Geography].CurrentMember.Name ="Canada"
    ),
  [Measures].[Reseller Sales Amount]
  )
```

- **Using subspace**:

```
(
[Measures].[Reseller Sales Amount],
[Geography].[Geography].[Country].&[Canada]
)
```

Using subspace will be faster since it is applied to entire set instead of calculating each member of the set.

Other common situations that causes Cell-By-Cell processing are:

- User Defined Stored Procedures process data Cell-By-Cell.
- Cell security cause Cell-By-Cell processing and slows down MDX query.
- Dynamic member, dimension or parameters cause Cell-By-Cell processing.

Tip #6: Hint Query Executor

Tip #6.1: Hint Query Executor for empty tuples using "Non Empty Behavior".

Query: Find "Net Sales Amount" for each country for fiscal year 2007.

Net Sales Amount = Reseller Sales Amount - Discount Sales Amount

You can hint "Query Executor" that "Net Sales Amount" is empty, if "Reseller Sales Amount" is empty. This will save time for "Query Executor", because query "Query Executor" will not spend time to calculate the "Net Sales Amount" if "Reseller Sales Amount" is empty. You can hint "Query Executor" by following the statement:

```
NON_EMPTY_BEHAVIOR =
 {
 [Measures].[Reseller Sales Amount]
 }
```

MDX

```
WITH
MEMBER [Measures].[Net Sales Amount] AS
[Measures].[Reseller Sales Amount]
-
[Measures].[Discount Amount],
NON_EMPTY_BEHAVIOR =
    {
    [Measures].[Reseller Sales Amount]
    }
SELECT
   {
   [Measures].[Reseller Sales Amount],
   [Measures].[Discount Amount],
   [Measures].[Net Sales Amount]
   } ON COLUMNS,
   {
   [Geography].[Geography].[Country].Members
   } ON ROWS
FROM
   [Adventure Works]
WHERE
    [Date].[Fiscal].[Fiscal Year].&[2007]
```

Result

	Reseller Sales Amount	Discount Amount	Net Sales Amount
Australia	(null)	(null)	(null)
Canada	$5,615,169.14	$12,203.14	$5,602,966.00
France	$1,428,020.38	$4,142.65	$1,423,877.73
Germany	(null)	(null)	(null)
United Kingdom	$1,406,491.96	$2,680.12	$1,403,811.84
United States	$19,335,397.26	$39,158.56	$19,296,238.70

Tip #6.2: Hint for expression of IIF statement.

IIF statement has two expressions <exp1> and <expr2>,

There are three types of hint you can provide with expressions in IIF statements which can help Query Executor to efficiently use resources:

- **EAGER**: The expression will be evaluated for the total subspace of IIF statement.
  For example,
  IIF (<condition>, <expr1> HINT EAGER, <expr2>)
  - <expr1> will not wait for <condition> to be evaluated.
  - This means, <expr1> will be evaluated even if <condition> returns false.
- **STRICT**: The expression will be evaluated for the resultant subspace of IIF statement.
  For example,
  IIF (<condition>, <expr1> HINT EAGER, <expr2> HINT STRICT)
  - <expr2> will wait for <condition> to be evaluated.
  - This means, <expr2> will only be evaluated if <condition> returns false.
- **LAZY**: In this case, the expression will be evaluated Cell-By-Cell basis.

Tip #7: Avoid Late-Binding

- Late bindings slow down MDX queries.
- Avoid late-binding while using MDX functions like LinkMember, StrToSet, StrToMember and StrToValue. It is important to understand not all usage of these functions creates late-binding (it depends on how the functions are used).
- Late bindings in a custom rollup expression will slow down a MDX query.

Query: Find "Reseller Sales Amount" for each product category for a given fiscal year. The fiscal year unique-name is passed as a string parameter.

In this example, both the following queries return the same result, the first query does not have any late binding, but one of the "StrToMember" in the second query creates late binding.

MDX

```
SELECT
   {
   [Measures].[Reseller Sales Amount]
   } ON COLUMNS,
   {
   [Product].[Product Categories].[Category]
   } ON ROWS
FROM
   [Adventure Works]
WHERE
   StrToMember
      (
      '[Date].[Fiscal].[Fiscal Year].&[2007]'
      )
```

Static Binding, **Good**

Result

	Reseller Sales Amount
Accessories	$124,433.35
Bikes	$22,417,419.69
Clothing	$750,716.33
Components	$4,629,101.14

MDX

```
WITH
MEMBER [Measures].[RSA-Product Category] AS
   (
   [Measures].[Reseller Sales Amount],
   StrToMember
      (
      [Product].[Product Categories].CurrentMember.UniqueName
      )
   ), FORMAT_STRING="Currency"

SELECT
   {
   [Measures].[RSA-Product Category]
   } ON COLUMNS,
   {
   [Product].[Product Categories].[Category]
   } ON ROWS
FROM
   [Adventure Works]
WHERE
   StrToMember
      (
      '[Date].[Fiscal].[Fiscal Year].&[2007]'
      )
```

Late Binding **Not Good**

Static Binding **Good**

Result

	RSA-Product Category
Accessories	$124,433.35
Bikes	$22,417,419.69
Clothing	$750,716.33
Components	$4,629,101.14

Tip #8: Use Members to Compare Instead Of String

It is always faster to compare a member with another member instead of converting a member to a string and then compare.

Query: Find "Reseller Sales Amount" for each product category for a given fiscal year. For product category "Accessories", show "Reseller Sales Amount" as 8.25% more than the existing "Reseller Sales Amount".

In this example, the following queries return same result:

- The first query compares by converting a member name to a string (this makes query slower).
- The second query compares a member with another member (this makes query faster).

MDX

```
WITH
MEMBER [Measures].[RSA-Product Category] AS
IIF
    (
    [Product].[Product Categories].CurrentMember.Name
    = 'Accessories',
    [Measures].[Reseller Sales Amount] * 1.825,
    [Measures].[Reseller Sales Amount]
    ), FORMAT_STRING="Currency"

SELECT
   {
   [Measures].[RSA-Product Category]
   } ON COLUMNS,
   {
   [Product].[Product Categories].[Category]
   } ON ROWS
FROM
   [Adventure Works]
WHERE
    [Date].[Fiscal].[Fiscal Year].&[2007]
```

Members converted to string before comparison **Slows down query**

Result

	RSA-Product Category
Accessories	$227,090.87
Bikes	$22,417,419.69
Clothing	$750,716.33
Components	$4,629,101.14

MDX

```
WITH
MEMBER [Measures].[RSA-Product Category] AS
IIF
    (
    [Product].[Product Categories].CurrentMember IS
    [Product].[Product Categories].[Category].[Accessories]
    ,
    [Measures].[Reseller Sales Amount] * 1.825,
    [Measures].[Reseller Sales Amount]
    ), FORMAT_STRING="Currency"

SELECT
   {
   [Measures].[RSA-Product Category]
   } ON COLUMNS,
   {
   [Product].[Product Categories].[Category]
   } ON ROWS
FROM
   [Adventure Works]
WHERE
    [Date].[Fiscal].[Fiscal Year].&[2007]
```

Members compared with a member **This is good**

Result

	RSA-Product Category
Accessories	$227,090.87
Bikes	$22,417,419.69
Clothing	$750,716.33
Components	$4,629,101.14

Tip #9: For Calculated Members, Cover All Boundary Conditions

For most of Year-To-Year, Quarter-To-Quarter , Month-To-Month calculations, the following boundary conditions need to be handled apart from normal calculations:

- **First Period**: For the first period, there is no previous period to compare. If the previous member does not have value, your code needs to handle this condition.
- **Future Period**: Future data may not be available, so you need to handle the calculation for future periods.
- **"All Level"**: A valid calculation for "All Level".

Some other common boundary conditions are:

- Handle Divide by zero.
- Handle null values.

Tip #10: Avoid Forward References

Forward references of members slow down a query.

Query: Display "Reseller Sales Amount" for all states of "United States" and compare with Country's "Reseller Sales Amount" for fiscal year 2008.

Both the following queries return same result,

- The first query has forward references (this makes query slower).

MDX

```
WITH
MEMBER [Measures].[PCT for Country] AS
[Measures].[Reseller Sales Amount]/
[Measures].[RSA for Country],
FORMAT_STRING='Percent'

MEMBER [Measures].[RSA for Country] AS
    (
    [Measures].[Reseller Sales Amount],
    ANCESTOR
        (
        [Geography].[Geography].CurrentMember,
        1
        )
    )

SELECT
   {
   [Measures].[Reseller Sales Amount],
   [Measures].[PCT for Country]
   } ON COLUMNS,
   {
   [Geography].[Geography].[Country].&[United States].Children
   } ON ROWS
FROM
   [Adventure Works]
WHERE
    [Date].[Fiscal].[Fiscal Year].&[2007]
```

Forward references

Result

	Reseller Sales Amount	PCT for Country
Alabama	$15,497.20	0.08%
Arizona	$448,353.42	2.32%
California	$3,860,128.46	19.96%
Colorado	$1,071,753.62	5.54%
Connecticut	$498,866.74	2.58%
Florida	$515,173.61	2.66%
Georgia	$345,141.06	1.79%
Idaho	$8,724.01	0.05%
Illinois	$103,451.65	0.54%
Indiana	$671,294.92	3.47%
Kentucky	$16,857.89	0.09%
Maine	$388,169.48	2.01%
Maryland	(null)	(null)
Massachusetts	$12,826.06	0.07%
Michigan	$590,727.99	3.06%
Minnesota	$216,514.67	1.12%
Mississippi	$145,196.69	0.75%
Missouri	$641,459.81	3.32%

* The second query does not have forward references (this makes query faster).

MDX

```
WITH
MEMBER [Measures].[RSA for Country] AS
    (
    [Measures].[Reseller Sales Amount],
    ANCESTOR
        (
        [Geography].[Geography].CurrentMember,
        1
        )
    )

MEMBER [Measures].[PCT for Country] AS
[Measures].[Reseller Sales Amount]/
[Measures].[RSA for Country],
FORMAT_STRING='Percent'

SELECT
   {
   [Measures].[Reseller Sales Amount],
   [Measures].[PCT for Country]
   } ON COLUMNS,
   {
   [Geography].[Geography].[Country].&[United States].Children
   } ON ROWS
FROM
   [Adventure Works]
WHERE
    [Date].[Fiscal].[Fiscal Year].&[2007]
```

No more forward references

Result

	Reseller Sales Amount	PCT for Cou
Alabama	$15,497.20	0.08%
Arizona	$448,353.42	2.32%
California	$3,860,128.46	19.96%
Colorado	$1,071,753.62	5.54%
Connecticut	$498,866.74	2.58%
Florida	$515,173.61	2.66%
Georgia	$345,141.06	1.79%
Idaho	$8,724.01	0.05%
Illinois	$103,451.65	0.54%
Indiana	$671,294.92	3.47%
Kentucky	$16,857.89	0.09%
Maine	$388,169.48	2.01%
Maryland	(null)	(null)
Massachusetts	$12,826.06	0.07%
Michigan	$590,727.99	3.06%
Minnesota	$216,514.67	1.12%
Mississippi	$145,196.69	0.75%
Missouri	$641,459.81	3.32%
M[illegible]ana	$5,30[illegible].34	0.03%

Tip #11: Utilize Cache

* Reuse of query engine cache makes query faster.
* To understand how the cache works, it is very important to understand the scope or boundary of a calculation. There are three possible scopes or boundaries of a calculation.

Scope	Example	Boundary Description	Cache Utilization	Search Order Of a Calculation
Global	Create member in cubes calculation.	Any query from any session that have same security role.	High	Third
Session	Create member in a session.	Any query in current session.	Medium	Second
Query	Create a member using "WITH MEMBER".	Only this query.	Low	First

- Calculations, which are frequently used by same security role users should be placed in global calculations.
- If a calculation is present in query scope, session scope and global scope, then the MDX query will use calculation from "Query Scope". The order of search of calculation is:
  - Query Scope
  - Session Scope
  - Global scope

Tip #12: Document Your MDX Code

- Document your MDX but not excessively.
- Assign short and meaningful names for members and sets.
- Indent your MDX code for readability.

Production Phase Tuning

It is very crucial that the production environment is tuned for the best possible performance.

Tip #13: Disable Query Logging If Possible

- Query logging always slows down queries.
- However, query log is needed for "Usage Based Aggregation" in production environment. So, query logging need to be enabled. In such a case, enable logging for a limited period of time and log infrequently, e.g. log once every 10 queries.
- Query logging is a property of SSAS server instance. This means that, you cannot selectively enable query log for a particular cube or SSAS database.

To disable query logging in an SSAS instance, follow these steps:

1. Open SQL Server Management Studio and connect to "Analysis Services" instance.
2. Right click on instance name in Object Explorer and select "Properties".
3. Go to "General" tab.
4. Set the property "Log\QueryLog\QueryLogSampling" to "false".

Figure 10-2 : Disable query log in an Analysis Services instance.

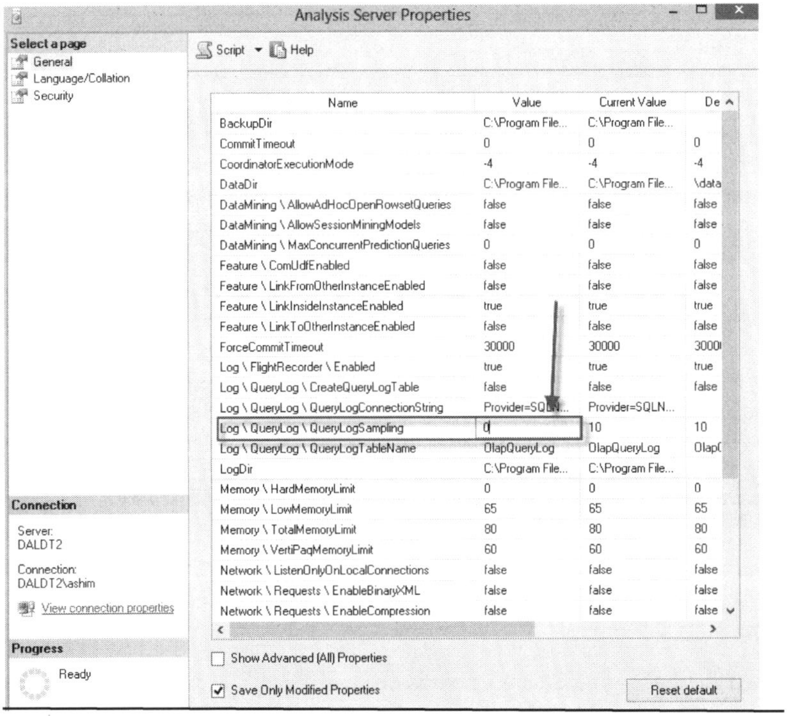

Tip #14: Usage Based Aggregation

Once the cube is deployed to production, the "Usage Based Optimization" wizard can be used to tune the cube for better performance. The following steps first enable query logging to save activity logs and then create aggregation using "Usage Based Optimization Wizard".

Step 1: Configure SQL Server Analysis Services instance to enable query log:

1 Open SQL Server Management Studio and connect to "Analysis Services" instance.
2 Right click on instance name in Object Explorer and select "Properties".
3 Go to "General" tab.
4 Set the property "Log\QueryLog\CreateQueryLogTable" to "true".
5 Set the property "Log\QueryLog\QueryLogConnectionString" by clicking on the ellipse and connect to a database.
6 Set the property "Log\QueryLog\QueryLogSampling" to "1".
7 Set the property "Log\QueryLog\QueryLogTableName" to "OlapQueryLog". Click OK.

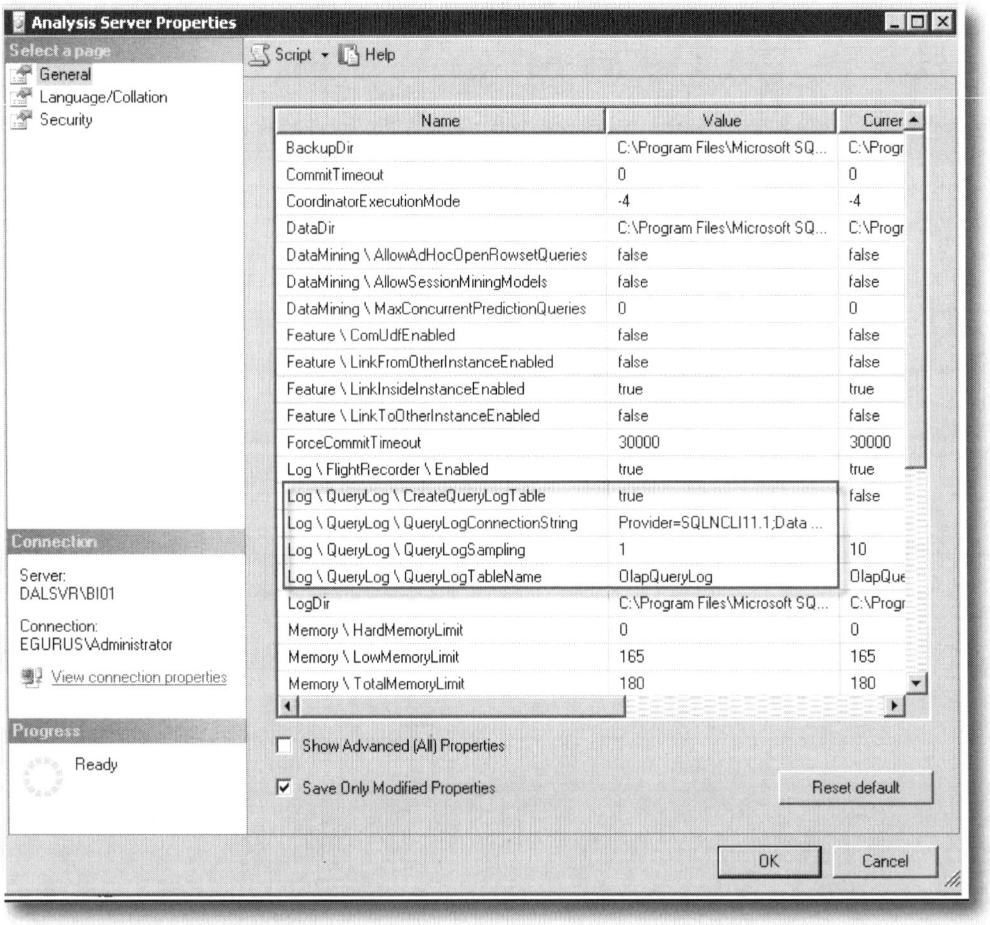

Step 2: Run some sample queries to record in query log:

1 Query 1:

```
SELECT
  {
  [Measures].[Reseller Sales Amount]
  } ON COLUMNS,
  {
  [Product].[Product Categories].[Category]
  } ON ROWS
FROM
  [Adventure Works]
```

2 Query 2:

```
SELECT
  {
  [Measures].[Reseller Sales Amount]
  } ON COLUMNS,
  {
  [Product].[Product Categories].[Category]
  } ON ROWS
FROM
  [Adventure Works]
WHERE
  (
  [Date].[Fiscal].[Fiscal Year].&[2008]
  )
```

3 Query 3:

```
SELECT
  {
  [Measures].[Reseller Sales Amount]
  } ON COLUMNS,
  {
  [Product].[Product Categories].[Subcategory]
  } ON ROWS
FROM
  [Adventure Works]
WHERE
  (
  [Date].[Fiscal].[Fiscal Year].&[2008]
  )
```

4 Query 4:

```
SELECT
  {
  [Measures].[Reseller Sales Amount]
  } ON COLUMNS,
  {
  [Product].[Product Categories].[Subcategory]
  } ON ROWS
FROM
  [Adventure Works]
WHERE
  (
  [Date].[Fiscal].[Fiscal Year].&[2008],
  [Geography].[Geography].[Country].&[United States]
  )
```

Step 3: Switch Off the Query Logging:

Do not enable query logging indefinitely, because query logging will slow down performance of the system.

1 Open SQL Server Management Studio and connect to "Analysis Services" instance.
2 Right click on instance name in Object Explorer and select "Properties".
3 Go to "General" tab.
4 Set the property "Log\QueryLog\CreateQueryLogTable" to "false".
5 Click OK.

Step 4: Run Usage Based Optimization Wizard:

1 Open SQL Server Management Studio and connect to "Analysis Services" instance.
2 Expand the node "Databases" in object explorer.
3 Expand "Adventure Works" -> "Cubes".
4 Expand "Measure Groups" --> "Reseller Sales".
5 Right Click on "Reseller_Sales_2008" and select "Usage Based Optimization".
6 Usage Based Aggregation Wizard will appear.

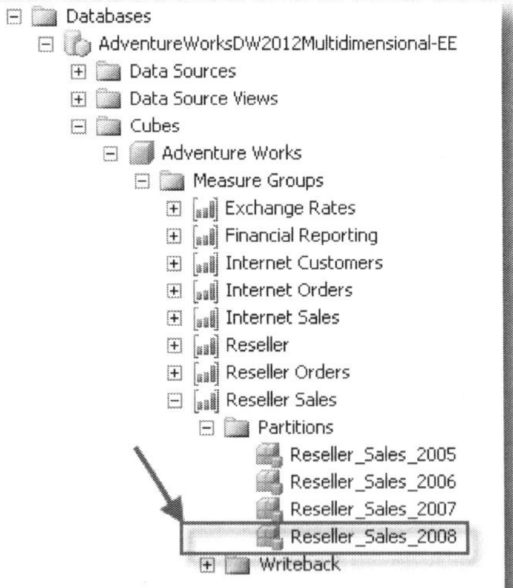

6 Click "Next" in welcome screen.

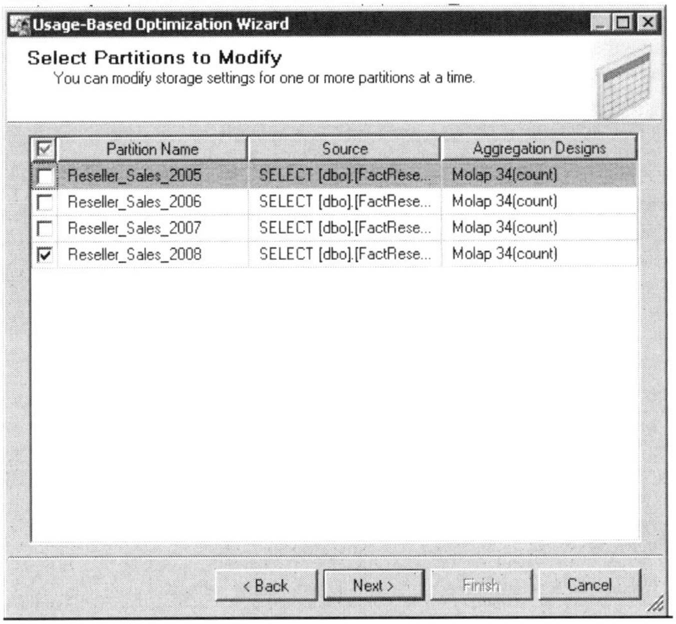

7 Select "Reseller_Sales_2008" partition.

8 Click "Next".

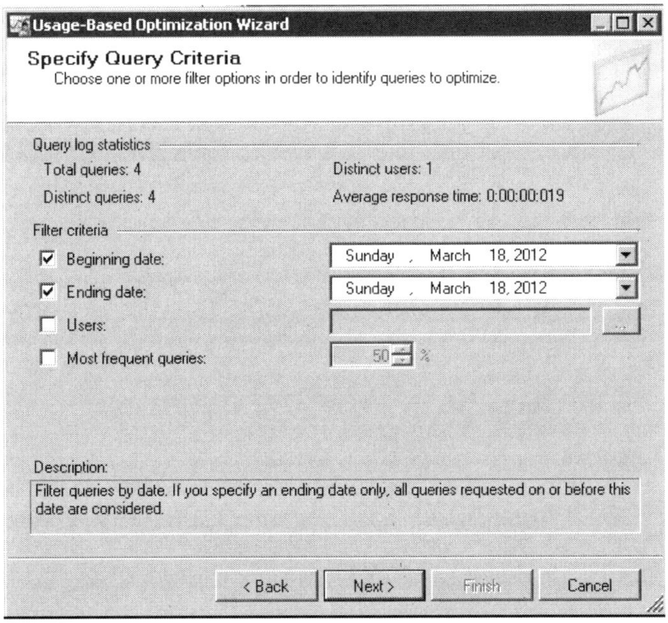

9 Select appropriate "Beginning Date" and "End Date".

10 Click "Next".

11 "Review the Queries that will be Optimized" screen will appear.

12 Select all queries and click "Next" button, "Specify Object Counts" screen will appear.

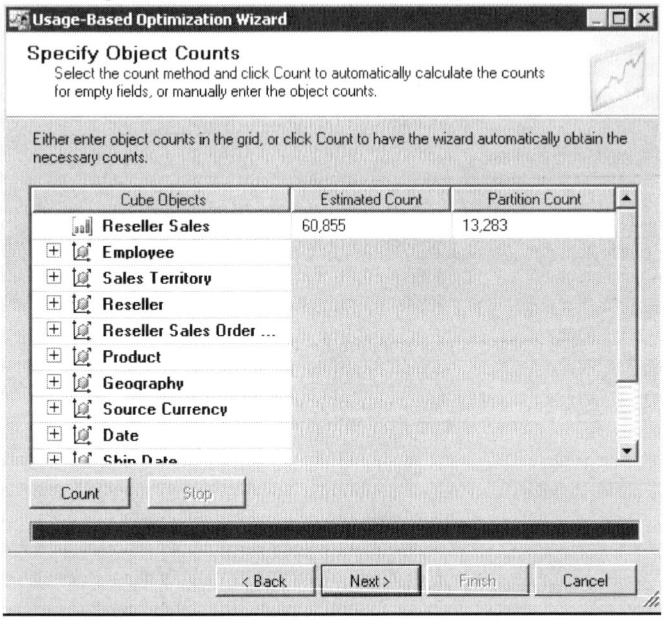

13 Enter the production value of "Estimated Count" and "Partition Count" or get count of the current system by clicking "Count" button".

14 Click "Next", "Set Aggregation Options" screen will appear.

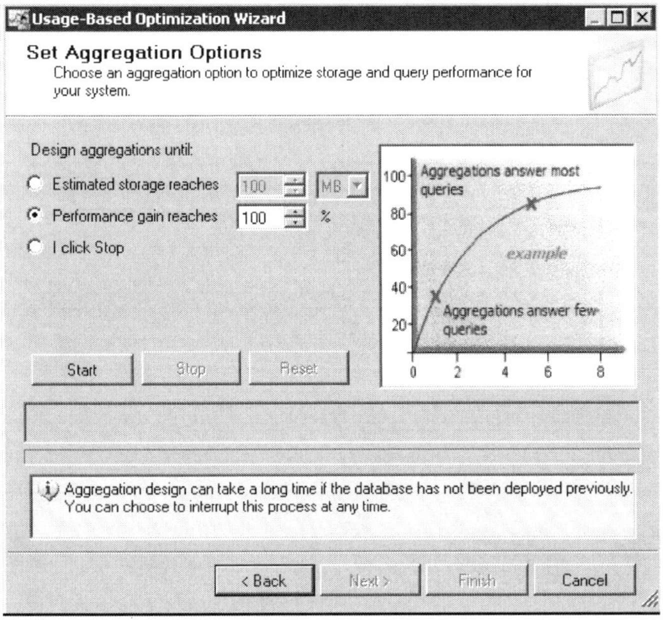

15 Click "Start" to create all aggregation and click "Next" and then click "Finish".

Tip #15: Utilize Parallelism

- Parallelism of tasks increases the performance of queries.
- Parallelism can be configured in properties of "SQL Server Analysis Services" instance.

Steps to set configurations for different ThreadPool:

1 Open SQL Server Management Studio and connect to "Analysis Services" instance.
2 Right click on instance name in Object Explorer and select "Properties".
3 Go to "General" tab.
4 Check "Show Advanced(All) Properties".
5 Go to the end of the list of properties.
6 You will see three sets of parameters.

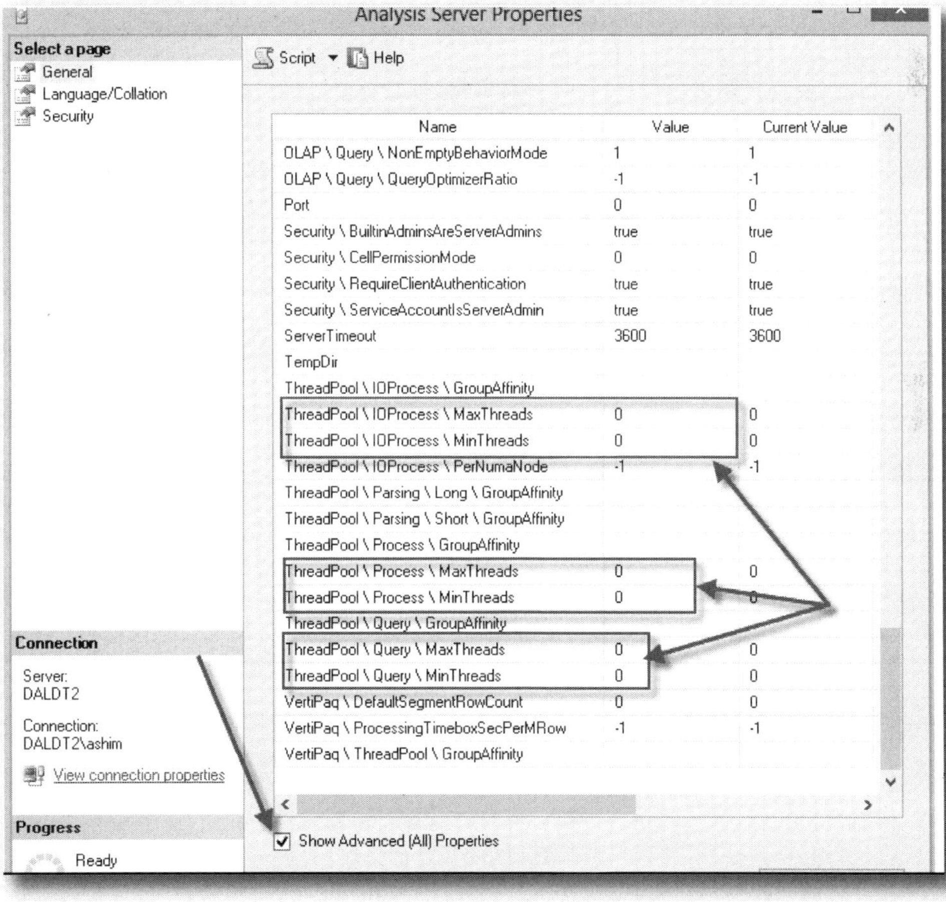

- "IOProcess" threadpools are used for read jobs.
- "Process" threadpools are used for ROLAP and processing related jobs, including writing new files.
- "Query" threadpools are used to connect to "Query Execution Engine".

Figure 10-2: ThreadPool mappings.

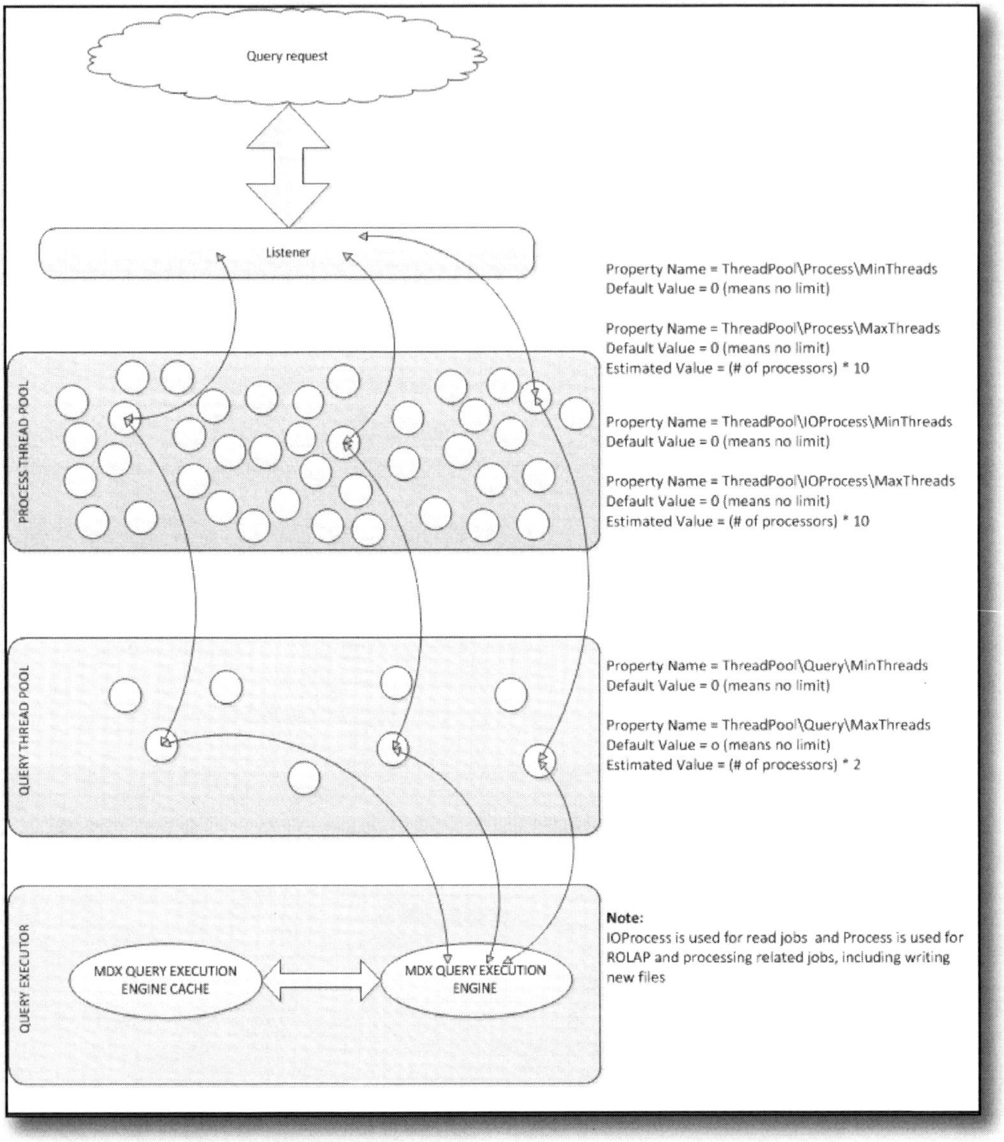

- IOProcess: Estimated MinThreads =1. Estimated MaxThreads = (Number of processors *10).
- Process: Estimated MinThreads =1. Estimated MaxThreads = (Number of processors *10).
- Query: Estimated MinThreads =1. Estimated MaxThreads = (Number of processors *2).

Appendix I: Excercise Answers

Exercise#1.1

Goal: Find [Reseller Sales Amount] for each product category for each country.

MDX

```
SELECT
  {
  [Product].[Product Categories].[Category]
  } ON COLUMNS,
  {
  [Geography].[Geography].[Country]
  } On ROWS
FROM
  [Adventure Works]
WHERE
 (
 [Measures].[Reseller Sales Amount]
 )
```

Result

	Accessories	Bikes	Clothing	Components
Australia	$23,947.53	$1,323,820.73	$42,915.80	$203,651.31
Canada	$118,127.35	$11,636,380.59	$378,947.63	$2,244,470.02
France	$48,031.73	$3,560,665.65	$128,092.22	$870,748.34
Germany	$35,083.07	$1,543,015.65	$71,619.43	$334,269.89
United Kingdom	$42,593.03	$3,405,747.21	$118,828.80	$711,839.79
United States	$303,515.23	$44,832,751.73	$1,037,436.95	$7,434,097.31

Exercise#1.2

Goal: Display sorted list of all states of "United States".

MDX	Result

WITH
MEMBER [Measures].[StateName] AS
[Geography].[Geography].[State-Province].Name
SELECT
  {
  } ON COLUMNS,
  {
  Order
    (
    [Geography].[Geography].[State-Province],
    [Measures].[StateName],
    BASC
)
  } On ROWS
FROM
  [Adventure Works]
WHERE ([Geography].[Country].&[United States])
	Alabama
	Arizona
	California
	Colorado
	Connecticut
	Florida
	Georgia
	Idaho
	Illinois
	Indiana
	Kentucky
	Maine
	Maryland
	Massachusetts

Exercise#1.3

Goal: Find the number of cities in the state of Florida.

MDX	WITH
	MEMBER [Measures].[City Count] AS
	Count
	  (
	  [Geography].[Geography].[State-Province].&[FL]&[US].Children
	  )
	SELECT
	  {
	  [Measures].[City Count]
	  } ON COLUMNS
	FROM
	  [Adventure Works]

Result	City Count 15

Exercise#2.1

Goal: Find "Bottom 5% products" based on "Internet Sales Amount" from the list of all products for fiscal year 2008. Do not include empty "Internet Sales Amount" values.

MDX

```
SELECT
 {
 [Measures].[Internet Sales Amount]
 } ON COLUMNS,
 {
 BOTTOMPERCENT
   (
   NonEmpty
     (
     [Product].[Product Categories].[Product],
     [Measures].[Internet Sales Amount]
     ),
   5,
   [Measures].[Internet Sales Amount]
   )
  } ON ROWS
FROM
  [Adventure Works]
WHERE
  [Date].[Fiscal].[Fiscal Year].&[2008]
```

Result

	Internet Sales Amount
Racing Socks, L	$2,355.38
Racing Socks, M	$2,526.19
Bike Wash - Dissolver	$6,868.80
Patch Kit/8 Patches	$6,892.90
Touring Tire Tube	$6,971.03
Road Tire Tube	$8,841.84
Classic Vest, S	$10,033.00
Half-Finger Gloves, L	$10,457.23
Half-Finger Gloves, S	$11,338.87
Half-Finger Gloves, M	$11,583.77
Classic Vest, L	$11,684.00
Classic Vest, M	$11,747.50
Mountain Tire Tube	$14,510.92
Road Bottle Cage	$15,300.98
AWC Logo Cap	$18,834.05
Mountain Bottle Cage	$19,390.59
Long-Sleeve Logo Jersey, XL	$19,546.09

Exercise#2.2

Goal: Find "Reseller Sales Amount", "Reseller Sales Quantity" for Texas , Florida and New York for fiscal years 2007, 2008 for the product categories "Bikes" and "Clothing".

Strategy:

- Columns: "Reseller Sales Amount", "Reseller Sales Quantity".
- Rows: Texas, Florida and New York.
- Where Clause: For fiscal years 2007, 2008 for the product categories "Bikes" and "Clothing".

```
(
 { [Date].[Fiscal].[Fiscal Year].&[2007], [Date].[Fiscal].[Fiscal Year].&[2008] },
 { [Product].[Product Categories].[Category].&[1], [Product].[Product Categories].[Category].&[3] }
)
```

MDX

```
SELECT
  {
  [Measures].[Reseller Sales Amount],
  [Measures].[Reseller Order Quantity]
  } ON COLUMNS,
  {
  [Geography].[Geography].[State-Province].&[TX]&[US],
  [Geography].[Geography].[State-Province].&[FL]&[US],
  [Geography].[Geography].[State-Province].&[NY]&[US]
  } ON ROWS
FROM
  [Adventure Works]
WHERE
  (
    {
    [Date].[Fiscal].[Fiscal Year].&[2007],
    [Date].[Fiscal].[Fiscal Year].&[2008]
    },
    {
    [Product].[Product Categories].[Category].&[1],
    [Product].[Product Categories].[Category].&[3]
    }
  )
```

Result

	Reseller Sales Amount	Reseller Order Quantity
Texas	$4,097,795.90	8,249
Florida	$1,135,444.74	3,429
New York	$904,037.14	2,962

Exercise#2.3

Goal: Find the number of days between 01/20/2008 and 03/15/2008.

MDX

```
WITH
MEMBER [Measures].[Number Of Days] AS
Count
  (
  [Date].[Calendar].[Date].&[20080315]
  :
  [Date].[Calendar].[Date].&[20080120]
  )

SELECT
  {
  [Measures].[Number Of Days]
  } ON COLUMNS
FROM
  [Adventure Works]
```

Result

Number Of Days
56

Exercise#2.4

Goal: Display "Reseller Sales Amount" for each product category for each country. Also sort the result by country and then by product category.

MDX

```
WITH
MEMBER [Measures].[CountryName] AS
[Geography].[Geography].CurrentMember.Name
MEMBER [Measures].[ProductcategoryName] AS
[Product].[Product Categories].CurrentMember.Name
SELECT
  { [Measures].[Reseller Sales Amount] } ON COLUMNS,
  {
  Order ([Geography].[Geography].[Country], [Mea-
sures].[CountryName])
  * Order ( [Product].[Product Categories].[Category],
          [Measures].[ProductcategoryName]  )
  } ON ROWS
FROM
  [Adventure Works]
```

Result

		Reseller Sales Amount
Australia	Accessories	$23,947.53
Australia	Bikes	$1,323,820.73
Australia	Clothing	$42,915.80
Australia	Components	$203,651.31
Canada	Accessories	$118,127.35
Canada	Bikes	$11,636,380.59
Canada	Clothing	$378,947.63
Canada	Components	$2,244,470.02
France	Accessories	$48,031.73
France	Bikes	$3,560,665.65
France	Clothing	$128,092.22
France	Components	$870,748.34
Germany	Accessories	$35,083.07

Exercise#2.5

Goal: Using "Exists" function display name of the states which have following cities: Columbus, San Jose, Tampa.

MDX	Result

SELECT
{
} ON COLUMNS,
{
EXISTS
(
[Geography].[Geography].[State-Province],
{
[Geography].[Geography].[City].&[San Jose]&[CA],
[Geography].[Geography].[City].&[Tampa]&[FL],
[Geography].[Geography].[City].&[Columbus]&[GA]
}
)
} ON ROWS
FROM
[Adventure Works]
	California
	Florida
	Georgia

Exercise#3.1

Goal: Find "Reseller Sales Amount" for all non-empty calendar weeks of calendar year 2008. Also, show start date and end date of each week.

Step 1: Find "Reseller Sales Amount" for all non-empty calendar weeks of calendar year 2008

```
SELECT
  {
  [Measures].[Reseller Sales Amount]
  } ON COLUMNS,
  {
  NonEmpty
    (
    [Date].[Calendar Weeks].[Calendar Week],
    [Measures].[Reseller Sales Amount]
    )
  } ON ROWS
FROM
  [Adventure Works]
WHERE
  [Date].[Calendar Year].&[2008]
```

Step 2: Find "Reseller Sales Amount" for all non-empty calendar weeks of calendar year 2008. Also show start date and end date of each week.

MDX

```
WITH
MEMBER [Measures].[First Day of Week] AS
[Date].[Calendar Weeks].CurrentMember.FirstChild.name

MEMBER [Measures].[Last Day of Week] AS
[Date].[Calendar Weeks].CurrentMember.LastChild.name

SELECT
   {
   [Measures].[First Day of Week],
   [Measures].[Last Day of Week],
   [Measures].[Reseller Sales Amount]
   } ON COLUMNS,
 {
 NonEmpty
   (
   [Date].[Calendar Weeks].[Calendar Week],
   [Measures].[Reseller Sales Amount]
   )
 } ON ROWS
FROM
  [Adventure Works]
WHERE
  [Date].[Calendar Year].&[2008]
```

Result

	First Day of Week	Last Day of Week	Reseller Sales Amount
Week 1 CY 2008	(null)	(null)	$1,662,547.32
Week 5 CY 2008	(null)	(null)	$2,699,300.79
Week 9 CY 2008	(null)	(null)	$2,738,653.62
Week 14 CY 2008	(null)	(null)	$2,206,725.22
Week 18 CY 2008	(null)	(null)	$3,314,600.78
Week 22 CY 2008	(null)	(null)	$755.78
Week 23 CY 2008	(null)	(null)	$3,415,479.07

Notes:

- First day of Week and Last day of Week is null because [Date] level is not present in hierarchy [Calendar Week]
- Following steps shows how to add [Date] level in hierarchy [Calendar Week].

Steps to add "Date" level below "Calendar Week" level:

1 Open SQL Server Data Tools.
2 Open analysis services project "AdventureWorksDW2012Multidimensional-EE".
3 In solution explorer, double click on dimension "Date" in "Dimensions" folder.
4 Drag "Date" from "Attributes" tab to bottom of hierarchy "Calendar Weeks", as shown in the figure below.
5 Go to "Attribute Relationship" tab and make sure
   - [Date] level rolls up to level "Calendar Week".
   - "Calendar Week" level rolls up to [Calendar Year].
   - Attribute relationship will be look like, Date --> "Calendar Week" --> "Calendar Year".

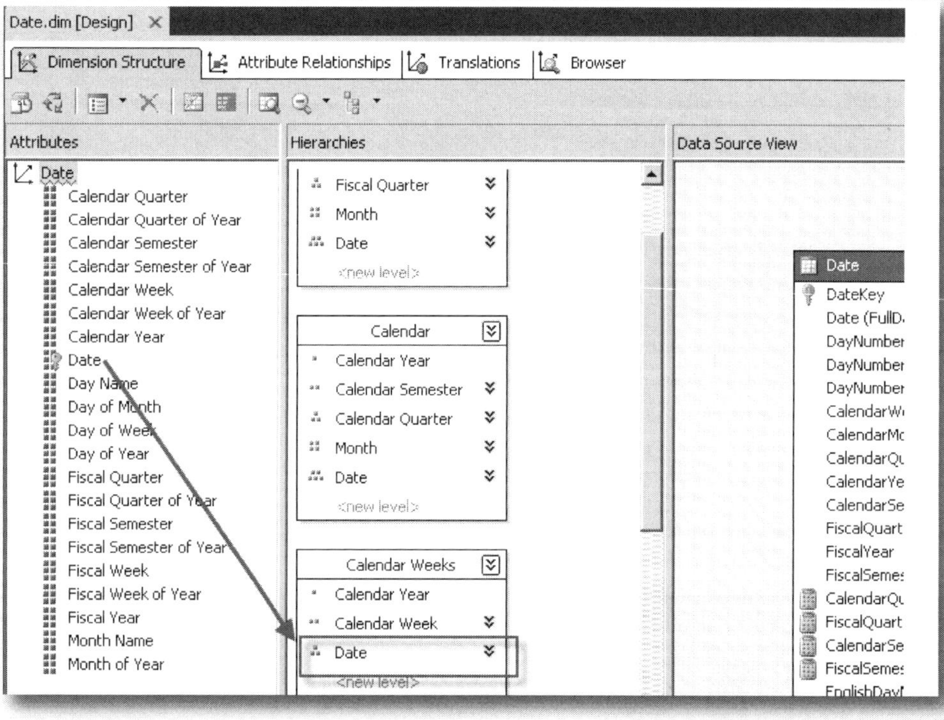

Last MDX query will now show data for first day of the week and last day of the week.

Result		First Day of Week	Last Day of Week	Reseller Sales Amount
	Week 1 CY 2008	January 1, 2008	January 5, 2008	$1,662,547.32
	Week 5 CY 2008	January 27, 2008	February 2, 2008	$2,699,300.79
	Week 9 CY 2008	February 24, 2008	March 1, 2008	$2,738,653.62
	Week 14 CY 2008	March 30, 2008	April 5, 2008	$2,206,725.22
	Week 18 CY 2008	April 27, 2008	May 3, 2008	$3,314,600.78
	Week 22 CY 2008	May 25, 2008	May 31, 2008	$755.78
	Week 23 CY 2008	June 1, 2008	June 7, 2008	$3,415,479.07

Exercise#3.2

Goal: Find the default member of attribute "Destination Currency" of dimension "Destination Currency".

MDX	
	``WITH MEMBER [Measures].[Default Currency] AS [Destination Currency].[Destination Currency].DefaultMember.Name SELECT { [Measures].[Default Currency] } ON COLUMNS FROM [Adventure Works]``
Result	Default Currency: US Dollar

```
WITH
MEMBER [Measures].[Default Currency] AS
[Destination Currency].[Destination Currency].DefaultMember.Name

SELECT
  {
  [Measures].[Default Currency]
  } ON COLUMNS
FROM
  [Adventure Works]
```

Result

Default Currency
US Dollar

Exercise#3.3

Goal: Find average list price of each product category.

MDX

```
WITH
MEMBER [Measures].[Avg List price] AS
AVG
  (
  DESCENDANTS
    (
    [Product].[Product Categories].Currentmember,
    [Product].[Product Categories].[Product]
    ) AS Set1,
    StrToValue(Set1.Current.Properties("List Price"))
  ), Format_string ="Currency"
SELECT
  {
  [Measures].[Avg List price]
  } ON COLUMNS,
  {
  [Product].[Product Categories].[Category]
  } ON ROWS
FROM
  [Adventure Works]
```

Result

	Avg List price
Accessories	$34.23
Bikes	$1,524.59
Clothing	$47.02
Components	$535.96

Exercise#3.4

Goal: Find **"Reseller Sales Amount" for each product category** for the state of California for the fiscal year 2008 and compare with **total "Reseller Sales Amount"** for the state of California for fiscal year 2008.

Step 1: Find "Reseller Sales Amount" for each product category for state of California for fiscal year 2008.

Columns: "Reseller Sales Amount".
Rows: Product categories.
Where Clause: For state of California for fiscal year 2008.

<table>
<tr><td>MDX</td><td><pre>SELECT
  {
  [Measures].[Reseller Sales Amount]
  } ON COLUMNS,
  {
  [Product].[Product Categories].[Category]
  } ON ROWS
FROM
  [Adventure Works]
WHERE
  (
  [Geography].[Geography].[State-Province].&[CA]&[US],
  [Date].[Fiscal].[Fiscal Year].&[2008]
)</pre></td></tr>
<tr><td>Result</td><td>

	Reseller Sales Amount
Accessories	$34,376.56
Bikes	$2,969,671.51
Clothing	$79,736.95
Components	$480,930.22

</td></tr>
</table>

Step 2: Create a calculated member "RSA-Total" for all product categories.

```
MEMBER [Measures].[RSA-Total] AS
SUM
    (
    [Product].[Product Categories].[Category],
    [Measures].[Reseller Sales Amount]
    )
```

Step 3: Create a calculated member "RSA-Percent" as [Reseller Sales Amount]/[RSA-Total] and format as a percentage.
MEMBER [Measures].[RSA-Percent] AS
[Measures].[Reseller Sales Amount]/[Measures].[RSA-Total],
Format_String = "Percent"

MDX

```
WITH
MEMBER [Measures].[RSA-Total] AS
SUM
  (
  [Product].[Product Categories].[Category],
  [Measures].[Reseller Sales Amount]
  )
MEMBER [Measures].[RSA-Percent] AS
[Measures].[Reseller Sales Amount]/[Measures].[RSA-Total],
Format_String="Percent"
SELECT
  {
  [Measures].[Reseller Sales Amount],
  [Measures].[RSA-Total],
  [Measures].[RSA-Percent]
  } ON COLUMNS,
  {
  [Product].[Product Categories].[Category]
  } ON ROWS
FROM
  [Adventure Works]
WHERE
  (
  [Geography].[Geography].[State-Province].&[CA]&[US],
  [Date].[Fiscal].[Fiscal Year].&[2008]
  )
```

Result

	Reseller Sales Amount	RSA-Total	RSA-Percent
Accessories	$34,376.56	$3,564,715.24	0.96%
Bikes	$2,969,671.51	$3,564,715.24	83.31%
Clothing	$79,736.95	$3,564,715.24	2.24%
Components	$480,930.22	$3,564,715.24	13.49%

Exercise#3.5

Goal: Find "Reseller Sales Amount", "Reseller Order Quantity" for states that contain following cities "Dallas" , "Austin", "Los Angeles", "Chicago" , "New York" , "Orlando", "Miami" for fiscal years 2007, 2008 for the product categories "Bikes" and "Clothing".

Strategy:

Columns: "Reseller Sales Amount", "Reseller Order Quantity".

Rows: States that contain following cities "Dallas" , "Austin", "Los Angeles", "Chicago" , "New York" , "Orlando", "Miami".

Where Clause: For fiscal years 2007, 2008 for the product categories "Bikes" and "Clothing".

MDX

```
WITH
SET [Cities] AS
{
[Geography].[Geography].[City].&[Dallas]&[TX],
[Geography].[Geography].[City].&[Austin]&[TX],
[Geography].[Geography].[City].&[Los Angeles]&[CA],
[Geography].[Geography].[City].&[Chicago]&[IL],
[Geography].[Geography].[City].&[New York]&[NY],
[Geography].[Geography].[City].&[Orlando]&[FL],
[Geography].[Geography].[City].&[Miami]&[FL]
}
SELECT
  {
  [Measures].[Reseller Sales Amount],
  [Measures].[Reseller Order Quantity]
  } ON COLUMNS,
  {
  EXISTS (
    [Geography].[Geography].[State-Province],
    [Cities]
    )
  } ON ROWS
FROM
  [Adventure Works]
WHERE
  (
  {[Date].[Fiscal].[Fiscal Year].&[2007],
  [Date].[Fiscal].[Fiscal Year].&[2008]
  },
  {
  [Product].[Product Categories].[Category].&[1],
  [Product].[Product Categories].[Category].&[3]
  }
  )
```

Result

	Reseller Sales Amount	Reseller Order Quantity
California	$6,233,038.85	14,104
Florida	$1,135,444.74	3,429
Illinois	$151,531.86	687
New York	$904,037.14	2,962
Texas	$4,392,911.50	8,713

Exercise#4.1

Goal: Find:

a. [Internet Order Quantity] for all products sold in June, 2008.

b. [Internet Order Quantity] for all products shipped in June, 2008.

c. [Internet Order Quantity] for all products sold in June 2008 and shipped in June, 2008.

Strategy:

- The [Date] dimension represents "Sale Date" and the [Ship Date] dimension represent "Ship Date".

Note: IOQ = "Internet Order Quantity".

MDX

```
WITH
MEMBER [Measures].[IOQ-SaleDate] AS
  (
  [Measures].[Internet Order Quantity],
  [Date].[Calendar].[Month].&[2008]&[6]
  )

MEMBER [Measures].[IOQ-ShipDate] AS
  (
  [Measures].[Internet Order Quantity],
  [Ship Date].[Calendar].[Month].&[2008]&[6]
  )
MEMBER [Measures].[IOQ-Sale-ShipDate] AS
  (
  [Measures].[Internet Order Quantity],
  [Date].[Calendar].[Month].&[2008]&[6],
  [Ship Date].[Calendar].[Month].&[2008]&[6]
  )

SELECT
  {
  [Measures].[IOQ-SaleDate],
  [Measures].[IOQ-ShipDate],
  [Measures].[IOQ-Sale-ShipDate]
  } ON COLUMNS
FROM
  [Adventure Works]
```

Result

IOQ-SaleDate	IOQ-ShipDate	IOQ-Sale-ShipDate
5,545	5,461	4,259

Exercise#4.2

Goal: Find [Reseller Sales Amount] for each month of calendar year 2008, and show the sum of [Reseller Sales Amount] for prior 12 months for each month.

Step 1: Find "Reseller Sales Amount" for each month of calendar year 2008.

MDX	Result
SELECT { [Measures].[Reseller Sales Amount] } ON COLUMNS, { DESCENDANTS ([Date].[Calendar].[Calendar Year].&[2008], [Date].[Calendar].[Month]) } ON ROWS FROM [Adventure Works]	(see result table below)

	Reseller Sales Amount
January 2008	$1,662,547.32
February 2008	$2,700,766.80
March 2008	$2,739,370.98
April 2008	$2,204,623.41
May 2008	$3,315,275.00
June 2008	$3,415,479.07
July 2008	(null)
August 2008	(null)
September 2008	(null)
October 2008	(null)
November 2008	(null)
December 2008	(null)

Step 2: Create a calculated member "RSA-12 Months" as sum of "Reseller Sales Amount" for prior 12 months of the current month.

```
WITH
MEMBER [Measures].[RSA-12 Months] AS
SUM
  (
    {
    [Date].[Calendar].CurrentMember.lag(13)
    :
    [Date].[Calendar].CurrentMember.lag(1)
    },
  [Measures].[Reseller Sales Amount]
  )
```

Current month is not included, sum of 12 months prior of the current month.

Step 3: Include all together, Find "Reseller Sales Amount" for each month of calendar year 2008, also show sum of "Reseller Sales Amount" for prior 12 months for each month.

MDX

```
WITH
MEMBER [Measures].[RSA-12 Months] AS
SUM
  (
   {
   [Date].[Calendar].CurrentMember.lag(13)
   :
   [Date].[Calendar].CurrentMember.lag(1)
   },
  [Measures].[Reseller Sales Amount]
  )
SELECT
  {
  [Measures].[Reseller Sales Amount],
  [Measures].[RSA-12 Months]
  } ON COLUMNS,
  {
  DESCENDANTS
   (
   [Date].[Calendar].[Calendar Year].&[2008],
   [Date].[Calendar].[Month]
   )
  } ON ROWS
FROM
      [Adventure Works]
```

Result

	Reseller Sales Amount	RSA-12 Months
January 2008	$1,662,547.32	$34,387,882.64
February 2008	$2,700,766.80	$33,865,216.75
March 2008	$2,739,370.98	$35,248,441.72
April 2008	$2,204,623.41	$35,602,966.11
May 2008	$3,315,275.00	$36,243,634.44
June 2008	$3,415,479.07	$37,693,631.01
July 2008	(null)	$38,228,357.40
August 2008	(null)	$36,240,484.70
September 2008	(null)	$33,574,834.16
October 2008	(null)	$29,361,862.65
November 2008	(null)	$25,314,288.61
December 2008	(null)	$23,032,172.73

Exercise#4.3

Goal:

a.Find [Internet Sales Amount] for the current year for the state of Texas.

b. Find [Internet Sales Amount] for the current month for the state of Texas.

c. Find [Internet Sales Amount] for today for the state of Texas.

Step 1:

a. Find "Internet Sales Amount" for the current year for state of Texas.

MDX

```
WITH
MEMBER [Date].[Calendar].[CurrentYear] AS
StrToMember
  (
  '[Date].[Calendar].[Calendar Year].'+ '&['+ CStr(Year(Now()))+']'
  )

MEMBER [Measures].[CurrentYearString] AS
'[Date].[Calendar].[Calendar Year].'+ '&['+ CStr(Year(Now()))+']'

SELECT
  {
  [Measures].[Internet Sales Amount],
  [Measures].[CurrentYearString]
  } ON COLUMNS,
  {
  [Date].[Calendar].[CurrentYear]
  } ON ROWS
FROM
  [Adventure Works]
WHERE
  (
  [Geography].[Geography].[State-Province].&[TX]&[US]
  )
```

Result

	Internet Sales Amount	CurrentYearString
CurrentYear	(null)	[Date].[Calendar].[Calendar Year].&[2012]

Note: As there is no data for year 2012, Internet Sales Amount shows as null.

Step 2:

b. Find "Internet Sales Amount" for the current month for state of Texas.

MDX	WITH MEMBER [Date].[Calendar].[CurrentMonth] AS StrToMember ('[Date].[Calendar].[Month].'+ '&['+ CStr(Year(Now()))+']&['+ IIF(Len(CStr(Month(Now()))) =1,"0","")+CStr(Month(Now()))+ ']') MEMBER [Measures].[CurrentMonthString] AS '[Date].[Calendar].[Month].'+ '&['+ CStr(Year(Now()))+']&['+ IIF(Len(CStr(Month(Now()))) =1,"0","")+CStr(Month(Now()))+ ']' SELECT { [Measures].[Internet Sales Amount], [Measures].[CurrentMonthString] } ON COLUMNS, { [Date].[Calendar].[CurrentMonth] } ON ROWS FROM [Adventure Works] WHERE ([Geography].[Geography].[State-Province].&[TX]&[US])
Result	(see table below)

	Internet Sales Amount	CurrentMonthString
CurrentMonth	(null)	[Date].[Calendar].[Month].&[2012]&[05]

Note: As there is no data for year 2012, Internet Sales Amount shows as null.

Step 3:

c. Find "Internet Sales Amount" for today for state of Texas.

MDX

```
WITH
MEMBER [Date].[Calendar].[Today] AS
StrToMember
  (
  '[Date].[Calendar].[Date].'+'&['+CStr(Year(Now()))+
  IIF(Len(CStr(Month(Now()))) =1,"0","")+CStr(Month(Now()))+
  IIF(Len(CStr(Day(Now()))) =1,"0","")+CStr(Day(Now()))+
  ']'
  )

MEMBER [Measures].[TodayString] AS
  '[Date].[Calendar].[Date].'+'&['+CStr(Year(Now()))+
  IIF(Len(CStr(Month(Now()))) =1,"0","")+CStr(Month(Now()))+
  IIF(Len(CStr(Day(Now()))) =1,"0","")+CStr(Day(Now()))+
  ']'

SELECT
  {
  [Measures].[Internet Sales Amount],
  [Measures].[TodayString]
  } ON COLUMNS,
  {
  [Date].[Calendar].[Today]
  } ON ROWS
FROM
  [Adventure Works]
WHERE
  (
  [Geography].[Geography].[State-Province].&[TX]&[US]
  )
```

Result

	Internet Sales Amount	TodayString
Today	(null)	[Date].[Calendar].[Date].&[20120503]

Note: As there is no data for year 2012, Internet Sales Amount shows as null.

Exercise#4.4

Goal: Find the first and last year, which have non-empty "Reseller Sales Amount" in [Adventure Works] .

MDX

```
WITH
MEMBER [Measures].[Year Name] AS
[Date].[Calendar].CurrentMember.Name
SELECT
 {
 [Measures].[Reseller Sales Amount],
 [Measures].[Year Name]
 } ON COLUMNS,
 {
 Head
   (
   Order
     (
     NonEmpty
       (
       [Date].[Calendar].[Calendar Year],
       [Measures].[Reseller Sales Amount]
       ),
     [Measures].[Year Name]
     )
   ),
 Tail
   (
   Order
     (
     NonEmpty
       (
       [Date].[Calendar].[Calendar Year],
       [Measures].[Reseller Sales Amount]
       ),
     [Measures].[Year Name]
     )
   )
 } ON ROWS
FROM
 [Adventure Works]
```

Result

	Reseller Sales Amount	Year Name
CY 2005	$8,065,435.31	CY 2005
CY 2008	$16,038,062.60	CY 2008

Exercise#5.1

Goal: Find “Reseller Sales Amount” for all products for calendar year 2008 which have string "Pedal" in the model name.

MDX

```
SELECT
  {
  [Measures].[Reseller Sales Amount]
  } ON COLUMNS,
  {
  FILTER
    (
    [Product].[Product Categories].[Product],
    InStr
    (
    [Product].[Product Categories].CurrentMember.Properties("Model Name"),
    "Pedal"
    )
    )
  } ON ROWS
FROM  [Adventure Works]
WHERE  (  [Date].[Calendar].[Calendar Year].&[2008]  )
```

Result

	Reseller Sales Amount
HL Mountain Pedal	$15,296.84
HL Road Pedal	$12,828.82
LL Mountain Pedal	$3,133.93
LL Road Pedal	$8,478.61
ML Mountain Pedal	$3,539.13
ML Road Pedal	$9,611.53
Touring Pedal	$534.53

Exercise#5.2

Goal: Find "Reseller Sales Amount" for all non-empty weeks for calendar year 2007. Week names are "Week 1 CY 2007", "Week 2 CY 2007" etc. Modify week names with two digits, padded with zero in the left, for example, "Week 01 CY 2007", "Week 02 CY 2007" etc.

Step 1: Find "Reseller Sales Amount" for all non-empty weeks for calendar year 2007.

MDX

```
SELECT
  {
  [Measures].[Reseller Sales Amount]
  } ON COLUMNS,
  {
  NonEmpty
  (
  [Date].[Calendar Weeks].[Calendar Year].&[2007].Children,
  [Measures].[Reseller Sales Amount]
  )
  } ON ROWS
FROM
  [Adventure Works]
```

Result

	Reseller Sales Amount
Week 1 CY 2007	$1,317,541.83
Week 5 CY 2007	$2,384,846.59
Week 9 CY 2007	$1,563,955.08
Week 14 CY 2007	$1,865,278.43
Week 18 CY 2007	$2,880,752.68
Week 22 CY 2007	$1,987,872.71
Week 27 CY 2007	$2,665,650.54
Week 31 CY 2007	$4,212,971.51
Week 35 CY 2007	$4,047,574.04
Week 40 CY 2007	$2,282,115.88
Week 44 CY 2007	$3,483,161.40
Week 48 CY 2007	$3,510,948.73

Step 2: Modify week names with two digits, padded with zero in the left.
See query in next page.

<table>
<tr><td>MDX</td><td>

```
WITH
MEMBER [Measures].[New Week Name] AS
Left([Date].[Calendar Weeks].CurrentMember.Name,4)+" "+
IIF(Len(Trim(Mid([Date].[Calendar Weeks].CurrentMember.Name,6,2))) =1,"0","")+
Trim(Mid([Date].[Calendar Weeks].CurrentMember.Name,6,2))+" "+
Right([Date].[Calendar Weeks].CurrentMember.Name,7)

SELECT
  {
  [Measures].[Reseller Sales Amount],
  [Measures].[New Week Name]
  } ON COLUMNS,
  {
  NonEmpty
    (
    [Date].[Calendar Weeks].[Calendar Year].&[2007].Children,
    [Measures].[Reseller Sales Amount]
    )
  } ON ROWS
FROM
  [Adventure Works]
```

</td></tr>
<tr><td>Result</td><td>

	Reseller Sales Amount	New Week Name
Week 1 CY 2007	$1,317,541.83	Week 01 CY 2007
Week 5 CY 2007	$2,384,846.59	Week 05 CY 2007
Week 9 CY 2007	$1,563,955.08	Week 09 CY 2007
Week 14 CY 2007	$1,865,278.43	Week 14 CY 2007
Week 18 CY 2007	$2,880,752.68	Week 18 CY 2007
Week 22 CY 2007	$1,987,872.71	Week 22 CY 2007
Week 27 CY 2007	$2,665,650.54	Week 27 CY 2007
Week 31 CY 2007	$4,212,971.51	Week 31 CY 2007
Week 35 CY 2007	$4,047,574.04	Week 35 CY 2007
Week 40 CY 2007	$2,282,115.88	Week 40 CY 2007
Week 44 CY 2007	$3,483,161.40	Week 44 CY 2007
Week 48 CY 2007	$3,510,948.73	Week 48 CY 2007

</td></tr>
</table>

Exercise#5.3

Goal: Display non empty "Reseller Sales Amount" for cities of the state of Texas.

a. Sort the list by "Reseller Sales Amount".

b. Sort the list by "City Name".

Step 1: Sort the list by "Reseller Sales Amount.

MDX

```
SELECT
  {
  [Measures].[Reseller Sales Amount]
  } ON COLUMNS,
  {
  Order
    (
    NonEmpty
      (
      [Geography].[Geography].[State-Province].&[TX]&[US].Children,
      [Measures].[Reseller Sales Amount]
      ),
    [Measures].[Reseller Sales Amount]
    )
  } ON ROWS
FROM
  [Adventure Works]
```

Result

	Reseller Sales Amount
Plano	$2,930.55
Fort Worth	$3,531.50
Cedar Park	$4,008.86
Sugar Land	$9,078.47
Killeen	$12,071.31
Baytown	$14,042.08
La Marque	$18,772.68
Arlington	$101,203.58
Carrollton	$138,416.15
Round Rock	$145,073.63
Laredo	$175,502.16
Dallas	$270,026.71
Corpus Christi	$278,412.80

Step 2: Sort the list by "City Name".

MDX	WITH MEMBER [Measures].[City Name] AS [Geography].[Geography].CurrentMember.Name SELECT { [Measures].[Reseller Sales Amount] } ON COLUMNS, { Order (NonEmpty ([Geography].[Geography].[State-Province].&[TX]&[US].Children, [Measures].[Reseller Sales Amount]), [Measures].[City Name]) } ON ROWS FROM [Adventure Works]
Result	(table below)

	Reseller Sales Amount
Arlington	$101,203.58
Austin	$586,524.95
Baytown	$14,042.08
Carrollton	$138,416.15
Cedar Park	$4,008.86
College Station	$617,340.46
Corpus Christi	$278,412.80
Dallas	$270,026.71
Fort Worth	$3,531.50
Garland	$1,123,139.92
Houston	$909,362.91
Humble	$294,389.81
Irving	$655,828.25
Killeen	$12,071.31

Exercise#5.4

Goal: For a given year and a state, both passed as string parameters, find "Reseller Sales Amount".

MDX

```
SELECT
  {
  [Measures].[Reseller Sales Amount]
  } ON COLUMNS
FROM
  [Adventure Works]
WHERE
  (
  StrToMember("[Date].[Calendar].[Calendar Year].&[2007]"),
  StrToMember("[Geography].[Geography].[State-Province].&[CO]&[US]")
  )
```

Result

Reseller Sales Amount
$1,086,727.75

Exercise#5.5

Goal: Display all states of United States and also display string length of each state name.

MDX

```
WITH
MEMBER [Measures].[StrLength] AS
LEN([Geography].[Geography].CurrentMember.Name)

SELECT
  {
  [Measures].[StrLength]
  } ON COLUMNS,
  {
  [Geography].[Geography].[Country].&[United States].Children
  } ON ROWS
FROM
  [Adventure Works]
```

Result

	StrLength
Alabama	7
Arizona	7
California	10
Colorado	8
Connecticut	11
Florida	7
Georgia	7
Idaho	5

Exercise#6.1

Goal: Find the monthly average of "Reseller Sales Amount" for fiscal year 2007 for the state of New York for following cases:

A. Include months with no sales.

B. Exclude months with no sales.

Case A: Find the monthly average of "Reseller Sales Amount" for fiscal year 2007 for state of New York, include months with no sales.

MDX	WITH MEMBER [Measures].[Avg Monthly Sale] AS AVG (DESCENDANTS ([Date].[Fiscal].[Fiscal Year].&[2007], [Date].[Fiscal].[Month]), CoalesceEmpty ([Measures].[Reseller Sales Amount], 0)), Format_string ="Currency" SELECT { [Measures].[Avg Monthly Sale] } ON COLUMNS FROM [Adventure Works] WHERE [Geography].[Geography].[State-Province].&[NY]&[US]
Result	Avg Monthly Sale $40,731.50

Case B: Find the monthly average of "Reseller Sales Amount" for fiscal year 2007 for state of New York, exclude months with no sales.

MDX

```
WITH
MEMBER [Measures].[Avg Monthly Sale] AS
AVG
  (
  NonEmpty
    (
    DESCENDANTS
      (
      [Date].[Fiscal].[Fiscal Year].&[2007],
      [Date].[Fiscal].[Month]
      ),
    [Measures].[Reseller Sales Amount]
    ),
  [Measures].[Reseller Sales Amount]
  )

SELECT
  {
  [Measures].[Avg Monthly Sale]
  } ON COLUMNS
FROM
  [Adventure Works]
WHERE
  [Geography].[Geography].[State-Province].&[NY]&[US]
```

Result

Avg Monthly Sale
$61,097.25

Exercise#6.2

Goal: Rank products based on "Reseller Sales Amount" for the state of Florida for fiscal year 2008. Do not show products that have no sales.

MDX

```
WITH
MEMBER [Measures].[The Rank] AS
Rank
  (
  [Product].[Product Categories].CurrentMember,
  NonEmpty
    (
    [Product].[Product Categories].[Product],
    [Measures].[Reseller Sales Amount]
    ),
  [Measures].[Reseller Sales Amount]
  )
SELECT
  {
  [Measures].[Reseller Sales Amount],
  [Measures].[The Rank]
  } ON COLUMNS,
  {
  NonEmpty
    (
    [Product].[Product Categories].[Product],
    [Measures].[Reseller Sales Amount]
    )
  } ON ROWS
FROM
  [Adventure Works]
WHERE
  (
  [Geography].[Geography].[State-Province].&[FL]&[US],
  [Date].[Fiscal].[Fiscal Year].&[2008]
  )
```

Result

	Reseller Sales Amount	The Rank
Hitch Rack - 4-Bike	$7,188.58	35
Water Bottle - 30 oz.	$290.49	126
Bike Wash - Dissolver	$391.20	123
Sport-100 Helmet, Black	$1,516.84	93
Sport-100 Helmet, Blue	$1,726.96	88
Sport-100 Helmet, Red	$1,415.58	96
Hydration Pack - 70 oz.	$1,937.94	86
Patch Kit/8 Patches	$46.72	142
Mountain-200 Black, 38	$35,801.84	4
Mountain-200 Black, 42	$23,408.90	11
Mountain-200 Black, 46	$11,015.95	21
Mountain-200 Silver, 38	$41,759.82	3
Mountain-200 Silver, 42	$12,527.95	19
Mountain-200 Silver, 46	$23,663.90	10
Mountain-400-W Silver, 38	$7,848.80	29
Mountain-400-W Silver, 40	$5,078.63	46
Mountain-400-W Silver, 42	$2,770.16	74
Mountain-400-W Silver, 46	$7,387.10	33
Mountain-500 Black, 40	$3,887.93	58
Mountain-500 Black, 42	$4,535.92	50
Mountain-500 Black, 44	$4,535.92	50

Exercise#6.3

Goal: The following result shows "Reseller Sales Amount" for "Bikes", "Clothing" and "All Products" for the state of Texas with "Reseller Sales Amount" of "All Products" as sum of all product categories. Modify the query to show "Reseller Sales Amount" of "All Products" as sum of product categories Bikes and Clothing.

MDX

```
SELECT
  {
  [Measures].[Reseller Sales Amount]
  } ON COLUMNS,
  {
  VisualTotals
    (
      {
      [Product].[Product Categories].[Category].[Bikes],
      [Product].[Product Categories].[Category].[Clothing],
      [Product].[Product Categories].[All Products]
      }
    )
  } ON ROWS
FROM
  [Adventure Works]
WHERE
  [Geography].[Geography].[State-Province].&[TX]&[US]
```

Result

	Reseller Sales Amount
Bikes	$5,176,738.21
Clothing	$105,216.45
All Products	$6,236,182.34

Using "VisualTotals" function, you can show "Reseller Sales Amount" of "All Products" as sum of product categories Bikes and Clothing. Important note is that, VisualTotals function required to arrange all members of given set ordered by hierarchy. There are two ways you can modify above query to get the expected result:

Solution 1: Modify the ordering of members in the above set as,

```
{
[Product].[Product Categories].[All Products],
[Product].[Product Categories].[Category].[Bikes],
[Product].[Product Categories].[Category].[Clothing]
}
```

Solution 2: Use the hierarchize function,

```
Hierarchize
 (
  {
  [Product].[Product Categories].[Category].[Bikes],
  [Product].[Product Categories].[Category].[Clothing],
  [Product].[Product Categories].[All Products]
  }
 )
```

<table>
<tr><td>MDX</td><td><pre>SELECT
  {
  [Measures].[Reseller Sales Amount]
  } ON COLUMNS,
  {
  VisualTotals
    (
    Hierarchize
      (
        {
        [Product].[Product Categories].[Category].[Bikes],
        [Product].[Product Categories].[Category].[Clothing],
        [Product].[Product Categories].[All Products]
        }
)
)
  } ON ROWS
FROM
  [Adventure Works]
WHERE
  [Geography].[Geography].[State-Province].&[TX]&[US]</pre></td></tr>
<tr><td>Result</td><td><table><tr><th></th><th>Reseller Sales Amount</th></tr><tr><td>All Products</td><td>$5,281,954.66</td></tr><tr><td>Bikes</td><td>$5,176,738.21</td></tr><tr><td>Clothing</td><td>$105,216.45</td></tr></table></td></tr>
</table>

Exercise#7.1

Goal: Find the weekly median of "Internet Order Quantity" for fiscal year 2008.

MDX

```
WITH
MEMBER [Measures].[The Median] AS
Median
  (
  [Date].[Fiscal Weeks].[Fiscal Year].&[2008].Children,
  [Measures].[Internet Order Quantity]
  )
SELECT
  {
  [Measures].[The Median]
  } ON COLUMNS
FROM
  [Adventure Works]
```

Result

The Median
1037

Exercise#7.2

Goal: Find weekly covariance of "Internet Sales Amount" and "Internet Tax Amount" for fiscal year 2008.

MDX

```
WITH
MEMBER [Measures].[The Covariance] AS
Covariance
  (
  [Date].[Fiscal Weeks].[Fiscal Year].&[2008].Children,
  [Measures].[Internet Sales Amount],
  [Measures].[Internet Tax Amount]
  )
SELECT
  {
  [Measures].[The Covariance]
  } ON COLUMNS
FROM
  [Adventure Works]
```

Result

The Covariance
637701855.85393

Exercise#7.3

Goal: Assume "Internet Sales Amount" is directy proportional to "Internet Tax Amount"and form linear regression equation y = mx + c, Given

- "Internet Sales Amount" and "Internet Tax Amount" for each week of fiscal year 2007.
- "Internet Sales Amount" for each week of fiscal year 2008.

Predict "Internet Tax Amount" for each week of fiscal year 2008.

MDX

```
WITH
MEMBER [Measures].[Predicted Internet Order Count] AS
Round
  (
  LinRegPoint
    (
    [Measures].[Internet Sales Amount],
    [Date].[Fiscal Weeks].[Fiscal Year].&[2007].Children,
    [Measures].[Internet Order Count],
    [Measures].[Internet Sales Amount]
    )
  )
SELECT
  {
  [Measures].[Internet Sales Amount],
  [Measures].[Predicted Internet Order Count],
  [Measures].[Internet Order Count]
  } ON COLUMNS,
  {
  [Date].[Fiscal Weeks].[Fiscal Year].&[2008].Children
  } ON ROWS
FROM
  [Adventure Works]
```

Result

	Internet Sales Amount	Predicted Internet Order Count	Internet Order Count
Week 1 FY 2008	$311,488.76	174	228
Week 2 FY 2008	$204,768.01	114	122
Week 3 FY 2008	$172,549.66	96	104
Week 4 FY 2008	$206,866.16	115	124
Week 5 FY 2008	$198,566.05	111	244
Week 6 FY 2008	$192,346.36	107	343
Week 7 FY 2008	$196,682.69	110	370
Week 8 FY 2008	$190,412.60	106	355
Week 9 FY 2008	$191,907.09	107	353
Week 10 FY 2008	$246,629.71	138	377
Week 11 FY 2008	$256,380.16	143	391
[illegible]	$249[illegible]	[illegible]	39[illegible]

Exercise#8.1

Goal: Write a scope statement to set "Reseller Sales Amount" to null for all products which have string "Pedal" in the product name for fiscal year 2008.

Step 1: Find "Reseller Sales Amount" for all products for calendar year 2008 which have string "Pedal" in the model name.

MDX

```
SELECT
  {
  [Measures].[Reseller Sales Amount]
  } ON COLUMNS,
  {
  FILTER
    (
    [Product].[Product Categories].[Product],
    InStr
      (
      [Product].[Product Categories].CurrentMember.Properties("Model Name"),
      "Pedal"
      )
    )
  } ON ROWS
FROM
  [Adventure Works]
WHERE
  (
  [Date].[Calendar].[Calendar Year].&[2008]
  )
```

Result

	Reseller Sales Amount
HL Mountain Pedal	$15,296.84
HL Road Pedal	$12,828.82
LL Mountain Pedal	$3,133.93
LL Road Pedal	$8,478.61
ML Mountain Pedal	$3,539.13
ML Road Pedal	$9,611.53
Touring Pedal	$534.53

Step 2: Add following MDX script at the end of calculations of the cube and save.

MDX SCRIPT	SCOPE (FILTER ([Product].[Product Categories].[Product], InStr ([Product].[Product Categories].CurrentMember.Properties("Model Name"), "Pedal")), [Date].[Calendar].[Calendar Year].&[2008]); THIS = null; END SCOPE;

Step 3: Verify "Reseller Sales Amount" is null for all products which have string "Pedal" in product name for fiscal year 2008. Run the MDX query from step 1.

Result

	Reseller Sales Amount
HL Mountain Pedal	(null)
HL Road Pedal	(null)
LL Mountain Pedal	(null)
LL Road Pedal	(null)
ML Mountain Pedal	(null)
ML Road Pedal	(null)
Touring Pedal	(null)

Exercise#8.2

Goal: Write scope statements for internet sales for year 2008 to:

a. Set Memorial Day weekend as tax free weekend.
b. Set 4th July weekend as tax free weekend for clothing.

Step 1: Display Internet Tax Amount for Memorial Day weekend and 4th July weekend for year 2008. Also display Internet Tax Amount for May, 2008 and July, 2008.

MDX

```
SELECT
  {
  [Measures].[Internet Tax Amount]
  } ON COLUMNS,
  {
  [Date].[Date].&[20080529],
  [Date].[Date].&[20080530],
  [Date].[Date].&[20080703],
  [Date].[Date].&[20080704]
  } ON ROWS
FROM
  [Adventure Works]
```

	Internet Tax Amount
May 29, 2008	$5,144.49
May 30, 2008	$3,661.67
July 3, 2008	$143.75
July 4, 2008	$104.11

MDX

```
SELECT
  {
  [Measures].[Internet Tax Amount]
  } ON COLUMNS,
  {
  [Date].[Calendar].[Month].&[2008]&[5],
  [Date].[Calendar].[Month].&[2008]&[7]
  } ON ROWS
FROM
  [Adventure Works]
```

	Internet Tax Amount
May 2008	$150,265.40
July 2008	$4,067.25

Step 2: Add following MDX script in end of "Calculations" of the cube and save.

MDX SCRIPT

```
SCOPE
  (
    {
    [Date].[Date].&[20080529],
    [Date].[Date].&[20080530],
    [Date].[Date].&[20080703],
    [Date].[Date].&[20080704]
    },
  [Measures].[Internet Tax Amount]
  );
THIS = null;
END SCOPE;
```

Step 3: To verify Internet Tax Amount present for Memorial Day weekend and 4th July weekend. Display Internet Tax Amount for Memorial Day weekend and 4th July weekend for year 2008. Also display Internet Tax Amount for May, 2008 and July, 2008.

MDX

```
SELECT
  {
  [Measures].[Internet Tax Amount]
  } ON COLUMNS,
  {
  [Date].[Date].&[20080529],
  [Date].[Date].&[20080530],
  [Date].[Date].&[20080703],
  [Date].[Date].&[20080704]
  } ON ROWS
FROM
  [Adventure Works]
```

	Internet Tax Amount
May 29, 2008	(null)
May 30, 2008	(null)
July 3, 2008	(null)
July 4, 2008	(null)

MDX

```
SELECT
  {
  [Measures].[Internet Tax Amount]
  } ON COLUMNS,
  {
  [Date].[Calendar].[Month].&[2008]&[5],
  [Date].[Calendar].[Month].&[2008]&[7]
  } ON ROWS
FROM
  [Adventure Works]
```

	Internet Tax Amount
May 2008	$141,459.25
July 2008	$3,819.40

Analysis:

- "Internet Tax amount" for Memorial Day weekend and 4th July weekend is null.
- "Internet Tax amount" for May, 2008 is reduced by $5144.49 +$3661.67 = $8806.16.
- Before scope statement, "Internet Tax amount" for May, 2008 = $150,265.40.
- After scope statement, "Internet Tax amount" for May, 2008 = $150,265.40 - $8806.16 = $141,459.24
- "Internet Tax amount" for July, 2008 is reduced by $143.75+$104.11 = $247.86.
- Before scope statement, "Internet Tax amount" for July, 2008 = $4067.25.
- After scope statement, "Internet Tax amount" for May, 2008 = $4067.25 - $247.86 = $3819.39

Exercise#8.3

Goal: Write a scope statement to set followings for the state of California:

a. Set "Reseller Sales Amount" as null for any dates before December 17, 2007.

b. Modify last scope statement to set "Reseller Sales Amount" to null for all dates between December 17, 2007 and March 5, 2008.

c. Modify last scope statement to set "Reseller Sales Amount" to null for any dates after March 5, 2008.

Step 1: Find

a. Total "Reseller Sales Amount" before December 17, 2007.

b. Total "Reseller Sales Amount" between December 17, 2007 and March 5, 2008.

c. Total "Reseller Sales Amount" after March 5, 2008.

MDX

```
WITH
MEMBER [Date].[Date].[Before 12/13/2007] AS
SUM(Null:[Date].[Date].&[20071213])

MEMBER [Date].[Date].[Between 12/13/2007-03/05/2008] AS
SUM([Date].[Date].&[20071213]:[Date].[Date].&[20080305])

MEMBER [Date].[Date].[After 03/05/2008] AS
SUM([Date].[Date].&[20080305]:Null)

SELECT
  {
  [Measures].[Reseller Sales Amount]
  } ON COLUMNS,
  {
  [Date].[Date].[Before 12/13/2007],
  [Date].[Date].[Between 12/13/2007-03/05/2008],
  [Date].[Date].[After 03/05/2008]
  } ON ROWS
FROM
  [Adventure Works]
```

Result

	Reseller Sales Amount
Before 12/13/2007	$64,412,534.38
Between 12/13/2007-03/05/2008	$7,100,501.74
After 03/05/2008	$8,937,560.86

Step 2: Add following MDX script in "Calculations" tab of the cube and save.

MDX SCRIPT	SCOPE ({Null:[Date].[Date].&[20071213]}, [Measures].[Reseller Sales Amount]); THIS = null; END SCOPE;

Step 3: Run the MDX query from Step 1 and verify "Reseller Sales Amount" is null for any dates before December 17, 2007.

Result

	Reseller Sales Amount
Before 12/13/2007	(null)
Between 12/13/2007-03/05/2008	$7,100,501.74
After 03/05/2008	$8,937,560.86

Step 4: Modify MDX script from Step 2 in calculations of the cube and save.

MDX SCRIPT	SCOPE ({[Date].[Date].&[20071213] :[Date].[Date].&[20080305] }, [Measures].[Reseller Sales Amount]); THIS = null; END SCOPE;

Step 5: Run the MDX query from Step 1 and verify "Reseller Sales Amount" is null for any dates between December 17, 2007 and March 5, 2008.

Result

	Reseller Sales Amount
Before 12/13/2007	$64,412,534.38
Between 12/13/2007-03/05/2008	(null)
After 03/05/2008	$8,937,560.86

Step 6: Modify MDX script from Step 4 in "Calculations" tab of the cube and save.

MDX SCRIPT	SCOPE ({[Date].[Date].&[20080305] : Null }, [Measures].[Reseller Sales Amount]); THIS = null; END SCOPE;

Step 7: Run the MDX query from Step 1 and verify "Reseller Sales Amount" is null for any dates before December 17, 2007.

Result

	Reseller Sales Amount
Before 12/13/2007	$64,412,534.38
Between 12/13/2007-03/05/2008	$7,100,501.74
After 03/05/2008	(null)

Notes:

- To change all measures of measure group "Reseller Sales" as null for any dates after March 5, 2008, use MeasureGroupsMeasures in scope statement.

MDX SCRIPT	SCOPE ({[Date].[Date].&[20080305] : Null }, MeasureGroupMeasures("Reseller Sales")); THIS = null; END SCOPE;

Exercise#8.4

Goal: Create an MDX scope statement to set "Reseller Tax Amount" for the month of March of each year as null.

Step 1: Display "Reseller Tax Amount" for the month of March of each calendar year.

<table>
<tr><td>MDX</td><td><pre>SELECT
  {
  [Measures].[Reseller Tax Amount]
  } ON COLUMNS,
  {
  FILTER
    (
    [Date].[Calendar].[Month],
    [Date].[Calendar].CurrentMember.Properties("Month of Year")="March"
)
  } ON ROWS
FROM
  [Adventure Works]</pre></td></tr>
<tr><td>Result</td><td>

	Reseller Tax Amount
March 2005	(null)
March 2006	$116,422.43
March 2007	$125,116.40
March 2008	$219,149.67
March 2009	(null)
March 2010	(null)

</td></tr>
</table>

Step 2: Add following MDX script in "Calculations" tab of the cube and save.

MDX SCRIPT	SCOPE (FILTER ([Date].[Calendar].[Month], [Date].[Calendar].CurrentMember.Properties("Month of Year")="March"), [Measures].[Reseller Tax Amount]); THIS = null; END SCOPE;

Step 3: Run the MDX query from Step 1.

Result

	Reseller Tax Amount
March 2005	(null)
March 2006	(null)
March 2007	(null)
March 2008	(null)
March 2009	(null)
March 2010	(null)

Exercise#8.5

Goal: Create a calculated measure [Measures].[Management Bonus Pct]. Write scope statement to set:

a. [Measures].[Management Bonus Pct] for leaf level to zero.
b. [Measures].[Management Bonus Pct] for first level to 0.05%.
c. [Measures].[Management Bonus Pct] for each level to 0.03% more than the lower level.

Step 1: Add following MDX script in "Calculations" tab of the cube to create calculated member.
See the solution in next page.

MDX SCRIPT

```
CREATE MEMBER CURRENTCUBE.[Measures].[Management Bonus Pct] AS
0.5;

CREATE MEMBER CURRENTCUBE.[Measures].[IsGeneration0] AS
IsGeneration
  (  [Employee].[Employees].CurrentMember,  0  );

CREATE MEMBER CURRENTCUBE.[Measures].[IsGeneration1] AS
IsGeneration ( [Employee].[Employees].CurrentMember,  1  );

SCOPE  (  [Employee].[Employees].Members  );
  IF ([Measures].[IsGeneration0]= true)
  Then
  [Measures].[Management Bonus Pct] =0.0
  End If;

  IF ([Measures].[IsGeneration1]= true)
  Then
  [Measures].[Management Bonus Pct] =0.3
  End If;
End Scope;
```

Step 2: Display [Management Bonus Pct] for all employees.

MDX

```
SELECT
  {
  [Measures].[Management Bonus Pct]
  } ON COLUMNS,
  {
  DESCENDANTS
    (
    [Employee].[Employees].[All Employees].Children
    )
  } ON ROWS
FROM
  [Adventure Works]
```

Result

	Management Bonus
Ken J. Sánchez	0.3
Brian S. Welcker	0.5
Amy E. Alberts	0.3
Jae B. Pak	0
Rachel B. Valdez	0
Ranjit R. Varkey Chudukatil	0
Stephen Y. Jiang	0.3
David R. Campbell	0
Garrett R. Vargas	0
Jillian Carson	0
José Edvaldo. Saraiva	0
Linda C. Mitchell	0
Michael G. Blythe	0

Exercise#9.1

Goal: Using Alter Cube statement in calculation of cube, change default destination currency as Euro.

Step 1: Find default member of destination currency.

MDX	WITH MEMBER [Measures].[Default Currency] AS [Destination Currency].[Destination Currency].DefaultMember.Name SELECT { [Measures].[Default Currency] } ON COLUMNS FROM [Adventure Works]
Result	Default Currency US Dollar

Step 2: Add following MDX script at the end of cube calculations of the cube and save.

MDX SCRIPT	Alter Cube CurrentCube Update Dimension [Destination Currency].[Destination Currency], Default_Member = [Destination Currency].[Destination Currency].&[EURO];

Analysis:

- Above script set default member of hierarchy [Destination Currency].[Destination Currency].
- Update Dimension clause applies to dimension or hierarchy.

Step 3: Verify default member of destination currency changed from US Dollar to Euro.

MDX

```
WITH
MEMBER [Measures].[Default Currency] AS
[Destination Currency].[Destination Currency].DefaultMember.Name

SELECT
      {
      [Measures].[Default Currency]
      } ON COLUMNS
FROM
      [Adventure Works]
```

Result

Default Currency
EURO

Step 4: Once verified, remove following MDX script from end of cube calculations and save.

MDX SCRIPT

```
Alter Cube   CurrentCube
Update Dimension [Destination Currency].[Destination Currency],
Default_Member = [Destination Currency].[Destination Currency].&[EURO];
```

Exercise#9.2

Goal: Find "Reseller Sales Amount" in GBP for "United Kingdom" for March, 2008.

MDX

```
SELECT
  {
  [Measures].[Reseller Sales Amount]
  } ON COLUMNS,
  {
  [Geography].[Geography].[Country].&[United Kingdom]
  } ON ROWS
FROM
  [Adventure Works]
WHERE
  (
  [Date].[Calendar].[Month].&[2008]&[3],
  [Destination Currency].[Destination Currency].&[United Kingdom Pound]
  )
```

Result

	Reseller Sales Amount
United Kingdom	£198,099.41

Exercise#9.3

Goal: Find "Customer Name", "Source Currency" and "Sales Order Number" for all internet sales for product "Water Bottle - 30 oz." in June 1, 2008.

Step 1: Find Internet Sales Amount for product "Water Bottle - 30 oz." in June 1, 2008.

MDX

```
SELECT
  {
  [Measures].[Internet Sales Amount]
  } ON COLUMNS
FROM
  [Adventure Works]
WHERE
  (
  [Date].[Date].&[20080601],
  [Product].[Product].&[477]--Water Bottle - 30 oz.
  )
```

Result

Internet Sales Amount
$49.90

Step 2:

- Add DRILLTHROUGH at the beginning of the MDX.
- Add following fields with RETURN clause
  - [$Customer].[Customer] AS [Customer Name]
  - [$Source Currency].[Source Currency Code] AS [Source Currency]
  - [$Internet Sales Order Details].[Internet Sales Order]
- Add aliases "Customer Name", "Source Currency" and "Sales Order Number" for above fields.

MDX

```
DRILLTHROUGH
SELECT
  {
  [Measures].[Internet Sales Amount]
  } ON COLUMNS
FROM
  [Adventure Works]
WHERE
  (
  [Date].[Date].&[20080601],
  [Product].[Product].&[477]--Water Bottle - 30 oz.
  )
RETURN
[$Customer].[Customer] AS [Customer Name],
[$Source Currency].[Source Currency Code] AS [Source Currency] ,
[$Internet Sales Order Details].[Internet Sales Order] AS [Sales Order Number]
```

Result

Customer Name	Source Currency	Sales Order Number
Vanessa J. Diaz	AUD	SO71956 Line 1
Deanna N.. Sabella	USD	SO71959 Line 3
Teresa A. Gutierrez	GBP	SO71960 Line 3
Caleb Zhang	USD	SO71961 Line 6
Richard L. Patterson	USD	SO71968 Line 2
Jordan Gonzales	CAD	SO71971 Line 1
Trevor B. Diaz	CAD	SO71973 Line 3
Gavin M. Powell	GBP	SO71994 Line 3
Dominique L. Prasad	USD	SO71995 Line 3
Virginia Gonzalez	AUD	SO71997 Line 3

References

Books:

- Microsoft SQL Server 2008 MDX Step by Step. Author: Bryan C.Smith, C.Ryan Clay, Publisher: Microsoft Press.
- Microsoft SQL Server 2008 Analysis Services Step by Step. Author: Scott Cameron, Publisher: Microsoft Press.
- Microsoft SQL Server 2012 Book online and white papers.
- Practical MDX Queries: For Microsoft SQL Server Analysis Services 2008. Author: Art Tennick.
- MDX with Microsoft SQL Server 2008 R2 Analysis Services Cookbook. Author: Tomislav Piasevoli, Publisher: PACKT.
- Expert Cube Development with Microsoft SQL Server 2008 Analysis Services. Author: Marco Russo, Alberto Ferrari and Chris Webb, Publisher: PACKT.

Websites:

- MSDN Forum: http://social.msdn.microsoft.com/Forums/en-US/sqlanalysisservices
- MSDN webcasts: http://msdn.microsoft.com/en-us/events
- Adventure works, sample projects from: http://www.codeplex.com
- http://ssas-info.com
- Chris Webb's BI Blog: http://cwebbbi.wordpress.com/
- Craig Utley's site : http://www.LearnMicrosoftBI.com
- http://ssas-wiki.com

Index

Printed in Dunstable, United Kingdom

91342622R00219